PRAISE FOR
All This Safety Is Killing Us

"This collection offers an ensemble of analysis, reflection, and grounded theory that radically extends the aspirational and strategic horizons of contemporary abolitionist projects."

> **—DYLAN RODRÍGUEZ,** distinguished professor at UC Riverside and author of *White Reconstruction*

"A stark first-hand look at the ways policing and carcerality negatively impact health care delivery and patient well-being, and evidence-based steps we can take to create safer and healthier medical settings."

> **—ALEX S. VITALE,** author of *The End of Policing*

"Contributors to this impressive anthology show how health and well-being are not separate from violence . . . [and] how health institutions and inequities are linked fundamentally to the state violence of prisons, policing, border fortification, and deportation. Health justice means abolishing these systems of oppression and transforming health systems."

> **—JENNA M. LOYD,** associate professor at University of Wisconsin–Madison and author of *Health Rights Are Civil Rights*

"What does health mean in a sick society? Who survives in an economy that renders lives disposable? Can anyone be safe within structures that exacerbate harm? This critical text unites organizers, medical practitioners, incarcerated writers, and disability justice advocates to offer a radical revisioning of health and healing."

> **—CHRISTINA HEATHERTON,** Elting Associate Professor of American Studies and Human Rights at Trinity College and editor of *Policing the Planet*

"A compelling must-read for anyone committed to health justice. The book offers a deep, intersectional exploration of our current carceral health system, alongside compelling case studies of groundbreaking abolitionist practice. A wide range of perspectives and lenses are represented in thoughtful, intentional ways—all clearly, accessibly, and beautifully written."

—**MAKANI THEMBA**, chief strategist at Higher Ground Change Strategies

"This creative and innovative volume brings together an unusually wide range of voices to make a clear case that police, prisons, and borders are racist structures that not only fail to keep us safe, but also kill the most vulnerable members of our communities. Anyone who wants to understand and confront how carceral systems exacerbate health inequalities should read this book."

—**TANYA GOLASH-BOZA**, author of *Race and Racisms*

"A much-needed analysis of the inextricable entanglements between the violence of policing and prisons to the slow violence of health injustice, all of which lead to the premature deaths of millions. Case studies and analyses offer concrete examples of the tactics and tools health care practitioners and organizers are already using to dismantle systems of carceral safety and replace them with abolition medicine. I hope this book becomes required reading for all health workers."

—**A. NAOMI PAIK**, author of *Bans, Walls, Raids, Sanctuary*

"Grounded in everyday practice and struggle, this engaging collection persuasively demonstrates that abolitionist frameworks are invaluable for health care justice and the collective labor of living otherwise."

—**ALYOSHA GOLDSTEIN,** professor of American Studies at the University of New Mexico

"This timely, incisive, and necessary anthology articulates the imperative of abolition as a public health mandate, featuring compelling narratives, innovative research, critical interviews, illuminating zines, and evocative art contributed by health care and anti-carceral practitioners, educators, and activists. Accessible for everyone, from college campuses to health departments, this instructive text needs to be read and applied with urgency for abolition now and everywhere."

—**WHITNEY PIRTLE,** associate professor at UC Merced

ALL THIS SAFETY IS KILLING US

ALL THIS SAFETY IS KILLING US

HEALTH JUSTICE BEYOND PRISONS, POLICE, AND BORDERS

Edited by Ronica Mukerjee and Carlos Martinez

North Atlantic Books

Huicåhin, unceded Ohlone land
Berkeley, California

North Atlantic Books
Huichin, unceded Ohlone land
2526 Martin Luther King Jr Way
Berkeley, CA 94704 USA
www.northatlanticbooks.com

Cover design by John Yates
Book design by Happenstance Type-O-Rama
Printed in Canada

All This Safety Is Killing Us: Health Justice Beyond Prisons, Police, and Borders is sponsored and published by North Atlantic Books, an educational nonprofit based in the unceded Ohlone land Huichin (Berkeley, CA) that collaborates with partners to develop cross-cultural perspectives; nurture holistic views of art, science, the humanities, and healing; and seed personal and global transformation by publishing work on the relationship of body, spirit, and nature.

CONTENT DISCLAIMER: This book contains material that may be triggering, including references to self-harm, sexual abuse, or trauma.

North Atlantic Books's publications are distributed to the US trade and internationally by Penguin Random House Publishers Services. For further information, visit our website at www.northatlanticbooks.com.

Library of Congress Cataloging-in-Publication Data

Names: Mukerjee, Ronica, editor. | Martinez, Carlos (Writer on public health), editor.
Title: All this safety is killing us : health justice beyond prisons, police, and borders : abolitionist frameworks and practices from clinicians, organizers, and incarcerated activists / edited by Ronica Mukerjee and Carlos Martinez.
Description: Berkeley, CA : North Atlantic Books, [2024] | Includes bibliographical references and index.
Identifiers: LCCN 2024045623 (print) | LCCN 2024045624 (ebook) | ISBN 9798889841401 (trade paperback) | ISBN 9798889841418 (ebook)
Subjects: LCSH: Prisoners—Medical care. | Prison reform.
Classification: LCC HV8833 .A45 2024 (print) | LCC HV8833 (ebook) | DDC 365/.667—dc23/eng/20250109
LC record available at https://lccn.loc.gov/2024045623
LC ebook record available at https://lccn.loc.gov/2024045624

The authorized representative in the EU for product safety and compliance is Eucomply OÜ, Pärnu mnt 139b-14, 11317 Tallinn, Estonia, hello@eucompliancepartner.com, +33757690241.

The interior of this book is printed on 100 percent recycled paper, and the cover is printed on material from well-managed forests.

1 2 3 4 5 6 7 8 9 FRIESENS 30 29 28 27 26 25

ACKNOWLEDGMENTS

The ideas and visions for different futures proposed in this book could not have coalesced without the spark of revolutionary potential that emerged in the heated summer months of 2020. As the Movement for Black Lives galvanized public attention with mass mobilizations demanding justice for George Floyd and others sacrificed to the altar of "safety," new political possibilities and horizons of struggle suddenly burst forth and took center stage. This book owes its existence to this unique moment in time as well as to a much longer and broader lineage of organizing that had been building momentum for years and is now encapsulated by the term "abolition."

While the mass mobilizations of 2020 forced a national (and international) conversation on the violence of policing onto hitherto unsympathetic ears, collectives and organizations across the country had already been engaged in campaigns to challenge various manifestations of the prison industrial complex for decades—often with little attention or fanfare. The seeds of the multifaceted movement we see today, and by extension this book, were sown by the uncompromising ideas and actions of generations of organizers, thinkers, and dreamers.

While the editors of this book initiated this project, it is in reality a collaborative product that is far larger than the sum of its parts. The contributors to this volume engaged in painstaking work to write, draw, and repeatedly revise their pieces. All of the contributors also served as peer reviewers, providing crucial feedback to other contributors on their manuscripts. Jennifer Gottlieb helped us move this project forward under a tight deadline by conducting a first-round review of the full book manuscript. Keosha Bond reviewed and provided feedback on early drafts of several book chapters. This book would not have been possible without all of these efforts at multiple stages of its development.

This book was enriched not only by the contributions of health justice activists but also by the brilliance and imagination of radical artists and cultural workers, many of whom are incarcerated. We would like to thank ABO Comix, a collective of creators and activists who work to amplify the voices of LGBTQ+ prisoners through art, for their support in helping us to include several artists in their network. Please visit www.abocomix.com to support their work. In particular we want to honor the memory of Edee Allynnah Davis, a Native American trans woman, artist, poet, and abolitionist, as well as an advisory board member for ABO Comix who passed away while being held captive in the Texas prison system. We would also like to thank E. T. Russian and Juliet McMullin for their support in connecting us to several artistic contributors.

This book ultimately came to completion because several people and institutions believed in its value, which was critical for moving us along even when the road ahead felt long and uncertain. The Alpha Zeta chapter of the Sigma Theta Tau Honors Society provided us with important early seed funding for developing the project. We are profoundly grateful to our publisher, North Atlantic Books, for ushering this book into the world. In particular we would like to thank Margeaux Weston for seeing the potential for this project and getting other NAB editors on board. Both Jasmine Respess and Trisha Peck played critical roles in helping us to shape the manuscript and bringing the book into its final form. Working with them has been an honor and a pleasure.

We would also like to thank Rachel Herzing for being willing to open the book with her wisdom and insights from years of on-the-ground organizing against the prison industrial complex. Her foreword has helped us to convey the book's primary message that abolitionism is not just a distant fantasy but rather a movement that is being built brick by brick within our lifetimes.

The editors would each like to extend gratitude to a number of individuals for their support in moving this book from being an idea into a reality. Ronica would like to thank her dazzlingly courageous queer, trans, BIPOC (and other) community of friends, including Ronni T. for last-minute editing, Goutami S. for even more last-minute editing, and Melissa M. for reading and critiquing her work. Ronica would also like to thank Zena Sharman for believing in her and writing and curating the important and inspiring book *The Care We Dream Of*. Lastly, Ronica would like to thank Loretta for their tenacious love and constant support, and for all of the adventures, with more to come.

Carlos would like to thank his friends and comrades (too many to list here) who inspire him to maintain radical optimism even in such politically dangerous times. His colleagues and comrades at the UC San Francisco REPAIR Project created a critical space for theorizing the concept and practice of medical abolition, which provided him with an important conceptual foundation for working on this project. In particular, he would like to thank Aimee Medeiros, Antoine Johnson, Bonnie Wong, Kara Zamora, Nadia Gaber, Vincanne Adams, and several others for their ideas and imaginations. He would also like to thank Rafik Wahbi and Lauren Textor for their sharp thinking and organizing experiences that shaped our chapter on abolitionist harm reduction. Last, but not least, he would like to thank Katynka Martinez for her love, laughter, kindness, and companionship that make anything feel possible, even in the most challenging moments.

If nothing else, we hope this book serves as an archive and testament to the yearning, theorizing, and organizing among a large swath of health justice activists for a world in which safety is not defined by policing, prisons, or borders. We thank all of those pushing the boundaries of what is considered possible from their various positions and locations in ways both big and small. This book is inspired by and dedicated to you and the work you've done and will continue to do.

TABLE OF CONTENTS

LIST OF ILLUSTRATIONS

FOREWORD

The prison industrial complex (PIC) does not provide safety or well-being. The phrase "PIC" describes the interdependent relationship between public and private interests that use imprisonment, policing, surveillance, the courts, and the cultural tools associated with them to build and maintain social control and power differences. It is designed for containment and control and must be abolished. The harms of the punishment system have been enumerated many times over. We know, for example, that for the millions of people held in cages in prisons, jails, detention centers, and other locked institutions, life is bare. We also know that who gets targeted by cops, who gets sentenced, and who gets caged (or killed) is highly racialized. The editors of this volume refer to the PIC as *the* racial justice issue of our time. The durability of the punishment system's deeply rooted racism persists despite the impacts of the 2020 racial justice uprisings—the largest protests in US history.

Imprisonment compromises people's health through factors including transmission of communicable diseases within crowded spaces; denial of necessary medicines and preventive care; forced sterilization; medical experimentation, and through the deprivation of fresh air, nutritious food, and quality sleep. The psychological harms of imprisonment have been linked to everything from stress to suicide. Similar effects plague survivors of the violence of policing. As Mukerjee and Martinez note in their preface, policing and deportation are *disease-producing* practices. The PIC also harms the loved ones of people in the closest proximity to the system's harms—causing stress and trauma or drawing resources from already overstretched households. Most of us are somehow ensnared in the tentacles of the PIC and made to confront crises created, exploited, and exacerbated by agents of the prison industrial complex that purposefully leave us fearful, weaker, poorer, and sicker.

The PIC does not generate these harms accidentally. Because the function of the system is containment and control, it has violence baked into it. When we understand the violence inherent in surveillance programs, imprisonment and detention, policing and border control, and courts and deportation, attempts to reform or improve the punishment system should give us pause. Reformist goals intend to improve or "fix" elements of the system to make it work better. Better in this case, however, improves the punishment system's ability to cage, criminalize, and kill. If we truly care about safety, the only logical choice is to dismantle this killing machine.

PIC abolitionist politics are often met by detractors and skeptics asking how we'll stay safe without prisons and police. This question rests on a disingenuous presumption that the punishment system has anything to do with safety. Lasting safety, by contrast, is found through caring social relationships, stable, reliable physical shelter, equitable means of participating in the economy, and the ability to maintain physical, emotional, spiritual, and mental health. Agents of the PIC have dedicated substantial time and energy to portraying the system as the only trustworthy means of ensuring safety, security, and well-being. However, the system offers only containment, control, violence, and death—and it doesn't even wield those reliably in direct relation to harms that have occurred. Promoting containment in the sheep's clothing of safety perpetuates the idea that criminalized actions continue to increase despite data from US law enforcement agencies indicating that "crime" rates continued to trend downward over the last thirty years. The actions most frequently used to stoke fear, such as rape and murder, are also least frequently resolved by law enforcement. "Broken windows" policing, a dominant policing approach in the US and increasingly around the world, also stokes fear by suggesting that houses with untended gardens or broken windows are a gateway to chaos. This policing approach equates protection of property and the emptying of public space with safety, laying bare the motivating forces behind policing—not human care but preservation of private property.

PIC abolition is the political praxis that seeks to eliminate the use of surveillance, policing, sentencing, imprisonment, and execution *and* to build healthy, stable, self-determined societies that do not rely on coercion and vengeance to address harm. PIC abolition is a political vision, but it is also a pragmatic approach to building the futures we need and deserve. This praxis has been developed through struggle over decades and been put to work by organizers, advocates, activists, and cultural and legal workers across many sectors bound together by a commitment to developing new ways of living together and in relationship to the natural world that elevate care, transformation, and well-being above vengeance and retribution.

Even if we accept that the PIC must be abolished, we may still wonder how that might be achieved. For many of us, imagining uprooting and eliminating a system as ubiquitous and powerful as the punishment system is overwhelming. Every single day, people around the world are organizing campaigns against the expansion of prisons, jails, and detention centers, making interventions to disrupt policies and practices that criminalize survival, offering supports that create buffers between targeted communities and police, and generating knowledge that helps us move toward a PIC abolitionist horizon.

All This Safety Is Killing Us: Health Justice Beyond Prisons, Police, and Borders—Abolitionist Frameworks and Practices from Clinicians, Organizers, and Incarcerated Activists joins this conversation, contributing insights from pandemic- and racial rebellion–era health practitioners and health justice activists committed to ending the violence of the PIC and fortifying our abilities to stay safe and well. While the collection acts as a primer, delineating the substantial harms of the punishment system, many of the pieces also offer concrete, practical means through which actors in medical and public health systems might prevent, interrupt, and repair harms done by the PIC. These include decriminalization to disability justice; decarceration; removal of cops from schools, hospitals, clinics, and similar public-serving spaces; border justice; de-escalation; and language and communication strategies, among others. The contributors to this collection understand that abolishing the punishment system requires collective action rather than having the correct political line, using the correct words, or reading the right feeds, essays, or books.

Health practitioners and health justice advocates are essential to advancing PIC abolition. They not only help us care for our bodies and minds but assist us in practicing the skills necessary for collective care. They offer alternative means of thinking about repair, resilience, and healing. They also have a sober understanding of what it takes to stay alive and well. When they describe the punishment system as one that produces disease, we should pay attention. When they tell us that policing and imprisonment are incompatible with authentic health-care provision, it comes from direct experience addressing the effects of the violence of the PIC.

Insights from the health justice movement add a welcome dimension to broader discussions of abolitionist politics and practice. They encourage us to imagine the ways, big and small, that all of us, from within our own contexts, can do things that make sustaining the punishment system impossible. They also help us remember that this system touches all of us, albeit with different impacts, depending on who and where we are. This book offers perspectives from nurses, doctors, clinicians, public health workers, artists, social workers, academics, teachers, researchers, activists, and organizers (with a range of experiences of the violence of the punishment system). Despite the fact that PIC abolitionist organizers and activists have long articulated health care and well-being as essential to a future that does not rely on the punishment system, practitioners in this sector have been less visible actors in campaigns and projects. *All This Safety Is Killing Us* refocuses the spotlight on the important lessons and practices people advancing health justice are contributing to the movement for PIC abolition. The collection is right on time to continue expanding the circles of influence advancing abolitionist politics in a period in which the politics are essential.

As you engage with the pieces in this important collection, I encourage you to consider the following questions and considerations:

- ▸ **Abolition of what and for what?** What is to be abolished, and what is worth preserving? What opportunities does abolition make possible?

- ▸ **Alternatives to what?** Not all alternatives are the same. With that in mind, we need to ask, Are we simply replacing a bad thing with a bad alternative or displacing problems rather than addressing them directly? How can we avoid accidentally building a new PIC instead of eliminating it completely? Is an alternative really necessary to establish *before* we attempt to eliminate part or all of this harmful system?

- ▸ **What are *all* the borders?** As we challenge the legitimacy of national borders, what other boundaries are important to keep in mind (between local geographies, between movement sectors, between departments in hospitals, etc.)? How can we keep these different scales of borders and boundaries in mind even as we acknowledge that they may require different approaches?

- ▸ **Are we accessing the full range of available tools?** Have we imagined their full potential and considered using them in unconventional ways before putting them down?

- ▸ **Are we engaging the full range of people we should be?** Who may not yet understand their vested interest in fighting for PIC abolition? How can we bring them in?

The PIC creates, maintains, and aggravates the problems its proponents claim it solves. It does not provide safety. It cannot be deployed in its own elimination. Without being overly rigid or purist, we must attempt to dismantle the PIC and develop new ways of living. This is possible.

Rachel Herzing, author of *How to Abolish Prisons: Lessons from the Movement Against Imprisonment*
New York, New York
July 2024

PREFACE

BY CARLOS MARTINEZ AND RONICA MUKERJEE

In our social media-saturated society, it's now taken for granted that police violence is widespread and deadly. The endless surfacing of new videos capturing instances of heinous violence against Black, Indigenous, and Latinx people at the hands of police officers have made such images appear as an almost predictable feature of modern life. The names of the victims of police violence have become well known to us—Oscar Grant, Tamir Rice, Alex Nieto, Ta'Kiya Young, Michael Brown, Sean Monterrosa, Eric Garner, Breonna Taylor, George Floyd, among too many others to list here. A seemingly infinite stream of reports on the systematic abuses and harms experienced by prisoners at the hands of prison guards across the country, from New York to Atlanta to California, has similarly made the harms associated with incarceration seem uneventful. Likewise, the violence experienced by migrants and asylum seekers crossing ever more militarized borders, whether in the form of migrant detention, family separation, deportation, or death caused by heat stress while walking through the Sonoran Desert, has become a commonplace occurrence. While this violence became acutely visible to people in the United States under the first Trump administration, it continues today.

Police, prisons, and borders—structures ostensibly designed to keep our society safe—kill, and they disproportionately kill people of color. For better or worse, this is no longer a surprising fact. Of course, the far-reaching circulation of violent stories and imagery emanating from these systems is not the only, or even primary, reason why they are now perceived by large swaths of society as harmful. The social movements that have emerged to resist them—the Movement for Black Lives, anti-prison organizations such as Critical Resistance, and immigrant and refugee rights movements, among others—prevent us from forgetting the names of victims or from presuming that their deaths were somehow justified.

Moreover, critical insights from movement activists and scholars, both inside and outside of academic institutions, have helped us understand that these systems are, in their origin and at their core, structured by racism. The morbid data, though incomplete and insufficient, speaks for itself—Black people are more than three times as likely as white people to be killed during police encounters, and Latinx, Indigenous, and Pacific Islander people are also killed at higher rates compared to white people.[1,2,3] Undoubtedly, police killings cross racial lines, but they also sharpen the dividing lines between racial groups.

The harms associated with these structures are now well understood by many to be a central, if not *the* central, racial justice issue of our time. However, only recently have these structures been more widely scrutinized as having any relationship to health injustice—the unequal patterns of disease and death produced by racial, class, gender, and other social inequalities. The profoundly unequal stratification of disease that we see in our society is unjust because it is the avoidable result of policies that could be modified. Being killed by a police officer can perhaps be easily comprehended as a matter of health justice. But the more subtle, slow, and less palpable physical and mental harms associated with policing, prisons, and border enforcement have often fallen out of view.

In 2009 geographer and political organizer Ruth Wilson Gilmore articulated a key insight that mass incarceration is "a machine for producing and exploiting a group-differentiated vulnerability to premature death."[4] However, the inherent harms of such institutions went largely ignored within the public health and medical fields.

This has changed in the last few years, thanks in no small part to an upsurge in organizing and activism by public health and medical trainees and practitioners. Just as broader racial justice movements have forced a national conversation on police violence, health-care activists have organized to demand that their respective fields break free from their historic silence. As physician Vanessa K. Ferrel discusses in an interview with scholar and activist Alexia Arani in chapter 3 of this book, activist groups such as White Coats for Black Lives (WC4BL) were formed by medical students in 2014 in the wake of the deaths of Michael Brown and Eric Garner. WC4BL chapters sprang up throughout the country and began to conduct "die-ins," in which protesters simulate being dead, at medical schools to pressure their institutions and the field of medicine at large to confront structural racism in their curriculum and practice.[5] The End Police Violence Collective, contributors to this collection, waged a multiyear campaign demanding that the American Public Health Association recognize police violence as constituting a racialized health crisis.[6] Amid the rise of the COVID-19 pandemic, several scholars and activists across the country documented the acute perils faced by incarcerated communities and began to advocate for immediate decarceration, aimed at reducing the number of people held in jails and prisons.[7, 8]

An ever-growing cohort of researchers, clinicians, community groups, and public health advocates have joined forces to investigate and address the physical and psychological harms produced by police violence, incarceration, and border enforcement practices. This book, *All This Safety Is Killing Us: Health Justice Beyond Prisons, Police, and Borders—Abolitionist Frameworks and Practices from Clinicians, Organizers, and Incarcerated Activists*, was inspired by these activities and emerged as a collaborative effort to document, expand upon, and propagate this growing area of research, practice, and activism to a broader public. Collectively, the contributors to this edited volume seek not only to document the harms to health produced by mass criminalization but to demonstrate that a different way forward is possible and that those of us working within the public health, clinical, and mental health care fields have critical roles to play in that project.

In this book, you will hear from a wide range of health practitioners, clinicians, and activists at the frontlines of care who are asking questions, organizing, theorizing, and strategizing in various ways to confront the harms of policing and incarceration. Based on our experiences, we recognize that to defy this seemingly omnipotent security apparatus, we first must undo dominant political and cultural frameworks that continue to equate safety with punishment.

Beyond Carceral Safety

Beginning in 2020, news media outlets began heralding the onset of a "crime wave" engulfing cities across the United States, purportedly the outcome of movement demands to "defund the police" that emerged in the wake of George Floyd's murder.[9] Despite the fact that widespread defunding never took place and only a few cities have implemented modest proposals to shift funds away from police, this narrative has proven eminently useful for "tough on crime" politicians and advocates.[10] We will only be safe again, they tell us, by inflating police budgets and putting more cops on the street. This outcry for safety delivered through the path of policing is, of course, not a new phenomenon. Safety, though a seemingly ever-elusive goal, has long served as a prime motivator for the expansion of policing, prisons, and immigration enforcement. From Lyndon B. Johnson's "War on Crime" in the 1960s to Richard Nixon's and Ronald Reagan's "War on Drugs" to the anti-immigrant policies of every recent president, the promise and principle of safety has been at the heart of successive administrations' punitive proposals.

As a result of this long history, safety is now viewed by much of the public as being synonymous with "carcerality"—a logic and form of governance premised on using punishment, incarceration, surveillance, and militarized force toward improving society. Police and prisons are the most easily recognized carceral institutions in our society. But carcerality encompasses a much wider range of systems and practices (several of which implicate and involve health practitioners), including migrant detention centers, compulsory drug treatment and psychiatric care, family policing, and deportation, among several others.

Safety, of course, is desired by all, and the desire to acquire it seems commonsensical enough. For several generations, we have only been offered a limited version of safety by our political leaders. Meghan McDowell uses the term "carceral safety" to describe this "control-based approach to public safety," which "requires a material and ideological commitment to punishment, security (i.e. police, military, surveillance), and self-defense."[11] Like a bottomless pit that can never be filled, the greatest power of these carceral systems is their ability to entice us to keep shoveling more resources into them, even though their promise to make us safer always seems to be out of reach. The outcomes of our political and societal infatuation with carceral safety are astounding.

With over two million people being held in the nation's prisons and jails—nearly one out of every 100 people,[12] the United States claims the dubious honor of incarcerating more people than any other country on the planet.[13] Indeed, every state in the country "incarcerates more people per capita than virtually any independent democracy on earth."[14] While we comprise less than 5 percent of the global population, our country now incarcerates 20 percent of all the world's prisoners.[15] The United States has become the world's largest jailer by increasing the nation's incarcerated population by 500 percent over the last forty years,[16] and we spend approximately $182 billion every year to perpetuate this unimaginable feat.[17]

Along with incarceration, our border and immigration enforcement regime has grown to unprecedented levels in recent years. Between 1993 and 2021, the US Border Patrol's annual budget has increased over tenfold, from $363 million to nearly $4.9 billion.[18] Around the turn of the twenty-first century, deportations of undocumented immigrants increased dramatically. Between 1997 and 2012 alone, the US carried out 4.2 million deportations—over twice the total of every deportation documented in this nation's history prior to 1997.[19] The country now spends more on immigration enforcement, the largest portion of the federal law enforcement budget, than at any other point in history.[20]

Meanwhile, our police forces have become far more militarized than in other wealthy countries, affecting both morbidity and mortality rates in the US. While several countries do not even routinely arm their officers, including most of the United Kingdom and Norway,[21] police officers in the United States are increasingly armed with military-grade equipment.[22] The fatal outcomes of this militarization are clear. In 2019 rates of fatal police shootings in the United States were five times and twenty-two times higher than Australia's and France's rates respectively, prompting criminologists to refer to America's police as "exceptionally lethal."[23]

Despite these world-historic outlays of money and resources, people in the United States are less safe and have poorer health outcomes than people in similar nations. For example, the United States has the highest homicide rate compared to other wealthy industrialized nations, which experience a fraction of this country's violence.[24]

While the financial cost to support these bloated carceral systems has only grown, throughout the country municipalities and states have seen their budgets for other critical social services, including education and public health, consistently cut in recent decades.[25] Unfortunately, the cost for this trend has not been solely financial. Policing, mass incarceration, deportation, and border enforcement have not only required billions of taxpayer dollars to maintain, but they have also come at the cost of tremendous suffering and illness. Though much of this suffering is unquantifiable, the existing evidence makes clear that policing and prisons are profound vectors of disease that produce premature death.

Several studies have indicated that incarceration devastates the physical and mental health of prisoners[26, 27] as well as their families.[28, 29] Compared to the general population, incarcerated people experience higher rates of chronic diseases, such as diabetes, cardiovascular disease, high blood pressure, asthma, arthritis, and cancer.[30, 31] As was made brutally evident during the early stages of the COVID-19 pandemic, prisons are also breeding grounds for a wide range of infectious diseases due to their poor ventilation and overcrowding. "Carceral institutions worldwide," Eric Reinhart writes, "have long functioned as disease multipliers and epidemiological pumps for surrounding communities in relation to HIV, tuberculosis, hepatitis C, influenza, and other infectious diseases."[32] Moreover, as Aminah Elster and her colleagues describe in painstakingly deep detail in chapter 7, prisoners are routinely victimized by systemic acts of medical violence and neglect, reproducing the trauma and abuse that many of them already experienced prior to incarceration.

Policing and deportation, we also know, are disease-producing practices. Aside from the physical violence associated with policing, people who experience abuse on behalf of law enforcement exhibit higher levels of mental distress and biological markers of stress, such as shortened telomeres.[33, 34] Men who have been stopped by police more often in their lifetimes are three times more likely to exhibit symptoms of post-traumatic stress disorder.[35] Simply living in a neighborhood where invasive policing practices are more prevalent has been shown to make individuals more likely to suffer from high blood pressure, diabetes, and other health issues.[36] Similarly, deportation and even the mere threat of deportation are associated with increased levels of mental distress, anxiety, and high blood pressure among undocumented individuals.[37, 38] Moreover, children with one or more deported parents experience a significant deterioration in their mental and physical health.[39, 40, 41]

Members of our society who are already socially and politically marginalized are made even more vulnerable by carceral systems. For example, members of the LGBTQ+ community are overrepresented at every stage of the criminal justice system, beginning with juvenile justice. LGBTQ+ people, particularly trans people and queer women, experience significantly higher rates of arrest, imprisonment, and community supervision than straight and cisgender people.[42] They also experience harsher treatment and systemic discrimination while in police custody and incarceration.[43, 44] As writer, poet, and activist Leroy Moore discusses in an interview in chapter 5, people with a variety of disabilities, including physical, psychological, and learning differences, are disproportionately targeted and harmed by the police. Indeed, half of all people killed by police have a disability.[45]

All these forms of carceral safety are killing too many of us, and some of us more than others—sometimes quickly and at other times slowly and imperceptibly. Despite that, the harms of carceral safety are not something we hear discussed often in public policy circles or mass media outlets. In part, this is because those who are overwhelmingly targeted and undermined by carceral safety tend to belong to groups that have always been cast as inherently threatening in the US political and racial order—Black and Latinx people, immigrants, substance users, sex workers, and various subsets of the population preemptively charged with being deviant and dangerous. Even if unnecessary harm has been wrought against them, we are told that the project of carceral safety—an ever-expanding experiment in mass punishment—is an inevitability that we have no choice but to pursue. To think otherwise must just be naive utopianism.

In reality, pursuing carceral safety is an exercise in cynical utopianism, which would have us maintain faith, despite all evidence to the contrary, that we can use militaristic force and punishment to create a safer society. But how do we free our societies and the institutions we work within from the stranglehold of carceral safety, and how can health activists and practitioners contribute to such an effort? While this book does not intend to provide a definitive answer to this question, we do draw hope and important lessons from the anti-carceral activists who have been leading this charge for several years.

Beyond Reformism

As the social movements and thinkers that inspired this book have clearly articulated, we can no longer hinge all our hopes on reducing the harms from law and immigration enforcement by attempting to reform them into more humane institutions. Indeed, the elusive promise of reform has been a recurrent means of quelling concerns when the violence associated with policing and prisons becomes too apparent and disturbing for liberal sensibilities. As Geo Maher reminds us, "police reform is as old as policing itself," pointing out that the very institution of policing was first established as an effort by the British Crown to control and professionalize groups who brutalized poor people on its behalf.[46] Prisons, too, have their origins in the reformist impulse to bureaucratize social control and end bodily torture as a means of punishment, which they did not do, as is made painfully evident in the ceaseless reports of violence still experienced by prisoners.[47]

Today, every time images of killing by law enforcement go viral, leading to protests, "popular reforms go on tour," as Derecka Purnell writes.[48] In the 1960s urban upheavals in response to systematic police brutality against Black communities brought forth an era of reformist proposals to make policing "race-neutral." In the 1970s and '80s lawmakers proposed sentencing reforms that sought to "modernize the criminal code and reduce racial disparity" in response to a series of prison rebellions against inhumane conditions and racialized violence against prisoners, such as the historic 1971 uprising at New York's Attica prison. Several police reform proposals have been put forward in recent years, such as requiring that police have body and dashboard cameras, banning the use of chokeholds, limiting no-knock warrants, conducting bias trainings, diversifying police departments, and ending racial profiling, among others. In the end, as Naomi Murakawa argues, many of these administrative fixes have simply had the effect of making "violence appear less emotional and more rights-laden."[49]

Many such reforms were included in the proposed George Floyd Justice in Policing Act of 2021. While the bill was fiercely debated in Congress, as Mariame Kaba and Andrea Ritchie contend, "nothing in the legislation named for him would have prevented George Floyd's murder, nor changed the conditions that brought him into contact with the cops who killed him."[50] Derek Chauvin, the officer who killed George Floyd, they point out, was thoroughly trained in implicit bias and de-escalation techniques, and his department had already undergone years of reform efforts, claiming to have "adopted 90 percent of the policies promoted by Obama's Task Force on 21st Century Policing."[51] Writing in response to the countless reforms proposed in the wake of the 2014 Ferguson uprising, Rachel Herzing, cofounder of Critical Resistance, explains, "This orientation toward police reform imagines that documentation, training or oversight might protect us from the harassment, intimidation, beatings, occupation and death that the state employs to maintain social control under the guise of safety."[52]

Aside from being ineffective, this reformist approach to "tweaking Armageddon," as Ruth Wilson Gilmore describes it, plays a more pernicious role: it distracts our focus from the structural inequalities that produce the cycles of economic deprivation, social abandonment, and dehumanization impacting racialized communities that allow policing and incarceration to appear as necessary.[53] Reforms, Purnell explains, seek to "make police polite managers of inequality." Moreover, by perpetuating the assumption that small tweaks to policing and incarceration practices are sufficient for remedying their harms, the totality of these structures is left unexamined and unchallenged.[54] Reforms to the prison-industrial complex, Herzing argues, "may run the risk of exceptionalizing or isolating negative elements of the system, while normalizing its overall operation and underwriting its future."[55] The violence stemming from policing and incarceration, in other words, is a feature of those systems, not an aberration that can be reformed away.

But most alarmingly, reformism has served as a key mechanism by which prisons and policing have been fortified and expanded. As Gilmore recounts in her groundbreaking text *Golden Gulag*, after federal courts directed California to relieve overcrowding in its prisons in the 1970s (a seemingly positive reform), politicians used this dictate as an opportunity to embark on "the biggest prison-building project in the history of the world."[56] Between 1982 and 2000, California built twenty-three new prisons and the state's prisoner population grew nearly 500 percent.[57] In a similar sleight of hand, in 2006 California governor Arnold Schwarzenegger proposed moving 4,500 incarcerated "non-violent" women into forty new smaller "community correctional facilities" in response to overcrowding and deplorable conditions in existing state prisons.[58] Advocates for this expansion claimed that such facilities represented a form of "gender-responsive justice" necessary for reducing violence against women in prisons and meeting their specific needs. However, incarcerated people in women's prisons did not agree, so they engaged in an organizing and petition-signing campaign to fight against what Rose Braz, a cofounder of Critical Resistance, referred to as "kinder, gentler, gender-responsive cages."[59] Likewise, police reforms, as Geo Maher argues, have attempted to "wash away the sins of the past by rewarding the most ineffective and violent departments with grants, advanced weaponry, and new technological fixes."[60]

Rather than seeking to merely mitigate harm while leaving these overall structures of violence intact, the contributors to this collection are motivated by the politics and practice of abolitionism—a movement and theoretical framework that demands a revolutionary transformation in social relations to break with the dominant logic of punishment that merely perpetuates cycles of violence and continues to fail us.[61] As Ronald Leftwich, a restorative justice advocate and prisoner, writes in chapter 1, "Abolition is about changing the ways we currently respond to harm without creating more."

For abolitionists, movements against policing, prisons, and borders are part of a historic lineage of revolt against oppressive institutions and practices that have terrorized racialized communities since the advent of settler colonialism—chattel slavery, convict leasing, lynching, Jim Crow, segregation, etc.[62] Grounded in this genealogy of struggle, abolitionists view contemporary institutions of policing and punishment as reconstituted vestiges of a society founded on colonial exploitation and still shaped by racial capitalism.

Policing, prisons, and borders have served as instruments of racial control and human dehumanization targeting populations that have been deemed disposable and dangerous throughout the history of the United States.[63, 64, 65, 66] This tendency toward making racialized groups disposable does not emerge solely out of racist animosity, nor a long, torturous history of white supremacy—though these elements are certainly part of the equation. Racialized disposability is also a requirement of our capitalist society's need to rationalize the dramatic inequalities and health disparities that it produces. As Ruth Wilson Gilmore explains, "Put simply, capitalism requires inequality and racism enshrines it. Thus, criminalization and mass incarceration are class war."[67] While this class war via mass criminalization has communities of color at the center of its crosshairs, white people from socially and economically abandoned communities are also targets, as made evident by the nearly four hundred thousand white prisoners in federal prisons as of 2022.[68]

With this magnified view of the legacies and foundations of mass criminalization and confinement, abolitionists understand that only a project that aims to reshape our society can produce a different outcome. Fundamentally, abolitionists recognize that punishment, surveillance, and incarceration will never make us safer or remedy the violence and other social ills that plague us. But abolition is not simply about tearing down police stations, prisons, and detention centers. It requires confronting our society's deadly inequalities while constructing new structures of care, mutual aid, and community restorative justice. As a scholar and political organizer, Dylan Rodríguez explains, "Abolition is not merely a practice of negation—a collective attempt to eliminate institutionalized dominance over targeted peoples and populations—but also a radically imaginative, generative, and socially productive communal (and community-building) practice."[69]

Toward an Abolitionist Health Justice

In our view, the goals guiding health justice and abolitionism are inextricably intertwined. Both approaches aim to challenge the mental, corporeal, and social harms produced by existing inequalities. Health justice is grounded in movements seeking transformational social change by "addressing the structural determinants of health that are the root cause of health inequities, such as the social and economic policies that create unequal conditions in health care, employment, housing, and education."[70] A health justice perspective recognizes that the health inequalities that pervade our society, resulting in worse disease outcomes and shorter life expectancies for those inhabiting a marginalized socioeconomic status, reflect and reinforce inherited social and political hierarchies. Abolitionist theory and practice can provide health justice advocates with a sharpened analysis and broader framework for understanding and confronting the central role that carceral systems play in causing and exacerbating health inequalities. Until we address, abolish, and replace these systems, health justice cannot be reached.

An abolitionist perspective beckons health justice advocates to contend with the ways that science and medicine have historically served to justify and exploit the oppression and confinement of racialized communities. Since at least the eighteenth century, scientists and physicians have played a central role in constructing spurious notions of Black people's "biological inferiority" that have fueled their associations with crime and pathology.[71, 72, 73] As Liat Ben-Moshe explains in her writing and discusses in her interview in chapter 11, racism, ableism, and sanism (the imperative to be sane and rational) have served as intersecting axes of oppression over time, resulting in a logic of "racial criminal pathologization."[74] In the early twentieth century, southern physicians, influenced by evolutionary science and the rising popularity of eugenics, warned of the growing threat of purportedly "degenerate" genes spread by Black as well as poor and disabled white people.[75] Associating Blackness with "born criminality," they argued that the only solution was to implement eugenic segregation, incarceration, and sterilization in response.[76, 77]

Medical institutions have served as primary sites of incarceration throughout US history. In California, where the highest number of eugenic sterilizations were conducted in the country, psychologists played a central role in categorizing working-class Latinxs as "criminally inclined" and "sexually deviant," leading to their disproportionate institutionalization and sterilization between 1920 and 1945.[78] During the Civil Rights and Black Power era, Black men who engaged in political activity began to be diagnosed by psychiatrists with schizophrenia, which became viewed as a disease associated with their perceived anger and mistrust, resulting in lifelong confinement in mental institutions for some.[79]

Although the forty-year racist history of the US Public Health Service's study on six hundred Black men in Tuskegee is well known, prisons have also served as hubs of unethical medical experimentation. Until the last few decades of the twentieth century, prisoners were widely used as test subjects in biomedical experiments in the United States.[80] An estimated 90 percent of pharmaceutical drugs licensed before the 1970s were first tested on prison populations.[81] While apologists have argued that prisoners participated in experiments voluntarily, true consent can hardly be considered to exist inside an inherently coercive institution.[82] Moreover, prisoners were often uninformed about the potential harms they might experience as research subjects.[83] Examples of the harms inflicted upon prisoners abound. But the experiments conducted by University of Pennsylvania–affiliated dermatologist Albert Kligman on hundreds of prisoners at Holmesburg Prison for over twenty years are among the most notorious. Kligman's test subjects were exposed to various radioactive and carcinogenic chemicals, such as dioxin, resulting in debilitating chronic pain, illnesses, and psychological trauma for many.[84]

Recognizing the ways that science and medicine have been key purveyors of carceral violence is critical for health and medical practitioners seeking to engage in abolitionist practice today. Despite important reforms, our contemporary health and medical institutions continue to serve, reproduce, and intersect with an array of punitive institutions and practices. As several contributors to this book address, a primary task facing abolitionists working in public health and medicine is to unlink and replace these chains of punishment and human coercion. Scholars and health practitioners have increasingly adopted the concept of "abolition medicine" to consider how the health-care profession can confront the legacies of racism in medicine and contemporary practices of race-based surveillance, policing, and incarceration in health-care settings. As Zahra Khan, Yoshiko Iwai, and Sayantani DasGupta write, "If abolition is the framework that confronts the carceral system by deconstructing oppressive systems and envisioning new ways of addressing harm without reproducing oppression, then abolition medicine is the organizing tool and response to the structural and historical violence reproduced by the US health-care system that envisions care delivery without oppression."[85]

While discussions of abolitionism and medicine have grown in recent years, much of this writing has been confined to articles in academic journals, making it largely inaccessible to a broader audience of activists and practitioners. Bridging abolitionism with health justice will necessitate challenging and altering many of the ways that people working in public health organizations and medical institutions conceive of and do their work. We hope to contribute to the necessary task of building a collective and widely available organizing toolbox for putting abolitionist health justice into practice. Just as health justice will not be achieved without abolishing harmful punitive systems, the abolitionist project will require the involvement of health practitioners to support the development for new structures of care, healing, and solidarity outside the reach of prisons, police, and borders.

Practicing Abolitionist Health Justice

Pursuing abolitionism necessarily involves acts of speculation to imagine a world in which punishment, confinement, surveillance, and coercion are not the default mechanisms we use to create a safe and just society. But abolitionists are not content with simply conjuring up visions of a distant utopia. Abolitionism is fundamentally rooted in praxis—an iterative and cyclical process of putting theoretical ideas into practice and reflecting on this implementation to inform future actions.[86] As Rose Braz reminds us, "Abolition is not just an end goal but a strategy today."[87] The practice of abolition involves building organizational infrastructures, launching campaigns, developing community protocols for building safety and accountability, and putting forward discrete challenges to carceral power. Only through engaging in such activities can we get a clearer picture of the possible horizons beyond carcerality, the strategies that will be necessary to get there, and the capacities that our movements must develop. Perhaps most importantly, abolitionist activities widen movement participation by demonstrating that creating safety without prisons and policing is possible. As Rachel Herzing emphasizes, "If [prison-industrial complex] abolitionists are to dispel the idea that our political aspirations are more than science fiction fantasies, putting them into practice is essential."[88]

But just as we can't hinge our hopes on reformist tweaks to carceral systems, we also can't expect or wait for an abolitionist society to be established in one fell swoop. Rather, abolitionists seek to advance changes that chip away at the presence, reach, and influence of carceral structures and practices in our daily lives, whether in our communities, schools, workplaces, or hospitals. "Rather than aiming to improve police through better regulation and more resources," Amna Akbar explains, "reform rooted in an abolitionist horizon aims to contest and then to shrink the role of police, ultimately seeking to transform our political, economic, and social order to achieve broader social provision for human needs."[89]

Such reforms aim to divert existing public resources away from policing and prisons toward alternative structures of communal power and nonpunitive social welfare and public health infrastructures. This process seeks to reverse the tendency that has dominated our society since at least the 1970s, in which public resources have been progressively siphoned from our social safety net toward the financing of ever larger systems of policing, immigration enforcement, and imprisonment. Ruth Wilson Gilmore has drawn from political theorist André Gorz's concept of non-reformist reforms to describe such abolitionist change strategies, which "unravel rather than widen the net of social control through criminalization."[90]

In recent years, we have seen several important examples of non-reformist reforms being advanced by health and medical practitioners. Across the country, clinicians, public health advocates, and medical students have allied with grassroots organizations to halt the expansion of carceral institutions and call for alternative models of care and transformative justice. In Georgia, health-care workers joined forces with a grassroots coalition, the Communities Over Cages Campaign, to push back against several proposals by the Fulton County Sheriff's Department to acquire and construct new jail spaces to relieve overcrowding. Unswayed by the sheriff's claims that these proposals are born out of humanitarian concerns, the coalition "held press events, wrote opinion pieces, held teach-ins for other health-care workers, and showed up to city hall consistently for public comment" to demand that the county invest instead in the development of a community resource and wellness center.[91]

In 2018 the Los Angeles County Sheriff's Department sought to respond to an acute and ever-growing mental health-care crisis within its jail system by proposing the development of a nearly $2 billion "treatment-oriented" jail for prisoners with psychiatric and substance use issues. Many health practitioners, unconvinced by the county's claim that such an institution would be guided by a new vision of "social justice" jail medicine, joined an alliance of grassroots organizations, the JusticeLA Coalition, to resist the project. A varied group of "medical students, nurses, psychiatrists, emergency physicians, social workers, and others" worked with the coalition to write letters, submit public comments, and participate in demonstrations emphasizing the dire need for non-carceral mental health and substance use services for the county's marginalized communities.[92] Their resistance pushed the county to "pivot away from their plan for a more 'caring' jail system and toward a 'care first, jail last' approach."[93]

In addition to these hopeful mass campaigns, clinicians are organizing inside emergency departments, intensive care units, community health centers, and other sites of care to limit and remove the presence and influence of policing and surveillance. For example, clinicians in San Francisco formed the DPH (Department of Public Health) Must Divest coalition to demand that the San Francisco Sheriff's Department be removed from the city's DPH clinics and San Francisco General Hospital and that these resources be used to fund the expansion of behavioral health care. Meanwhile, a growing number of community health centers that serve undocumented communities, such as the Monsignor Oscar A. Romero Clinic in Los Angeles, have developed protocols to ensure safety and legal representation for their patients in the scenario of an Immigration and Customs Enforcement agent visit.[94]

In chapter 2, Mihir Chaudhary discusses the organizing strategies that he and other surgical residents employed at Highland Hospital in Oakland, California, to regulate and limit police presence in the emergency department trauma bay while seeking to create "counter-surveillance" tools that would allow providers and patients to report police misconduct. In chapter 6, Jenna Heath, Elizabeth Hur, and Nicole Mitchell Chadwick examine the harmful and racist entanglements between child protective services and perinatal care that conspire to "control and separate structurally marginalized racial and ethnic minority groups' families." Drawing from their experiences working in inpatient settings during the perinatal period, they provide a series of instructive "mechanisms of resistance" that clinicians can use to limit their collusion with family policing systems.

With the rise of abolitionist campaigns and a growing awareness of the inherent violence of policing, some cities have begun to establish non-police mental and behavioral crisis teams to respond to emergencies. While such interventions are an important advance in limiting the presence of police, in chapter 12 Naomi Schoenfeld and Jennifer Esteen, nurses who have worked in such teams, warn of the limitations of reforms that require health-care workers to continue to work in "systems governed by similar carceral logics and biases." A truly abolitionist behavioral health infrastructure, they contend, will require a shift in myopic focus from "crisis care," an outcome of chronic underfunding of social welfare services, toward "broad investment in community-based support and significant expansion of easily accessible and free mental health care and substance use treatment." Their provocation calls on clinicians interested in building abolitionist alternatives to be wary of having their vision for non-carceral medicine limited to the proposals that are currently on offer.

Similarly, in chapter 10 Rafik Wahbi, Carlos Martinez, and Lauren Textor draw on historical and contemporary examples of radical health organizing to argue that our efforts to respond to urgent material needs should not be divorced from broader movement-building work. Inspired by the examples set forth by the Black Panther and Young Lords Parties, they discuss the radical potential of an abolitionist harm reduction movement to respond to our current opioid overdose disaster that "serves the people" using mutual aid models while building expansive coalitions that challenge the criminalization of homeless people and substance users. As Onyịnye Alheri also reminds us in chapter 9, the global War on Drugs, spearheaded and funded by the United States for over fifty years, has been a disaster for communities outside of the United States as well, particularly in Latin America and Africa. To advance international drug policy changes, she insists, we will also need a cultural "paradigm shift" from the still-dominant view of substance use as a disease.

Ultimately, practicing abolitionist health justice will require the proliferation of innumerable ongoing projects that confront dominant carceral logics while experimenting with new models of care both inside and outside of existing health institutions. This unending praxis will require the consistent development and revision of new strategies to maneuver through resistance and attempts at co-optation. Abolition, Charmaine Chua asserts, "is a constant struggle, waged in battle after battle against the morphological, shape-shifting power of repressive state forces and legitimated state violence."[95] In chapter 4, the End Police Violence Collective provides us with several examples of existing interventions aimed at putting abolitionist health justice into practice. As these interventions make evident, abolition is far from science fiction.

But multiplying and escalating these actions, as they write, will require the involvement of a wider range of public health activists working in collaboration with grassroots demands to divest from carceral systems. As chapter 8 by Tien Pham, Amber Akemi Piatt, and Nate Tan on their advocacy efforts to abolish the prison-to-ICE pipeline emphasizes, this work must also include impacted communities in all aspects of the work, including conducting research on the harms of carcerality. Moreover, the inherently creative work of abolitionism must involve the contributions of artists. In this vein, we feature artwork throughout this book created by visual artists, some of whom are currently prisoners, who have been impacted by and resist carceral systems in a variety of ways.

This collection of writing is not meant to be an exhaustive review of all the abolitionist projects, campaigns, and practices being launched and implemented across the United States. It's merely a snapshot in time meant to provide a glimpse, however partial and incomplete, of the many important experiments that abolitionist health justice activists in and out of prison are pursuing to help guide and inspire kindred efforts. We hope it becomes clear to readers that health is fundamentally a social and political phenomenon, and visionary movements that challenge our current political common sense are the strongest medicines we have available to advance health justice for all. This book is our collective attempt to nurture the conversations, reflections, creativity, and radical planning necessary for making abolitionist health justice a reality and to build a world of true safety beyond prisons, police, and borders.

PREFACE NOTES

1. Foster-Frau, Silvia. "Latinos Are Disproportionately Killed by Police but Often Left Out of the Debate about Brutality, Some Advocates Say." *The Washington Post* (Washington, DC), June 2, 2021.
2. Schwartz, Gabriel L., and Jaquelyn L. Jahn. "Mapping Fatal Police Violence across U.S. Metropolitan Areas: Overall Rates and Racial/Ethnic Inequities, 2013–2017." *PLOS ONE* 15, no. 6 (June 24, 2020): e0229686.
3. Schwartz, Gabriel L., and Jaquelyn L. Jahn. "Disaggregating Asian American and Pacific Islander Risk of Fatal Police Violence." *PLOS ONE* 17, no. 10 (October 10, 2022): e0274745.
4. Gilmore, Ruth Wilson. "Race, Prisons and War: Scenes from the Gilmore History of US Violence." *Socialist Register* 45 (March 19, 2009).
5. Charles, Dorothy, Kathryn Himmelstein, Walker Keenan, and Nicolas Barcelo. "White Coats for Black Lives: Medical Students Responding to Racism and Police Brutality." *Journal of Urban Health : Bulletin of the New York Academy of Medicine* 92, no. 6 (December 2015): 1007–10.
6. Conner, Cheryl, Christine Mitchell, Jaquelyn Jahn, and on behalf of the End Police Violence Collective. "Advancing Public Health Interventions to Address the Harms of the Carceral System: A Policy Statement Adopted by the American Public Health Association, October 2021." *Medical Care* 60, no. 9 (September 2022): 645.

7. Barsky, Benjamin A., Sunny Y. Kung, and Monik C. Jiménez. "COVID-19, Decarceration, and Bending the Arc of Justice—The Promise of Medical-Legal Partnerships." *Health Affairs Forefront*. (May 28, 2021).

8. Franco-Paredes, Carlos, Nazgol Ghandnoosh, Hassan Latif, Martin Krsak, Andres F. Henao-Martinez, Megan Robins, Lilian Vargas Barahona, and Eric M. Poeschla. "Decarceration and Community Re-entry in the COVID-19 Era." *The Lancet Infectious Diseases* 21, no. 1 (January 2021): e11–16.

9. Baptiste, Nathalie. "Stop Blaming Crime Rates on Defunding the Police." *Mother Jones* (San Francisco, CA), July 2, 2021.

10. Friedman, Andy and Mason Youngblood. "Nobody Defunded the Police: A Study." *The Real News Network*, April 18, 2022.

11. McDowell, Meghan G. "Insurgent Safety: Theorizing Alternatives to State Protection." *Theoretical Criminology* 23, no. 43–59 (February 2019).

12. Wagner, Peter and Wanda Bertram. "What Percent of the U.S. Is Incarcerated?" *Prison Policy Initiative* (Northampton, MA), January 16, 2020.

13. Law, Victoria. *Prisons Make Us Safer: And 20 Other Myths about Mass Incarceration*. New York: Penguin Random House, 2021.

14. Widra, Emily and Tiana Herring. "States of Incarceration: The Global Context 2021." *Prison Policy Initiative* (Northampton, MA), September 2021.

15. Cloud, David H., Ilana R. Garcia-Grossman, Andrea Armstrong, and Brie Williams. "Public Health and Prisons: Priorities in the Age of Mass Incarceration." *Annual Review of Public Health* 44 (April 3, 2023): 407–28.

16. The Sentencing Project. "Trends in U.S. Corrections." *The Sentencing Project*, 2020.

17. Wagner, Peter and Bernadette Rabuy. "Following the Money of Mass Incarceration." *Prison Policy Initiative* (Northampton, MA), January 25, 2017.

18. American Immigration Council. *The Cost of Immigration Enforcement and Border Security*. Washington, D.C.: American Immigration Council, 2021.

19. Golash-Boza, Tanya, and Pierrette Hondagneu-Sotelo. "Latino Immigrant Men and the Deportation Crisis: A Gendered Racial Removal Program." SSRN Scholarly Paper. Rochester, NY: Social Science Research Network, 2013.

20. Akkerman, Mark. "Global Spending on Immigration Enforcement Is Higher than Ever and Rising." *Migration Information Source* (Washington, D.C.), May 31, 2023.

21. Fox, Kara. "How US Gun Culture Compares with the World." *CNN* (Atlanta, Georgia), July 19, 2017.

22. Cheatham, Amelia and Lindsay Maizland. "How Police Compare in Different Democracies. Council on Foreign Relations." *Council on Foreign Relations* (New York, NY), March 29, 2022.

23. Hirschfield, Paul J. "Exceptionally Lethal: American Police Killings in a Comparative Perspective." *Annual Review of Criminology* 6, no. 1 (January 27, 2023): 471–98.

24. Chamie, Joseph. "America's High Homicide Rate." *N-IUSSP* (Florence, Italy), February 6, 2023.

25. Weber, Lauren, Laura Ungar, Michelle R. Smith, Hannah Recht, and Anna Maria Barry-Jester. "Hollowed-Out Public Health System Faces More Cuts amid Virus." *KFF News Reports* (San Francisco, CA), July 1, 2020.

26. Cunha, Olga, Andreia de Castro Rodrigues, Sónia Caridade, Ana Rita Dias, Telma Catarina Almeida, Ana Rita Cruz, and Maria Manuela Peixoto. "The Impact of Imprisonment on Individuals' Mental Health and Society Reintegration: Study Protocol." *BMC Psychology* 11, no. 1 (July 25, 2023): 215.

27. Novisky, Meghan A, Kathryn M Nowotny, Dylan B Jackson, Alexander Testa, and Michael G Vaughn. "Incarceration as a Fundamental Social Cause of Health Inequalities: Jails, Prisons and Vulnerability to COVID-19." *The British Journal of Criminology* (April 8, 2021): azab023.

28. Beresford, Sarah, Nancy Loucks, and Ben Raikes. "The Health Impact on Children Affected by Parental Imprisonment." *BMJ Paediatrics Open* 4, no. 1 (February 10, 2020): e000275.

29. Turney, Kristin. "Family Member Incarceration and Mental Health: Results from a Nationally Representative Survey." *SSM - Mental Health* 1 (December 1, 2021): 100002.

30. Hewson, Thomas, Matilda Minchin, Kenn Lee, Shiyao Liu, Evelyn Wong, Chantal Edge, Jake Hard, Katrina Forsyth, Jane Senior, and Jennifer Shaw. "Interventions for the Detection, Monitoring, and Management of Chronic Non-communicable Diseases in the Prison Population: An International Systematic Review." *BMC Public Health* 24 (January 24, 2024): 292.

31. Wang, Emily A., Nicole Redmond, Cheryl R. Dennison Himmelfarb, Becky Pettit, Marc Stern, Jue Chen, Susan Shero, Erin Iturriaga, Paul Sorlie, and Ana V. Diez Roux. "Cardiovascular Disease in Incarcerated Populations." *Journal of the American College of Cardiology* 69, no. 24 (June 20, 2017): 2967–76.

32. Reinhart, Eric. "How Mass Incarceration Makes Us All Sick." *Health Affairs Forefront*. (May 28, 2021).

33. DeVylder, Jordan E., Hyun-Jin Jun, Lisa Fedina, Daniel Coleman, Deidre Anglin, Courtney Cogburn, Bruce Link, and Richard P. Barth. "Association of Exposure to Police Violence with Prevalence of Mental Health Symptoms among Urban Residents in the United States." *JAMA Network Open* 1, no. 7 (November 21, 2018): e184945.

34. McFarland, Michael J., John Taylor, Cheryl A. S. McFarland, and Katherine L. Friedman. "Perceived Unfair Treatment by Police, Race, and Telomere Length: A Nashville Community-Based Sample of Black and White Men." *Journal of Health and Social Behavior* 59, no. 4 (December 2018): 585–600.

35. Hirschtick, J. L., S. M. Homan, G. Rauscher, L. H. Rubin, T. P. Johnson, C. E. Peterson, and V. W. Persky. "Persistent and Aggressive Interactions with the Police: Potential Mental Health Implications." *Epidemiology and Psychiatric Sciences* 29 (February 5, 2019): e19.

36. Sewell, Abigail A. and Kevin A. Jefferson. "Collateral Damage: The Health Effects of Invasive Police Encounters in New York City." *Journal of Urban Health: Bulletin of the New York Academy of Medicine* 93, no. Suppl 1 (April 2016): 42–67.

37. Artiga, Samantha and Barbara Lyons. "Family Consequences of Detention/Deportation: Effects on Finances, Health, and Well-Being." *KFF News Reports* (San Francisco, CA), September 18, 2018.

38. Torres, Jacqueline M., Julianna Deardorff, Robert B. Gunier, Kim G. Harley, Abbey Alkon, Katherine Kogut, and Brenda Eskenazi. "Worry about Deportation and Cardiovascular Disease Risk Factors among Adult Women: The Center for the Health Assessment of Mothers and Children of Salinas Study." *Annals of Behavioral Medicine* 52, no. 2 (February 5, 2018): 186–93.

39. Allen, Brian, Erica M. Cisneros, and Alexandra Tellez. "The Children Left Behind: The Impact of Parental Deportation on Mental Health." *Journal of Child and Family Studies* 24, no. 2 (2015): 386–92.

40. Lopez, William D., Pilar Horner, John Doering-White, Jorge Delva, Laura Sanders, and Ramiro Martinez. "Raising Children amid the Threat of Deportation: Perspectives from Undocumented Latina Mothers." *Journal of Community Practice*, April 3, 2018.

41. Martinez-Donate, A., J. Tellez Lieberman, L. Bakely, C. Correa, C. Valdez, E. McGhee Hassrick, E. Gonzalez-Fagoaga, A. Asadi Gonzalez, and

G. Rangel Gomez. "Deporting Immigrant Parents: Impact on the Health and Well-Being of Their Citizen Children." *European Journal of Public Health* 30, no. Supplement 5 (September 1, 2020): ckaa165.203.

42. Jones, Alexi. "Visualizing the Unequal Treatment of LGBTQ People in the Criminal Justice System." *Prison Policy Initiative.* March 2, 2021. https://www.prisonpolicy.org/blog/2021/03/02/lgbtq/.

43. Donohue, Gráinne, Edward McCann, and Michael Brown. "Views and Experiences of LGBTQ+ People in Prison Regarding Their Psychoso-cial Needs: A Systematic Review of the Qualitative Research Evidence." *International Journal of Environmental Research and Public Health* 18, no. 17 (September 3, 2021): 9335.

44. Mallory, Christy, Amira Hasenbush, and Brad Sears. "Discrimination and Harassment by Law Enforcement Officers in the LGBT Community." The Williams Institute, 2015. https://williamsinstitute.law.ucla.edu /publications/lgbt-discrim-law-enforcement/.

45. Thompson, Vilissa. "Understanding the Policing of Black, Disabled Bodies." *Center for American Progress.* February 10, 2021.

46. Maher, Geo. *A World Without Police: How Strong Communities Make Cops Obsolete.* New York: Verso Books, 2021.

47. Gilmore. "Race, Prisons and War."

48. Purnell, Derecka. *Becoming Abolitionists: Police, Protest, and the Pursuit of Freedom.* New York: Verso Books, 2021.

49. Murakawa, Naomi. *The First Civil Right: How Liberals Built Prison America.* Oxford: Oxford University Press, 2014.

50. Kaba, Mariame and Andrea J. Ritchie. "Why We Don't Say 'Reform the Police.'" *The Nation* (New York City, NY), September 2, 2022.

51. Kaba and Ritchie. "Why We Don't Say 'Reform the Police.'"

52. Herzing, Rachel. "Big Dreams and Bold Steps toward a Police-Free Future." *Truthout* (Sacramento, CA), September 16, 2015.

53. Gilmore, Ruth Wilson. Speech delivered at the "Revolution Will Not Be Funded: Beyond the Nonprofit Industrial Complex" conference. University of California, Santa Barbara, April 30 to May 1, 2004.

54. Purnell. *Becoming Abolitionists.*

55. Herzing, Rachel. "Commentary: 'Tweaking Armageddon': The Potential and Limits of Conditions of Confinement Campaigns." *Social Justice* 41, no. 3 (137) (2014): 190–95.

56. Gilmore, Ruth Wilson. *Golden Gulag: Prisons, Surplus, Crisis, and Opposition in Globalizing California.* Berkeley: University of California Press, 2007.

57. Gilmore. *Golden Gulag*.

58. Braz, Rose. "Kinder, Gentler, Gender Responsive Cages: Prison Expansion Is Not Prison Reform." *Women, Girls, and Criminal Justice* 7, no. 6 (2006): 87–88.

59. Braz. "Kinder, Gentler, Gender Responsive Cages." 87–88.

60. Maher. *A World Without Police*.

61. Carrier, Nicolas, and Justin Piché. "The State of Abolitionism." *Champ Pénal/Penal Field*, no. Vol. XII (March 23, 2015).

62. Rodríguez, Dylan. "Abolition as Praxis of Human Being: A Foreword." *Harvard Law Review*, April 10, 2019.

63. Akers Chacón, Justin and Mike Davis. *No One Is Illegal: Fighting Racism and State Violence on the U.S.-Mexico Border*. Chicago: Haymarket Books, 2006.

64. Jett, Brandon T. *Race, Crime, and Policing in the Jim Crow South: African Americans and Law Enforcement in Birmingham, Memphis, and New Orleans, 1920–1945*. Louisiana: LSU Press, 2021.

65. Muhammad, Khalil Gibran. *The Condemnation of Blackness: Race, Crime, and the Making of Modern Urban Americas.* Cambridge: Harvard University Press, 2019.

66. Wacquant, Loïc. "Deadly Symbiosis: When Ghetto and Prison Meet and Mesh." *Punishment & Society* 3, no. 1 (January 1, 2001): 95–133.

67. Gilmore, Ruth Wilson. "The Worrying State of the Anti-Prison Movement." In *Abolition Geography: Essays Towards Liberation*, edited by Brenna Bhandar and Alberto Toscano, 449–453. New York: Verso Books, 2022.

68. Carson, E. A. and Kluckow, R. *Prisoners in 2022: Statistical Tables*. Washington, D.C.: U.S. Department of Justice, Bureau of Justice Statistic, 2023. https://bjs.ojp.gov/document/p22st.pdf.

69. Rodríguez. "Abolition as Praxis of Human Being."

70. Wiley, Lindsay F., Ruqaiijah Yearby, Brietta R. Clark, and Seema Mohapatra. "Introduction: What Is Health Justice?" *The Journal of Law, Medicine & Ethics* 50, no. 4 (n.d.): 636–40.

71. Cooper Owens, Deirdre. *Medical Bondage: Race, Gender, and the Origins of American Gynecology*. Georgia: University of Georgia Press, 2017.

72. Hogarth, Rana A. *Medicalizing Blackness: Making Racial Difference in the Atlantic World, 1780–1840*. North Carolina: UNC Press Books, 2017.

73. Washington, Harriet A. *Medical Apartheid: The Dark History of Medical Experimentation on Black Americans from Colonial Times to the Present*. New York: Anchor, 2008.

74. Ben-Moshe, Liat. *Decarcerating Disability: Deinstitutionalization and Prison Abolition*. Minnesota: University of Minnesota Press, 2020.

75. Dorr, Gregory Michael. "Defective or Disabled?: Race, Medicine, and Eugenics in Progressive Era Virginia and Alabama." *The Journal of the Gilded Age and Progressive Era* 5, no. 4 (2006): 359–92.

76. Dorr. "Defective or Disabled?" 359–92.

77. Nelson Butler, Cheryl. "Blackness as Delinquency." *Washington University Law Review* 90, no. 5 (2013): 1335–1397, 2013.

78. Lira, Natalie. *Laboratory of Deficiency: Sterilization and Confinement in California, 1900–1950s*. California: University of California Press, 2021.

79. Metzl, Jonathan. *Protest Psychosis: How Schizophrenia Became a Black Disease*. Massachusetts: Beacon Press, 2011.

80. Hornblum, Allen M. "They Were Cheap and Available: Prisoners as Research Subjects in Twentieth Century America." *BMJ* 315, no. 7120 (November 29, 1997): 1437–41.

81. Harkness, Jon M. "Nuremberg and the Issue of Wartime Experiments on US Prisoners: The Green Committee." *JAMA* 276, no. 20 (November 27, 1996): 1672–75.

82. Lerner Barron H. "Subjects or Objects? Prisoners and Human Experimentation." *New England Journal of Medicine* 356, no. 18 (2007): 1806–7.

83. Hornblum, Allen M. *Acres of Skin: Human Experiments at Holmesburg Prison*. New York: Routledge, 1998.

84. Hornblum. *Acres of Skin*.

85. Khan, Zahra H., Yoshiko Iwai, and Sayantani DasGupta. "Abolitionist Reimaginings of Health." *AMA Journal of Ethics* 24, no. 3 (March 1, 2022): 239–46.

86. Rodríguez. "Abolition as Praxis of Human Being."

87. Samuels, Liz and David Stein. "Perspectives on Critical Resistance." In *Abolition Now!: Ten Years of Strategy and Struggle Against the Prison Industrial Complex* by The CRI0 Publications Collective. California: AK Press, 2008.

88. Herzing, Rachel. "Abolition Is Practical." *Inquest* (Cambridge, MA), July 11, 2023.

89. Akbar, Amna A. "An Abolitionist Horizon for (Police) Reform." *California Law Review* 108 (2020): 1781.

90. Gilmore. *Golden Gulag*.

91. Spencer, Mark. "Beware the Healthier Cage." *Inquest* (Cambridge, MA), Aug. 31, 2023.

92. Levenson, Jeremy, and Shamsher Samra. "Organized Care as Antidote to Organized Violence: An Engaged Clinical Ethnography of the Los Angeles County Jail System." *Culture, Medicine, and Psychiatry* (2023): 1–26.

93. Levenson and Samra. "Organized Care as Antidote to Organized Violence." 1–26.

94. Garcia, Jacqueline and Virginia Gaglianone. "Sanctuary Clinics Offer Respite for Undocumented Residents amid Immigration Raids." *CapRadio*, June 22, 2019.

95. Chua, Charmaine. "Abolition Is a Constant Struggle: Five Lessons from Minneapolis." *Theory & Event* 23, no. 4 Supplement (2020): S-127–S147.

1
TRAUMA, RESTORATIVE JUSTICE, AND ABOLITION

Overcoming Cycles of Violence
with Community Care

BY RONALD LEFTWICH WITH HANNAH MICHELLE BROWER

Ronald Leftwich leads Restorative Justice programming at Massachusetts Correctional Institution at Norfolk, where he is incarcerated. Ron has spent the majority of his life behind prison walls and is currently serving a life sentence without possibility of parole. Ron believes that the only way out of violence is to talk about it. This chapter was written by Ron and edited by Hannah Michelle Brower.

Over two million people are incarcerated in US prisons and jails currently, and a staggering number of them are people of color. Besides this, our cities and communities of color continue to be marginalized and remain locked in cycles of often deadly violence. The mass imprisonment of Black and Brown people, the working poor, the unemployed, the unhoused, transgender and queer people, Indigenous Americans, and other marginalized people of all stripes does not and has never provided us with real safety. This reality points to a colossal failure of the state, since it almost exclusively employs carceral systems to keep people safe. Our criminal justice system, the police, our courts, and prisons all view violence as a simple, unforgivable crime—and they view prosecution, imprisonment, and death as the only solutions.

In this chapter, I argue that it is the failure of the state to recognize and treat the trauma that precedes violence, which denies us real safety and keeps us locked in perpetual cycles of violence. The connection between trauma experienced, trauma left untreated, and violence committed toward people in the carceral system becomes evident as I detail the traumatic, dark past of my personal life. If, as I assert, trauma is at the root of violence, we must abolish the current system, which neither recognizes nor is designed to treat the trauma in our communities.

Finally, I argue that the only way to truly achieve safety is by completely dismantling or abolishing the carceral system. In its place, I propose restorative justice and abolitionist principles as the transformative foundations for communities of care. Communities supported by restorative justice principles begin with the premise that everybody matters, so when harm is committed, the entire community has a stake in the outcome.

Restorative justice asks us to first address the needs of the harmed person or persons. It asks, What do they need for healing? How can the harm be repaired, or is it even repairable? We are also asked to address the needs of the person or persons who committed the harm. Why did they commit this harm? How do we prevent this harm from ever being repeated? What does the person who committed the harm need to heal? Also, community members are asked what it will take to make the community feel safe again. Coupled with restorative justice principles, abolitionist ideals weave a strong foundation for transformative change in our communities.

Abolition is about changing the ways we currently respond to harm without creating more. Our courts, prisons, and jails create more harm by resting on a system of retributive justice that continues cycles of violence. While abolition is concerned with abolishing prisons and jails, this is not all it is concerned with. Abolitionist principles also begin with the idea that everyone matters, and no one is expendable. Through abolitionist understanding, we don't put people to death or incarcerate people forever to solve our problems. In communities of care where restorative justice and abolitionist principles are the norm, violence is viewed from a perspective of health, and the current retributive form of justice is eschewed in favor of a system characterized by healing, restoration, dialogue, and truth-telling.

I begin with truth-telling: the traumatic, dark past of my personal life and my connection to violence. I write from a prison cell where I now sit, serving a life sentence without the possibility of parole. There are no words to adequately express the remorse, shame, or anguish I feel. Still, I can only begin by saying I'm deeply sorry for the harm, pain, and trauma I've caused. The man I brutally killed and the woman I attacked and brutalized did not deserve any of this violence. This man and woman, their families and friends, are all victims and survivors, and I'm deeply sorry for leaving them with lifetimes of pain and loss. I can neither bring back a life nor repair the physical and psychological harm I've left behind, but I can accept responsibility for my actions and hold myself accountable.

Part of my accountability and responsibility is to share my story. I'm hopeful it will convince us to develop communities of care where health-care justice is available for every community member. I'm also hopeful that the story of my dark past will shed some light on our misguided reliance on the carceral systems, which have been a fixture in my life since I was four years old. As a survivor and perpetrator of deadly violence, I know firsthand how the carceral state—the courts, police, and prisons—fails to provide real safety.

Cycles of Trauma and Violence

I was five years old when I witnessed the shooting death of my father at the hands of my thirteen-year-old brother, his eldest son. I know now that it didn't have to be this way.

My father left to fight in the Korean War a kind, gentle, and intelligent man. He returned brutal and sadistic, suffering from post-traumatic stress disorder (PTSD) and an alcohol addiction. Despite the trauma he experienced in the war, he was never offered any treatment. Instead, he sought comfort in alcohol to calm his nightmares and put out the fires in his brain.

The psychological pain he experienced showed itself through violence. My father would take his pain out on Mom, my brothers, and me. If Mom served him cold food or if it didn't taste right to him, he would slam the plate to the floor, grab her, and hit her repeatedly, blackening her eyes, and busting open her lips and nose. Without fail, each time Junie, my oldest brother—then thirteen years old—would run into the kitchen to protect our mom. My father, often intoxicated and furious, would seize Junie and beat him even more severely than he beat my mother.

My father would beat me and my brothers for sucking our thumbs, wetting our beds, or for any reason he deemed necessary. He would beat us with his hands, his belt, or switches, which would leave thick, red welts all over our bodies that stung. My father was unaware of our crippling fear of him or the fact that he was the underlying cause of our bed-wetting and thumb-sucking. He was never aware that the trauma and PTSD that caused so much of his suffering, he was now beating into us on a daily basis.

As time passed, the beatings, fear, and chaos in our house grew worse. The mere sight or sound of my dad filled me with fear and dread, and I continued to watch my mom and Junie endure their beatings. Some incidents were seared into my memory. For example, the numerous times he yelled at Junie, my older two brothers, Barry and Peewee, and me to get outside. But before we left, he would make Mom strip naked in front of us, then he would get naked, put his penis in his hand, glare at us and say, "Now, I'm going to show you how to treat a woman." Then he'd push Mom toward the bedroom and tell us to "get the hell out."

This was yet another difficult and dangerous lesson implanted in my developing mind. How could I understand my naked father, his penis in hand, telling me "how to treat a woman" when I was four years old? I can recall the police showing up at our house so many times, with their red and blue lights flashing. After entering our home, two imposing white police officers would lead our father outside. I can still remember their words, "Come on, Ray, this has got to stop. You can't keep doing this." They would then walk him back inside, telling him to "go to bed and sleep it off." I don't ever remember these policemen walking our mom out of the house to talk with her, nor them asking her or Junie if they needed help. The police would drive off, leaving our father to repeat his brutal, drunken behavior a day or two later. My mom and brother, with their black eyes and busted noses and lips, were always left sitting on the couch.

Then it happened. The day was bright, sunny, and warm as I walked home from pre-school. I was five years old.

I knew before I bounded up the four steps to our front door that Mom was in the kitchen cooking. I could smell the hamburgers, onions, and peppers as I picked up my pace. When I raced up the steps and pulled open the screen door, I saw my three older brothers—Junie, Peewee, and Barry—sitting on the couch. A quick glance down the hallway confirmed that Mom was in the kitchen, but then my attention was suddenly caught when I saw Junie. In his hand he had my father's big, black gun, and in the other was a big, red bullet with a gold end. On the end table was another big, red bullet that looked like the one Junie was holding. As the screen door closed behind me, Junie, who was thirteen at the time, said, "Ronnie, you better go outside and play." I always did what Junie told me to do, so I turned right back around and went outside to play. In my stomach, I had a bad feeling. I knew something bad was going to happen.

I played in front of our house until our father came home. He got out of the car, covered from head to toe in mud from his job as a ditch digger. He walked toward the steps, and as he glared down at me, I looked up at him. For a split second, I thought about telling him, "You better not go in that house." But I didn't say anything. He walked up the steps and pushed the screen door open. As he stepped inside, I slipped in behind him. Looking between my father's legs, I could see Junie, tears streaming down his face, holding our dad's gun, and pointing it at my dad and me. Dad said, "What are you going to do with that?"

Through his tears, Junie said, "Shoot you." I thought I heard my father laugh as he reached for the gun, then BLAM!!!—the loudest sound I ever heard, as the gun went off and my dad flew backward, past me, and hit the floor. I was paralyzed and scared. I wet myself. Mom came running out of the kitchen screaming for help. Junie put the gun on the couch where Peewee and Barry remained sitting, then he went outside to sit on the steps. I went outside and sat beside him.

The police arrived, red and blue lights flashing, along with an ambulance. Junie was put in the back of the police car, and my father was wheeled out and put into the ambulance. Mom got in the back of the ambulance with him. I watched as the police car, with Junie in the back, and the ambulance, with my dad and mom in the back, both drove off.

The Aftermath of Trauma

I sat on our front steps with Peewee and Barry. Our neighbor came to sit with us too. None of us said a word. I sat on those steps for a long time, afraid to go back into our house. No one spoke to me, asked me if I was all right, or held me. I was left to deal with this violent, horrific, and cataclysmic event on my own. It was getting dark when I got the nerve to walk back into our house. The first thing I saw was the white chalk outline of where my father's body had fallen and a pool of blood, now blackish red, leaking over the chalk line. My mom came home late that night, gathered my brothers and me on the couch, and told us, "Your father is gone." She was crying, but I can remember feeling two things: a huge sense of relief and overwhelming fatigue. I fell asleep on the couch as I watched our mother, with a bucket of soapy water and rags, crying on her knees as she scrubbed away the white chalk outline of our father and that blackish-red pool of blood.

At the age of five, this day completely turned my already chaotic world upside down. I needed to process what I'd witnessed, to make sense out of chaos. The first thing I had to do was deal with the fear. I was paralyzed with fear when that gun went off, an overwhelming fear. WAS I DEAD? I couldn't move. How could I be relieved that our dad was no longer alive? I felt confused, crazy, and out of control. I couldn't deal with these emotions, these thoughts, so I did everything I could to turn them off.

On this dreadful day, my developing brain and body were taught the most erroneous lesson imaginable. I learned that one could kill another person to solve a problem. After witnessing this event, I became hypervigilant and super-attuned toward anything and anyone that I perceived as a threat. I could never again allow myself to experience those feelings that made me feel insane, out of control, paralyzed with fear, and completely vulnerable. My only goal in life was to protect this extremely vulnerable self. These traumatic experiences stayed with me as I grew older, influencing my choices and decisions for decades. I only became an adult in physical age. The horrific traumas of my past had shackled and anchored me to my five-year-old self, no matter how many years passed.

I grew up to commit two horrible and violent crimes, twenty-two years apart, not because I was born to be a murderer or a monster. I committed these harms because I failed to overcome the debilitating and horrific effects of the traumas I experienced as a young child. In many ways, I grew up to reenact the same traumas I had witnessed in my home. I saw a woman abused—my mom—and I went on to assault and abuse a woman in her home. I saw a murder—the killing of my father—and I went on to commit the murder of a man who was like a father to me.

My brother, Junie, fared no better. After shooting my father, he was incarcerated in a detention home for juveniles until he turned eighteen. This notoriously violent juvenile detention facility provided no assistance to my brother. He never recovered from the horror he had experienced at the hands of our dad, nor from the consequences of taking our dad's life. After being released, Junie developed gambling and alcohol addictions and abused each of his wives, much like our father had done to our mother. Junie would later die from alcohol-related illnesses.

The State's Failure to Address Trauma

It's impossible to know what would have gone differently if we lived in a country that prioritized safety over punishment. However, we can only work to make that place a reality if we are aware of the instances in which a different course of action might have resulted in greater safety.

My father experienced the trauma of war. If the state had provided him with the services and support that he needed to heal—including access to psychotherapy and addiction treatments—then he may never have committed violence against my mom and his children. The impact of my father's ongoing assault profoundly harmed my mother, my brothers, and me. We might not have endured this horrible abuse, and Junie and I might not have committed acts of violence if the state had sent professionals with training in family abuse and trauma instead of police. This cycle of harm may have been prevented if the state had provided my mom with assistance and other options, as well as allowed my dad the opportunity to get therapy.

Junie was the victim of my father's violence and the perpetrator of his murder. If, instead of being sent to a brutal juvenile detention, Junie had been treated like a thirteen-year-old child who had been victimized by ongoing violence, he may not have gone on to abuse the women in his life. After the violent trauma I experienced as a child, I committed a horrible and violent crime, and I went to prison for eighteen years. I would not have committed another murder within a year of leaving prison if, instead of incarceration, I had participated in a restorative justice process that required me to face the consequences of my actions and accept true accountability.

It's possible that the outcomes for my family, and thousands of families like ours, could have been drastically different if the state had responded with care, treatment, and restorative justice methods instead of relying on carceral institutions at every turn. We need to imagine a world in which this is possible to make it a reality. To create that world, I believe we must abolish carceral systems and replace them with something completely different: communities of care that are guided by restorative justice approaches.

Prison Abolition and Communities of Care: A Restorative Justice Approach

Since I've spent nearly forty-five years locked up behind prison walls, one would think that prison abolition would seem like a fantastic idea to me. But to the contrary, my belief in abolition did not come easy. I simply couldn't understand how anyone would suggest that abolishing our prisons and setting free dangerous people who had committed violence against others was a good idea. After all, I was living proof that it wasn't. I had spent eighteen years in prison for a violent sexual attack on an innocent woman, and less than a year after my release, I was back in prison serving a life sentence for killing a man who had only tried to help me. No, abolishing prisons just didn't seem reasonable.

Then something happened in 2013. I had served fifteen years of this life sentence when I found myself at the Massachusetts Correctional Institution in Norfolk. One Saturday morning, I sat in an auditorium filled with more than 250 incarcerated men and some seventy people from surrounding communities. I listened as two mothers, one after the other, stood up and talked about how their sons were murdered and how it affected them. They shared their grief, anguish, anger, and the unrelenting pain and suffering of their loss. On this day, like no other, I was confronted with the harm, pain, and suffering I had caused. Even though they were not related to the man I had killed or the woman I had attacked, as I listened to their words, I saw the horror, shock, terror, and pain that the victims, their family members, and their friends had to deal with as a result of offenses like the ones I committed.

The suffering, pain, and anguish that these mothers shared convicted me far more harshly than the judge's pronouncement of my life sentence. Their grief, pain, and suffering split me wide open emotionally, and, for the first time in my life, I truly allowed myself to feel what others felt. As I sat there and connected with their loss and hurt, I came face-to-face with my depravity and realized how disconnected I had become from humanity, my own and others'.

At the same event, Norfolk's annual Restorative Justice Retreat, I witnessed six men, who had committed horrible crimes, stand up in front of other incarcerated men, survivors, and victims from the community, including these two mothers, and take responsibility for their crimes. They described the harm they committed and promised to hold themselves accountable for their actions. These men received no compensation for their admissions, no "good time served" or early parole. They were simply attempting to repair any harm they had caused while continuing with their personal transformations.

It was on this day that I discovered the philosophy and a practice called restorative justice. This is where I began my true journey of personal healing, and where my thoughts and opinions about prison abolition and communities of care were formed. It was a life-changing experience for me, and by the end of the day, I was convinced that I wanted and needed more restorative justice. I've come to understand that restorative justice is a philosophy, a practice, and a way of relating to each other that seeks to transform the current systems that handle interpersonal and group conflict. It provides us with a way to shift our thinking in a new direction, away from punitive, retributive justice, and invites us to think more carefully about how we respond to violence, crime, and conflict.

Based in traditional Indigenous tribes' methods of community justice, restorative justice provides a way for all communities to respond to harms with a needs-based approach. In restorative justice when harm has been committed, addressing the needs of everyone involved is of paramount importance. But we begin by first addressing the needs of the person or persons harmed. This is a victim/survivor-centric philosophy and practice. When a person is harmed in our community, restorative justice recognizes immediately that there are certain obligations to the harmed party, and their needs must be addressed first in every instance. This approach requires us to ask questions that reach far beyond blame and punishment. How can the harm be repaired? Is it possible to repair the harm? What does a harmed person need for healing?

In the case of a murder, how do we meet the needs of family members and friends? Do they need to speak to the offender? What does a harmed party/victim/survivor need from the person or persons who harmed them?

Restorative justice recognizes that harms and crimes are not committed against the state—they are committed against people. Restorative justice aims, then, to address people's needs as thoroughly as possible. This also means addressing the needs of those people who commit harm against others. Prisons and jails are located in communities all across America. They are not designed for rehabilitation; instead, they are places where incarcerated people are held until their sentences, or their bodies, expire. People are generally left to their own devices when and if they are released from prison, and in far too many cases there is very little if any support for reintegrating back into our communities. While this is unsustainable, most of the damage is done prior to release.

Typically, behind prison walls, people who have hurt others are not required to talk about their offense or do any meaningful, introspective work. They are not required to answer important questions, including questions like these: What led up to your offense? Why did you offend? How did your offense affect the victim/survivor, their family, and the community? Why won't you offend again? How did your offense affect your own family? It's no surprise that large numbers of released folks return to prison. If you're not required to uncover the reasons why you offended, what is to prevent you from repeating the same behavior once released? Restorative justice practice not only provides a space and place to do this deep introspective work, but also provides us with a philosophy and principles to live by. My engagement in the philosophy allows me to share about my life, my trauma, and the heinous actions I committed in a way that I hope is accountable and responsible. Through victim offender empathy groups, participation in restorative justice reading and educational groups, as well as by learning to facilitate and lead such groups, I have immersed myself in the practice and philosophy. I've witnessed the transformations of many men who have committed violent offenses. In my ten-plus years in the program, I've never seen anyone who participated in a victim offender empathy group return to prison for committing a violent offense. While restorative justice is a powerful force that can heal the harmed person, the person who commits harm, and our communities, I argue that it works best, and would have the greatest impact, in a nonretributive system.

Building communities of care and imagining a different justice system is the answer.

Communities of Care

The only way to transform our reliance on prisons and our retributive system is to replace it with one that relies on opportunities for personal and community transformation. We need a philosophy for our communities that is based on truth-telling, where dialogue is the norm, where justice is focused on connection and relationship, and where all harms are obligated to be made as right as possible. I believe we are experiencing a zeitgeist moment in how we define community safety, responsibility, and accountability. In response to the murderous summer of 2020, with the killing of George Floyd and many others, community members, abolitionists, and people of every stripe are seeking and demanding change in our criminal justice system. They are not seeking cosmetic changes; they want real transformative change to a carceral system that does not provide us with real safety. Restorative justice and abolitionist principles provide the framework within which real safety can be attained. These principles will serve as the foundation for communities of care.

Using a restorative justice approach, we start from the premise that everyone matters and that "hurt people hurt people." Therefore, we are required to remedy the root causes of a person's harmful behavior, thus ensuring that the harmful behavior is not repeated. To do this, we must ensure that all community members have access to real safety such as affordable and high-quality health care, adequate housing, and employment. Two precepts of restorative justice are that it will center health-care justice as a fundamental requirement in any community of care:

1) When any harm is committed, the needs of the person(s) harmed must be the center of attention and must be addressed accordingly, and

2) Addressing the needs of the person(s) responsible for the harm is vital if we are to end cycles of violence.

We will not be able to address these needs without health-care justice. Affordable, accessible, and high-quality health care—including mental health treatment and trauma treatment centers—for everyone in the community is an essential component of healing.

Communities of care will originate anywhere like-minded people gather, so encourage one another and validate the overriding goals of health-care justice: true safety and freedom for all. Communities of care are formed wherever groups of people form relationships and where people are committed to working toward psychological and emotional healing. These groups may gather in any space or place: a living room, your apartment, your neighborhood, or in a park. The US has an overwhelming need for communities of care, especially for people and communities that have been harmed most by our punitive criminal legal systems. According to a 2016 report by the Annie E. Casey Foundation, over five million children in the US have experienced the incarceration of a parent during childhood.[1] Without communities of care, the consequences for many of these children will be devastating. These children are likely to "suffer poor academic outcomes, experience early pregnancies, experience PTSD, shame, self-loathing, and depression. Many will suffer abuse and neglect from one parent or others and at least half of these children will engage in criminal activity."[2] If these children end up in the juvenile system, they will be more than three times more likely to end up in prison than others, simply grist for the ever-churning human mill of the prison industrial complex.

We can change this. A restorative justice approach coupled with abolitionist ideals imagines communities where the needs of children are met, attended to, and nurtured. This means imagining a system that is not retributive and abolishing those carceral systems that perpetuate violence. This requires abolishing prisons. Abolition is not a far-fetched idea, but we must have the courage to imagine something better. As prison abolitionist and activist Mariame Kaba reiterates, and in the words of Michelle Kuo: "affluent communities—where police do not patrol school halls, where misbehavior in school results in counseling rather than jail, where people do not worry about their safety, and where addiction and mental illness are treated rather than criminalized—they are 'living abolition right now.'"[3]

Now we must expand abolition to all communities in this country. I'm actively engaged in making the Massachusetts Correctional Institution at Norfolk (MCI-Norfolk), where I live, a community of care. I'm a member of the restorative justice planning team. We develop and implement restorative justice programs designed to help men take responsibility and hold themselves accountable for the harms they've caused and to help them work toward healing. We work with and engage victims and survivors in all our programs, and we try to assist them in healing their trauma, pain, and suffering.

I've also joined hands with a spirited group of multigenerational, multiracial, incarcerated, and formerly incarcerated people and abolitionists known as the #DeeperThanWater coalition. This group was originally formed to bring attention to the fact that tap water at MCI-Norfolk was brown and filled with contaminants. #DeeperThanWater is now actively engaged in the fight for health-care justice in prisons in Massachusetts. We seek to bring attention to the inadequate and neglectful medical care that Wellpath, a for-profit health-care company, is providing at all Massachusetts state prisons. This company is destroying lives, and we have developed a campaign to push for change.

Our campaign team is a community of care, a community of like-minded individuals who are willing to fight for health-care justice until it is attained. Our community, supported by abolitionist and restorative justice principles, is a community of care in action! Building communities of care is movement work! We must work hard to build these communities into the fabric of our culture if we are to truly transform the way we respond to harm and violence. Without these communities, we will never fully confront the inequalities or injustices inherent in the carceral state. With them, there will no longer be a need for military police forces, countless jails and prisons, and a criminal justice system that does not provide real safety.

CHAPTER 1 NOTES

1. Annie E. Casey Foundation. "A Shared Sentence: The Devastating Toll of Parental Incarceration on Kids, Families and Communities" (2016). Retrieved from: https://assets.aecf.org/m/resourcedoc/aecf-ashared sentence-2016.pdf#page=7.
2. Wray, Harmon L. and Peggy Hutchinson. *Restorative Justice: Moving Beyond Punishment*. General Board of Global Ministries, the United Methodist Church, 2002.
3. Michelle Kuo. "What Replaces Prisons?" *The New York Review* (2020). Retrieved from: https://www.nybooks.com/articles/2020/08/20/what -replaces-prisons/.

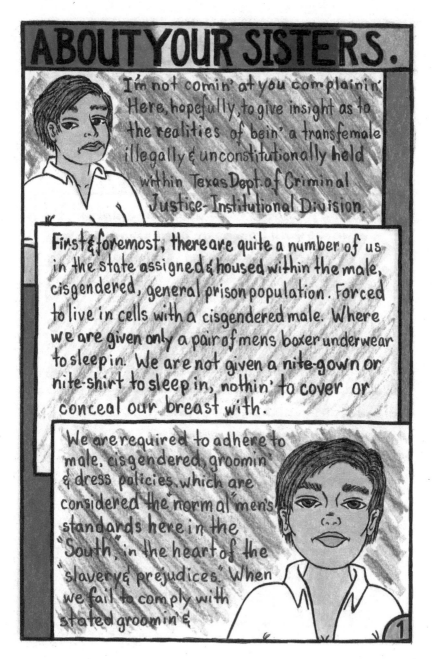

Figure 1.1: *About Your Sisters* mini-zine by Edee Allynnah Davis

dress policies we receive discipline, write-ups, & possible "loss of privileges." (L.O.P.), restriction where we are denied possession of our personal belongin's 'til compliance with the "normal" men's groomin' & dress policies forced upon us inspite of our feminine identities.
Now, take note, these brown-nose puppies are real, definitely quite real. Honestly, I cannot count the times that I have been required to strip nude for daily routine strip searches in the full view presence of cisgender males &/or right alongside of them, including cisgendered male officials
who I am "given orders" to strip for/in front of on a daily basis here. "Talk about a freakin' peep show!" Even though all the administrative & departmental authorities state/claim that there is a "ZERO TOLERANCE" policy in TDCJ-ID in accordance with the PREA (Prison Rape Elimination Act) laws set forth by the government, which includes the criminal act(s) of unconsented/unwanted "VOYERISM." & furthermore...
2

Figure 1.2

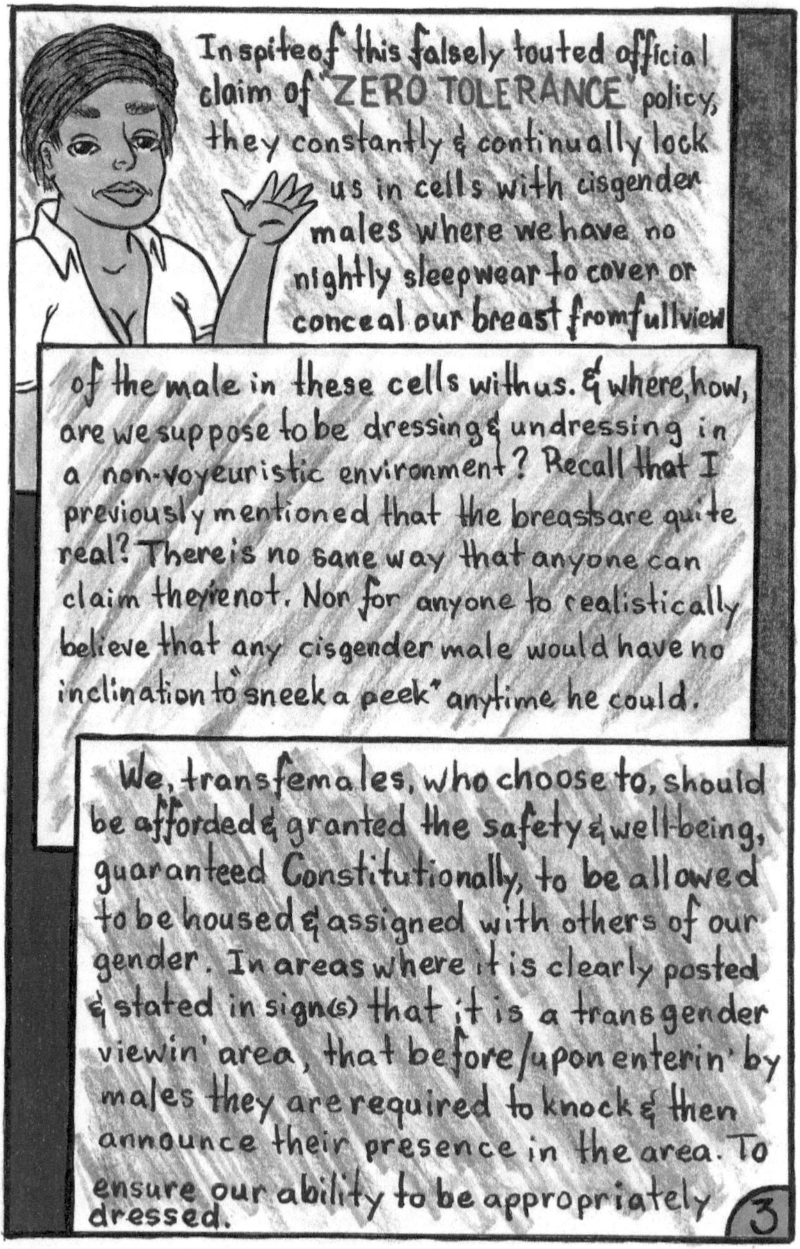

In spite of this falsely touted official claim of "ZERO TOLERANCE" policy, they constantly & continually lock us in cells with cisgender males where we have no nightly sleepwear to cover or conceal our breast from full view of the male in these cells with us. & where, how, are we suppose to be dressing & undressing in a non-voyeuristic environment? Recall that I previously mentioned that the breasts are quite real? There is no sane way that anyone can claim they're not. Nor for anyone to realistically believe that any cisgender male would have no inclination to "sneek a peek" anytime he could.

We, transfemales, who choose to, should be afforded & granted the safety & well-being, guaranteed Constitutionally, to be allowed to be housed & assigned with others of our gender. In areas where it is clearly posted & stated in sign(s) that it is a transgender viewin' area, that before/upon enterin' by males they are required to knock & then announce their presence in the area. To ensure our ability to be appropriately dressed. 3

Figure 1.3

We, trans females, should be afforded & granted Constitutional Rights to grow our hair, given nite wear for sleepin' in & female undergarments / panties / briefs.

Allowed to purchase & possess gender-related items from prison commissary / store. Such as, blow dryers, hair curlers, barrettes / hair ties, earrings, tweezers, emory boards, nail polish, make-up, feminine body care products, (lotions, soaps, shampoos, conditioners, deoderant, perfume). None of these items can be touted as a security risk to allow trans females to possess, as the cisgendered females within the prison system are allowed gender affirmative / appropriate products / possessions.

Allowing such will greatly attribute to our emotional / psychological well bein'. Reducin' the stress / strain placed upon the Mental Health Department(s) due to reduction of our anxieties & depression caused by being restricted from the

Figure 1.4

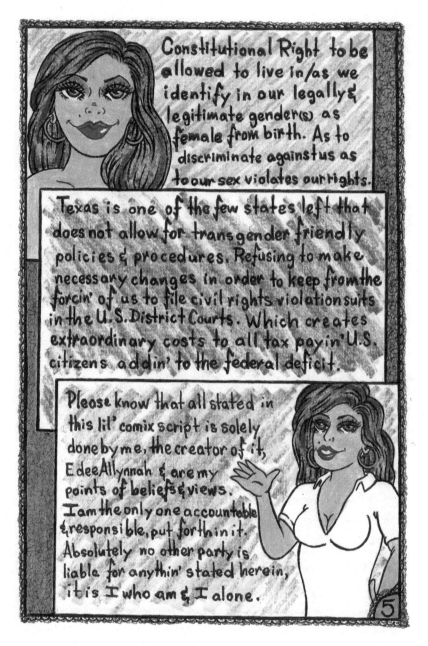

Figure 1.5

Figure 1.6

2

POLICING THE TRAUMA BAY

The Entanglement of the Carceral State and the Emergency Room

BY MIHIR CHAUDHARY

Shackles. The shackles that immobilized my patients in police custody and the daily oppression they produced felt wrong to me since I started surgical residency. When my patients were bound by shackles, they found it difficult to accomplish the simplest tasks, such as reaching for a meal tray, turning to sleep on their side, or scratching an itch on their nose. As I advanced in my training as a trauma surgeon, I developed a broader recognition of the far-ranging impacts of police presence during trauma patient care. This chapter is inspired by this broadening consciousness, further accelerated by the sweeping social movement in response to racialized police violence in the summer of 2020. In this chapter, I examine the complex interaction between the carceral state and the health-care system that begins once violently injured individuals arrive in hospitals. After being appointed chief resident in my hospital's trauma bay and developing a critical race lens to understand the carceral state, I sought to position myself as an active observer of the intersection between policing and trauma care. I took systematic notes and reflections during this period to understand police involvement in trauma patient care over a two-month period in the spring and early summer (April–May 2022) at our level 1 trauma center in Oakland, California—Highland Hospital. Highland Hospital exists within California's Alameda Health System—a public county health-care system. It is a 236-bed hospital with a regional trauma center that serves a broad catchment area, including the city of Oakland and out-lying suburban areas.

During this period, several insights about the operation of law enforce-ment personnel (LEP) inside clinical spaces emerged, including (1) the de facto power of police to violate the legal health-care privacy protec-tions of patients under custody, (2) the conflict of interest between law enforcement and trauma providers during the emergency care of trauma patients, and (3) strategies for health-care providers to build trust and advocate for their trauma patients impacted by the presence or actions of LEP. Using a critical race theory lens, this chapter seeks to explore how the carceral state is entangled within systems ostensibly designed for the provision of health care.

This chapter begins by traversing my own experiences as the chief resident on the trauma service during the participant period noted above, exploring the three emergent themes mentioned. Next, it broadens the view on violent injury, describing its epidemiology and how emergency departments and trauma centers become sites of policing. I then discuss the legal frameworks regulating law enforcement in health-care spaces. Next, the chapter will shift toward Highland Hospital, delving into in-depth interviews with trainees, senior doctors, and nurses to under-stand their views on LEP in health care. The final section will detail the ongoing, multiyear-long effort by specific emergency medicine providers to establish a set of hospital rules to regulate law enforcement activity during the acute care of trauma patients and how these activist provid-ers see their work within the context of abolitionist politics. The chap-ter concludes with a general review of hospital best practices that may allow trauma centers to work within an abolitionist framework to deliver care to acutely injured patients. As I hope becomes evident through this detailed analysis of the contemporary culture of trauma care and its links with policing, abolitionist politics are essential to the just transformation of trauma systems.

Experiences of a Trauma Surgery Resident

With few exceptions, police authority is widely accepted at Highland Hospital, including during trauma activations. Throughout my two months as the senior resident on trauma—that is, as the trauma chief—there were many instances of police entering the trauma bay to seek photographs of patients for evidence, and there was only one case where they were asked to leave during an acute phase of resuscitation by a nurse. Generally, residents would defer to perceived police authority, allowing them to seek whatever evidence or information they needed from patients, even during time-sensitive or critical junctures in care. One such instance involved a young Black man with a gunshot wound to the left upper arm suffering a brachial artery branch injury with ongoing blood loss. The patient's injury mandated an urgent operation. However, two officers stalled his transport to the operating room so they could have the wound dressings removed and have pictures taken. While these actions were not in keeping with hospital policies, which prioritize the immediate care of the injured patient, the police acted with de facto authority to delay the treatment for evidence capture. Another example involved a middle-aged Latino man shot through the right upper extremity and left back who was clinically stable. The patient initially opted to leave without receiving care unless his belongings were returned by law enforcement. While the team initially did not ask LEP to return the patient's belongings, it was clear that legally LEP had no basis to hold his belongings. As the chief resident, I was able to advocate for the patient's belongings to be returned, and the patient then cooperated with care. These instances speak to the informal, usually unquestioned, power of LEP within the clinical space.

The goal of police to criminalize and gather evidence often runs in direct contradiction to the patient care duties of clinicians. Specifically, in emergency trauma situations, while officers are seeking further information, clinicians are solely concerned with the care of the patient. When officers detain certain patients, the custodial duties of LEP may contradict the patient care duties of physicians. This was plainly illustrated to me in the instance of a twenty-year-old Black woman who was admitted following a gunshot wound to her thoracic spine, which left her paraplegic. Throughout her time at Highland Hospital, an officer was posted inside of her room at all times. The continual presence of police traumatized the patient. She reported psychological distress to the clinical team from her lack of privacy, which was specifically triggered by police presence. The trauma team advocated successfully for the officers to be seated outside of the room. Here, the policies of law enforcement to be directly posted in the patient's room were incongruent with the clinical reality that this patient would not walk again. Eventually, the patient received a placement in a rehabilitation center on a day of the week when officers were not present. This raised a legal and moral question for providers. The hospital clerk insisted the care team inform officers before discharge.

On the other hand, as the trauma chief, I identified with an abolitionist ethic and saw the police and carceral presence in this patient's room as actively traumatizing. The conscious decision was made to discharge without notification, and eventually, the patient left rehabilitation to go home. This episode raises the question of the possibility for abolitionist practice within health-care spaces: Can and should providers holding this form of radical politics facilitate the discharge of patients from carcerality? Is this a legitimate form of abolitionist direct action, despite, or rather in some ways *because* of its explicit illegality? As the corps of abolitionist providers grows, such questions of what forms of direct action are possible and legitimate deserve collective scrutiny and clarification.

During my time on the trauma service, LEP frequently violated patient rights in unlawful ways with impunity. The most common examples involved officers refusing to leave patient rooms and refusing to unshackle them even for history taking and physical exams—rights guaranteed to them by federal law and hospital policy. Another common violation was a refusal to facilitate a patient phone call. In all of these instances, a common solution would have been to question the officers' commanding supervisor and have a joint conference call with the patient, officer, and supervisor so they could clarify the patient's right to privacy and phone calls. To be sure, this takes extra time and effort, but this is the responsibility of the providers. One significant way this kind of advocacy is hampered is by the medical establishment itself.

To give one example, outside of the trauma service, I saw an incarcerated middle-aged white man for an anal fistula requiring an exam in the clinic. I asked the officers to leave the room, which they resisted and only acquiesced to after a phone call to their supervisor. After the exam, the patient eventually underwent surgery. I continued asking officers to grant patient privacy, and eventually, one set of officers filed a formal complaint. Then a meeting with program leadership ensued, and I was warned to cease asking officers for a private history and exam. They cited the dubious "morality" of incarcerated patients and the need to "watch out" for myself by having officers present.

These experiences reveal the complicity of providers in perpetuating carceral mindsets and practices. However, there is also a growing mutual solidarity network of abolitionist health-care workers and allies. In one case, one of my junior residents invoked this network by collaborating with abolitionist lawyers and doctors in the Bay Area after an incidence of police violence. Together, they strategized and assisted a young Black man who had been shot in the arm when trying to obtain his Air Jordan sneakers from police officers before discharge. Such examples demonstrate the power and potential for resisting police and carceral infiltration of health-care spaces.

Moving beyond my personal experiences as the trauma chief resident, the next section begins with a review of the scale of violent injury to give a sense of how emergency departments often function as sites of police and carceral intervention given the legal implications that follow such incidents.

Background: Violent Injury in the United States

The scale of violent injury in the United States is tremendous, and a significant portion of this injury is seen acutely in emergency departments. In 2021, the most recent year for which Centers for Disease Control and Prevention (CDC) public health data is available, over two million Americans suffered violent injury, and nearly seventy-five thousand of these Americans experienced a violent death.[1] On any given day, across the United States, an average of about 5,500 Americans arrive in emergency departments. To provide a sense of the scale of violence across the country—this equates to four Americans arriving to an emergency department *every minute* due to violent injury.[2]

The distribution of violent injury is racially inequitable. While homicide is the third leading cause of death for young Americans aged 15 to 34, it is the *leading* cause of death among Black Americans in this age group, according to the CDC's findings in 2021. Also, according to the CDC national database, for the year 2015, the first year for which race disaggregated data is available, Black Americans sustained over four hundred thousand nonfatal violent injuries out of the total 2.16 million nonfatal violent injuries.[3] This represents twice the rate of nonfatal violent injuries sustained by white Americans in 2015. Breaking the data down further, fifteen thousand of the total nonfatal violent injuries sustained by Black people were caused by the actions of LEP. To place this in a comparative context, Black people have a nearly three-fold greater rate of injury due to LEP action than white people.[4] Furthermore, the number of people truly injured by LEP remains unknown as over 90 percent of LEP voluntarily report violent crimes to the FBI Uniform Crime Reports with no designated category for LEP use of force (only 4 percent of law enforcement agencies reported police-involved shootings despite journalistic data indicating a far more widespread level of police-involved shootings).[5]

The incidence of violent injury rose significantly on a global scale in the wake of significant social and economic dislocation during the COVID-19 pandemic.[6,7,8] And, as one may imagine, each of these episodes of violent injury has a myriad of possible legal implications. The sheer magnitude of violent injury that is seen in emergency departments constructs the hospital setting as a key site of police and carceral state intervention. Violently injured patients are viewed as key sources of "evidence" or even suspects themselves.

As the theorizations of sociologist Johan Galtung emphasize, the etiology of such disproportionate violence among marginalized communities can only be understood through a broader social and political framework. For Galtung, episodes of interpersonal violence must be analyzed according to the social, political, and economic inequalities that give rise to them, which he refers to as *structural violence*.[9] Thus, health-care providers working among marginalized communities must find ways to attend to both the physical and the social wounds that our unequal society produces. I will now explore the legal landscape regulating LEP during patient care and delve into a case study of abolitionist providers and how they organized in the setting of Highland Hospital.

The Legal Landscape: HIPAA and EMTALA

In general, the profession of medicine lacks overarching norms to guide how physicians and hospitals should govern the intersection of police, carcerality, and patient care.[10] Nonetheless, federal laws exist that regulate LEP in the clinical setting to guide the interactions between LEP and trauma patients. Federal regulation of LEP in the emergency department is covered in the Emergency Medical Treatment and Labor Act (EMTALA) passed in 1986 and the Health Insurance Portability and Accountability Act (HIPAA) passed in 1996.[11] This section will specifically focus on how the scope of police officers is delimited within the context of these two pieces of health legislation. Such a policy review will better enable abolitionist trauma and emergency medicine providers to understand when officers may be acting explicitly outside the bounds of the law. The goal is to equip such providers regarding this knowledge to protect their patients from the violent repercussions of the police and carceral state. Concurrently, however, these are not meant to be normative descriptions of the legal regimes regulating LEP in health-care spaces, which, in certain ways, may be in direct contradiction to the ultimate vision of abolitionist trauma care, as will be explored later in the chapter.

EMTALA sets the limits of LEP involvement during the course of patient care. In general, EMTALA limits the ability of law enforcement to obtain tests from the hospital (such as blood alcohol level and imaging studies to localize bullets) solely for evidentiary use.[12] Once patients arrive in the hospital setting, the clinicians are responsible for their care and not beholden to and generally not advised to perform labs or studies for legal purposes. However, when certain tests are performed for indicated clinical care, LEP may use the collected data for evidentiary purposes without a warrant. An important exception to the limits on LEP requesting certain labs or studies is in the setting of a court-mandated subpoena, whereby those requests can be made for evidentiary purposes. Under EMTALA, a patient has the right to refuse any test or procedure if they are deemed to have medical competence.[13] Notably, EMTALA does not comment on patient rights in the setting of law enforcement questioning. However, most hospitals have institutional-level rules limiting law enforcement access to trauma patients during the acute phases of care. A recent analysis exploring how injured Black patients perceived their interactions with police indicates that trauma patients experience heavy questioning in the prehospital stage when LEP have exclusive access to the patient, especially in states where LEP are involved in prehospital transport.[14]

The other major law that regulates LEP in the emergency department (ED) and is relevant to violently injured patients is HIPAA. The major focus of HIPAA in this regard is custody over evidence that is also protected health information. According to HIPAA, health-care providers (HCPs) are required to provide personal health information (PHI) to LEP over a broad range of circumstances, including the following:[15]

1. It may prevent or lessen a threat to public safety.

2. It provides evidence linked to a crime.

3. It alerts LEP to a criminal death.

4. It alerts LEP to criminal activity.

5. It is in response to a subpoena.

6. It provides information about a criminal suspect.

7. An adult victim of a crime agrees to have their PHI given to LEP.

Of note, neither HIPAA nor EMTALA assigns any responsibility to trauma patients to provide information to LEP. At the same time, HIPAA does grant police officers with fairly broad powers to question HCPs. Nonetheless, police officers may find it *legally* expedient to gain direct testimony from patients, explaining their disproportionate focus on interrogating patients.[16]

Having explored HIPAA and EMTALA, the two primary legal authorities regulating the care and privacy of patients in custody, I now turn to the trauma bay itself. Specifically, Highland Hospital in East Oakland—a public safety-net trauma center—serves as our case study to unearth how the police and carceral state intersect with the care of injured patients.

Highland Hospital

The second portion of this piece will explore the experience of health-care professionals working at a public safety-net trauma center in East Oakland (Highland Hospital) that has an intimate administrative link to the county sheriff's department. The goal of this case study at Highland Hospital is to provide insight into the dynamics between police and HCPs that may exist in other clinical settings. I conducted in-depth, semistructured qualitative interviews with two different attending trauma surgeons,* a surgical resident, two ED resident physicians, and an ED nurse to understand the entanglement of police, carceral institutions, and trauma patients. All were involved in the care of trauma patients and had significant experience navigating LEP involvement during trauma patient care.

Additionally, I had many conversations with hospital administrators and legal counsels to uncover how institutional rules are established to regulate police officers in clinical spaces. Since Highland Hospital is a training institution, several interviews, as mentioned above, are with trainees—surgery and emergency medicine residents who are at the

---

* "Attending" refers to surgeons who have completed their training and are the lead physicians of a health-care team or service.

forefront of engaging with law enforcement during patient care. High-land Hospital sees a high volume of penetrating injury given its proximity to racially and economically marginalized neighborhoods in East Oakland[17] and has a continuous law enforcement presence from the sheriff's department. This case study explores how frontline nurses and physicians view patients, investigating how their attitudes are shaped within the structure and culture of health care to create complicity or foster resistance to the carceral state.

There is emerging evidence that the presence of law enforcement shapes clinical encounters and the comfort of providers in providing quality care.[18, 19, 20, 21, 22] Specific LEP practices such as shackling patients may induce bias in the doctor-patient relationship.[23] This section investigates how police presence impacts the care of trauma patients in particular. Our case study begins by delving into the experiences and insights of the various health-care providers involved in trauma patient care, punctuated with relevant data from participant observation. An important theme that emerges across interviews is how providers apply an individual responsibility frame to patients in legal custody—the idea that patients have caused and are accountable for their violation of the law. This frame is produced and reinforced in the way the clinical environment mystifies the social, economic, and political conditions leading to such actions. I conclude with an analysis of a resident-driven project to establish and enforce rules governing police officer activity during trauma resuscitations to offer a concrete example of abolitionist practice in trauma care.

Surgeons

In most trauma centers, the surgical team—residents, fellows, and attendings—are the primary hospital responders to high-acuity trauma activations and are supported by nurses and technicians. When a violently injured patient arrives to the trauma bay, surgical residents run the trauma code and manage the resuscitation. Simultaneous with the resuscitative efforts of surgical residents, law enforcement often seeks out violently injured patients to keep them in custody or seek further information from them. Within this context, I sought to understand how Highland trauma team members saw and experienced the police in the trauma bay. One former chief resident, now trauma attending, reflects on his time at Highland, noting the omnipresence of law enforcement as shaping the institution:

> *Sheriffs are basically there. The sheriff's office is right across the hallway from the social workers office. The cops are basically built into the structure of the health care institution and in those ways, they are just ever-present, they are always in the hallways, they are in the trauma bays, by the CT scanners and in the OR [operating room].* They are integrated into the hospital in a way we can't get case management into the hospital.*

These comments are insightful in that they describe an important visual disparity—the omnipresent sight of the punitive state—far more present in public safety-net institutions caring for economically and racially marginalized groups than in private health-care institutions caring for wealthier, white populations. Specifically, these comments raise the question of what the presence of the punitive state in certain health-care institutions does to form a specific relation between the state and racialized subjects. The safety-net hospitals where Black and Brown patients routinely receive care are often the most heavily policed, thereby allowing for criminalization to occur simultaneous to the receipt of health care.[24] What role is inscribed in the minds of Black and Brown patients receiving care at heavily policed hospitals? The previously mentioned trauma surgeon goes on to further characterize the county health-care space, stating: "Our care institutions damage relationships with patients. I don't know if they are seen as safe spaces." Such views on the presence of police defining the relationship between patients and institutions are

---

* The "CT scanner" refers to the medical imaging that many trauma patients undergo in evaluation of their injuries and is a separate part of the emergency department.

reiterated by an intern surgical resident who also feels like a surveillance target in highly policed clinical settings:

Their [LEP] presence, when they want to make it known, is definitely known and at least for me it's an intimidating presence. But then I remember that I am the patient's provider. So my feelings towards them [police] are—I'm unsure of how to interact with them in the setting of healing . . . I think their presence is always known when they are in the room.

Interviewer: How about in the trauma bay?

Trauma surgeon 1: Yes, like [their presence] in the [CT] scanner uninvited. And their presence is always known, but not the reason for their presence otherwise. I feel like they don't communicate with us why they need to be there.

Interviewer: Is there anything else?

Trauma surgeon 1: I just wish there was a way to separate these two systems in a way that is best for the patient at the end. How can we minimize the feelings of surveillance at all times? So, like, especially when the officer or whomever is in the room I have to actively remember not to act like I would otherwise because it, like, brings me discomfort . . . it takes extra mind energy to not focus my energy on another presence in the room that is not my patient.

The surgical resident here reiterates the co-constitution of the police surveillance state and public safety-net institutions ostensibly designed for caring and healing. She discusses the affective impact of feeling watched by police, in addition to the visual and signaling dimensions of their presence—their presence impacts both the provider and the patient.

In addition to this theme of surveillance, in interviews with the trauma attendings and residents, they all noted that trauma patients in custody often saw the trauma team in direct collusion with police officers. Because both officers and residents were in uniform, albeit different kinds, they were associated with institutional authority. Surgical residents struggled with how to explicitly demonstrate support or solidarity with patients to dispel this perception. One attending recalls the importance of taking action to demonstrate that the health-care team was not neutral and was, indeed, affirmatively on the patient's team. For example, this attending described that when she was a chief resident, a young Black man was shot through the head, dying in the trauma bay, and she fought to allow the family to stay in the ED with the patient and keep police out. This led to the officer filing a report against the chief resident. However, her actions and advocacy, ultimately, brought the patient's family closer to the trauma team. This trauma surgeon describes her experience as a resident at Highland:

> *I have been appalled at how unfair and aggressive the police have been at Highland during trauma activations. We, as the physicians, have been trained so differently. We take care of the patient first and foremost. If someone comes in as a Level 1 trauma, the last thing on our mind is, "Who did he/she shoot and why?" We are thinking about how to keep the patient alive.*

This trauma surgeon is speaking to a fundamental tension between the state interests of the police and carceral state and the ethical duties of health-care providers. Though the hospital sees police as functioning within a legitimate realm of "public safety," its analysis of police is structurally blind and unable to see "criminality" as emergent from the specific social conditions of race and class.[25, 26] Another trauma surgeon complicates the above perspective that physicians "have been trained so differently" by commenting on how the ideal of training conflicts with the culture of complicity that exists between health care and police:

> *Interviewer: Has your view of the police changed?*
>
> *Trauma surgeon 2: Pretty steady, though my view of health-care staff has changed. I knew that emergency nurses, emergency doctors, trauma doctors were kind of militarized in their thinking. But as I have become an attending, I see much more how it is entrenched. The trauma nurses are married to*

police officers, they are friends with police officers, and they know each other outside of the hospital.

These personal connections demonstrate that health-care providers in the trauma bay and police officers inhabit and share a class background that is often distinct from that of their patients. Violently injured patients often come from stigmatized race and class backgrounds separate from police, doctors, and nurses.

Historically, doctors, in particular, have often served as a dominant professional class and as a colonizing force in racially subjugated communities, as was explored by Frantz Fanon in his immersive study of the French colonization of Algeria and its subsequent struggle for liberation.[27] His analysis revealed how colonized Algerians saw French doctors as key actors in the imperial apparatus—seen to exist in complicity with the police and military as oppressive and alienating institutions. Analogously, as will be further explored, doctors in the urban safety net in the California context may be viewed as a formation acting in concert with other public authorities against racialized groups that have historically been excluded from mainstream institutions. Building on Fanon, scholar Carolyn Ureña argues that such exclusion produces not just physical but also epistemic "colonial wounds," whereby marginalized groups and their ways of knowing and being are systematically undermined relative to the dominant class of medical professionals.[28] Ureña's insights should compel health-care workers to recognize the deeper relational work needed to attend to the nonphysical wounds experienced by marginalized communities as well.

Emergency Room Physicians

While surgical residents' clinical experience in trauma is biased toward high acuity, time-sensitive patient care, emergency room residents, and physicians often care for a broader range of patients. This includes a diversity of patients implicated in the legal system—those with mental health crises and a variety of medical illnesses—in addition to those impacted by violent injury. Given their broader perspective, I sought to understand their experiences with law enforcement in the trauma bay.

Emergency physicians also describe interconnections between ED nursing and law enforcement that resonate with the previous trauma surgeon perspective. As one resident states:

> We even have a problem with the nursing staff a little bit. I know it sounds a little controversial, though we have nurses who wear sheriff badge necklaces or T-shirts that say, like, "Sheriff" or other crap on them, and it's super confusing to patients.

Such signaling may be "super confusing" to patients in that it erodes trust in health-care providers who, as the previously cited surgeon mentions, are seen as collusive with law enforcement. It resonates with the views of trauma surgeons on perceived and real complicity between health-care providers and law enforcement. Indeed, this emergency room resident also specifically notes personal relationships between nursing and police as a significant barrier to neutrality:

> I think there is a cultural allegiance. I think there are a lot of nurses who are literally married to cops. It is that simple. There's something there. I don't mean to sound classist; I mean a doctor can marry a cop, though a lot of nurses are.

This excerpt again references a broader social structure that aligns health-care institutions with punitive state institutions, both inside and outside of medical settings. It also demonstrates interdisciplinary divisiveness in perceived support of LEP. It is important to note, however, that many physicians, in addition to nurses, also have clear allegiance to police and carceral systems. Physicians working as emergency medicine doctors and trauma surgeons frequently have dual roles as police officers—further affirming Fanon's theorized links between the doctor and state systems of domination.[29, 30]

Nursing

Emergency department nurses, especially those in high volume trauma centers, are the clinical team members interfacing with patients over the longest periods and are often the most intimately involved in their care. How do their perspectives on trauma and law enforcement differ or converge with those of the physician teams? One theme explored earlier and shared by nurses, trauma surgeons, and emergency medicine physicians at Highland Hospital is the personal interconnections between law enforcement and HCPs. For example, many charge nurses at Highland are married to police officers and many more personally get to know the officers who frequently visit the emergency room as a site for searching for suspects and evidence. As one nurse describes:

> We deal with law enforcement when things are not chaotic, so we usually, the nurses usually, know who the police are when the police get there. So, on the nontrauma side, they [officers] come in with patients while they are in custody and often are there for twelve hours, sometimes if they [the patient] get admitted, for the entire day. The nurses or the EM [emergency medicine] providers may have more familiarity than the trauma team. A lot of times the officers will come to the nurse they know and be like, "Yo, what's happening?"

Relative to residents, especially surgical residents limited to encountering patients solely during trauma situations, nurses are consistently interacting with patients and officers. These interactions, especially during less acute circumstances, allow nurses and officers to develop relationships with each other. Another ED nurse independently confirmed that, beyond casual relationships, some nurses are personally connected to officers:

> Two charge nurses are married to police officers, but their husbands are not frequently in the hospitals because they are in higher-up positions. They are like sergeants or lieutenants or something.

Significantly this visible familiarity between nurses and officers is, again, seen as contributing to patient distrust of HCPs and the health-care system. As the same ED nurse notes:

> It feels like when you are talking to the police, they [the patients] think you are on their [the police's] team, and so then they don't want to tell you things that may be pertinent information because they think you will tell the police . . . I try not to make it obvious that I am friends with the officer. Because even if I am friends with the officer, I am not going to tell them information that the patient tells me; that's not my job. I mean I'll tell the officer like this person has three [gun]shots, but I'm not going to be, like, they smoked, like, meth or whatever.

This nurse expresses concern over the visible connections between nurses and officers and how this is perceived by patients with preexisting distrust of authoritarian institutions such as the police. This nurse makes a distinction between divulging what she thinks is legally pertinent information for the officer ("this person has three shots") and what is clinical information that may not be legally pertinent though has potential legal implications for the patient ("they smoke, like, meth or whatever"). Of note, HIIPA requirements mandate HCPs to provide LEP information that may be broadly linked to a crime. Within the broad scope of this requirement, reporting patient methamphetamine use in addition to bullet wounds could theoretically be included. However, such breadth of reporting carries the concern of seriously undermining patient trust while also contributing to a significant expansion of the carceral and surveillance state within health-care systems. The impact of reporting on trust is particularly true among marginalized communities who, for valid historical reasons, already harbor deep distrust of medical institutions.[31, 32, 33]

Often, nurses and doctors seeing patients decontextualized from the site of their original illness, injury, or mental health disorder only see their patients through a frame of individual responsibility. For example, a common phrase among ED nurses for patients cycling between prison or jail and the emergency room is *incarceritis*. Per the prior nurse:

> *We actually call it incarceritis. 'Cause what happens is people get arrested and come up with some medical complaint so they can go to the hospital instead of jail. "Oh, I got chest pain." "When did it start?" "As soon as I got arrested, I got chest pain." They'll come up with reasons to come here. Yeah, 'cause sometimes, like, they [the police] don't want to keep an officer off the street, so sometimes . . . depending on what the crime is they [the officer] may just sign them [the patient] out and ask them to come to court.*

The concept of *incarceritis* reveals how prevailing pro-carceral attitudes and cultures within emergency-health-care environments are formed. The incarcerated patient is seen as someone trying to manipulate the system and as not truly having an illness or injury. The fact that such a term exists in broad circulation speaks to the challenge of contextualizing structural violence within the more decontextualized episode of the clinical encounter. Again, structural blindness to the horrors of carceral confinement driving patients to seek escape, even if this means feigning medical illness, is captured by the colloquialism *incarceritis*.

The same nurse also later goes on to describe a case of an injured patient in custody for presumed child abuse. She explains that this narrative was passed on between nurses during their verbal handoff (i.e., how nurses transfer information about a patient during shift change) and affected treatment of the patient's pain. It was apparently common for nursing handoffs to include details on why a particular patient was in custody even if irrelevant to patient care. This, again, speaks to an individual responsibility frame that may permeate ED nursing and health care more generally. Such moral judgments naturally emerge within the course of ED care and, per this nurse, make it difficult to care for some patients. For example, this nurse explains that she wished she had never learned that her patient may have abused a child. She states, "If you don't know, you can treat them just regular. I pretend that everyone is in jail for a drug charge, so they are not bad people," revealing how some crimes more than others may trigger clinician bias.

Establishment of Emergency Department Guidelines

In order to learn more about the institutional policies and culture related to the regulation of police within Highland, I sought further information from hospital leadership. My email exchanges and conversations with administrators at Highland Hospital revealed the significant latitude that individual hospitals may have in regulating police interaction with patients. At Highland, a set of policies and rules theoretically govern the actions of patients in custody, including during trauma activations. These policies cover everything from patient privacy to the use of restraints and are devised by a committee of physicians and administrators. However, these policies are themselves not accessible unless specifically sought from hospital legal counsel. Additionally, it is unclear whether law enforcement is aware of these policies. When I began residency in 2016, historical incidents of police violations of patient rights fueled a movement to formalize and disseminate institutional policies regulating law enforcement at Highland Hospital. These efforts were reenergized following national movements against racialized police violence in 2020. Inspired by this, in the summer and fall of 2020, ED residents sought to create training for residents and a general reporting system to regulate law enforcement.

These efforts sought to prioritize the trauma patients' care and minimize law enforcement interference during the acute phases of resuscitation and intervention. This effort was primarily driven by a group of emergency medicine residents, many of whom explicitly identify as abolitionists. As such, they saw their efforts as a transitional strategy to a future hospital free from law enforcement all together. One of the founders of this project describes the initial motivation related to frequent violations of HIPAA standard of privacy for patients who were in custody. The project had two core components: (1) educating incoming residents of their responsibilities, under HIPAA, when caring for patients under law enforcement custody, and (2) providing a feedback mechanism to law enforcement for violations of HIPAA or institutional-level rules surrounding patient privacy. One of the founders of the effort describes the first component:

> We're trying to get a little bit more information out to people about what the policy is. It ended up being this resident pet project about getting it out to intern orientation. We worked with legal and security and HR [human resources] to include it at least in these annual training program things . . . we are trying to get them to own some of this training because it was really only happening for some residents at some times instead of being something that was owned by the hospital. It's a hospital responsibility, not a resident responsibility.

Given the hospital's failure to meet its obligations to patients under HIPAA, emergency medicine residents decided to self-organize and place this responsibility within the institution. As explained above, this was a multidisciplinary effort that involved multiple hospital departments (legal, security, and human resources) over multiple years. Specifically, part of the motivation for this project was a recognition that junior doctors were unknowingly violating patient privacy rights:

> I think people don't know how to act, so they end up treating law enforcement like another health-care professional, sharing patient information. And that has its own inherent risks. You can't get a good history if they [the officers] are there.

Given that interns and junior residents are socialized into the hegemonic authority of police officers, these ED activists recognized the explicit need for reeducation. As described in the previous section, it is often easy for clinicians to reflexively defer to the de facto power of law enforcement.

The second component of the emergency medicine resident project was to create feedback systems to alert the Oakland Police Department of violations of patient privacy or instances of patient harm following law enforcement action. This portion of the project was described by one of the ED resident activists:

And then also some sort of feedback mechanism. So something that would be training the residents, and the nurses, and the clerks. And then something that would have potential for feedback. And then, also, being able to communicate with sheriffs who are the liaisons and supposed to be in some ways the peacemakers who can help when OPD or some other law enforcement is in the ED and wilding out or doing something they're not supposed to be.

It is important to note that the liaisons regulating the emergency room providers and LEP are the sheriffs, who themselves are members of law enforcement. The lack of independent oversight speaks to the deep entrenchment of law enforcement in these spaces. Nonetheless, the resident project has now evolved such that quarterly meetings occur with hospital administration, resident leaders, and Oakland Police Department legal representation to review submitted reports of LEP misconduct. These resident activists saw their project as one of "harm reduction" within an ultimately abolitionist vision of eliminating police from the hospital. Though the Alameda Health System held explicitly progressive views of health equity, according to the activists, no one in the administration held abolitionist views. As one resident stated, "No one is able to say, 'No cops.' It's been about regulating the behavior of cops."

This reporting system project directly addresses physicians' concerns about police surveillance in health-care settings. Specifically, the reporting tool developed by the resident-activists provides a form of "counter-surveillance," a mechanism by which the surveilled providers can surveil the police. Of course, this project has yet to develop a means for patients under direct police supervision to report misconduct, though it offers one mechanism for rebalancing power by placing this tool in the hands of patient advocates.

Conclusion

The police and carceral state extend themselves into health-care spaces, particularly trauma bays, in distinct ways. Importantly, health care itself can become a mechanism for administering punishment by integrating and facilitating the omnipresence of law enforcement. Furthermore, certain health-care spaces—including emergency medicine and trauma surgery—may reproduce the punitive ideologies inherent to the police and carceral state. This is seen in explicit forms, such as including why someone is in custody within emergency nursing handoffs, or in implicit forms such as in the term *incarceritis,* which identifies people in jails and prisons coming to seek care as driven by false motivations. In these examples, we see many of the moral judgments inherent to the functioning of the police-carceral state also permeate and affect HCPs. Residents and attendings describe how police presence impacts their subjectivity within clinical spaces. It remains an ongoing and critical project to understand the specific relations that emerge from widespread police presence in hospitals serving marginalized communities.

Finally, on the level of practice, we have reviewed a concrete example of a resident-driven project in an ED serving a racialized and working-class community. This project seeks to disseminate legally driven guidelines regulating law enforcement presence. This project also created a health-care provider-reporting tool to identify concrete examples of law enforcement mistreatment of patients or violation of HIPAA duties. Such projects were viewed by residents as forming part of a broader abolitionist vision—facilitating the gathering of information and providing counter-surveillance to the punitive state. It provides one compelling example of a project grounded in an abolitionist ethic that may be reproduced to fit different local ED and trauma systems with frequent police contact. Specifically, this project begins the process of shifting power to trauma and emergency providers and, when paired with political education, can provide a tool that reduces the dominance of police in hospital spaces. This is just one example of a project with an abolitionist politic focused on reducing police power. Other efforts include shifting emergency response toward the community (such as the Anti-Police Terror Project in Oakland[34] or Chicago's Ujimaa medics[35]) and organizing to directly disembed the police from hospitals (See #DPHMustDivest[36] and the Beyond Do No Harm Collective[37]).

CHAPTER 2 NOTES

1. WISQARS (Web-Based Injury Statistics Query and Reporting System), CDC, accessed June 21, 2022, www.cdc.gov/injury/wisqars/index.html.
2. WISQARS.
3. WISQARS.
4. Lett, E., Asabor. E. N., Corbin. T., Boatright. D. "Racial Inequity in Fatal US Police Shootings, 2015–2020." *Journal of Epidemiology and Community Health*, jech-2020-215097 (October 27, 2020). Epub ahead of print. PMID: 33109524. https://doi.org/10.1016/j.surge.2020.07.004.
5. Richardson, J. B., St. Vil, C., Cooper, C. "Who Shot Ya? How Emergency Departments Can Collect Reliable Police Shooting Data." *Journal of Urban Health* 93, Suppl. 1 (April 2016): 8–31. https://doi.org/10.1007/s11524 -015-0008-7.
6. Olding, J., Zisman, S., Olding, C., Fan, K. "Penetrating Trauma during a Global Pandemic: Changing Patterns in Interpersonal Violence, Self-Harm and Domestic Violence in the Covid-19 Outbreak." *Surgeon* 19, no. 1 (February 2021): e9–e13. PMID: 32826157; PMCID: PMC7 392113. https://doi.org/10.1016/j.surge.2020.07.004.
7. Afif, I. N., Gobaud, A. N., Morrison, C. N., Jacoby, S. F., Maher, Z., Dauer, E. D., Kaufman, E. J., Santora, T. A., Anderson, J. H., Pathak, A., Sjoholm, L. O., Goldberg, A. J., Beard, J. H. (2022). "The Changing Epidemiology of Interpersonal Firearm Violence during the COVID-19 Pandemic in Philadelphia, PA." *Preventive Medicine* 158 (May 2022): 107020. PMID: 35301043; PMCID: PMC8920109. https://doi.org/10.1016/j.ypmed .2022.107020.
8. Sun, S., Cao, W., Ge, Y., Siegel, M., Wellenius, G. A. "Analysis of Firearm Violence during the COVID-19 Pandemic in the US." *JAMA Network Open* 5, no. 4 (April 2022): e229393. PMID: 35482307; PMCID: PMC9051986. https://doi.org/10.1001/jamanetworkopen.2022.9393.

9. Galtung, J. "Violence, Peace, and Peace Research." *Journal of Peace Research* 6, no. 3 (September 1969): 167–191. https://doi.org/10.1177/00223433 6900600301.

10. Tahouni, M. R. et al. "Managing Law Enforcement Presence in the Emergency Department: Highlighting the Need for New Policy Recommendations." *The Journal of Emergency Medicine* 49, no. 4 (June 2015): 523–29. https://doi.org/10.1016/j.jemermed.2015.04.001.

11. "Health Insurance Portability and Accountability Act (HIPAA) Privacy Rule: A Guide for Law Enforcement." HHS. www.hhs.gov/sites/default /files/ocr/privacy/hipaa/understanding/special/emergency/final_hipaa _guide_law_enforcement.pdf.

12. Brown, H. L., Brown, T. B. "EMTALA: The Evolution of Emergency Care in the United States." *Journal of Emergency Nursing* 45 no. 4 (July 2019): 411–14. https://doi.org/10.1016/j.jen.2019.02.002. PMID: 30902349.

13. Tahouni. "Managing Law Enforcement Presence in the Emergency Department." 523–529.

14. Jacoby, S. F., Richmond, T. S., Holena, D. N., Kaufman, E. J. "A Safe Haven for the Injured? Urban Trauma Care at the Intersection of Healthcare, Law Enforcement, and Race." *Social Science & Medicine* 199 (February 2018): 115–122. PMID: 28552292; PMCID: PMC5694382. https://doi.org/10.1016/j.socscimed.2017.05.037.

15. "Health Insurance Portability and Accountability Act (HIPAA) Privacy Rule."

16. Jacoby et al. "A Safe Haven for the Injured?" 115–22.

17. Alameda Health System. https://www.alamedahealthsystem.org/. Oakland, CA. Accessed June 21, 2022.

18. Harada, M.Y., Lara-Millán, A., Chalwell, L. E. "Policed Patients: How the Presence of Law Enforcement in the Emergency Department Impacts Medical Care." *Annals of Emergency Medicine* 78, no. 6 (December 2021): 738–48. https://doi.org/10.1016/j.annemergmed.2021.04.039. PMID: 34332806.

19. Haber, L. A., Erickson, H. P., Ranji, S. R., Ortiz, G. M., Pratt, L. A. "Acute Care for Patients Who Are Incarcerated: A Review." *JAMA Internal Medicine* 179, no. 11 (September 2019): 1561–1567. PMID: 31524937. https://doi.org/10.1001/jamainternmed.2019.3881.

20. Haber, L. A., Pratt, L. A., Erickson, H. P., Williams, B. A. "Shackling in the Hospital." *Journal of General Internal Medicine* 37, no. 5 (April 2022): 1258–1260. PMID: 35091917; PMCID: PMC8971251. https://doi.org /10.1007/s11606-021-07222-5.

21. Douglas, A. D., Zaidi, M.Y., Maatman, T. K., Choi, J. N., Meagher, A. D. "Caring for Incarcerated Patients: Can It Ever Be Equal?" *Journal of Surgical Education* 78 no. 6 (July 18, 2021): e154–e160. Epub. PMID: 34284945. https://doi.org/10.1016/j.jsurg.2021.06.009.

22. Brooks, K. C., Makam, A. N., Haber, L. A. "Caring for Hospitalized Incarcerated Patients: Physician and Nurse Experience." *Journal of General Internal Medicine* 37, no. 2 (January 6, 2021): 485–487. Epub. PMID: 33409890; PMCID: PMC7787594. https://doi.org/10.1007/s11606 -020-06510-w.

23. Haber et al. "Shackling in the Hospital." 1258–60.

24. International Healthcare Security and Safety Foundation. "Weapons Use Among Hospital Security Personnel" (Duke University Medical Center, 2014). https://www.iahss.org/resource/collection/48907176-3B11-4B24 -A7C0-FF756143C7DE/2014_Weapons_use_among_hosptial_security _personnel.pdf.

25. Gilmore, R. W. *Golden Gulag: Prisons, Surplus, Crisis, and Opposition in Globalizing California*. Berkeley: University of California Press, 2007.

26. Kundnani, A. "The Racial Constitution of Neoliberalism." *Race & Class* 63, no. 1 (2021): 51–69. https://doi.org/10.1177/0306396821992706.

27. Fanon, F. (1967). *A Dying Colonialism* (United Kingdom: Grove Atlantic. 1967).

28. Ureña, C. "Decolonial Embodiment: Fanon, the Clinical Encounter, and the Colonial Wound." *Disability and the Global South* 6, no. 1 (2019): 1640–1658.

29. "Hennepin Healthcare: Choose. Doctor or Police Officer?" Retrieved October 24, 2022, from https://www.fox9.com/news/hennepin-healthcare -choose-doctor-or-police-officer.

30. "To Serve and Protect, USC Trauma Surgeon Moonlights as a Cop." Retrieved October 24, 2022, from https://news.usc.edu/149005/to -serve-and-protect-usc-trauma-surgeon-moonlights-as-a-cop/.

31. Washington, H. A. *Medical Apartheid: The Dark History of Medical Experimentation on Black Americans from Colonial Times to the Present*. (New York: Knopf Doubleday Publishing Group, 2008).

32. Nelson, A. *Body and Soul: The Black Panther Party and the Fight Against Medical Discrimination*. (Minneapolis: University of Minnesota Press, 2011).

33. Armstrong, K., Karima, R. L., McMurphy, S., Putt, M. "Racial/Ethnic Differences in Physician Distrust in the United States." *American Journal of Public Health* 97, no. 7 (October 2011): 1283–89. PMID: 17538069.

34. *APTP: Anti-Police Terror Project*. APTP. (n.d.). Retrieved October 23, 2022, from https://www.antipoliceterrorproject.org/.

35. Wallace, G. "Bioethics Rooted in Justice: Community-Expert Reflections." *Hastings Center Report* 52, no. S1 (2022): S79–82. https://doi.org/10.1002/hast.1378.
36. *#DPHMustDivest*. Retrieved October 23, 2022, from https://www.dphmustdivest.com/.
37. Beyond Do No Harm. Retrieved March 15, 2023, from https://www.interruptingcriminalization.com/bdnh.

Figure 2.1: Artwork by Kristopher Storey

3

OUR WORK ENVIRONMENTS DO NOT HEAL

A Conversation on Carceral Health Care

BY ALEXIA ARANI AND VANESSA K. FERREL

Vanessa K. Ferrel, MD, MPH, is a Black queer HIV medicine and primary care physician, currently based out of Philadelphia. Vanessa has been on the frontlines of abolitionist medicine since 2014, organizing health-care workers for racial justice and striving to abolish carcerality from medical practice. On May 12, 2022, Alexia Arani, a queer mixed-race femme of color scholar-activist, interviewed Vanessa about their experiences applying abolitionist practices to health care. Alexia minimally edited the interview for length and clarity.

Alexia Arani (AA): *When we first met, you were a medical student in San Diego. Since then, you completed your residency in the Bronx and are now serving as an HIV medicine and primary care physician in Philadelphia. So can you talk a bit about the relationship between carcerality and medicine, as you've seen it play out across these various locations, over the course of your career?*

Vanessa Ferrel (VF): *I think we have to take a big step back and think about medicine itself as a structure that is very much founded in racism, genocide, ableism, and capitalism, like the whole United States. I think that I've always had a hard time in medicine because of those roots and because it's such an oppressive environment. Being a medical student, it's a really weird environment because you're always being evaluated. The threat of graduation is always being held over your head, and that really discourages any social-political advocacy work. Even basic patient advocacy* is seen as a waste of time and definitely discouraged, and then sociopolitical advocacy is seen as unprofessional because medicine should be an "apolitical" forum.

As far as my trajectory, I entered medical school as a very timid person, but I think I quickly enough found my footing and eventually decided that I would never put my career over my values. That's the decision that really enabled me to be more critical of the system, which I certainly participate in as a physician. But also, I'm personally affected by it because I love people who are patients, and I am a patient myself. And I think, also in the lines of training being a weird thing, residency really exploits you to the limits of being human. So you're sleep-deprived, hungry all the time, and you're mistreated; people are yelling at you. You don't really have the energy to do anything except to conform. Thinking about that stage of my life, I definitely would not have made it through without being able to build community with my patients and with other hospital workers who made that work environment much more tolerable. And I think, in this third stage as an attending, my work life will never be as difficult as it was as a resident or as a student, but I'm still within the system and fighting the same battles with different people.

I did a lot of inpatient work when I was a resident or a medical student, and now, I'm more in the outpatient center. I feel like people are criminalized in different ways, or the carcerality looks different in the inpatient versus outpatient environments. Within the inpatient environments, pretty much across the board, we do things to patients without their knowledge or consent or without really informing them. A really big thing is drug testing people. There are very few reasons to drug test people, in my opinion, especially if people tell you that they use drugs. There's constantly, "Oh well, they said they use drugs, so we need to drug test them." They already told us that they use drugs—what good is that going to do? Drug testing pregnant people without their consent and then reporting positive drug tests without informing people about the results is another huge way that we've criminalized people. It also perpetuates stigma for disabled folks, people who use drugs, and people with psychiatric illnesses. The way that we are trained to respond to people who may just be having a really hard day is, "Oh, call security because they're being 'non-compliant.'" They don't want to leave because they don't have a home to go to and instead of being like, "Let's find you a home," it's, "No, we need to physically remove this person from the property." And so it's the ways that we, every day, criminalize people that are magnified in health-care settings.

Another huge thing is when people can't afford to pay for services, a lot of the big institutions just sue them over their medical debt. This person doesn't have the money to pay the bills, so why would they have more money than what you're asking from them already? And another thing would be calling security to escalate a situation. I have rarely found that security, when called for emergency security purposes, has been able to deescalate, because you know, they're like the cops. They think they're the cops, and they just go in and make things worse, and people end up getting hurt. I remember very vividly, as a resident, I was rounding in the hallway, and we had left one patient, and the patient was having some verbal argument with one of the nursing staff, and then there was a security code called overhead. I remember hearing the security guard tackle the patient to the floor. I looked over, and this patient was just pinned to the floor by the security guard. I was like, "Why are we doing this in the fucking hospital?" My attending just kept going, and I was like, "No, no, I actually cannot continue my rounds; we need to acknowledge what happened to our patient here." I was surprised, but maybe not surprised, that the other people on the team were able to just keep going after witnessing something interpersonally violent happening to someone who was very vulnerable. That this happens to you in a place where you should be healing, that's absurd.

AA: *Those are really jarring examples of how medicine is complicit with the police and criminalization. Could you also speak to some of the more subtle ways that policing or ideas of deservingness of care or punishment get replicated in medicine?*

VF: *One thing is the idea of leaving against medical advice (AMA) and the conversations that we're trained to have with people who are leaving AMA. So usually, what has happened to me is someone will say, "Hey, I don't want to stay in the hospital because I hate it here" or "I have to go take care of something at home, and there's no one else to do this for me." Those have been, by and large, the reasons that people have told me they go against AMA. What we're supposed to tell people is that your treatment isn't quite complete yet. Of course, from a medical, legal perspective, we're covering our bases. If you leave, there's a potential that you could get sicker because your evaluation, diagnostics, or treatment haven't been completed yet, so we don't think it's safe for you to go. I think, unfortunately, the conversation that ends up happening is that people get threatened by their* medical team, "Well, if you leave now, you can't get a ride home, you can't get your medicine, you can't get care." When, really, it should be, "Go home and take care of things, and come back when you need to come back, when you're ready." And so I think that's huge, because people aren't responsible for their bills if they leave AMA. That's a huge misconception. Insurance still has to cover it, provided that they have insurance. The bill doesn't automatically go to the patient. And I think that's another way that they threaten people, like, "You're going to have to pay, and we're withholding other things from you." That's definitely something we could all be better at [communicating].

In terms of deservingness, for a lot of folks, especially people with chronic medical conditions who inevitably have a lot of psychosocial stressors; just a lot of shit going on with their lives, taking medicine is not the most important thing. They need to feed themselves, feed their families, be under a roof, and have shelter; just basic human needs. Maybe medicine is the last thing on their mind. If they feel comfortable being honest with their care team and saying, "Oh yeah, I'm not really taking these medications," the way that we're trained to respond is, "Well, you should really be taking your medications. Something is very wrong with you; this is your fault," and not, "It's the oppressive systems that are creating all of these issues that are making it hard for you to take your medications or for you to afford your medications." And when people advocate for themselves or their loved ones who are in the hospital, we call them disruptive, or aggressive, or combative. All they're trying to do is get the care that they deserve.

AA: So I'm curious, these patterns that you've talked about, have they been consistent across West to East Coast, medical school and residency, all these different environments that you've been working in? Or do you feel like you've had some experiences that are locally situated, in terms of how carcerality plays out in a health-care setting?

VF: I feel they've been pretty similar, with my personal experiences and also what I've heard from other people anecdotally, which I think cements the fact that this is a very structural [problem]. Because of the way that medical training is . . . we're working in US health care, which is racist and capitalist and ableist, so in the absence of doing exclusively free clinic work, everything that you do in the health-care setting has to be for profit. To generate profits, you have to ignore the *needs of the people in some vein. So, I think that this is where things start to get perpetuated. There may be some variations depending on how people's workloads are and what the staffing actually looks like because when you're really overworked and really tired, it's hard to be empathetic. Especially working as a physician in the inpatient setting, where every person who's being admitted to the hospital is having a terrible day because they're in the hospital, and you see twenty people, and everyone's having a bad day. You internalize how shitty everyone's feeling in addition to all the shit that you have to do, but you have to keep these things separate somehow. I think that the answer most people have is to dehumanize patients. And that's just how you get through your workday.*

AA: *You brought up the issue of medical training, and I know that's something you were really involved with during your residency at Montefiore* and at medical school at UC San Diego. Can you talk a little bit about your activism in these health-care settings?*

VF: *Yeah, we can throw it back to med school . . . [pauses, laughs] I'm remembering how much I hated it! It was a very dehumanizing environment for me as a person. I started around 2012 or 2013. Around 2014, when the Black Lives Matter movement was really sparking, and there were these very public executions of Black people, that all felt very personal to me. There was such a disconnect in what I was experiencing internally, and also socially, and what I was experiencing in the classroom, which was zero acknowledgment of what was happening, zero recognition. "We don't mention it because it's not relevant here." And I think that really was the point at which I just started to get mad. It was definitely the point at which I started being really radicalized. This is such a silent and complicit space, when medicine already has so much to contend with historically, and the fact that we still haven't learned our lesson, we would still willingly dehumanize as many people as possible as long as it upholds the status quo. So I just got mad.*

I started organizing with folks. It was initially a bunch of folks across schools within California, and then it became a more national movement. We coordinated

---

* The Montefiore Medical Center is the University Hospital for the Albert Einstein College of Medicine. Routinely described as one of the "premier academic medical centers" in the nation, its main campus is located in the northern Bronx, where the majority of the population is Black and Latine.

the first White Coat for Black Lives die-in in December 2014, and it was from
that that the national White Coats for Black Lives movement really started. Here,
eight years later, I'm thinking about the experience of organizing for Black lives
as a medical student and how much of that [reaction] was, again from medical
training: "Y'all are being unprofessional, this is irrelevant, what you're doing is
not only unimportant, but it's disruptive." "What you're doing is bad, and you
need to stop because it can affect your future and your career." I'm thinking about
how these institutions were suppressing us—and it was very much a shared experience; this was happening to everyone who was organizing around White Coats
for Black Lives—but then, in 2020 with the acute anti-racism movement, [those
same institutions were like] "We're anti-racist, we're #WhiteCoats4BlackLives."
I'm like, weren't y'all just silencing us, you know, less than ten years ago?

So the national White Coats for Black Lives movement started from that. It
was very much a Black, student-led organization that's really grown as people
have gone through the next stage of training, from medical school to residency. But
they still kept this radical tradition of, "We're explicitly an abolitionist organization, we take our teachings from radical Black feminist theory, our priorities are to
center and liberate Black people and acknowledge what happens to Black people
in health care as patients and as workers." I don't know what I would have done
without having that cross-campus/national solidarity, that opportunity to build
with people.

After my third year of medical school, I took a year off to do a [Master of
Public Health] (MPH) degree in New York, and I was seeing the same things.
It was 2016. The same shit was still happening, because the same shit has been
happening to Black people for forever. So again, [all] these very high-profile cases,
and, again, silence in the classroom. So I was able to take what we had done with
White Coats for Black Lives and implement it into the setting at Columbia under
the title of Health Equity for Black Lives, thinking about [the questions], "What
does it mean for a public health institution, and especially an Ivy League, to be
completely silent on the matter of Black lives? What does it mean for us, as Black
students, to be navigating these classrooms that center white experience and white
comfort and white fragility? What about our comfort and what about our safety?
What about our fragility?"

And then moving into residency, it was so much harder to organize. I think a lot of that is because residency is supposed to burn that out of you completely. It's designed in a way that you're working bananas hours and people are mad at you for things that you don't have control over. People that should be taking the blame aren't taking the blame, and so you're just tired all the time and it's very hard to organize. The first year and a half leading up to right before COVID started, I just really needed to get through it. And then COVID fucked everyone up and is fucking everyone up still. I think the COVID situation in the Bronx, plus the acute anti-racism movement simultaneously—with a social, radical national uprising (which was the good part)—institutions were like, "We'll try the mild version of that." I'm seeing these two things together, and seeing the hypocrisy of the institutions, where what we were doing back in 2014 was actually right and it's really fucked up of y'all to try to steer us away from doing these things and then co-opting our slogans and co-opting our movements. Now there are all these really woke institutions because they have the language that they've stolen, and they don't understand what [the language] means. Residency is a hard place to organize, and power to the people that are able to do it.

I think the only other organizing part of residency that I found helpful for my own politics was supporting the labor organizing that was happening among other health-care workers, especially the nursing union. Because of COVID and working in hospitals that were already understaffed [and functioning] with complete misallocation of resources, I supported labor unions. Seeing the people who are on the frontlines—as physicians we do maybe the least important job on the care team, and it is really everybody else running the show—and especially witnessing how poorly nurses are treated from the top down also led to my support of labor organizing. We all do the same job, which is taking care of patients, so seeing how shittily they were treated constantly and then seeing how much worse that got during and after COVID added to my politics. Some residents are like, "Nurses are so demanding, I can't believe they don't draw blood," pitting workers against each other. No, we all have the same enemy, which is the CEO who made $6 million—during a pandemic. So that's where an additional part of my politics was strengthened in the last few years, which I'm certainly grateful for.

AA: *And if I'm remembering correctly, haven't you also been really involved with curriculum development and trying to foreground less oppressive approaches to medicine, both at UCSD and in your residency?*

VF: *So, within UCSD, a colleague and I created a preclinical elective titled "Intersections of LGBTQ Health," which was created to address the huge disparity—huge lack of queer and trans health education that existed—and the elective especially focused on different populations within the queer and trans community and thinking about intersectional identities and what health looks like, or could look like, in each of those communities. And then in residency at Monte, I worked with a couple of colleagues to reinvent the social medicine immersion month, which is a mandatory one-month-long orientation for incoming or first-year family medicine, internal medicine, and pediatrics residents. And so the social medicine orientation was founded back in the '80s, and I think it just stayed that way for thirty years. When we went through it as first-years, it was, of course, white-centered. It really didn't capture the realities of the people who live in the Bronx. That was the biggest problem. This is a disservice to our patients. So we worked together to create a curriculum that was founded on the principles of intersectionality, critical race theory, and centering of the margins, and we tried to recruit people that were from the Bronx or people of color who could speak to the realities of the different levels of oppression that our patients were experiencing in the Bronx. And so we were really changing the way that that specific curriculum operated. I think that specific curriculum is not dissimilar to most other medical education curriculum, which is inevitably created to coddle white people and make them feel comfortable, because the last thing we want is for white people to feel uncomfortable in the classroom, since that's who deserves to be in these classrooms.*

AA: *What did you feel like the reception was to those changes in curriculum? What were the effects you noticed?*

VF: *For the queer health elective, because it was an elective, it didn't get as much pushback from the faculty, and the students really had a great time. That curriculum is still being run and is still a student-led curriculum, which is really great. But the social medicine month was such a shit show. So much of that had to do with the faculty who run the program being mostly older white people who are* like, "This is where I went for residency, this is such a great place, and all we have to do is stay exactly the same, because on paper, for the last forty years, we've been the premier social justice residency program." And then it's us, a group of young Black and Brown people being like, "Y'all are fucked up for this, and what you're doing is a disservice to everybody." Maybe our approach could have been different [laughs], maybe there was a reason the reception was bad. But it was really hard, to the point that I was like, "I am definitely not doing that again next year." Every meeting became an interrogation. We came with these very thoughtful, detailed plans, and they would just do everything that they could to tear it apart.

There was a time that this was contrasted so deeply and so clearly when there was a group of white residents who were going to do this queer health session for an elective. The faculty response was just so loving. When one of the young white people left crying, one of the older white people went out to comfort them. I was like, "Y'all are a mess. So you're telling me all I have to do is cry?" I would have done that if we could have saved all of the arguments [laughs]. [W]e did this curriculum change early first year and late second year, so it was 2020 when it was delivered. COVID had started maybe a few months before the planning session began for next year. When we hopped on these meetings like, "We're going to do that again, right?" The faculty was like, "Yeah." They didn't put up a fight. Maybe they were tired from working too much, because we were all working too much.

AA: I want to follow that thread because you've mentioned a few times some of the co-optation that happens, like how White Coats for Black Lives is something that these institutions are now getting behind after the uprisings that we've seen since 2020. So I'm curious about that shift you've noticed. It seems like you're not impressed by it [laughs]. Can you talk a little bit more about what the difference is between being abolitionist in your approach versus this lip-service, superficial, anti-racist sloganism that's been happening?

VF: You're right to say I'm not impressed, because I'm not. It has been very transparent what these institutions have chosen to say, or chosen to do, or chosen to show in the last couple of years. But this isn't the first time you're learning about racism. We know that this is not the first time [laughs], and then I haven't really seen good evidence of sustaining that change. Everybody had these incredible mission statements, they had promises: "We're gonna make reparations." And then as *quickly as it came, it was gone. So what are you doing now? It's been two years. How are you still being anti-racist? What are you doing to uphold that?*

I will say, I think the only thing that I've seen that has been sustained has been the race correction and renal function. In early 2021, after years and years of advocacy and organizing around this, the American Society of Nephrology and National Kidney Foundation adopted the stance that we are no longer recommending that kidney function be race corrected.* So prior to that official recommendation, there were a few institutions that were like, "We're going to stop doing this." That was, of course, because of many years of student activist organizing. The most impressive case that I've seen is Labcorp, which is a big, national community-based lab. That's where all the blood work in the US goes to—it's either Labcorp or Quest. This past January, they were like, "We're moving away from using this race correction factor; we will no longer be running labs with the race correction factor." That's huge. That is a national lab. But other than that, I haven't really seen people or institutions sustain a meaningful response.

In thinking about what a sustained or principled response would be, Cops Out of Care had a conference last April, and they ran through a bunch of different scenarios on what we can do to be principled abolitionists. The main argument was that a lot of hospitals or health-care institutions contract with police officers to provide their security, so how do we use this growing abolitionist movement as a way to promote defunding the cops by targeting the cops that are in hospital systems? I think, at Monte, after the whole acute anti-racism movement, there were

---

* Medical institutions in the United States have historically estimated kidney function (glomerular filtration rate or GFR) using calculations developed with the assumption that Black people biologically have increased muscle mass. When this "race correction" is applied to kidney function, the "African American GFR" is higher than the "non-African American GFR," which falsely overestimates the kidney function of Black patients. Overestimating GFR in Black patients not only delays diagnosis of early chronic kidney disease and preventative measures for progression, but it also precludes a significant number of Black patients from being eligible for organ transplant even with identical severity of disease compared to non-Black populations. For more information, see Tsai, Jennifer W., Jessica P. Cerdeña, William C. Goedel, William S. Asch, Vanessa Grubbs, Mallika L. Mendu, and Jay S. Kaufman. "Evaluating the Impact and Rationale of Race-Specific Estimations of Kidney Function: Estimations from U.S. NHANES, 2015–2018." *E Clinical Medicine* 42 (December 1, 2021): 101197; and "Removing Race from Estimates of Kidney Function," National Kidney Foundation, March 9, 2021. https://www.kidney.org/news/removing-race-estimates-kidney-function.

just more cops. There were suddenly NYPD officers at the front desk. I was like, this is the opposite!

I think if you have a contract with a police force, stop having that contract. Get rid of that shit. When you have security, what are they securing? What are their jobs? What are their intentions? If there's a person who is being "aggressive" or is doing something that is making people feel unsafe, what is the security going to do to make everybody feel safe? I think that's de-escalation. If hospitals are like, we're not getting rid of security, then the approach has to be different. I think also having clearer protocols around the little things we do to surveil people, like drug testing. Who are we testing, why, and how many of those drug tests are necessary? In medicine, we're always asking, "If I do this thing, how does that change management?" And why don't you ask yourself that question about simple things like this, drug testing: "How is this going to change my management? They already told me they use drugs. This is a waste of money."

I think another thing that would be cool would be just letting people wear their own clothes in the hospital, letting people go outside. Some people are in the hospital for weeks, months at a time; they are so restricted. They're physically, geographically restricted. There's no fresh air in a hospital; you forget what outside smells like. That would be just a nice and simple thing that we could do to make the environment feel less like we need to surveil you all the time and more like, yeah, it's shitty to be here; why don't we do something that can potentially be healing? Imagine!

AA: *So, what about individual health-care workers? Perhaps you can draw on your own experiences. How do you move in an abolitionist way as you are caring for your patients?*

VF: *I think it always starts with killing the cop in your head. For me, I really had to train myself to unlearn what could be my first responses. What am I trained to do that could make a person feel unsafe or stigmatized or judged? Because all of that is how we criminalize people. We reinforce stigma or we judge them or we withhold services or something. So, first of all, I try to make people feel comfortable, which is not a skill that every provider has [laughs]. What I find helpful is talking through my thinking process with people before I ask something that could be a stigmatizing topic for them. So, "The reason that I'm going to ask you this is* because, from a medical standpoint, I need to know x, y, z to determine whatever the next step would be." So it doesn't feel like, "Why is this person asking me this question, and what are they going to do with that information?" Something that I've really enjoyed doing is encouraging people to sign up for portals and letting them know you can read everyone's notes in the portal.[*] I don't know how much accountability there is for other people, but it does help me be more thoughtful in writing my notes, especially when I'm tired.

And I think, just generally practicing harm reduction in every sense of the word. So, of course, harm reduction applies to people who are using drugs and approaching that in a very nonjudgmental way and making sure that they're using safely and have the tools, physical and emotional, to use safely. But then other kinds of harm reduction, like using PrEP, using drugs and sex, how to make people safer and still get pleasure from the things that they enjoy. But I think all of that requires thinking about patients in a very human-centered way, which is something that you have to be really intentional about, because it's not the way that our work environments are set up to be. Our work environments are not set up to be healing places, so it's hard to want to heal in a place that doesn't feel healing for anybody. So we have to have a little bit of self-accountability to really try it.

AA: *And how do you navigate your role as a gatekeeper of medication, resources, diagnoses, all of that?*

VF: *I have been struggling with this a little bit in the last few weeks. I definitely feel weird about saying no, and sometimes okay, this is actually unsafe for a medical reason, but I have to be sure to explain that, "This is why we can't do this thing." But there's other things that we will gatekeep for no reason. Like sick notes. I will write anybody a sick note for any amount of time. It fucking sucks to work; tell*

---

[*] In April 2021, the 21st Century CURES Act (AKA Open Notes Act) mandated that clinical documentation in any electronic health record must be made available immediately to a patient via an online patient portal. Patients have had the right to obtain their medical information for decades, but the process to make a formal request had a lengthy timeline and often cost money. All patients of health-care institutions that utilize electronic health record systems now have the ability to access key aspects of their health in near real time without being subjected to the gatekeeping or bureaucracy of requesting paper records.

me how much time you need. My schedule right now allows me to see people as frequently as they like, and so instead of being like, "I can only see you every three to six months," some people need a little bit more attention and care, and I think that allows me to be more attentive and thoughtful with them and make a plan that feels realistic or feasible. That actually works, because you have x resources and don't have y resources. It's a weird thing, especially as a new attending, because I'm only practicing under my own license, and I don't have supervision. So, in the beginning, I was questioning myself a lot: "Is this the right thing to do?" Now I'm like, "Okay, why do I feel like I shouldn't do this? If it's not medically unsafe, why do I want to have control over this? Does it make sense for me to do that?" So, I'm recognizing when I'm having that feeling and being like, actually that feeling is bullshit [laughs]. So it's a constant battle for me.

AA: *Yes, and you're recognizing, too, how much of this really depends on the institutional context because, as you mentioned, part of you being able to have those personalized relationships is because you have openings in your schedule. And I remember when I interviewed you the first time, you mentioned getting negative feedback on being too casual or too unprofessional because you were relating to your patients and trying not to be this authoritative figure.*

VF: *Totally, yeah. It's so funny that you said that because I was also thinking about that earlier today, as I now have students shadowing me, and I remember when I was a med student, I was always so impressed if the doctor just sat next to the patient and made meaningful eye contact [laughs]. It gives people a sense of being a human. But people are like, "Why are you doing that? You sit where you sit, and the patient sits where they sit." These things are structured. You shouldn't slouch, you should face the computer and not the patient, there's all this hidden curriculum of what a doctor should be. Especially as a Black person, I'm missing the mark on so many levels because I'm not white. It's the way you talk to patients, you need to be more formal, you can't say "yeah," which is this weird, respectability, tone-policing thing. That was really irritating for me, and very upsetting to me as a med student. But it was what I felt most comfortable with, and the feedback from preceptors or the people who were supervising me was always so different from the feedback that I was getting from patients. Patients' feedback was that I made them feel comfortable. And I was like, why the fuck do I care what* *the person evaluating thinks if the patient, who is the most important person in this room, feels safe?*

AA: *This is just so interesting, thinking about the microscale of these interactions, because I'm thinking about abolition and how so often folks can feel like, "Oh that's overwhelming. Are you telling me we have to tear down the hospital? How would you even do that?" And I think you're opening up that there are all of these super small, little ways that you can disrupt whiteness and carcerality. Literally just taking the time to look someone in their eyes and slow down and ask how they're doing can make such a difference in disrupting that whole dehumanizing framework that medicine is built on.*

VF: *Totally, yeah. I'm still reading* We Do This 'Til We Free Us,[1] *but one of the things that I've read lately that really stuck out to me was that we have to focus on the mundane and not the spectacle or the excess. What are we doing every day that is harmful and oppressive to people? What are we normalizing every day that we could just change really easily? That's the same conversation I have with my patients about changing lifestyle—like incorporating exercise or eating a couple of vegetables. What's one small thing that you can change? If you change one small thing every week, in eight weeks you'll have a lot of changes. There are little things that we can do to change our environments, and those little changes still have the potential to make a big difference.*

AA: *Absolutely. Building on that, the abolitionist project is not just about destroying but building, so making those changes is what's so important. I'm curious to hear about some of the grassroots, community-based, abolitionist health-care projects that are being built, organizations you've worked with, or just projects you want to uplift that health-care workers can possibly learn from or give their time and labor to help out with.*

VF: *Definitely Cops Out of Care and the Beyond Do No Harm Coalition.* Folks in the Bronx and New York City, I'm thinking about Movement for Family*

---

* To learn more about Cops Out of Care, see interruptingcriminalization.com /cops-out-of-care; for the Beyond Do No Harm Coalition, see https://www .interruptingcriminalization.com/do-no-harm

Power, JMACforFamilies, those folks are really addressing the issue of family separation as systemic with the drug testing of parents and, what would it mean to provide resources instead of criminalizing parents who use drugs? And then the Eyes on You Committee / Root and Branch and Take Back the Bronx who are working directly with folks that are in Rikers—we gotta free them all.[†] Those are the highly recommended folks.*

AA: *Was there anything else you wanted to talk about?*

VF: *I just have another quote. I was reading through the list of quotes that I've really enjoyed from this book* [We Do This 'Til We Free Us], *that I haven't finished reading in a year and a half [laughs]. But the core tenets of abolitionist practice are, "Refusal, or only evil will collaborate with evil. Care, and care is the antidote to violence. And collectivity. Everything worthwhile is done with others."[2]*

AA: *I love that. What a beautiful way to end the interview.*

CHAPTER 3 NOTES

1. Kaba, M and Nopper, T. K. *We Do This 'Til We Free Us: Abolitionist Organizing and Transforming Justice* (Chicago: Haymarket Books, 2021).
2. Murakawa, N. (2021). Foreword. In M. Kaba and T. K. Nopper (Ed). *We Do This 'Til We Free Us: Abolitionist Organizing and Transforming Justice* (Chicago: Haymarket Books, 2021), xvii–xx.

---

* To learn more about Movement for Family Power, see https://www .movementforfamilypower.org/; for JMACforFamilies, see https://jmacforfamilies.org/.

† To learn more about the Eyes on You committee, see https://medium.com /@eyesonyounyc and https://twitter.com/Eyes_On_You_NYC; for Root and Branch, see https://linktr.ee/root_branchnyc or https://www.instagram.com/root_branchnyc; for take Back the Bronx, see https://www.instagram.com/takebackthebronx/.

Figure 3.1: *High Rates* mini-zine by E.T. Russian,
Juliet McMullin, and Delight Satter

Figure 3.2

Boarding schools, and the displacement of Indigenous people from the lands that sustained them since the beginning of time,

not only resulted in negative health effects,

they also resulted in ethnocide — the intentional destruction of their culture.

Figure 3.3

In the 1918 flu epidemic many Indigenous people passed.

We are missing those generations that are essential

for supporting knowledge sharing and healthy lives.

Doctors are seeing echoes of the policies that were designed for genocide and ethnocide. Not to mention the ongoing aggressions we see today.

Figure 3.4

For example, the Dakota Access Pipeline and threats to the Indian Child Welfare Act.

Also, Indian Health service receives diminished funding, despite those health services being part of the U.S. treaty obligations with Indigenous Nations.

And the microaggressions Indigenous people experience daily.

Stereotypes linked to spiritualism or casinos are used to deny resources or take meaningful input from Indigenous communities.

Figure 3.5

Programs that claim to help Indigenous people are developed, yet the resources often never make their way to the tribes or individuals.

Figure 3.6

Figure 3.7

In a historical context, doctors are seeing a different age distribution than they are used to seeing. Honestly, doctors should be thinking about these patients as ten years older, and screening appropriately.

How should they be working with their patients and talking to them about healthy lifestyles or prevention?

Figure 3.8

Figure 3.9

Figure 3.10

Figure 3.11

4

ABOLITION IS PUBLIC HEALTH

BY END POLICE VIOLENCE COLLECTIVE

"Abolition is about presence, not absence.
It is about building life-affirming institutions."

—RUTH WILSON GILMORE, ABOLITIONIST SCHOLAR AND ACTIVIST

In October 2021, the American Public Health Association (APHA)—the largest professional association of public health professionals, at twenty-five thousand members—permanently passed a statement outlining the health harms of carceral settings, including prisons, jails, immigration detention centers, parole, probation, and E-carceration. Through the statement—entitled "Advancing Public Health Interventions to Address the Harms of the Carceral System"[1]—APHA calls for measures to be taken by public health and other decision-making bodies across the US to "move towards the abolition of carceral systems and build[ing] in their stead just and equitable structures that advance the public's health." The statement argues these public health solutions are long-overdue measures needed to address the longstanding, widespread health harms of carceral systems on individuals, families, and communities.

Guided by an understanding that abolition is public health, in this chapter we will discuss why it is important for a professional public health organization like APHA to take this stance. We will then delve into the practical application of the action steps to demonstrate their feasibility and support their implementation, including successful emergent examples from ongoing community organizing for non-police, non-carceral alternatives. We will urge the public health field to quickly adopt these strategies grounded in equity and community care. Finally, we will conclude with examples of how researchers, organizers, educators, and policymakers have used the statement since its adoption to support ongoing work in communities.

The adoption of APHA's policy statement on carceral systems would not have been possible without the decades of abolitionist organizing that came before it and without the immense efforts of movement leaders, who are largely Black women. Many of us had been coauthors of the 2018 policy statement, *Addressing Law Enforcement Violence as a Public Health Issue*,[2] which similarly called for a paradigm shift within public health to reject reinforcement of punitive approaches to social and economic injustices. The policing statement took three years to pass and faced significant pushback despite a groundswell of support. In deciding to move forward on a statement about the harms of carceral systems, we imagined a similarly protracted process. But the specific political moment made it possible.

In 2020 the onset of the COVID-19 pandemic and the acute threat posed by its rapid spread in carceral settings initially brought urgency to organizers' demands for immediate decarceration. Shortly after, the police murders of Breonna Taylor, George Floyd, Tony McDade, and many other Black people set off a tidal wave of unprecedented uprisings around the globe. In mourning, outrage, and sharp clarity, organizers in the streets, in city hall hearings, and across media platforms unapologetically named the immediate need for abolitionist approaches to harm and accountability and made explicit connections between state violence and public health. The conditions were set for the field of public health to unapologetically name abolition as a public health strategy.

The statement is now permanent APHA policy, meant to represent the association's position on related policies and guide their lobbying efforts. However, statements and positions are only as good as the additional and continual actions to put them into practice. The statement affirms, as organizers have for decades, that 1) criminalized actions arise from conditions of inequity, interpersonal, and structural harms, and 2) existing systems do not address or prevent these underlying conditions, and certainly not in humanistic or restorative ways. We also sought to reinforce that abolition is not solely aimed at dismantling these structures, but also at building and growing structures and systems that create the conditions for people and communities to have what they need to be healthy and safe *without* carceral systems.

A Summary of the Action Steps

Through its fifteen action steps, APHA's policy statement serves as guidance to medical and public health practitioners, researchers, educators, organizers, policymakers, and others in their work to decrease reliance on the criminal legal system and build in its stead just and equitable systems that advance safety, public health, and well-being. They are intended for comprehensive implementation over time, such that the success of any one action step is rooted in efforts to effectively implement all others. These action steps can be broadly grouped within the following categories: (1) decarceration; (2) divesting from carceral systems and investing in the social determinants of health; (3) committing to non-carceral measures for accountability, safety, and well-being that are aligned with survivors' justice goals; and (4) decriminalization (Table 4.1).

Table 4.1. *Advancing Public Health Interventions to Address the Harms of the Carceral System*
Action Steps

CATEGORY	ACTION STEPS
Decarceration	**APHA urges federal, state, tribal, territorial, and local governments and agencies to:** ▶ End the practice of cash bail and pretrial incarceration. ▶ Significantly and continually reduce the number of people incarcerated in jails, prisons, and detention centers through release.

CATEGORY	ACTION STEPS
Decarceration *continued*	**APHA urges Congress, the Centers for Disease Control and Prevention, and the National Institutes of Health, in collaboration with community organizations, survivors, and formerly incarcerated individuals, to:** ▶ Put forth a set of recommendations that will decrease the population within carceral settings based on the principles of human rights and health justice. **APHA calls on state and local health departments to:** ▶ Provide accurate, timely, and publicly available data on incarcerated, detained, and released populations at the state and facility levels.
Divesting from carceral systems and investing in social determinants	**APHA urges federal, state, tribal, territorial, and local governments, and agencies to:** ▶ Meet patient rights requirements for people with mental illness and substance use disorder to be in the least restrictive environment for care by redirecting funding and referrals from jails, prisons, and involuntary and/or court-mandated inpatient psychiatric institutions to inclusive, community-based living and support programs. ▶ Reallocate funding from the construction of new jails, detention centers, and prisons to the societal determinants of health, including affordable, quality, and accessible housing and health care, employment, education (including in early childhood), and transportation. ▶ Adopt policies to ensure employment and economic security for the individuals and local communities affected by reductions in staff and/or closures of prisons, jails, and detention facilities.

CATEGORY	ACTION STEPS
	▶ Develop, implement, and support community-based programming interventions to address the medical, social, and financial needs of people who have been harmed by the criminal legal system, including those transitioning from incarceration. **APHA calls on state and local health departments to:** ▶ Advocate for, collaborate and educate around, and support both the decarceration and defunding of all carceral facilities and systems in the ongoing mission to advance the public's health, regardless of jurisdiction, and invest in programs and interventions that better address human needs (e.g., mental health rapid response) rather than deploying the carceral system.
Committing to non-carceral measures for accountability, safety, and well-being	**APHA urges federal, state, tribal, territorial, and local governments, and agencies to:** ▶ Develop, implement, and support non-carceral measures to ensure accountability, safety, and well-being of varying degrees to meet different levels of individual and community needs for support (e.g., programs based in restorative and transformative justice). **APHA urges Congress, the Centers for Disease Control and Prevention, and the National Institutes of Health, in collaboration with community organizations, survivors, and formerly incarcerated individuals, to:** ▶ Fund research on the effectiveness of alternatives to incarceration (e.g., transformative justice) and how to effectively change carceral policies and perceptions of criminality in society.

CATEGORY	ACTION STEPS
Decriminalization	**APHA urges federal, state, tribal, territorial, and local governments and agencies to:** ▶ Decriminalize activities shaped by the experience of marginalization, such as substance use and possession, housing insecurity, and sex work. ▶ Implement policies and practices designed to remove barriers to stable employment and housing for formerly incarcerated people, including expungement of criminal records. ▶ Restore voting rights for all formerly or currently incarcerated people to ensure their basic democratic right to participate in elections. **APHA urges Congress, the Centers for Disease Control and Prevention, and the National Institutes of Health, in collaboration with community organizations, survivors, and formerly incarcerated individuals, to:** ▶ Fund research on policy determinants of exposure to the carceral system.

Source: (Advancing Public Health Interventions to Address the Harms of the Carceral System, 2020)[3]

Considering Opposition to the Action Steps

Pushback surrounding the policy statement's action steps primarily stem from questioning either (1) whether the steps are supported by sufficient evidence or (2) whether they can be "safely" or "feasibly'" implemented.[4] With regard to its evidence base, the statement draws on a comprehensive research and practice literature, which finds that divesting from carceral practices and investing in public health priorities (e.g., housing, health care, education, etc.) advances safety, reduces incarceration rates, and improves population health.[5] It is worth noting, however, that standards for sufficient evidence are often not uniformly applied. Proponents of carceral systems need not demonstrate such practices are more effective in reducing harm and increasing safety and well-being relative to abolitionist approaches.

Carceral systems persist despite evidence of their inability to meaningfully stem structural and interpersonal harm, their perpetuation of structural marginalization, and their adverse effects on currently and formerly incarcerated individuals, survivors of harm, and the general public.[6] Taken together, evidence, to date, supports not only the promise of abolition for maximizing health, safety, and well-being, but documents the myriad and far-reaching harms of carceral systems.

As for their feasibility, the action steps are modeled after existing domestic or global policy, state, and local programming, or community-led, noncarceral measures for accountability, safety, health, and well-being. Thus, to support efforts to understand, implement, and evaluate the efficacy of the action steps, the remainder of this chapter presents some of the existing practical examples that inspired APHA's recommendations, followed by a discussion of how the statement has been applied since its adoption.

Practical Applications of the Action Steps

This section provides examples of existing interventions to demonstrate the action steps' feasibility and provide guidance on their implementation. We organize these examples by the four main categories of the action steps (Table 4.1). Each example is a commitment to divesting from carceral systems and investing in abolitionist alternatives to prevent and account for harm, ensure safety, and maximize health and well-being.

Decarceration

The extensive harms of carcerality make decarceration a public health imperative. Conditions of confinement such as overcrowding, poor ventilation, toxic water, extreme temperatures, aging infrastructure, and poor nutrition are associated with a number of unfavorable health outcomes, including the increased risk of infectious disease exposure—most recently evidenced during the COVID-19 pandemic.[7, 8] Research also documents how these health harms extend beyond carceral settings, affecting individuals upon their release,[9] their families and communities,[10] and the broader population.[11]

The policy statement urges significant and continuous decarceration via unconditional large-scale releases bolstered by appropriate community-based support, as well as reducing the number of new jail and prison admissions by ending carceral policies and practices such as pretrial incarceration, criminalization of substance use, houselessness, and sex work, among others. Importantly, the policy statement is clear that other forms of at-home surveillance and control, such as electronic monitoring or parole, are still carceral in nature. The following examples illustrate what decarceration looks like in practice.

DECARCERATION DURING COVID-19

When COVID-19 began to spread in the US in March 2020, many activists, organizers, public health professionals, clinicians, and concerned community members called for immediate, urgent, and drastic decarceration efforts. After its inevitable spread through congregate settings—including jails, prisons, and detention centers—nearly three thousand people have died from COVID-19 in carceral settings, likely an underestimate due to state failure to report data transparently and by releasing people just before they died in custody.[12, 13, 14] In the first year of the pandemic in the US, the rate of COVID cases in prisons was 3.3 times higher than the US general population, and 5 times higher during a December 2020 surge.[15]

However, during this time, the incarcerated population in the US was reduced by only around 16 percent[16] via fewer prison admissions due to court closures and delays,[17] compassionate release for eligible medically vulnerable individuals, and limited release of those incarcerated pretrial or convicted of nonviolent offenses.[18] Failure to significantly reduce the incarcerated population often hinged on concerns around public safety. However, evaluations of release efforts found that in eleven cities and counties where jail populations decreased during COVID-19, crime rates and arrest rates also declined.[19] An earlier study, published in July 2020 by the American Civil Liberties Union, looked at data from jails in twenty-nine different cities. The study found that most county jails did some measurable amount of decarceration with no correlated surge in crime rates.[20] Unfortunately, by 2021, incarceration rates had returned to prepandemic levels.

ENDING CASH BAIL AND PRETRIAL INCARCERATION

The stated purposes of the US bail system are 1) to ensure that people appear in court after they are released from jail pretrial and 2) to detain someone a judge determines may pose danger to another person or to the community.[21] However, a significant majority of people released pretrial *without* bail still return to trial and are not rearrested. For example, Washington, DC, eliminated cash bail in 1992 and now releases 94 percent of all people arrested without using bail. Still, 90 percent of people return to every court appearance, and 98 percent of people are not rearrested for what courts consider a "violent crime" pretrial.[22] The Bronx Freedom Fund, which—before shutting down in 2020—used to be a community bail fund that paid bail for those who could not afford it, found that 95 percent of the people they bailed out of jail returned for their court dates, and less than 2 percent were later convicted.[23] In Kentucky, around 70 percent of arrested people are released pretrial, with only half of 1 percent of those people rearrested for a "violent crime."[24] With 482,000 people incarcerated pretrial in the US each day, ending cash bail and pretrial incarceration is one successful mechanism for decarceration.

Divesting from Carceral Systems and Investing in the Social Determinants of Health

The only sustainable way to achieve public safety is ensuring all community members have the resources they need to thrive. However, most cities invest far more into policing and punishment than the systems people need, like housing, health care, transportation, and education.[25] Removing the main drivers of criminalized behaviors by providing necessary resources is a large task, but many communities are already doing this work. The following examples are some ways that communities are divesting from punishment in educational and health-care settings and investing in non-carceral strategies to prevent and address harm. These initiatives are new and ongoing. When possible, we present process and short-term outcome indicators of their effectiveness, but for most it is too early to evaluate their impact on health outcomes. As recommended in the APHA statement action steps, ongoing research and evaluation efforts will ensure the interventions are achieving their stated goals or adapt accordingly.

POLICING IN SCHOOLS: OAKLAND AND CHICAGO

Oakland, California. Black Organizing Project (BOP) is a grassroots organization that started the Bettering Our School System campaign to dissolve the Oakland Unified School District's dedicated police force after the Oakland School Police Department (OSPD) murdered twenty-year-old Raheim Brown in 2011. The success of BOP's campaign was due to years of building and organizing. This included setbacks, such as advocating for a school board proposal to eliminate OSPD in March 2020 that was defeated by one vote, but it also included wins. Indeed, with mounting support following the 2020 uprisings against police violence, the school board unanimously adopted BOP's proposed policy to dissolve the OSPD and reinvest its $6 million budget into a new safety plan focused on "supporting students and fighting the school to prison pipeline."[26] Key parts of this plan included having social workers or psychologists respond to students experiencing a mental health crisis. It also included the creation of a Culture and Climate Department to retrain unarmed, non-police school security as "Culture Keepers" and "Culture and Climate Ambassadors," building relationships with students, supporting a healthy school culture, and mediating conflicts using restorative justice practices.[27]

Three years after adopting the resolution, several of its stipulations have been achieved, including (1) the dissolution of OSPD, (2) the introduction of Culture and Climate Ambassadors, and (3) the "redesign of school district–wide safety plans, police-free policies and trainings, and a transformative school safety budget."[28] Notably, while these "divest" stipulations have been met, in light of budget cuts proposed by the Oakland Unified School District (OUSD) that threaten to renege on the "invest" stipulations, BOP activists have reaffirmed their commitment to hold the district accountable to ensuring investment in academic and mental health resources for the safety, health, and well-being of all OUSD students.[29]

Chicago, Illinois. In Chicago, the mayor and her appointed school board declined to make an overarching decision on the presence of police in Chicago public schools (CPS) and instead decreed that local school councils (LSCs)—composed of the principal, teachers, staff, parents, and community members associated with each school—could decide for themselves whether to keep police in their schools. Out of the seventy-seven schools with two officers, thirty-three LSCs voted to remove both officers, twenty-three voted to remove one officer, and twenty-one voted to keep both officers. This resulted in the Chicago Police Department (CPD) receiving $12 million from CPS compared to $33 million in the year prior. CPS then provided $3 million divided between thirty-one schools for implementation of alternative safety plans, such as establishing a dean of culture and climate or a restorative justice coordinator.[30, 31] It must be noted, however, that when schools went back to in-person instruction in August 2021, the twenty-three schools that voted to have only one officer did not have their votes respected. Instead, two officers were placed in their schools for the year because CPD refused to allow officers to work alone; per CPS, there were "concerns raised by CPD to ensure the safety of schools and their school community" in the decision but noted that the police department was not charging the schools for the additional police officer.[32]

NON-POLICE MENTAL HEALTH CRISIS HOTLINES

Minneapolis, Minnesota. Relationships Evolving Possibilities (REP) formed in the wake of the uprisings in Minnesota after the police murder of George Floyd. An explicitly abolitionist organization, REP set up an emergency hotline to respond to nonviolent emergencies such as noise complaints, neighbor complaints, and mental health crises, and to provide conflict de-escalation and referral to community resources. The hotline is live in Minneapolis and St. Paul via text or phone on Friday and Saturday evenings from 7 p.m. to midnight.[33] The power of this hotline is its availability, not just for mental health crises, but also for any nonviolent interpersonal conflict. Having a trusted community member intervene and offer assistance is safer than involving law enforcement. It also builds the community support networks that abolitionists envision as a way to ensure true public safety.

Oakland and Sacramento, California. MH First, a project of the Anti Police-Terror Project, provides a non-police hotline response to mental health crises, including psychiatric emergencies, substance use support, and domestic violence safety planning, available from 8 p.m. to 8 a.m. every Friday and Saturday night in Oakland and Sacramento. The aims of MH First are "to interrupt and eliminate the need for law enforcement in mental health crisis first response by providing mobile peer support, de-escalation assistance, and non-punitive and life-affirming interventions, therefore decriminalizing emotional and psychological crises and decreasing the stigma around mental health, substance use, and domestic violence, while also addressing their root causes: white supremacy, capitalism, and colonialism."[34] While the available services are currently limited, the Anti Police-Terror Project is actively working to expand the reach of MH First and other non-police crisis hotlines across California.

Non-carceral Measures for Accountability, Safety, and Well-Being Aligned with Survivors' Justice Goals

While acknowledging that every survivor's experience of healing from harm is unique, concerns surrounding the misalignment of carceral practices with survivors' justice goals are consistent. These concerns include how seeking justice, safety, and accountability through carceral practices (1) restricts survivor agency, (2) is limited in achieving lasting safety, (3) risks exacerbating the harm, (4) retraumatizes survivors, and (5) contributes to nonreporting of harm among survivors.[35, 36, 37, 38, 39] Still, with incarceration often the only available recourse for harm, carceral interventions are commonly pursued as an alternative to "nothing."[40, 41]

Recognizing this gap between what is materially invested and what is needed, survivors, organizers, practitioners, and others have coalesced in support of abolitionist alternatives to incarceration in ways responsive to the complexity of survivors' justice goals. These approaches prevent, create accountability for, and heal harm through (1) structural interventions to support access to necessary resources (e.g., housing, employment, immigration status) known to prevent or mitigate harm, (2) using support-oriented frameworks (e.g., rehabilitation, mental health treatment, voluntary drug use disorder treatment, community service) to account for harm, and (3) survivor-centered approaches (e.g., validating experiences of harm, acknowledging agency, repairing harm, preventing further harm) to promote healing.[42, 43, 44, 45, 46] The following examples illustrate what this looks like in practice.

Project NIA. Founded by abolitionist organizer, educator, and curator Mariame Kaba in Chicago in 2009, with the goal of "ending youth incarceration through transformative justice,"[47] Project NIA helps build community support systems as a way to prevent young people's involvement with the criminal legal system. Rather than perpetuating carceral responses to harm, transformative justice is a nonpunitive process of addressing harm and fostering accountability that centers survivors of harm and brings together everyone affected to decide collectively how to heal and repair the harm done interpersonally, as well as the larger systems and structures that created the conditions for harm to occur. Communities have been practicing transformative justice for generations. To foster spaces for transformative justice processes, Project NIA launched the NYC Transformative Justice Hub, which provides political education and training to facilitate and support those engaged in transformative justice processes when harm has been done.[48] Multiple other projects have arisen from Project NIA's efforts, including Liberation Library, which provides books to young people who are incarcerated; Circles and Ciphers, which supports the development of youth leadership through "hip-hop infused restorative justice;" and campaigns to shut down youth detention centers in Chicago.[49]

One Million Experiments. One Million Experiments is a virtual zine and online repository of community-based and community-built safety strategies without policing and punishment.[50] To expand societal ideas about what keeps us safe, the site captures examples of community safety responses outside of the carceral system being developed across the US, including mutual aid programs, non-police crisis response programs, and support for healing from harm and stepping into accountability. The site arises from the idea that abolition becomes possible with the building of many new strategies for addressing harm and supporting survivors. As Mariame Kaba names in the One Million Experiments podcast, "The point is many containers are needed for different kinds of things, and you shouldn't be afraid to start new containers because new containers are needed."[51]

Decriminalization

Criminalization is the deliberate categorization of certain activities—often activities necessary for survival in the presence of structural marginalization—as unlawful and the codification of punitive responses to those activities. Scholars have critiqued criminalization as a political tool to establish dominance and exert control implemented without regard for adverse effects on the safety, health, and well-being of marginalized populations.[52, 53] Decriminalization, by contrast, is the act of repealing criminalizing legislation, thus reversing justification for legal system involvement and creating opportunities for evidence-based intervention to maximize population safety, health, and well-being. The following section provides a set of examples for how decriminalization has been implemented to date.

DECRIMINALIZATION OF DRUG USE

In the US, the War on Drugs, and the resulting surge in criminalization, has been routinely identified as racist, harming communities of color and fueling systemic racism by way of the carceral system.[54, 55, 56] To counter this, decriminalization of drug use in the US becomes an urgent step to support population health and to address structural harms and racial inequities. The following are two examples of global decriminalization of drug use.

Portugal. In 2001 Portugal initiated a health-centered approach and dropped criminal charges for anyone found in possession of drugs for personal use. Though Portugal was not the first country to do this, they have remained a model for countries across the world. Research found incarceration rates fell by half, uptake in drug treatment increased, and significant cost savings materialized due to redirecting resources from the carceral system to the health system.[57] Furthermore, rates of drug use did not significantly increase in adult populations and actually decreased for adolescents.[58] As rates for drug deaths in the EU increased, rates in Portugal fell dramatically following the reforms and have remained below average for the region in the decades since.[59]

Oregon. In 1973, the state of Oregon decriminalized the possession of cannabis. Research comparing medically related hospital admissions before (1970) and after (1975) found a decrease in medically significant problems from cannabis after decriminalization.[44] In 2021, Oregon voters approved a state measure to decriminalize all drugs, with a plan to redirect funding from the state legalization of cannabis sales toward recovery services.[60] In a landmark victory, implementation was sought quickly, yet practitioners on the ground faced difficulties around decriminalizing drugs without the proper systemic support in place.[61] A lack of access to qualified addiction specialists, treatment centers, and health care compounded during the COVID-19 pandemic. Further exacerbating the issue, the state cannot use Medicaid funds to expand treatment for drugs federally classified as illegal.[62] While decriminalization is crucial, it is just one part of the larger systemic solution. The example in Oregon highlights the need to radically equip and mobilize various systems (including health care, treatment services, mental health, and transitional living housing) to support successful implementation. Still, early evaluations of Oregon's policy suggest that drug overdoses did not increase after decriminalization, contrary to opposing political arguments that warned of decriminalization worsening fatal drug use.[63]

DECRIMINALIZATION OF SEX WORK

Sex workers, trafficking survivors, activists (e.g., Amnesty International), and public health officials (e.g., World Health Organization) have long advocated the decriminalization of sex work, defined as "the removal of all sex work-related activities from criminal law and the regulation of sex work as a form of legitimate labor."[64, 65, 66] In 2020, the ACLU conducted a review of over eighty studies, also concluding that the optimal strategy for enhancing health and safety for people in the sex trade is the full decriminalization of sex work.[67] Eliminating punitive methods, including police harassment, arrests, and incarceration, creates greater access to legal protections, health and social services, community support, and other resources without fear of legal repercussions.[67, 68, 69, 70] It also allows public health strategies to emerge, by redirecting energy and resources toward necessary and practical approaches to address the root causes of health and safety issues within the sex trade, including poverty, intimate partner violence, grooming and coercion, housing insecurity, queer and transgender discrimination, racism, and social stigma.[71, 72, 73] These collective efforts contribute to the improvement of working conditions, health, safety, and overall well-being for individuals engaged in the sex trade, particularly trans women of color, who experience higher rates of violence.[74]

Decriminalization across Five Jurisdictions Globally. In 1995, the Australian state of New South Wales became the first jurisdiction to decriminalize sex work.[75] In 2003 New Zealand followed suit, becoming the first country to decriminalize sex work through the New Zealand Prostitution Reform Act (PRA), drafted in collaboration with the New Zealand Prostitutes Collective.[76] Since then, three additional jurisdictions—the Northern Territory of Australia (in 2019), Victoria, Australia (2022), and Belgium (2022)—have also implemented sex work decriminalization models.[77] While published evaluations of decriminalization in the latter three jurisdictions are not yet available, there has been extensive research conducted within New South Wales and New Zealand.[78] One such study examining the more immediate onset implications of sex work decriminalization found that five years after the passage of the PRA, 90 percent of sex workers in New Zealand reported the PRA gave them employment, legal, health, and safety rights, and 64 percent found it easier to refuse unsafe or undesirable clients.[79]

A 2023 scoping review of the academic and gray literature published between 1995 and 2022 on outcomes in both New South Wales and New Zealand found persistent health, safety, and wellness benefits over time following decriminalization in both sites, including improvements in access to health services, improvements in sexual health testing rates and outcomes, and decreased vulnerability to exploitation and trafficking.[80] The authors conclude—and leading health organizations concur—that decriminalization continues to be a necessary first step to address the health and social harms disproportionately affecting this diverse and stigmatized population.[81, 82]

DECRIMINALIZATION OF HOUSELESSNESS

Houselessness is a systemic inequity perpetuated by the criminalization of poverty.[84] Poverty, alongside systematic marginalization based on race, gender, sexuality, disability, age, and drug use, fuels the rising prevalence of houselessness while exacerbating health inequities. Law enforcement across the country are sanctioned to arrest people for lying down, sleeping, camping, begging, living in cars, or even sharing food in some cities.[85]

Housing Not Handcuffs Campaign. Initiated in 2016 by the National Homelessness Law Center and the National Coalition for the Homeless, Housing Not Handcuffs is a coalition of over three thousand organizations, professionals, and community members united to end houselessness and its criminalization in the United States.[86] The campaign advocates for affordable housing and offers advocacy tools and model policies for legislation centered on three pillars: preventing houselessness by strengthening housing protections and eliminating unjust evictions, shortening houselessness by stopping criminalization, and ending houselessness by increasing access to and availability of affordable housing.[87]

Moms 4 Housing. In 2019, Dominique Walker and three other mothers and their children occupied a house owned, but left vacant, by a real estate investment company in Oakland, California. Their actions highlighted the housing crisis in Oakland created by the predatory investment of real estate speculators, leaving an estimated four vacant houses for every unhoused resident.[88] The mothers demanded safe housing and, despite eviction notices, garnered widespread community support resulting in the community crowdfunding for the successful purchase of their home.[89] Their actions sparked policy changes at the city, state, and federal levels, including legislation that offers tenants the first right to buy their home, makes corporations who buy multiple properties during foreclosures less lucrative, and an amendment to the California constitution naming housing as a human right.[90]

Applications of the APHA Statement to Support Ongoing Work in Communities

Just as the work of generations of activists and organizers informed the content of the policy statement, we hope that it further amplifies community work and serves as an evidence base that organizers, teachers, researchers, policymakers, and others can draw upon. Since APHA adopted the policy statement in 2021, people across sectors from around the world have used the statement to support their work. In Table 4.2, we present a noncomprehensive set of examples of how the statement has been used in research, advocacy, education, and media.

Table 4.2. Examples of How the Statement Has Been Used in Research, Advocacy, Education, and Media

SECTOR OF WORK	EXAMPLES OF HOW THE STATEMENT HAS BEEN USED
Research	▶ An article in the *Lancet* about incarceration and structural racism during the COVID-19 pandemic.[91] ▶ An article in the *Lancet* about tuberculosis in prisons in Brazil.[92] ▶ A case study of a COVID outbreak in a California prison published in *BMC Public Health*.[93] ▶ An article in *PLOS One* about the global impact of COVID-19 in prisons.[94] ▶ An article in *PLOS One* about the role of Medicaid expansion in reducing police arrests.[95] ▶ An opinion piece about non-police opioid responses in *Proceedings of the National Academy of Sciences of the United States of America*.[96]

SECTOR OF WORK	EXAMPLES OF HOW THE STATEMENT HAS BEEN USED
	▶ An article in the *Journal of Indigenous Social Development* about incarcerated Indigenous people in New Zealand during the COVID-19 pandemic.[97] ▶ An article about abolitionist alternatives to involuntary commitment published by Cambridge University Press.[98]
Advocacy	▶ Organizers from the Brooklyn Movement Center cited the statement in a report released in response to NYC Mayor Eric Adams's "Blueprint to End Gun Violence," which would increase NYPD presence in predominantly Black and Latinx communities.[99] ▶ Policy analysts at the Texas Center for Justice and Equity cited the statement in a report urging investment in non-police, non-carceral responses to harm in San Antonio, TX.[100] ▶ Policy analysts from Policy Matters Ohio cited the statement in a brief about the health benefits of ending money bail in Ohio.[101] ▶ The president and CEO of Howard Brown Health used the statement in public comment urging divestment from policing and investment in the social determinants of health in Chicago city budget.[102] ▶ Researchers used the statement in a policy brief against the Police, Crime, Sentencing and Courts Bill, which broadly expanded the power of police and the criminal legal system, including against protesters, in the UK.[103] ▶ Several groups of organizers and researchers in Massachusetts cited the statement in support letters urging a moratorium on building more prisons and jails in the state.[104, 105]

SECTOR OF WORK	EXAMPLES OF HOW THE STATEMENT HAS BEEN USED
Advocacy *continued*	▶ Public health organizers with the Public Health Justice Collective in San Francisco used the statement in public comment, speaking to the Human Rights Commission's Close Juvenile Hall Working Group.
Education	▶ A course at the University of Michigan (Dr. Paul Fleming's "Historical Roots of Health Inequities") includes a discussion of the statement as part of class conversations.
	▶ A lecture in the University of Chicago's Epidemics of Injustice course was dedicated to the policy statement and to uplifting the experience of formerly incarcerated speakers.
	▶ The statement was cited by Dr. Mark Spencer in a Medicine Grand Rounds lecture at Emory School of Medicine.
	▶ The statement is included in the online curriculum "Towards Abolition," built by and for public health workers to learn about abolition.[106]
Media	▶ In the widely shared Ed Yong piece "How Public Health Took Part in Its Own Downfall," published in *The Atlantic*, the statement is named as an example of radical public health work focusing on the broader social issue of incarceration.[107]
	▶ An article in *Mic* focused entirely on APHA's adoption of the policy statement and outlines its content.[108]
	▶ An article from *Prison Policy Initiative* on prisons and jails that have refused to decarcerate during COVID-19 names the statement as an example of the recommendations for decarceration from public health officials.[109]

SECTOR OF WORK	EXAMPLES OF HOW THE STATEMENT HAS BEEN USED
	▶ The authors of the policy statement co-authored the aforementioned article in *Inquest* about the process of getting the statement adopted by APHA.[110]

Conclusions

While a surge of support following the 2020 uprisings directed momentum toward addressing the harms of carceral systems with an explicit and unprecedented focus on abolition across the US, a politically motivated shift back to a more familiar "tough on crime" rhetoric has already begun.[111, 112, 113] To sustain that initial energy and commitment, we call on the field of public health to leverage its much-espoused and now mainstream social determinants of health, prevention, and equity frameworks to join demands to divest from limited, ineffectual, and actively harmful "downstream" interventions that, at best, tacitly reinforce or, at worst, directly collude with carceral systems and punishment-based approaches.

We also call on the field of public health to again heed the guidance from its evidence base by joining demands to invest in the societal determinants of health (e.g., affordable, quality, and accessible housing and health care, employment, education, transportation, etc.) that have been shown to create necessary conditions for collective thriving and well-being. In embracing the field's commitment to safeguarding the public's health, public health professionals have a key role to take up in the multivoice, multisector, community-led movement toward abolition. The policy statement provides recommendations to move toward public health and abolition's shared goal of creating a world in which jails, prisons, and detention centers are obsolete by building and sustaining just and equitable societal systems that advance the public's health, safety, and well-being.

CHAPTER 4 NOTES

(Epigraph) Gilmore, Ruth Wilson. "No Easy Victories: Fighting for Abolition," (lecture hosted by Critical Resistance, Chicago, IL, November 8, 2017). https://www.youtube.com/ watch?v= FGPV PrJG XsY.

1. American Public Health Association. (2020). *Advancing Public Health Interventions to Address the Harms of the Carceral System*. Retrieved December 7, 2020. from https://www.apha.org/policies-and-advocacy/public-health -policy-statements/policy-database/2021/01/14/advancing-public -health-interventions-to-address-the-harms-of-the-carceral-system.

2. American Public Health Association. (2018) *Addressing Law Enforcement Violence as a Public Health Issue*. Retrieved December 7, 2020. from https://www.apha.org/policies-and-advocacy/public-health-policy -statements/policy-database/2019/01/29/law-enforcement-violence.

3. American Public Health Association. *Advancing Public Health Interventions to Address the Harms of the Carceral System*.

4. *Abolition Is Public Health*. (2022). Inquest. Retrieved June 14, 2022, from https://inquest.org/abolition-is-public-health/.

5. American Public Health Association. *Advancing Public Health Interventions to Address the Harms of the Carceral System*.

6. American Public Health Association. *Advancing Public Health Interventions to Address the Harms of the Carceral System*.

7. American Public Health Association. *Advancing Public Health Interventions to Address the Harms of the Carceral System*.

8. Barsky, B. A., Reinhart, E., Farmer, P., and Keshavjee, S. (2021). "Vaccination plus Decarceration—Stopping Covid-19 in Jails and Prisons." *New England Journal of Medicine, 384*(17), 1583–1585. https://doi.org/10.1056 /NEJMp2100609.

9. Patterson, E. J. (2013). "The Dose-Response of Time Served in Prison on Mortality: New York State, 1989–2003." *American Journal of Public Health, 103*(3), 523–28. https://doi.org/10.2105/AJPH.2012.301148.

10. American Public Health Association. *Advancing Public Health Interventions to Address the Harms of the Carceral System*.

11. Wildeman, C. (2016). Incarceration and population health in wealthy democracies. *Criminology* 54(2), 360–82.

12. Dolovich, S., Tyagi, E., and Marquez, N. (2021). *The States That Lead the Nation in COVID-19 Cases Are Hiding Their Prison Data*. UCLA Law COVID Behind Bars Data Project. Retrieved June 14, 2022, from https://uclacovidbehindbars.org/delta-surges-hiding-data.

13. Florko, N. (2022). *Despite Biden's Big Promises and a Far Better Understanding of the Virus, Covid-19 Is Still Raging through the Nation's Prisons.* STAT. Retrieved June 14, 2022, from https://www.statnews.com/2022/02/02/biden-promises-covid19-prisons/.

14. Turcotte, M., Sherman, R., Griesbach, R., and Klein, A. H. (2021). "The Real Toll from Prison COVID Cases May Be Higher than Reported." *New York Times.* Retrieved June 14, 2022, from https://www.nytimes.com/2021/07/07/us/inmates-incarcerated-covid-deaths.html.

15. Marquez, N., Ward, J. A., Parish, K., Saloner, B., and Dolovich, S. (2021). "COVID-19 Incidence and Mortality in Federal and State Prisons Compared with the US Population, April 5, 2020, to April 3, 2021." *JAMA, 326*(18), 186–1867. https://doi.org/10.1001/jama.2021.17575.

16. Klein, B., Ogbunugafor, C. B., Schafer, B. J., Bhadricha, Z., Kori, P., Sheldon, J., Kaza, N., Wang, E. A., Eliassi-Rad, T., Scarpino, S. V., and Hinton, E. (2021). "The COVID-19 Pandemic Amplified Long-Standing Racial Disparities in the United States Criminal Justice System." *medRxiv*, 2021.2012.2014.21267199. https://doi.org/10.1101/2021.12.14.2126719.

17. Sharma, D., Li, W., Lavoie, D., and Lauer, C. (2020). *Prison Populations Drop by 100,000 during Pandemic but not because of COVID-19 Releases.* The Marshall Project. Retrieved June 14, 2022, from https://www.themarshallproject.org/2020/07/16/prison-populations-drop-by-100-000-during-pandemic.

18. Klein, B. et al. "The COVID-19 Pandemic Amplified Long-Standing Racial Disparities in the United States Criminal Justice System."

19. *The Impact of COVID-19 on Crime, Arrests, and Jail Populations.* (2021). Safety & Justice Challenge, JFA Institute. Retrieved June 14, 2022, from https://safetyandjusticechallenge.org/resources/the-impact-of-covid-19-on-crime-arrests-and-jail-populations/.

20. ACLU. (2020). *Decarceration and Crime during COVID-19.* Retrieved June 14, 2022, from https://www.aclu.org/news/smart-justice/decarceration-and-crime-during-covid-19.

21. H.R. 5865 - Bail Reform Act of 1984. (1984). US Congress, House of Representatives. Retrieved June 14, 2022, from https://www.congress.gov/bill/98th-congress/house-bill/5865.

22. Doyle, C., Bains, C., and Hopkins, B. (2019). *Bail Reform: A Guide for State and Local Policymakers.* Criminal Justice Policy Program, Harvard Law School. Retrieved June 14, 2022, from https://docslib.org/doc/2562074/bail-reform-a-guide-for-state-and-local-policymakers-by.

23. The Bronx Freedom Fund. (2020). *Legacy*. Retrieved June 14, 2022, from http://www.thebronxfreedomfund.org/legacy.

24. Doyle, C. et al. (2019). *Bail Reform: A Guide for State and Local Policymakers.*

25. Fassler, E. (2021). "10 Largest US Cities Will Spend More on Police than Public Health This Year." Truthout. Retrieved June 14, 2022, from https://truthout.org/articles/10-largest-us-cities-will-spend-more-on -police-than-public-health-this-year/.

26. Getachew, S. (2021). "Oakland Eliminated Its School Police Force—So What Happens Now?" KQED. Retrieved June 14, 2022, from https:// www.kqed.org/arts/13893831/oakland-eliminated-its-school-police -force-so-what-happens-now.

27. Sinnamon-Johnson, E., and McSwain-Mims, D. (2023). "Oakland Schools Made a Promise to Black Students—It's Time to Deliver." *San Francisco Bay View National Black Newspaper.* https://sfbayview.com/2023/08 /oakland-schools-made-a-promise-to-black-students-its-time-to-deliver/.

28. Sinnamon-Johnson and McSwain-Mims. "Oakland Schools Made a Promise to Black Students—It's Time to Deliver."

29. Sinnamon-Johnson and McSwain-Mims. "Oakland Schools Made a Promise to Black Students—It's Time to Deliver."

30. Karp, S. (2021). "Chicago Police to Continue Sending 2 Officers to Schools That Voted to Have Just 1." WBEZ Chicago. Retrieved June 14, 2022, from https://www.wbez.org/stories/chicago-police-to-continue -sending-two-officers-to-schools-that-voted-to-have-just-one/ef3a89c3 -434b-490d-b226-e7357d2b6915.

31. Sherry, S. (2020). "Pull Chicago Police from CPS Schools and Use That $33 Million on Mental Health Services Instead, Activists and Elected Leaders Say." *Chicago Tribune.* Retrieved June 14, 2022, from https:// www.chicagotribune.com/news/breaking/ct-george-floyd-chicago -police-schools-mental-health-cps-20200609-2reexackwzegjmtr3jyem okt34-story.html?msclkid=c6f2468bc73011eca38a6d0adc66ffc5.

32. Karp, S. "Chicago Police to Continue Sending 2 Officers to Schools That Voted to Have Just 1."

33. REP. (2022). *Our Hotline.* Retrieved June 14, 2022, from https://repformn .org/hotline/.

34. Anti Police-Terror Project. (2022). *M.H. First: Community First Response.* Retrieved June 14, 2022, from https://www.antipoliceterrorproject.org /mental-health-first.

35. American Public Health Association. *Advancing Public Health Interventions to Address the Harms of the Carceral System.*

36. Decker, M. R., Holliday, C. N., Hameeduddin, Z., Shah, R., Miller, J., Dantzler, J., and Goodmark, L. (2020, 2022/03/01). "Defining Justice: Restorative and Retributive Justice Goals Among Intimate Partner Violence Survivors." *Journal of Interpersonal Violence, 37*(5–6), NP2844-NP2867. https://doi.org/10.1177/0886260520943728.

37. Goodmark, L. (2018). *Decriminalizing Domestic Violence: A Balanced Policy Approach to Intimate Partner Violence* (Vol. 7). University of California Press.

38. Goodmark, L. (2020). *How Representing Victims of Domestic Violence Turned Me into a Prison Abolitionist.* University of California Press. Retrieved June 14, 2022, from https://www.ucpress.edu/blog/51224/how-representing -victims-of-domestic-violence-turned-me-into-a-prison-abolitionist/.

39. Kulkarni, S. (2019, 2019/01/01). "Intersectional Trauma-Informed Intimate Partner Violence (IPV) Services: Narrowing the Gap between IPV Service Delivery and Survivor Needs." *Journal of Family Violence, 34*(1), 55–64. https://doi.org/10.1007/s10896-018-0001-5.

40. Decker, M. R. et al. "Defining Justice: Restorative and Retributive Justice Goals Among Intimate Partner Violence Survivors."

41. Sered, D. (2017). *Accounting for Violence: How to Increase Safety and Break Our Failed Reliance on Mass Incarceration.* New York: Vera Institute of Justice.

42. American Public Health Association. *Advancing Public Health Interventions to Address the Harms of the Carceral System.* (2020).

43. Goodmark. *Decriminalizing Domestic Violence: A Balanced Policy Approach to Intimate Partner Violence* (Vol. 7). University of California Press.

44. Goodmark. *How Representing Victims of Domestic Violence Turned Me into a Prison Abolitionist.*

45. Kulkarni. "Intersectional Trauma-Informed Intimate Partner Violence (IPV) Services."

46. Housing not Handcuffs. (2021). *Crime Survivors Speak: The First-Ever National Survey of Victims' Views on Safety and Justice.* Criminalization Fact Sheet. Retrieved June 14, 2022, from https://housingnothandcuffs.org /wp-content/uploads/2021/06/HNH-One-Pager-June-2021-1.pdf.

47. Project NIA. (2022). *Project NIA.* Retrieved June 14, 2022, from https:// project-nia.org/mission-history.

48. NYC Transformative Justice Hub. (2022). *The NYC Transformative Justice Hub Serves Three Primary Purposes.* Retrieved June 14, 2022, from https:// nyctjhub.com/public_whatwedo.html.

49. Project NIA. (2022). *Past Projects.* Retrieved June 14, 2022, from https:// project-nia.org/past-projects.

50. *One Million Experiments.* (2022). One Million Experiments. Retrieved June 14, 2022, from https://millionexperiments.com/.

51. Kisslinger, D. and Williams, D. (Hosts). (October 28, 2021). Episode 1 - The Hypothesis with Mariame Kaba [Audio podcast episode]. In *One Million Experiments Podcast.* Retrieved June 14, 2022, from https://soundcloud.com/one-million-experiments.

52. Davis, A.Y. (1971). *Political Prisoners, Prisons, and Black Liberation.* Boston Anarchist Black Cross.

53. Hinton, E. and Cook, D. (2021). "The Mass Criminalization of Black Americans: A Historical Overview." *Annual Review of Criminology, 4*(1), 261–86. https://doi.org/10.1146/annurev-criminol-060520-033306.

54. Alexander, M. (2010). *The New Jim Crow : Mass Incarceration in the Age of Colorblindness.* New York: New Press, 2010. [Jackson, Tennessee]: Distributed by Perseus Distribution. https://search.library.wisc.edu/catalog/9910095136402121.

55. Bailey, Z. D., Krieger, N., Agénor, M., Graves, J., Linos, N., and Bassett, M. T. (2017, 2017/04/08/). "Structural Racism and Health Inequities in the USA: Evidence and Interventions." *The Lancet, 389*(10077), 1453–63. https://doi.org/https://doi.org/10.1016/S0140-6736(17)30569-X.

56. Lusane, C. and Desmond, D. (1991). *Pipe Dream Blues: Racism and the War on Drugs.* South End Press.

57. American Public Health Association. (2013). *Defining and Implementing a Public Health Response to Drug Use and Misuse.* Retrieved June 14, 2022, from https://www.apha.org/policies-and-advocacy/public-health-policy-statements/policy-database/2014/07/08/08/04/defining-and-implementing-a-public-health-response-to-drug-use-and-misuse.

58. Hughes, C. E. and Stevens, A. (2010). "What Can We Learn from the Portuguese Decriminalization of Illicit Drugs?" *The British Journal of Criminology, 50*(6), 999–1022. https://doi.org/10.1093/bjc/azq038.

59. Transform Drug Policy Foundation. (2021). *Drug Decriminalisation in Portugal: Setting the Record Straight.* Retrieved June 14, 2022, from https://transformdrugs.org/blog/drug-decriminalisation-in-portugal-setting-the-record-straight.

60. US Department of Justice, Office of Justice Programs. (1976). *Effects of Decriminalization of Marijuana in Oregon.* Retrieved June 14, 2022, from https://www.ojp.gov/ncjrs/virtual-library/abstracts/effects-decriminalization-marijuana-oregon.

61. Westervelt, E. (2021). "Oregon's Pioneering Drug Decriminalization Experiment Is Now Facing the Hard Test." NPR. Retrieved June 14, 2022,

from https://www.npr.org/2021/06/18/1007022652/oregons-pioneering
-drug-decriminalization-experiment-is-now-facing-the-hard-test.

62. Westervelt. "Oregon's Pioneering Drug Decriminalization Experiment Is
Now Facing the Hard Test."

63. Joshi, S., Rivera, B. D., Cerdá, M., Guy, G. P., Jr., Strahan, A., Wheelock,
H., and Davis, C. S. (2023). "One-Year Association of Drug Possession
Law Change with Fatal Drug Overdose in Oregon and Washington."
JAMA Psychiatry. https://doi.org/10.1001/jamapsychiatry.2023.3416.

64. Amnesty International. (2016). *Q&A: Policy to Protect the Human Rights of
Sex Workers*. Retrieved June 14, 2022, from https://www.amnesty.org/en
/documents/pol30/4173/2016/en/.

65. Macioti, P. G., Power, J., and Bourne, A. (2023, 2023/09/01). "The
Health and Well-Being of Sex Workers in Decriminalised Contexts: A
Scoping Review." *Sexuality Research and Social Policy, 20*(3), 1013–1031.
https://doi.org/10.1007/s13178-022-00779-8.

66. World Health Organization. (2023). *Sex Workers*. Retrieved December
22, 2023, from https://www.who.int/teams/global-hiv-hepatitis-and-stis
-programmes/populations/sex-workers.

67. Amnesty International. *Q&A: Policy to Protect the Human Rights of Sex
Workers*.

68. Macioti, P. G. et al. "The Health and Well-Being of Sex Workers in
Decriminalised Contexts."

69. Sakha, S., Greytak, E., and Haynes, M. (2020). *Is Sex Work Decriminalization
the Answer?* ACLU. Retrieved June 14, 2022, from https://www.aclu.org
/sites/default/files/field_document/aclu_sex_work_decrim_research
_brief_new.pdf.

70. Platt, L., Grenfell, P., Meiksin, R., Elmes, J., Sherman, S. G., Sanders,
T., Mwangi, P., and Crago, A. L. (2018, Dec). "Associations between
Sex Work Laws and Sex Workers' Health: A Systematic Review and
Meta-analysis of Quantitative and Qualitative Studies." *PLoS Med,
15*(12), e1002680. https://doi.org/10.1371/journal.pmed.1002680.

71. Amnesty International. *Q&A: Policy to Protect the Human Rights of Sex
Workers*.

72. Macioti, P. G. et al. "The Health and Well-Being of Sex Workers in
Decriminalised Contexts."

73. World Health Organization. *Sex Workers*.

74. Sakha, S. et al. *Is Sex Work Decriminalization the Answer?*

75. Macioti, P. G. et al. "The Health and Well-Being of Sex Workers in
Decriminalised Contexts."

76. Abel, G., Fitzgerald, L., and Brunton, C. (2007). *The Impact of the Prostitution Reform Act on the Health and Safety Practices of Sex Workers.* https://www.otago.ac.nz/christchurch/otago018607.pdf.

77. Macioti, P. G. et al. "The Health and Well-Being of Sex Workers in Decriminalised Contexts."

78. Macioti, P. G. et al. "The Health and Well-Being of Sex Workers in Decriminalised Contexts."

79. Abel, G. et al. (2007). *The Impact of the Prostitution Reform Act on the Health and Safety Practices of Sex Workers.*

80. Macioti, P. G. et al. "The Health and Well-Being of Sex Workers in Decriminalised Contexts."

81. Macioti, P. G. et al. "The Health and Well-Being of Sex Workers in Decriminalised Contexts."

82. World Health Organization. *Sex Workers.*

84. Herring, C., Yarbrough, D., and Marie Alatorre, L. (2019). "Pervasive Penality: How the Criminalization of Poverty Perpetuates Homelessness." *Social Problems, 67*(1), 131–49. https://doi.org/10.1093/socpro/spz004.

85. National Law Center on Homelessness and Poverty and Housing not Handcuffs. (2018) *Housing not Handcuffs: Ending the Criminalization of Homelessness in US Cities.* Retrieved June 14, 2022, from https://homelesslaw.org/wp-content/uploads/2018/10/Housing-Not-Handcuffs.pdf.

86. Housing not Handcuffs. (2021). *Crime Survivors Speak: The First-Ever National Survey of Victims' Views on Safety and Justice.*

87. Housing not Handcuffs. (2018). *Policy Solutions.* Retrieved June 14, 2022, from https://housingnothandcuffs.org/policy-solutions/.

88. Brinklow, A. (2019). "San Francisco Has Nearly Five Empty Homes per Homeless Resident." Curbed San Francisco. Retrieved June 14, 2022, from https://sf.curbed.com/2019/12/3/20993251/san-francisco-bay-area-vacant-homes-per-homeless-count.

89. Colorado, M. (2019). "Mothers Who Took over Abandoned Oakland Home Say They'll Stay Put despite Eviction Notice." NBC Bay Area. Retrieved June 14, 2022, from https://www.nbcbayarea.com/news/local/mothers-who-took-over-abandoned-oakland-home-say-theyll-stay-put-despite-eviction-notice/2190757/.

90. Baldassari, E. and Solomon, M. (2020). "How Moms 4 Housing changed laws and inspired a movement." KQED. Retrieved June 14, 2022, from https://www.kqed.org/news/11842392/how-moms-4-housing-changed-laws-and-inspired-a-movement.

91. LeMasters, K., Brinkley-Rubinstein, L., Maner, M., Peterson, M., Nowotny, K., and Bailey, Z. (2022, Mar). "Carceral Epidemiology: Mass Incarceration and Structural Racism during the COVID-19 Pandemic." *Lancet Public Health, 7*(3), e287–e290. https://doi.org/10.1016/s2468 -2667(22)00005-6.

92. Walter, K. S., Dos Santos, P. C. P., Gonçalves, T. O., da Silva, B. O., da Silva Santos, A., de Cássia Leite, A., da Silva, A. M., Figueira Moreira, F. M., de Oliveira, R. D., Lemos, E. F., Cunha, E., Liu, Y. E., Ko, A. I., Colijn, C., Cohen, T., Mathema, B., Croda, J., and Andrews, J. R. (2022, May). "The Role of Prisons in Disseminating Tuberculosis in Brazil: A Genomic Epidemiology Study." *Lancet Regional Health—Americas, 9.* https://doi.org /10.1016/j.lana.2022.100186.

93. Duarte, C., Cameron, D. B., Kwan, A. T., Bertozzi, S. M., Williams, B. A., and McCoy, S. I. (2022, 2022/05/14). "COVID-19 Outbreak in a State Prison: A Case Study on the Implementation of Key Public Health Recommendations for Containment and Prevention." *BMC Public Health, 22*(1), 977. https://doi.org/10.1186/s12889-022-12997-1.

94. Kim, H., Hughes, E., Cavanagh, A., Norris, E., Gao, A., Bondy, S. J., McLeod, K. E., Kanagalingam, T., and Kouyoumdjian, F. G. (2022). "The Health Impacts of the COVID-19 Pandemic on Adults Who Experience Imprisonment Globally: A Mixed Methods Systematic Review." *PLoS One, 17*(5), e0268866. https://doi.org/10.1371/journal.pone.0268866.

95. Simes, J. T. and Jahn, J. L. (2022). "The Consequences of Medicaid Expansion under the Affordable Care Act for Police Arrests." *PLoS One, 17*(1), e0261512. https://doi.org/10.1371/journal.pone.0261512.

96. Allen, B., Feldman, J. M., and Paone, D. (2021). "Public Health and Police: Building Ethical and Equitable Opioid Responses." *Proceedings of the National Academy of Sciences, 118*(45), e2118235118.

97. King, P., Cormack, D., and Keenan, R. (2020). COVID-19 and the mass incarceration of Indigenous peoples. *Journal of Indigenous Social Development, 9*(3), 141–157.

98. Wahbi, R., and Beletsky, L. (2022). "Involuntary Commitment as 'Carceral-Health Service': From Healthcare-to-Prison Pipeline to a Public Health Abolition Praxis." *Journal of Law, Medicine & Ethics, 50*(1), 23–30.

99. Piere, A., Haile, R., Ferguson, L., Williams, M., and X, D. (2022). *Invest in Black Futures.* Brooklyn Movement Center. Retrieved June 14, 2022, from https://brooklynmovementcenter.org/wp-content/uploads/2022 /04/BMC_BlackFuturesReport_v5_Exe_Summary.pdf.

100. Martinez, J. (2022). *San Antonio Must Pursue Public Safety Solutions Outside of Arrest and Incarceration.* Texas Center for Justice and Equity. Retrieved June 14, 2022, from https://texascje.org/system/files?file=publications /2022-02/policy-brief-san-antonio-must-pursue-public-safety-solutions -outside-arrest-and-incarceration.pdf.

101. Johnson, S., Pruitt, T., and van Lier, P. (2021). *Bail reform will make Ohioans healthier.* Policy Matters Ohio. Retrieved June 14, 2022, from https:// www.policymattersohio.org/research-policy/quality-ohio/justice-reform /bail-reform-will-make-ohioans-healthier.

102. Munar, D. E. (2020). *Public Comment on Proposed City Budget.* Howard Brown Health. Retrieved June 14, 2022, from https://howardbrown.org /wp-content/uploads/2021/07/Howard-Brown-city-budget-proposal -comment.pdf.

103. Aked, H., Blell, M., Cheung-Judge, R., Kaner, E., Luasabanathan, K., Palmer, C., van den Berghe, C., and Wondrack, J. (2021). *The Public Health Case against the Policing Bill.* MedAct. Retrieved June 14, 2022, from https://www.medact.org/2021/resources/briefings/public-health -case-against-policing-bill/.

104. Jimenez, M., Buttler, B., Graves, J., Lewin, V., and Takinami, E. (2022). *Public Health Harms of Prison and Jail Investment.* FXB Center for Health & Human Rights at Harvard University. Retrieved June 14, 2022, from https://cdn1.sph.harvard.edu/wp-content/uploads/sites/2464/2022/01 /Prison-RecommendationsFINAL-1-21-22.pdf.

105. *Public Testimony of 55 Organizations Submitted to the Special Commission on Department of Correction and Sheriff's Department Funding.* (2022). Retrieved June 14, 2022, from https://correctionalfunding.com/wp-content /uploads/2022/01/PLS-Testimony-1.14.22-Final.pdf.

106. *Towards Abolition: A Learning and Action Guide for Public Health.* Retrieved June 14, 2022, from https://www.towardsabolition.com/.

107. Yong, E. (2021). "How Public Health Took Part in Its Own Downfall." *The Atlantic.* Retrieved June 14, 2022, from https://www.theatlantic .com/health/archive/2021/10/how-public-health-took-part-its-own -downfall/620457/.

108. Uyeda, R. L. (2020). "Prisons Are a Public Health Crisis, the American Public Health Association Says." MIC. Retrieved June 14, 2022, from https://www.mic.com/impact/prisons-are-a-public-health-crisis-the -american-public-health-association-says-40336505.

109. Widra, E. (2020). *State Prisons and Local Jails Appear Indifferent to COVID Outbreaks, Refuse to Depopulate Dangerous Facilities*. Prison Policy Initiative. Retrieved June 14, 2022, from https://www.prisonpolicy.org/blog /2022/02/10/february2022_population/.

110. *Abolition Is Public Health*.

111. Fuller, T., Dewan, S., and Browning, K. (2021). "San Francisco Mayor Declared State of Emergency to Fight City's 'Nasty Streets.'" *New York Times*. Retrieved June 14, 2022, from https://www.nytimes.com /2021/12/17/us/san-francisco-state-of-emergency-crime.html.

112. Michaels, S. (2021). "Biden Said He'd Cut Incarceration in Half. So Far, the Federal Prison Population Is Growing." *Mother Jones*. Retrieved June 14, 2022, from https://www.motherjones.com/crime-justice/2021/07 /biden-said-hed-cut-incarceration-in-half-so-far-the-federal-prison -population-is-growing/.

113. Wootson, C. R. (2022). "Biden Makes His Midterm Message Clear: 'Fund the Police.'" *Washington Post*. Retrieved June 14, 2022, from https://www.washingtonpost.com/politics/2022/03/05/biden-fund -the-police/.

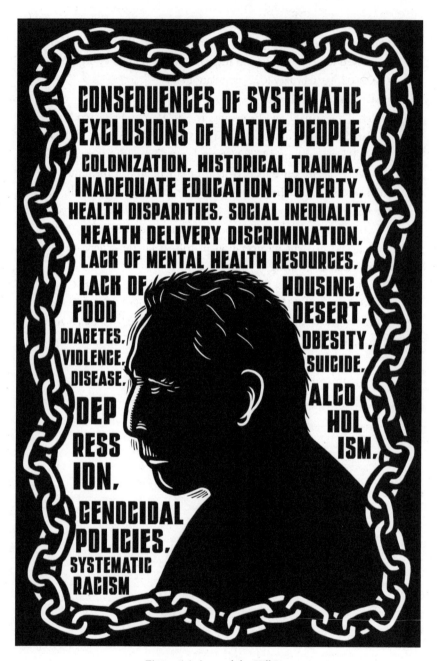

Figure 4.1: Artwork by Kill Joy

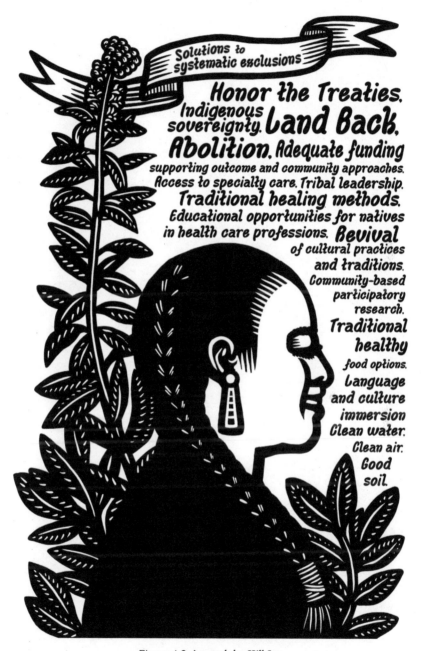

Figure 4.2: Artwork by Kill Joy

5

INTERVIEW WITH LEROY F. MOORE JR.

BY RONICA MUKERJEE

Ronica Mukerjee (R): *Hello, Leroy. Can you tell me a little about yourself and your background?*

Leroy F. Moore Jr.: *I am an activist, poet, author, and cofounder of Krip-Hop Nation, and cofounder of Sins Invalid. My activist work has been around police brutality around people with disabilities since the 1980s.*

My dad was loosely involved with the Black Panthers and Rainbow Push in the 1970s.

I was involved with overturning a wrongful incarceration of a Black disabled man in the late 1990s and was one of the key players in challenging police brutality cases in San Francisco involving the targeting of Black men with disabilities during that same time period. POOR Magazine, which I was involved with at its very beginnings, came up with the idea of never calling the police around this same time as well.

Recently I have chosen to be a PhD student at UCLA. They came to me because of my work with Krip-Hop Nation in order to open up the Krip-Hop Institute in Los Angeles. Krip-Hop Nation is an international network of hip-hop artists and other musicians with disabilities. We created a documentary called Where Is Hope: The Art of Murder about police brutality against people with disabilities.

All of my writing and poetry are focused on issues with disability, and I have written six books. I was awarded the United States Artist award for my writing.

I was there in the beginning with Patty Berne and Leah Lakshmi Piepzna-Samarasinha and Mia Mingus. You know we thought about disability justice (DJ) because the disability rights movement was too white and too straight, so Patty

Berne, with her excellent mind, thought about disability justice for people of color, people who are queer, who are transgender, people who are poor. People know disability rights as something you use in the courts, or you use it to sue people, but really disability justice is something that you live by.

In the late '90s, I was corresponding with disabled prisoners through connections from the San Francisco Bayview newspaper. Disability justice in terms of police brutality means that we control our own communities without police and that we need to be the overseers of our own communities. After decades of being an activist against police brutality, I know that trying to change police policies through forums and conferences is bullshit. I would say that people with disabilities are about 70 percent of all recorded deaths from police brutality. There is no appropriate data, and no one is counting, but that's my estimate.

R: How are people with disabilities affected by the criminal justice system?

Leroy: Big time. Especially Black and Brown people with disabilities. In these last couple of months Alabama executed a Black disabled man. It's been like one after another. They're caught up in the system because Black disabled people are funneled into the system by the school-to-prison pipeline. So the systems have no clue around race and disability—this includes the courts, schools, and even the NAACP has no clue around disability. When you're in those systems and you try to get some justice—for example in the courts—the judges all the way down to lawyers all have no clue about disability, and this is humongous because the civil rights of people with disabilities are very often violated.

In the late '90s, there was a disability organization that was educating courts around disability and how to communicate and the applicable civil rights. I was involved with Michael Manning's case. Michael Manning was and is a Black disabled man. He was at a gasoline station just getting gas, and all of a sudden he was attacked from behind, and he ended up railroaded because the judge was a racist white disabled man. So for years we stayed on his case, and he finally got free because we pushed the system to realize that the judge was racist and ableist, even though he was disabled. So Michael Manning is now out and free. And that's only one case, you know, and especially for Black and Brown disabled men it's a constant struggle to not be shot by police. I have sat with lawyers, like police *brutality lawyers who downplay and disregard disability, and we had to educate them as activists about disability rights and needs. Disabled men, women, non-binary and trans people, but especially disabled Black and Brown men and trans/ nonbinary people, get caught up in the injustice system, and they spend their life trying to get out.*

R: *In terms of disability in the media, who actually gets to have a valid intersectional experience? Can you speak to the parts that are allowed to be visible and not allowed to be visible when there is violence perpetrated against a person of color (Black, Indigenous, Latinx people, etc.) who has disabilities?*

Leroy: *When there's a national or local issue related to disability, people with disabilities are never on the media, even though there are scholars; they talk to everyone except the person with a disability.*

> **When there's a national or local issue related to disability, people with disabilities are never on the media, even though there are scholars; they talk to everyone except the person with a disability.**

And it's not only the legal system or media, it's also the activists. I was in so many protests with—I can say his name, I don't care—Van Jones. He used to tell me, "Oh be quiet around the disability stuff." It's like, dude, someone needs to stand up to the police, come on.

Even some parents in Black and Brown communities don't want to mention disability or mental health because of the lack of disability education in their communities, and so people echo the slave master's thinking around disability where people with disabilities were not seen as useful or were put to death. Because of the racism in the disability institutions who did not focus on educating Black communities, Black communities still have the slave master's and religious thinking around people with disabilities; people are seen as either "overcoming" or collecting services from the government. It is still like that within the Black community.

That's why I say that Black disabled people can't go home because the homes they come from are so ableist. I came up with the term "Black ableism" because the Black community never got the education around the negative effects of ableism. Because of the lack of appropriate political lens, police brutality and the racism of the justice system, the effects are that a lot of social justice movements do not realize the disability component to their movements. Including within #MeToo movements and many other social justice movements.

I'm being honest, I was never a fan of Black Lives Matter, because they never talked about disability. We tried with Sins Invalid twice to educate them, but they never got back in touch with us. When we tried to promote our film on police brutality and disability, we got no love from BLM. It was shocking to me that these organizations didn't want to bring in a disability component to their work. It should not have been shocking, because I've been doing activism against police brutality since the '80s. So it's not only the justice system, it's also mechanisms outside the justice system that keep disability invisible, especially in the Black community.

I love disability justice, and I also have some critiques about disability justice. I love what Sins Invalid has done with disability justice. I also see that DJ has been hijacked by white disabled women. DJ is educating a lot of white people, but once again the Black community is left out. Because white people have the funds, have the stable organizations, and could collaborate and fund educating their own organizations. It's a commitment when you say, "OK, I am going to educate the Black community." You, as a white person, are going to your own community to educate about disability, but if you're going to a community that doesn't see you as part of it, a community that doesn't have the solid foundation of trust needed to be created by you, you need to do the work. We live in a capitalist society, you have to get paid, but there is no organization like the NAACP for Black disabled people where Black disabled people can be paid to do work that uplifts our communities.

What I'm seeing now, which is so fucked up under new inclusionary/equity shit policies, is that once again Black disabled people are not getting the jobs for disabled people; it's mostly white disabled women who are benefiting from new inclusionary policies. It's particularly fucked up because it came from Black death from police brutality but doesn't actually include the people that it should be benefiting.

> What I'm seeing now, which is so fucked up under new inclusionary/equity shit policies, is that once again Black disabled people are not getting the jobs for disabled people; it's mostly white disabled women who are benefiting from new inclusionary policies. It's particularly fucked up because it came from Black death from police brutality but doesn't actually include the people that it should be benefiting.

R: *Can you talk about the interconnections between racism, eugenics, and disability?*

Leroy: *Every oppression against us, as disabled people, has an element of eugenics. Police brutality, medical systems, every element has some portion of eugenics. Especially now with gentrification. I see it a lot with poor people, these backward laws that have been placed in cities that don't get any bling-bling because of poor people. When I lived in San Francisco I was on the mayor's Board of Commissioners on Disability, and during the height of the gentrification, that whole board except for me and one other activist agreed to take out the benches in downtown San Fran. That's eugenics because it leads to people getting ticketed and criminalized. You can't stand, you can't sit.*

I think it also speaks to specifically how poor and disabled people of color are over-policed. We have architecture that overpolices people, like I said about the benches. We have anti-homeless architecture, which is essentially anti-disability as well. Like the sweeps where they are cleaning out encampments—it's like, what the hell?! I see that as eugenics. I call it soft eugenics. Because when most people think about eugenics, they just think about, you know, Nazi Germany gas chambers, but there are many types of soft eugenics that slowly kill us.

R: *How do police being in the hospital affect BIPOC people with disabilities?*

Leroy: *Police in the hospital?! That shit doesn't make sense at all! A couple of years ago, Krip-Hop had this exhibit in the children's hospital, and we did an*

*event there. I was shocked because, God! There were so many cops. This is a chil-
dren's hospital! I was like, why are cops around in the freaking children's hospital?
Wow! So that concept alone. Cops in hospitals? How did that become a reality?*

*The police have been like Pac-Men, gobbling up everything. You know right
now the police are involved with workplaces, clinics for physical health, mental
health centers; now they are in the hospitals, in nursing homes, police are in schools,
what's going on? Especially in Georgia, there are a lot of Black disabled youth in
nursing homes, not in their own homes because there is no funding or support to
do community living. You know in SF the mayor thinks he slick; he tried to cut
the police budget and put that money to this program that hires people coming out
of incarceration settings. So it's very hard to come out against the organization, but
he is hiring them to do security work in SF. So it's like, what the hell, you cut the
police budget then you're gonna hire ex-prisoners to do police work? It's really slick
how mayors have been trying to keep the police budget the same so they go in a
circle. You think, oh yes, we want that budget cut, but you come to find out they're
making more police. It makes it hard to go against, because it's prisoners coming
out and having work, and so many prisoners have disabilities.*

R: *And these people now have to put their life on the line with not much training. They are making people do police officers' jobs with less training and more
expendability . . . In terms of police in health-care settings, how does it affect Black
and Brown people with disabilities accessing health care when health-care systems
have police in them?*

Leroy: *We can go back to the mental health budget in San Francisco. There was a
case I was involved in that was in POOR Magazine, Cameron Boyd. The young
man had a mental health disability, and the mother was trying to get services from the
mental health board and couldn't get it for years, and the result is the police shot him
because he didn't get the mental health services he needed. So the mixing of police and
mental health police in the hospitals doesn't make sense. Especially if we are trying to
have alternatives to police. If we are going to have alternatives, then let's have alternatives. If we are just going to put police everywhere, that's not an alternative.*

R: *White women and white men have taken over the disability conversation, as
you said, and it also feels like health-care settings are much more accessible for cis*

white men and white women. And policing and the possibility of being policed in those settings for people of color is much more likely because of the invisibility of disability in BIPOC people. What are your thoughts about that?

Leroy: *We see that a lot of Black disabled women don't get good services in the hospital system; this was an issue that I covered for years. Hospitals dump Black disabled women on the streets, and that just doesn't happen to white women. Once again it's the system who sees us as not worthy of health care. Not worthy to extend a hand and say, "We can't find you a place right this moment, but we will try something else." Just dumping Black persons with disabilities out on the streets constantly, it's ludicrous. That's the system we live in.*

There was a video a couple of years ago, Three Generations of Black Men. Have you seen it? It's about three generations of Black men in my family and how we all fought against police brutality. We have the same cycles today.

Why are we continuing to do police brutality activist work in the same cycle? That's one issue I have with BLM: addressing police brutality as a career. We saw this before, with Jesse Jackson, with Al Sharpton, people using police brutality as a J-O-B. It's not.

It's like, what's the question? The question is not what the police need to do their jobs better. The question is: How can you be our neighbor so we don't have to call the police? And POOR Magazine has been working on this actively since the '90s, including teaching a workshop that says, "Never call the police." We all know that police are covered financially and politically by local, state, and federal government. If we know that, then why are we always trying to get police reform, because the people who are asking for reform are the people who fund the police. We should forget that tactic and come back to our community and teach our community about mental health, including autism.

There was one case outside of Denver about six years ago that I covered on my radio show. There was an autistic Black teenager [who was targeted/shot by the police], and as a result of what happened, the community got together—including a lot of Black churches—and they said no, we don't want the police. In this case, the parents had called the police for help. The police knew the kid and were aware of the situation because they had been to that family's place many times, and they shot the kid anyway. So for two years a group of church and community members did this program where they taught the whole community about autism, and they said they only wanted community involvement in future incidents and not police involvement. This only lasted two years because of funding.

Mass media attention always focuses on police training, and you know all that bullshit that has been there since the '80s without much success. So when it comes to the alternative plans outside of the police, they rarely get national media attention or funding, or if they do it's going to last only a couple of years. But this should be a more mainstream response, because we've done everything to try to do police reform. We've done trainings for the police; we've done so many other things. The system keeps us on what the police need, and then we go home and we don't have enough for our communities.

> **We've done everything to try to do police reform. We've done trainings for the police; we've done so many other things. The system keeps us on what the police need, and then we go home and we don't have enough for our communities.**

So, let's cut the cycle and say we are going back to the community and training our neighbors so we can call our neighbors and not the police. The thing about that is the police don't want us to do it because it cuts into their budget. And that's it right there. We've got Congressman James Clyburn talking about we all need alternatives, and he's a Black man pushing for more police. It's a cycle that keeps on going. My father saw it back in the '70s, how Jesse Jackson would come in and take up all the media and the activists on the ground would be like, who is him?! He just came in and he flew out and that's it.

R: *Can you talk about the process around divesting from carceral systems?*

Leroy: *When Reagan was in office, he just closed mental health facilities, but the thing that people don't discuss is that America doesn't do the transition in a sustainable way. There needed to be a better transition period.*

Americans think we will do this tomorrow and do that tomorrow and don't realize there is a process they have to go through. Americans can't deal with the transition process that is needed, for example, in abolition. That's why COVID is so rampant, because people don't understand there is a process that includes behavior changes. Americans want it yesterday. So when we cut large mental health institutions, during Reagan, there was no transition to help those people get housing because of the welfare budget cuts at the same time. So no wonder we have houselessness. And under gentrification, there is no community left.

R: *How do concepts of health and healthiness, which often have a racist component, lead to carceral violence for Black people with disabilities?*

Leroy: *We can't put the term health on people if we are not looking at institutional -isms—the -isms that are going to form when we put that word out there. A lot of institutions don't want to do the work to look at that. That is to say that when institutions put out their version of what is healthy, we gotta realize that healthy from their standpoint is not going to be healthy for the Black community or the disabled community. Especially coming from medical institutions. You know medical institutions have bad representation of board members and staff when it comes to people with disabilities. A couple of weeks ago I found an article, of course it was in Miami, Florida, and, oof, the governor was whacked. This is a case where they are trying to take a child away from this Black woman because she was disabled. I was like, what?! This is 2022 eugenics.*

We already had the Americans with Disabilities Act enacted. And still all these organizations and child protective services are gonna try to take away this Black disabled woman's child. Once again this is institutional thinking and bias against their own client.

R: *Why is a disability justice perspective necessary and integral to an abolitionist medicine framework?*

Leroy: *Disability justice looks at the people that are more oppressed: people of color, people that are queer, people that are trans. Disability justice creates a platform to really talk back to ableist, racist standpoints and how we give justice principles. Sins Invalid, for example, has principles that people outside of disability justice can* *follow. Those principles can change the whole way you're thinking about doing service, putting out statements or policies, or anything. Follow those principles—they are going to change everything. [See the DJ principles below.]*

Disability justice has been very co-opted recently and feels like a concept that people throw around without understanding it or paying respect to its founders and without understanding that it doesn't come from the academic community. I see white women taking it over, and it didn't have a chance to be fully processed by communities of color before it was co-opted by white women. We did not have a chance for Black communities to process disability justice before this happened.

R: *Disability justice is such a comprehensive movement—it encompasses almost everything that we actually need to center. I'm curious about your perspective on that.*

Leroy: *I think it's hard work. For one, people in the Black community and people of color communities have to deal with their own ableism. You can't exist in disability justice if you're ableist. It's totally impossible. I think Black and Brown communities need a national educational campaign around disability and disability justice. I see other countries do it—South Africa did it. I see people in London doing it. Because it has to happen. It can't happen comprehensively in and around white organizations. But how can we do it? How can you do it when you're living in a capitalist world and you need to get paid? There is very little money for disability justice. I see more disability community members working to educate foundations to increase funding for disability work and to look at the disability community as something that needs funding, but disability activists should not look at the nonprofit model to do their work because that goes against basic abolitionist principles. I do think disability justice is impossible to do under capitalism.*

And if you're talking about doing a national movement with Black and Brown communities around disability justice, where is that money going to come from? That is the thing that I really bang my head against the wall about. Back when I was like ten years old—this was before computers—me and two other friends did another campaign to a lot of national Black orgs like NAACP, Urban League, a bunch of them. We asked: Where are the Black disabled people? And we got back nothing. And then Keith Jones did it in the '90s after I did it. This just tells you about the lack of community and awareness around disability. You got Jesse Jackson, who is now disabled—and one of the persons that I wrote that letter to in the '80s—and is scared to talk about disability. It's like, you have Parkinson's now, dude! To see it come full circle and he is now disabled, and he still can't talk about it. It's like, wow! We have all these Black civil rights leaders who are now disabled and don't see disability as an activist place to do their work. This is linked to white supremacy because they don't see disability as a political, cultural, historical, artist place to do activism. It's also a lack of DJ education in the Black community.

> **We have all these Black civil rights leaders who are now disabled and don't see disability as an activist place to do their work. This is linked to white supremacy because they don't see disability as a political, cultural, historical, artist place to do activism.**

R: *How does the US compare to other parts of the world in terms of policing Black and Brown bodies and people with disabilities?*

Leroy: *Krip-Hop Nation, which I cofounded with Keith Jones, has been doing some excellent work internationally in Africa and other places when it comes to police brutality. I see police brutality a lot in other places against people with disabilities. I interviewed three Black disabled activists in London a couple of years ago. They talked about how the UK does a lot of studies on disability and race, but no one wants to implement the needed changes seen in the studies.*

Even in an international context, white disabled organizations take all the resources and take all the money, so this prevents addressing race and disability disparities and it also kills Black disabled movements. And there's no history on Black disability movements.

In the '90s I traveled to London, Canada, and South Africa, and all those places had rich Black disabled movements. And they all fell because of lack of support, lack of funding, and white national disabled organizations squashed them. In

2016 we at Krip-Hop Nation had an all-disabled African musicians tour in the Bay Area, including people from Tanzania, the Congo, and South Africa. We did this through Krip-Hop on an SSI budget. People came and slept on the floor of my one-room apartment, but we did it. Those are the kinds of stories that keep me going, because I think that was something very special, and Krip-Hop organized a campaign for two years to make that happen.

The UN has the treaty on disability, a disability treaty from five years ago called Convention on the Rights of Persons with Disabilities (CRPD). A lot of countries signed on to this treaty, but the US hasn't signed it yet. A country can sign all kinds of laws, but if there is no implementation, then it is useless. So a part of that treaty is arts, music, and entertainment. In Krip-Hop we believe that if you have not prioritized it in your budget, who is going to do the programs to make the treaty work? Krip-Hop has been doing that to help implement a little piece of this treaty, but it really goes to the fact that implementation is everything.

Disability laws and disability policies passed in the US are not funded or fully implemented, including the Individuals with Disabilities Education Act that passed in 1975 that hasn't been fully funded or fully implemented. And that affects a lot of Black and Brown people who get trapped in special education. And our so-called president ran his campaign saying we were going to finally implement that education law and the community is so excited—what are they excited for? This law has been on the books since 1975. Biden had been in some capacity in office since the '70s, and they just woke up and say now they are going to implement this law? This a key issue that leaves especially Black and Brown people under the bus. We have the highest rate of poverty, the highest rate of police brutality, we have the highest rate of everything because our laws are not being implemented.

R: *Are there any changes that you think would make the United States safer and more livable for Black people with disabilities?*

Leroy: *Wow, "more livable." That's a big one.*

I think when one can implement everything—it's weird to say this, because for a lot of people, when you think of disability you only think of the dollar sign, how much will it cost to do this or that—what makes us safe is when society steps up and accounts for how we're really living.

An example: during COVID, all of a sudden, people found Zoom, which is something that people with disabilities had already been using and trying to advocate for [working from home], and then all of a sudden it became normal for everyone. So now there is an emergency and other people are using accessible resources like video communication. It's when the issues hit white able-bodied people then those white able-bodied people are taking up this issue of access. Because it went into the homes of white people. I keep on saying if you want things to change, if you want laws to change, make it happen to white people and you will have a complete change overnight.

10 PRINCIPLES OF DISABILITY JUSTICE (FROM SINS INVALID)[1]	
INTERSECTIONALITY	"We do not live single issue lives"—Audre Lorde. Ableism, coupled with white supremacy, supported by capitalism, underscored by heteropatriarchy, has rendered the vast majority of the world "invalid."
LEADERSHIP OF THOSE MOST IMPACTED	"We are led by those who most know these systems."—Aurora Levins Morales
ANTI-CAPITALIST POLITIC	In an economy that sees land and humans as components of profit, we are anti-capitalist by the nature of having non-conforming body/minds.
COMMITMENT TO CROSS-MOVEMENT ORGANIZING	Shifting how social justice movements understand disability and contextualize ableism, disability justice lends itself to politics of alliance.
RECOGNIZING WHOLENESS	People have inherent worth outside of commodity relations and capitalist notions of productivity. Each person is full of history and life experience.
SUSTAINABILITY	We pace ourselves, individually and collectively, to be sustained long term. Our embodied experiences guide us toward ongoing justice and liberation.

10 PRINCIPLES OF DISABILITY JUSTICE (FROM SINS INVALID)[1]	
COMMITMENT TO CROSS-DISABILITY SOLIDARITY	We honor the insights and participation of all of our community members, knowing that isolation undermines collective liberation.
INTERDEPENDENCE	We meet each others' needs as we build toward liberation, knowing that state solutions inevitably extend into further control over lives.
COLLECTIVE ACCESS	As Brown, Black, and queer-bodied disabled people we bring flexibility and creative nuance that go beyond able-bodied/minded normativity, to be in community with each other.
COLLECTIVE LIBERATION	No body or mind can be left behind—only moving together can we accomplish the revolution we require.

CHAPTER 5 NOTES

1. Sins Invalid, Skin, Tooth, and Bone: The Basis of Movement Is Our People: A Disability Justice Primer (Berkeley, CA: Sins Invalid, 2019).

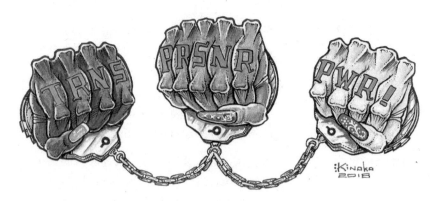

Figure 5.1: Artwork by Glenn "Kinoko" Tucker

6

FROM POLICING TO PROVIDING

How Hospitals Act as Entry Points to the
Family Policing System and Opportunities
for Harm Reduction

BY JENNA HEATH, ELIZABETH HUR,
AND NICOLE MITCHELL CHADWICK

In 2020 the medical field was seemingly galvanized to action in the wake of widespread protests of several highly publicized murders of Black people by police, including those of George Floyd and Breonna Taylor. Activists in and out of hospitals drew renewed attention to the history and current reality of medical racism, the field's neglect and exploitation of Black communities, and the violent disparities in disease and death caused by the COVID-19 pandemic. The movement highlighted important connections between anti-racism efforts in medicine and prison/police abolition: the American Public Health Association released the strong recommendation to move "toward the abolition of carceral systems and building in their stead just and equitable structures that advance the public's health."[1] The American Psychological Association similarly released a statement asserting that "the only way [. . .] to move toward an antiracist psychological practice is to embrace an abolitionist framework."[2] Though comparatively lukewarm, major medical associations such as the Association of American Medical Colleges (AAMC) and the American Medical Association (AMA) released statements addressing systemic racism and discrimination in medicine along with recommending all health-care organizations and systems apply these guidelines to help promote cultural change and safety.[3]

As prison and policing abolition have become widely recognized in the United States, abolitionist frameworks are increasingly being applied to, or finally acknowledged by, members of the medical system. Abolition-oriented analysis highlights how the medical system paradoxically commits harm against the people it is supposed to help. It is in this context that the decades-long critique of child welfare services (CWS)— or as legal scholar Dorothy Roberts calls it, the "family policing system" (FPS)—has captured national attention.

Roberts's seminal work *Shattered Bonds* and her most recent book *Torn Apart* reveal how the FPS mirrors the prison/policing system and contributes to the prison industrial complex (PIC) by overwhelmingly targeting Black families, punishing them for exploitative social conditions that ultimately act in service to uphold racial capitalism and white supremacy.[4] Multiple authors have argued for the abolition of the FPS on the grounds that it is fundamentally rooted in racism and capitalism and serves only to police disproportionately disenfranchised Black and Brown communities. Grassroots organizers have, for decades, worked against this system to keep families together through decreasing mandated reporting, overturning the Child Abuse Prevention and Treatment Act (CAPTA), and providing communal support and resources to prevent contact with the FPS. Roxanna Asgarian recently outlined a brief history of the movement against the FPS, following critical figures Dorothy Roberts's and Alan J. Dettlaff's journeys from desiring reform of the child welfare services to their convictions that abolition of the system at large is the only way forward.[5] This analysis has entered national discourse naturally alongside abolitionist frameworks, fiercely intersecting professional communities across the United States.

One professional stronghold seemingly impermeable to these analyses is the hospital. Medical staff are one of the most common referring parties to the FPS, frequently consulting child welfare services to "help" their patients in a hospital setting. This commonly occurs in the perinatal period, in which women are increasingly monitored before and after delivery, thus interacting with a variety of mandated reporters and at increased risk of referral to FPS. This is particularly true for those parents who use drugs, have been socioeconomically disenfranchised, or are victims of racism within the health-care system.[6] This chapter discusses mechanisms by which medical providers connect families to the FPS, specifically in the inpatient setting during the perinatal period. In doing so, we hope to provide practical ways for providers to practice harm reduction.

First, we examine abolitionist theory and key data surrounding the FPS, the harm it causes to Black and Brown families and children, and evidence that children do better when they stay with their families. Second, we review how medical personnel providing perinatal care in an inpatient setting directly connect families to the FPS through urine drug screens (UDS) and mandated reporting, thus introducing families to the FPS and accelerating harmful outcomes, directly opposing the purported goal to do no harm. Last, we echo the chorus of organizers to resist corroboration with the FPS through refusal to order toxicology screens when not medically indicated (or perform rigorous consent processes if medically indicated), limiting unnecessary exposure to other hospital-mandated reporters, and collaborating with other hospital workers to decrease exposure to the FPS.

All hospital staff are crucial in protecting patients from the harms of the FPS. Harm reduction will require robust protest and active engagement from hospital administrators, nurses, physicians, medical assistants, midwives, social workers, and others who interact with patients in the perinatal period. Considering the toxic hierarchy the medical system upholds, it bears saying that there is no one group of hospital staff that is more or less important than another in this fight. The three authors are physicians with lived experience in mechanisms by which physicians specifically contribute to harm. Thus, the intended audience for this article is physicians working in hospitals in perinatal care in the United States seeking to prevent harm to their patients. However, we hope that all those seeking to abolish partnerships between medicine and the PIC may benefit from this analysis.

Finally, we acknowledge that not all people who carry pregnancies or are able to be pregnant identify as women. When citing research that divides people into the categories "women" and "men," we will use "women" to identify people to be consistent with the language of the research cited. Otherwise, we will use "pregnant person/people." Additionally, we will refer to the FPS, child welfare services, and child welfare system interchangeably throughout the piece.

The FPS as Central to the Prison Industrial Complex

Medical staff must be grounded in the history and outcomes of the FPS. Confidently challenging normative assumptions that child welfare services exist to benefit patients requires understanding the formative forces surrounding the development of the modern-day child welfare system. To this end, we will briefly review abolitionist theory and data surrounding the FPS to orient those who may be unaware of its effects on patients.

Historical Context: FPS Roots and Parallels to the PIC

In *Torn Apart: How the Child Welfare System Destroys Black Families—and How Abolition Can Build a Safer World,* Roberts outlines a devastating history that traces the origins of the FPS from slavery to the child welfare system today.[7] The practice of family separation in the United States originated with chattel slavery, when Black families were involuntarily separated according to the whim of white slave owners. After emancipation, apprenticeship laws were put in place that continued the practice of family separation. As components of Black Codes central to the Jim Crow regime, apprenticeship laws gave judges the discretion to remove Black children from parents deemed unfit and place them on white planters' farms without their parents' consent. Most children under this law were returned to their former enslavers.[8]

With the Civil Rights movement, Jim Crow laws were formerly eliminated, but their social implications persisted. Simultaneously, for the first time, the provisions of welfare became available to Black families. Roberts points out that while it was a small victory to be included in welfare provision, the state benefits came at the cost of yet another form of state surveillance and control. Welfare provision was dependent on social service providers' highly subjective evaluation, and "unsuitable" housing was frequently met not with welfare provision but with the removal of children from those homes that were deemed unsafe. Removal was routinely justified through the longstanding narrative of the unfit Black parent, mirroring the prior apprenticeship laws.[9]

Removing Black children from homes further increased with the passage of the Adoption and Safe Families Act of 1997, which incentivized states to increase adoption rates. Simultaneously, major legislation like the Personal Responsibility and Work Opportunity Reconciliation Act resulted in massive cuts to welfare support. The result was a punitive response to poverty: less money was given to families in need, and when parents subsequently struggled to support their families, instead of receiving support, their children were removed.[10]

This historical background lays foundational groundwork to understanding how the FPS reflects the same carceral logic as the (PIC). Though a full review of the development of the PIC is outside the scope of this article, the same policies that gave rise to mass incarceration and the modern-day PIC also define the development of the FPS.

Redlining practices in the early twentieth century led to the development of predominantly low-income, urban, Black neighborhoods through nefarious and explicit refusal to provide home ownership loans to Black families. This was followed by predatory lending practices that trapped Black families in disenfranchised neighborhoods.[11] Nixon's War on Drugs, commonly recognized as a crucial cog in the development of mass incarceration, subsequently increased policing of those neighborhoods, disproportionately incarcerating Black people for drug use despite equal rates of drug use among white people. These same neighborhoods were and are the sites of increased surveillance of welfare recipients. Combined with the Adoption and Safe Families Act, the result was increased policing, fewer resources, more subjectively unsafe houses, and disproportionate removal of Black children from homes. The PIC and

FPS worked synergistically to increase the surveillance, control, and punishment of Black families.[12]

The historical context of the FPS reveals its intended function as a mechanism of surveilling and controlling Black families in collusion with the PIC. While the name "child protective services" suggests the system was designed to protect, historical analysis reveals that child protection was never an intended function of the FPS. The FPS is better understood as a central feature of the PIC in its routine surveillance and social control of Black bodies. Joyce McMillian, founder of JMACforFamilies and an advocate working to abolish the FPS and support families and communities, comments that "any system built to protect children should in no way mimic a system that purposefully punishes adults."[13] Roberts mirrors this sentiment:

> Family policing, though taking various historical forms, has always served to subjugate the most politically marginalized groups and maintain an unjust political structure in the name of saving children. [. . .] Family policing is not just similar to the parts of the carceral regime abolitionists are working to tear down. Family policing is *part of* the carceral regime.[14]

In summary, the FPS has historical roots in the practice of separating families for profit during chattel slavery; following the Civil Rights Act, it transformed into a system that stripped families of welfare provisions and then punished them for poverty by separating families in the name of child protection. It grew alongside the PIC with the War on Drugs via longstanding narratives regarding Black families being unfit parents. In doing so, the FPS grew into a "benevolent terror,"[15] functioning to disproportionately increase surveillance and punishment of Black families, unequivocally devoid of intention to provide care or harm reduction for children.

Harmful Impacts of the FPS on Children

In light of this grounding knowledge of history and function of the FPS, we will next consider the alarming disparities represented across FPS referrals, investigations, and family separation statistics.

National data suggests that roughly one in three children will undergo an FPS investigation.[16] Disparities in the FPS process begin at the investigation stage: by the time they reach the age of eighteen years old, 53 percent of Black children in the United States will have been subjected to at least one child protective services (CPS) investigation, as compared with 28 percent of white children and 37 percent of all children.[17] In a study examining CPS contact prevalence in the twenty most populous counties in the US, Black families had the highest risk of enduring an investigation, ranging from 39 percent to 62 percent depending on the county, which is double the risk white children faced (15 percent to 35 percent depending on the county).[18]

Of the children investigated nationally, one in seventeen children will be placed in foster care, meaning they will be removed from their birth parents and placed in the care of family members, nonfamily member foster parents, or group homes. Black children are two times more likely than white children to be subjected to family separation.[19] In 2018, Black children made up 23 percent of the foster care population and 14 percent of the population of children in the US.[20]

Locally, rates become significantly more disproportionate: for example, in Los Angeles, in July 2021 Black children made up 7 percent of LA County children, yet 27 percent of the foster care population.[21, 22] In New York in 2017, 25 percent of children were Black, yet Black children made up 53 percent of the foster care population.[23] Finally, not only are Black children more likely to be investigated and more likely to be separated from their families, but they are also less likely to return to their biological parents. Black children are 2.4 times more likely to experience parental termination, meaning the family suffers a court-ordered permanent termination of a parent's rights to their child.[24]

Cited reasons that children end up in foster care are important: as of 2020 nationwide, 73 percent of children in foster care are placed for neglect or housing issues, most of which are related to poverty or inability to provide food or childcare for dependents.[25] Three separate studies have shown that 30 percent of children are placed into foster care because they don't have housing.[26] As various organizers have pointed out, the practice of removing children from families who suffer from state-imposed socioeconomic conditions results in the criminalization of poverty, with the punishment being family separation, consistent with the history previously discussed.[27]

Though poverty, masqueraded as neglect, is frequently the reason for separation, once children are removed from homes and placed with foster families, *those families are then paid for the care of those children*. Erin Cloud saliently points out that in New York City over a two-year period, a parent on welfare allowed to keep their child would receive just over $22,000 from the state. A foster care parent would receive over $150,000 in that same time period.[28] Cloud concludes that while there are plenty of resources for the care of children, those resources are preferentially given to white strangers over Black parents.

The egregious nature of the FPS continues after children are removed from their families. *The FPS is violent by nature and leads to enormous disparities in health outcomes.* Time spent in foster care is associated with high risks of abuse, including sexual abuse,[29] homelessness,[30] mental illness and elevated rates of suicide,[31] as well as the likelihood of incarceration,[32] though data on outcomes for children in foster care are difficult to evaluate due to inconsistent or nonexistent FPS reporting systems. In 2016 one study compared mental and physical health-care outcomes between children in and out of foster care. Authors found that children in foster care were twice as likely to have learning disabilities, developmental delay, asthma, obesity, and speech problems; they were three times as likely to have ADD/ADHD, hearing problems, and vision problems; they were five times as likely to have anxiety, six times as likely to have behavioral problems, and seven times as likely to have depression.[33] The idea that the foster care system protects children insinuates that children do better in the foster care system than outside of it. The negative health outcomes experienced by children in foster care suggests otherwise. But what about the risk of leaving children in homes under suspicion of neglect or abuse?

Though as seen above, the FPS doesn't address these issues since it comes with an independent risk of harm, there also exists evidence that children at risk of foster care placement may do better when they remain with their parents. A 2007 retrospective study by Joseph Doyle used data from children in foster care in Illinois between 1990 and 2001 to look at outcomes for cases of "marginal" children or cases in which the investigators disagreed on the recommendation for placement.[34] Doyle compared the long-term outcomes of marginal children and found that children placed in foster care had higher incarceration rates, higher teen births, and were lower-earning when compared to similarly situated children who remained at home. In a follow-up study in 2008, Doyle looked at the effects of foster care on eventual interactions with the PIC, finding that as adults, children who had been placed in foster care had arrest, conviction, and imprisonment rates that were three times higher than those of similarly situated children who remained at home.[35]

Finally, the effects of COVID-19 also provide an important perspective in studying the abolition of the FPS. Legal scholar Anna Arons argues that in New York City COVID acted as an experiment in the abolition of the child welfare system: despite concern that children being quarantined at home would mask abuse, there were instead decreased reports of physical abuse, a decrease in reports deemed to be substantiated by evidence, and an absence of a rebound increase in reports of abuse when the quarantine ended. She concluded that we can envision a world in which CPS is abolished "because for a short time in 2020, we lived it."[36]

The FPS as Central to the Prison Industrial Complex: Conclusion

Medical providers must urgently transition their moral framework from understanding the child welfare system as a benevolent entity to condemning the family policing system as an entity of harm against families. The above review on the historical context of the FPS, the disparities in investigations and family separation, and the negative health effects of foster care should compel medical providers to understand the FPS as a facet of the deadly carceral web, with which collaboration should be vehemently avoided. This transition requires a tangible commitment to no longer support, collude with, or comply with the FPS. In order to extricate ourselves from complicity, we must understand specific mechanisms by which medical providers actively collude with the FPS. It is to these mechanisms that we will turn next.

Medical Providers as a Key Entry Point to the FPS

Despite an oath to do no harm, hospital staff function as *key entry points* connecting families to the FPS by acting as the initial actor entangling families in the carceral web. This section illuminates ways in which medical providers, and more specifically physicians, do this in the context of perinatal care in a hospital setting.

The hospital, and specifically the perinatal period, has long been a site rife with the peril of losing autonomy and losing children for Black and Brown communities. In *Killing the Black Body,* Roberts explores the criminalization of pregnant people who use substances and the medical personnel who assisted in their punishment. Her analysis includes chilling examples of medical collusion with the PIC: in 1989 at the Medical University of South Carolina, physicians and nurses aligned themselves with police to discreetly test pregnant patients for substance use when they presented in labor, reporting all those positive directly to police, which led to their immediate arrest after delivery. There are horrific stories of pregnant patients chained to beds during labor, forced out of the hospital and into jail mere hours after delivery, and bleeding through towels sitting in jail cells. She outlines how the power of the physician position led to violent collaboration with the state against Black patients: physicians assisted in legal testimony that patients using substances during pregnancy intentionally harmed their fetuses, and disproportionately overrode Black patients' autonomy by appealing for forcible substance use treatment. Roberts's work highlights how medical staff have historically prioritized compliance with law enforcement goals over caring for their patients.[37]

In *Policing the Womb,* Dr. Michele Goodwin, leading expert in fetal protection laws and their consequences, similarly identifies the hospital as a central actor connecting families to the FPS. With the rise of fetal protection laws criminalizing pregnant patient substance use, there emerged dual responsibility of the physician as both care provider and law enforcer. This duality became possible because the evidence for the "crime" is obtained in the context of a medical visit. The evidence was 1) a biologic specimen obtained in a hospital (the urine toxicology screen) or 2) patient reports of substance use in the context of the physician-patient confidentiality agreement. When acting as a physician, substance use elicits a treatment plan; but as a member of law enforcement, it results in punitive action. This dual responsibility, Goodwin explains, ultimately results in physician betrayal of patient trust:

> A key link in the numerous arrests and prosecutions of pregnant women throughout the United States is their medical providers, whose roles as undercover informants and modern day "snitches" belie their sacred fiduciary obligations. From their once revered roles as fiduciaries, duty-bound with tasks of protecting and promoting the interest of their female patients, some medical providers now police their pregnant patients' conduct and even serve as quasi law enforcers for the state.[38]

When physicians prioritize compliance or sense of duty to the punitive carceral state over their patient's best interest, they distort the patient-physician confidentiality agreement and ultimately, patient-physician trust.[39]

There are many ways in which a family can be referred to the FPS from a hospital; in the context of perinatal care, this often happens from a labor and delivery floor or a neonatal intensive care unit. These mechanisms are well documented by organizing groups such as Movement for Family Power, JMACforFamilies, and others who have detailed and organized around the impact of hospital actions on families. National Harm Reduction Coalition, along with Academy of Perinatal Harm Reduction, developed a "Pregnancy and Substance Use Toolkit" to help people navigate these potential hospital-based harms.[40] The following example will look at some of these mechanisms from the perspective of the medical provider. By pulling back the veil on how hospital staff approach these decisions, there is increased opportunity for accountability and harm reduction.

Connections to FPS in Perinatal Care

How does a patient receiving perinatal care become involved with the FPS in the hospital setting? How do routine procedures performed by physicians in a hospital setting condemn patients to the violence of the FPS?

Consider this common scenario on a labor and delivery floor: a pregnant patient arrives in labor. They are registered and checked in by a nurse, who takes their vital signs and often reviews a standard set of questions that frequently includes screening for recent drug use. Next, medical providers review previously documented history and review that history with the patient, including a verbal screen for drug/alcohol/tobacco use.

Providers then craft a plan for intervention. Concern for substance use will be based on certain medical conditions pregnant people present with (for example, placental abruption has higher associations with cocaine use), their admission of substance use, a history of substance use previously charted, or physical exam findings (for example, if someone has altered mental status).

What if the patient admits to substance use, has one of these medical conditions that indicates possible substance use, or otherwise gives cause for concern of substance use?

At that time, medical providers decide whether to obtain a urine toxicology screen on the pregnant person, a decision imbued with subjectivity in the absence of clear testing guidelines. If pursued, the order for a toxicology screen is often placed without consent, given that in most states there are no legal mandates to obtain a patient's consent. The urine is collected, and within several hours the results are available; if positive for a substance, this may trigger a reflex referral to child welfare or be grounds for a hospital social worker to see the patient.

In most labor and delivery settings, if there are complications during the delivery process or concern for the baby's well-being, the newborn may go to the neonatal intensive care unit (NICU) for close monitoring. In some hospitals, all babies admitted to the NICU get screened for toxicology with a meconium test (the baby's first passage of feces). If not reflexively collected, a rotating team of medical providers become familiar with the maternal and neonatal history, including any concern for substance use or any medical conditions that have been associated with substance use. New teams can decide to test neonates of mothers at any time for substance use. Each opportunity for testing matters because resultant referrals to the FPS are commonplace in cases of positive toxicology tests, often out of sight of the birthing parent and rarely with consent.

Another mechanism by which patients are connected to the FPS is through hospital social workers. Particularly in public hospitals, patients largely utilize public health insurance and may require social services that are often accessed through social workers. Hospital social workers are consulted by physician care teams to assist patients for many reasons, including teen pregnancy, substance use, depression, homelessness, domestic violence, etc. Often a history of drug use—regardless of use during pregnancy—can result in a social work consult. Given that the social worker (and all hospital workers) is also a mandated reporter, their conversation with the patient can also result in reporting to FPS for a variety of nonstandardized reasons. Though patients can refuse social work consults, they are frequently not given that option prior to a social worker arriving to their room; they may need additional services social work has to offer; and they may not be aware of the possibility of an FPS referral resulting from their conversation.

Though not all encompassing, this sketch of a typical series of events that occur when pregnant people seek care reveals two distinct mechanisms by which medical providers connect patients to the FPS: neonatal/perinatal toxicology screening and mandated reporting. It reveals how patients are surrounded by providers without protocols for biological testing despite intense legal ramifications, "deputized agents"[41] concerned about the consequences of failing to report, and perhaps well-intentioned medical providers ignorant of the FPS's destructive characteristics. A closer look at these two mechanisms can elucidate ideas for positive change.

Maternal and Neonatal Toxicology Screening: Discouraged, Discriminatory, Yet Persistent

The FPS is designed to control and separate structurally marginalized racial and ethnic minority groups' families; the urine toxicology screen generates biological evidence by which the FPS can do so. Testing is wildly discriminatory, exists largely because of a failure to standardize screening protocol, and results in the disproportionate reporting and punishment of people of color in the perinatal period.

Perinatal and neonatal toxicology screening is a test conducted on biologic specimens including urine, feces, or hair that informs providers about drug metabolites in the body. Tests vary but typically include cannabis, benzodiazepines, amphetamines, and opioids. As the most common and well-known mechanism by which physicians connect people to the FPS, maternal/neonatal toxicology screening is also the most widely denounced. National medical organizations, including the American College of Obstetrics and Gynecology and the National Perinatal Society, have released position/policy statements denouncing the criminalization of substance use in pregnancy. They formally recommend obtaining informed consent for all testing and suggest considering maternal reporting of substance use in place of toxicology screening.[42]

It is important to establish the variable understanding of the effects of substances on a developing fetus. The effects of alcohol use in pregnancy are best understood and studied. Fetal alcohol syndrome is the most severe result of prenatal alcohol use, but exposure to alcohol in utero is associated with growth deformities, facial abnormalities, and intellectual impairment, among other deficits.[43] Notably, recent data suggests the highest prevalence of late-pregnancy alcohol use was by white college graduates aged thirty-five and older; yet this group was also the least likely to be screened for alcohol use by their health-care provider.[44] The effects of other substances on fetuses is much less clear. Despite widely perpetuated narratives of the "crack baby" myth in the 1990s—used to uphold the myth of Black women as unfit mothers—the known effects of cocaine on developing pregnancies are poorly understood. Studies to date have not been able to show a significant relationship between cocaine use in pregnancy and negative obstetric or neonatal outcomes, largely due to lack of controlling for other factors such as age, socioeconomic factors, and exposure to other substances.[45] Impacts of opioid use in pregnancy include neonatal abstinence syndrome at time of delivery, of which long-term effects are also poorly understood due to small study size and confounding factors, and marijuana use is similarly poorly understood.[46, 47]

Regardless of known or unknown effects of substance use on pregnancy, the solution for any substance use disorder is substance use disorder treatment. Yet the fear of criminalization causes pregnant people to delay and avoid prenatal care, leading to overall poorer maternal and neonatal outcomes.[48] Even if women do pursue treatment, prenatal drug treatment programs are limited, with only nineteen states offering drug treatment programs specifically for pregnant people.[49]

In Tennessee, the Safe Harbor Act was passed in 2021, stating that if women using substances in pregnancy seek treatment, the FPS cannot remove their children due to drug use alone; yet journalists from *America Tonight* found that only five programs confirmed they enrolled pregnant people, two of which were completely full, and in total, only fifty available beds in Tennessee were available to pregnant people using drugs.[50] The discrepancy between the criminalization of substance use during pregnancy and the limited access to treatment programs makes clear that legislation and infrastructure are designed to punish, not treat, women with substance use disorders in pregnancy.

Currently, there are no standardized screening protocols for who, when, and on which patients to obtain UDS. Standardized screening protocols are beneficial for reducing bias when deciding to screen[51] and thus in their absence, decisions to screen are individualized and imbued with bias/racism. A landmark study showed that among pregnant people anonymously tested for drugs, the prevalence of use was found to be similar between Black and white populations; however, Black women were ten times more likely to be reported to law enforcement as a result.[52] If the design of the FPS is to surveil and control, then preferential screening and reporting of families who belong to racial and ethnic minority groups operationalizes surveillance and control.

In the absence of clear state and local guidelines, screening protocols change state by state and even hospital by hospital. A 2009 US Department of Health and Human Services report of state policy regarding prenatal substance exposure screening protocols found enormous variation in state screening protocols, hospital practices surrounding prenatal substance exposure protocols, reporting/referral protocols to the FPS, and the definition of substance exposure in utero as child abuse.[53] Eight states required health-care professionals to test for prenatal drug exposure if they suspect drug use,[54] and in Louisiana, suspicion of drug use is grounds for explicitly unconsented toxicology screening, of which positive tests trigger immediate reporting to the FPS.[55] A 2002 review of hospital protocol found that of 510 hospitals, only *one-third* reported even having a prenatal substance exposure protocol. Notably, protocols were most likely to be found in hospitals with a majority of white patients, and those were more likely to have detailed consent processes.[56]

In the absence of state or local screening protocols, screening practices encountered in hospitals are frequently *norms*, *not* hospital protocol, and frequently have no basis in evidence. This point can empower medical providers working in hospitals on labor and delivery and NICU floors to solidify or implement protocols that encourage medically indicated urine toxicology only.

How Medical Providers Should Proceed When Deciding Whether to Order Toxicology Screens

First, **providers should be aware of their hospital protocol regarding prenatal substance exposure and toxicology screening.** Compare these to state and county protocols. If hospital protocol is more punitive than either county or state, this is an area for advocacy and change for which multidisciplinary action will be required,[57] specifically collaboration with obstetrics and gynecology, pediatric teams, social work teams, and ideally with the input of local FPS abolition organizing groups. Alternatively, if there is no protocol, then providers should identify their hospitals' practices to be habitual rather than codified. In this case, providers should simply refuse to order toxicology screens that are not medically indicated.

In this vein, **the development of a medically indicated protocol for toxicology screening is urgently needed.** Medical providers rely on evidence for medical decision-making; decisions for toxicology screens must be shown to improve outcomes or prevent harm. Currently medical indications include conditions that are historically associated with drug use. However, more evidence to guide creation of a medically indicated standardized protocol (that acknowledges the legal dangers of urine drug screening) is desperately needed. Several county systems, including the LA Department of Health, have released expected practices regarding medically indicated reasons for performing urine toxicology screening in the perinatal period.

If a test is deemed medically indicated, consult with the patient and undergo a rigorous consent process indicating the medical reason behind the testing, the right to refuse testing, and the potential legal outcomes (including connection to family policing that can result in action from a home visit up to removal of the child) if testing is positive. Physicians should understand that a positive test is not sufficient evidence alone for a referral to family policing in some states, which will be discussed further in the next section.

The above recommendations are not new and have been made repeatedly by grassroots organizations working toward the abolition of the FPS from outside hospitals. Most notably, Beyond Do No Harm, through Interrupting Criminalization, explicitly addressed this in their third principle, calling for 1) explicit consent for urine toxicology screening and 2) medical personnel to refuse to report results to the police. Groups such as JMAC and Movement for Family Power recently fought for and achieved a new policy for New York City hospitals that standardizes testing and requires written informed consent from mothers.[58] They are further organizing around Senate Bill S4821, which would mandate informed consent prior to testing.[59] A Los Angeles–based coalition called Reimagine Child

Safety has specifically called for the board of supervisors to eliminate the routine screening of pregnant patients and neonates unless medically indicated and with informed consent.[60] Medical providers can support these groups and actively reduce harm by decreasing the number of urine toxicology screens ordered on pregnant people and their children.

Simply refusing to order a toxicology screen is one mechanism of harm reduction. But, in the event of a positive toxicology screen, what happens next? This leads us to the topic of mandated reporting.

Mandatory Reporting in the Hospital Setting: Legal Inconsistencies and Logistics of Reporting

Mandated reporters are people required by law to report any suspected or known instances of abuse or neglect among children, elders, or dependent adults. Health-care workers are one of the most common mandated reporters of cases of child abuse or neglect (third to education and law enforcement personnel).[61] In 2019 11 percent of child maltreatment reporters were medical personnel, accounting for nearly five hundred thousand reports in 2019.[62] In a 2007 study of the effects of foster care on over fifteen thousand children, there were more physician reports among the first-investigated children that ended up in foster care than among children who did not end up in foster care (17 percent vs. 10 percent). Physician (and notably, police) reporting was associated with an increased likelihood of children ending up in foster care.[63] It is difficult to know how many reports come from inside hospitals since no state has a centralized system for reporting FPS referrals from hospitals.[64]

Often operating under the assumption that the FPS helps families, both medical providers and hospital social workers may report families to the FPS with the assumption that FPS will determine whether or not abuse, neglect, or another problem is present. However, as Roberts explains, the FPS often takes those referrals as evidence of abuse:

> While doctors assume the FPS will respond to their concerns appropriately, caseworkers and judges assume doctors have accurately evaluated

the risks to children. *This mutually misguided deference leads many doctors to be shocked that their gut feelings caused the state to traumatize the very children they worried about.* These faulty judgments are made most frequently about Black mothers, who experience the double whammy of fewer resources for caregiving as well as stereotypes about their caregiving deficits.[65]

Specifically, pregnant people who use substances or have substance use disorders are frequently reported to the FPS by hospital-mandated reporters, often in the context of a positive UDS immediately before or after delivery. *But is maternal substance use evidence of abuse or neglect, and thus grounds for a referral to the FPS?* A review of legal inconsistencies and lack of standardization regarding reporting of positive UDS reveals the enshrined subjectivity at play with these decisions, leading to biased and discriminatory reporting.

A CAPTA Review: Federal, State, and Local Inconsistencies

Though medical providers may be under the assumption that they are complying with legal mandates by reporting patients with positive toxicology screens, there is little consistency between federal, state, and county reporting systems. In the 1990s state legislatures across the country passed laws criminalizing substance use in pregnancy. In 2003 Congress responded by amending and reauthorizing the Child Abuse Prevention and Treatment Act of 1974, which originally stated that to receive federal funding for state child welfare services, states must have policies that receive and respond to allegations of abuse/neglect. The 2003 amendment widened the definition of who must respond, requiring states to implement "policies and procedures to address the needs of the infants born and identified with fetal alcohol effects, fetal alcohol syndrome, neonatal intoxication or withdrawal syndrome, or neonatal physical or neurological harm resulting from prenatal drug exposure"[66] and that providers involved in their care subsequently notify child protective services.

In practice, medical personnel and policy makers interpret this law to mean that any infant with a positive UDS or infant born to a person with a positive UDS must be reported to child welfare services. *This common misinterpretation is evidenced by the varied manifestations of this law.*[67]

In California, the California Child Abuse and Neglect Reporting Law specifically states that a positive test is not indication of child abuse or neglect; however, any positive toxicology screen requires "an assessment of the needs of the mother and child."[68] The law does not give guidelines as to standard assessment or reporting practices. It also defers definition of the "needs assessment" to each county, further eliminating any standardization. In Los Angeles, the only publicly available county protocol regarding reporting practices is established by the Los Angeles Department of Child and Family Services (DCFS),[69] which also states that for any positive urine toxicology screen the child social worker (CSW) must conduct a needs assessment (the details of which are not publicly available). In Los Angeles, there are no publicly available standardized criteria for when a CSW needs to report a patient with a positive UDS to DCFS.[70]

Like nonstandardized toxicology testing protocols, nonstandardized reporting protocols invite and facilitate discriminatory reporting. There is a significant body of evidence reporting that medical staff (which includes CSWs) are anywhere from two to ten times more likely to report Black and Brown women with positive toxicology screens to the FPS compared to white women.[71, 72, 73, 74] Medical providers must practice harm reduction through decreased reporting, empowered with the knowledge of inconsistent and highly subjective, and resulting widespread discrimination around, reporting practices.

Logistics of Mandated Reporting in the Hospital Setting

Though positive toxicology screens are one of the most common reasons for referral to the FPS, there are many other reasons a patient may be connected to the FPS in the perinatal setting. Any medical provider or hospital staff member may report families to the FPS for a variety of reasons: vague unease regarding a family's ability to care for a child and misunderstanding of definitions of *neglect* or *abuse* may all result in FPS referral. One common mechanism by which this happens is via medical social workers, since in many public hospitals social support is offered to them. Medical providers may order social work consults for situations such as unstable housing, a history of domestic violence, diagnoses of depression and anxiety, complicated domestic relationship settings, and any indication of past or present substance use. During these interviews, other history components are often solicited, like prior FPS removal of children, history of incarceration, or history of domestic violence. As previously discussed, socioeconomic instability (which may manifest as homelessness or food instability) often is framed as neglect in the setting of a new infant and is a frequent reason for referral to the FPS; history of prior FPS involvement can also be enough to trigger an FPS report.

Whether direct medical providers or otherwise, all hospital staff must be engaged in the work of decreasing exposure to the FPS. There is inspiring work being done in the social work community regarding the integration of abolition into social work. In a recent webinar, "From Complicity to Resistance: Demanding an Abolitionist and Ethical Model of Social Work in Justice," panelists discussed educating and training social workers in the violent impact of the family policing system and mechanisms of operating outside of the current system in order to make change.[73] This sentiment is one the medical community must learn from, particularly through following the lead of grassroots organizers.

How can providers limit the harmful effects of mandated reporting in a hospital setting? Similar to the call to action in decreasing unconsented drug testing of pregnant people, Beyond Do No Harm has called for the elimination of mandated reporting, identifying both immediate actions in the hospital as well as organizing around changing hospital and state policies regarding mandated reporting.[76] Several groups call for mandated supporting as opposed to mandated reporting, citing a need for shifting the focus from policing to providing resources for families with needs.[77]

Legislation supporting this shift exists, and there are thirty-nine states approved to receive federal funds from the Family First Prevention Act of 2018, which allots funds for the prevention of family separation, though these funds are not immediately available and evidence of implementation is lacking.[78]

There are steps the health-care worker can take starting today to protect people from mandated reporting.

Do Not Report People to the FPS

When feeling concerned about a child, interrogate this suspicion; remember that as previously mentioned, the vast majority of referrals are made for neglect, which acts a proxy for poverty. **Clearly communicate with the variety of care team members in terms of your suspicion for abuse/neglect**. Be clear in your documentation regarding lack of suspicion of abuse/neglect when none exists. Resist when other members of care teams want to report patients to the FPS for anything other than explicit abuse or neglect. If a provider finds themselves concerned about abuse, consider first the evidence that children in foster care suffer devastating health outcomes and that children at high risk for abuse who stay with families may do better than those in foster care. **Then do not report families.**

If after all of these considerations a provider believes that a parent/family is committing willful abuse to a child, be explicit in your conversation to patients about why you believe an FPS referral to be necessary; tell them what to expect; and provide them with the contact information for National Advocates for Pregnant Women. *It cannot be overstated here that if a provider does decide to refer to the FPS, they are still actively subjecting a family to a violent system.* The calculus can only be that it leads to violence that is *less* than the violence of the current conditions.

The lurking dangers of the hospital need to continue to be fleshed out and resisted. For now, providers seeking to practice harm reduction for their patients will not refer patients to the FPS and will protect them from the other deputized agents within the hospital setting who may try to.

Conclusion: Abolition as the Only Answer

Though hypothetically filled with people desiring to heal, hospitals function paradoxically as sites where biological evidence and supposedly confidential information is relayed to authorities with capacity to tear apart families. *The medical community has long operated under the sense that they are the good actors, ones primarily operating in healing, yet the ways in which providers and hospitals act as initial actors in connecting people to the FPS dismantles this belief.* The therapeutic, confidential relationship sacred to the oath of a physician is compromised and bastardized when allegiance to the prison industrial complex is prioritized over patient health.

There are organizations mentioned throughout this article already working toward the abolition of the FPS. JMACForFamilies is an organization focused on abolishing current reporting and investigations as well as building holistic networks of support for families living in poverty.[77] Movement for Family Power is a grassroots activism organization that centers on raising awareness of the harms of the FPS and currently working on a bill that will require New York medical care providers to obtain informed consent for toxicology screening.[80] upEND is a University of Houston Graduate College of Social Work and Center for the Study of Social Policy collaboration also raising awareness of the harms of the FPS through community events and production of key resource guides.[81] Beyond Do No Harm has created entire infrastructure and training surrounding decreasing policing of patients by health-care workers in multidisciplinary spaces.[82] The National Advocates for Pregnant Women provides legal resources for people involved in or at risk of involvement with the FPS.[83] The authors cited in this article have been illuminating these harms for decades, and their work will continue to act as guiding lights for those of us seeking to reduce harm.

We join the calls of those pleading for the medical field to intervene in the violence caused by the FPS. We take for granted that the ultimate solution to the FPS is its abolition while also building systems of

accountability, care, and safety that reject punitive action and instead promote community thriving via community organizing. We have examined
mechanisms by which hospital staff often unwittingly or unintentionally
introduce families to the FPS through toxicology screenings and mandated reporting. We have shown that there are mechanisms of resistance
by which providers can practice harm reduction in the hospital setting
through decreasing toxicology screening, rigorous consent processes,
avoiding mandated reporting, and if reporting is necessary, pursuing
transparency with families alongside practical resources to organizations
that will support them legally and materially.

To close, it is worth considering the Movement for Family Power's
commentary on the entanglement between medical providers and the FPS:

> We have seen little evidence that medical providers engage in harm
> reduction strategies [. . .] Medical systems take these actions in con-
> travention of their ethical and legal obligations to patients; with knowl-
> edge of the harms the foster system will inflict on their patients; and
> with knowledge that such actions are well-documented to deter women
> from seeking prenatal and postpartum care—thereby isolating even more
> mothers at crucial times in their lives.[84]

This chilling account ignites moral urgency for providers to act now.
This conversation has taken center stage in abolition circles, and hospitals
and staff must respond to the patient call to do better. We must understand that *our patients do not trust us with good reason.* If we are to truly
live out the call to do no harm, we must understand how harm happens
regardless of intention, and we must resist corroboration with carceral
systems designed to harm and exploit.

The call is urgent because the dangers of the hospital abound. It is
time for providers to practice harm reduction today and support work in
abolition of the FPS. Together, we can build a society in which medical
care providers and patients trust one another, keep families together, and
work together for the thriving of communities. We can work toward a
society in which "do no harm" transitions from distantly aspirational to
definitively descriptive of the hospital's role in families' lives.

CHAPTER 6 NOTES

1. Conner, Cheryl, Christine Mitchell, Jaquelyn Jahn, and on behalf of the End Police Violence Collective. 2022. "Advancing Public Health Interventions to Address the Harms of the Carceral System: A Policy Statement Adopted by the American Public Health Association, October 2021." *Medical Care* 60 (9): 645–47. https://doi.org/10.1097/MLR.0000000000001756.

2. Klukoff, Hannah, Haleh Kanani, Claire Gaglione, and Apryl Alexander. 2021. "Toward an Abolitionist Practice of Psychology: Reimagining Psychology's Relationship with the Criminal Justice System." *Journal of Humanistic Psychology* 61: 451–69. https://doi.org/10.1177/00221678211015755.

3. "AMA Adopts Guidelines That Confront Systemic Racism in Medicine | American Medical Association." n.d. Accessed May 23, 2022. https://www.ama-assn.org/press-center/press-releases/ama-adopts-guidelines-confront-systemic-racism-medicine.

4. Roberts, Dorothy. 2022. *Torn Apart: How the Child Welfare System Destroys Black Families—and How Abolition Can Build a Safer World.* Basic Books; Roberts, Dorothy E. 2002. *Shattered Bonds: The Color of Child Welfare.* Basic Books.

5. Asgarian, Roxanna. "The Case for Child Welfare Abolition." In These Times, October 3, 2023. https://inthesetimes.com/article/child-welfare-abolition-cps-reform-family-separation.

6. Karvonen, Kayla L., Erica Anunwah, Brittany D. Chambers Butcher, Lydia Kwarteng, Tameyah Mathis-Perry, Monica R. McLemore, Sally Oh, Matthew S. Pantell, Olga Smith, and Elizabeth Rogers. "Structural Racism Operationalized via Adverse Social Events in a Single-Center Neonatal Intensive Care Unit." *The Journal of Pediatrics* 260 (September 2023): 113499. https://doi.org/10.1016/j.jpeds.2023.113499.

7. Roberts, Dorothy. 2022. *Torn Apart: How the Child Welfare System Destroys Black Families—and How Abolition Can Build a Safer World.* New York: Basic Books.

8. Roberts. *Torn Apart.* 90–102.

9. Roberts. *Torn Apart.*115–18.

10. Roberts. *Torn Apart.* 115–18.

11. For an in-depth discussion of the development of racial residential segregation and how racist exclusion gives way to predatory inclusion, see Dr. Keeanga-Yamahtta Taylor's *Race for Profit;* also see her interview; Democracy Now! 2019. *Race for Profit: Keeanga-Yamahtta Taylor on How Banks &*

Real Estate Biz Undermined Black Homeowners. https://www
.youtube.com/watch?v=DwOrGpVLeN4.

12. Roberts. *Torn Apart*. 123.
13. NAPW. 2022. From Complicity to Resistance: Demanding an Abolition-
    ist and Ethical Model of Social Work in Reproductive Justice. Webinar.
    https://www.youtube.com/watch?v=Ko4YX4DtVOc. (36:30).
14. Roberts. *Torn Apart*. 28–29.
15. Roberts. *Torn Apart*. 24.
16. H. Kim, C. Wildeman, M. Jonson-Reid, B. Drake. 2017. "Lifetime Preva-
    lence of Investigating Child Maltreatment among US Children." *Ameri-
    can Journal of Public Health* 107: 274–280.
17. Hyunil Kim et al. 2017. "Lifetime Prevalence of Investigating Child Mal-
    treatment Among US Children." *American Journal of Public Health* 107:
    274, 278.
18. "Contact with Child Protective Services Is Pervasive but Unequally
    Distributed by Race and Ethnicity in Large US Counties." n.d. *PNAS*.
    Accessed March 1, 2022. https://www.pnas.org/doi/abs/10.1073/pnas
    .2106272118.
19. Wildeman, Christopher, and Natalia Emanuel. 2014. "Cumulative Risks of
    Foster Care Placement by Age 18 for U.S. Children, 2000–2011." *PLOS
    ONE* 9 (3): e92785. https://doi.org/10.1371/journal.pone.0092785.
20. "Black Children Continue to Be Disproportionately Represented in
    Foster Care | KIDS COUNT Data Center." n.d. Accessed May 31, 2022.
    https://datacenter.kidscount.org/updates/show/264-us-foster-care
    -population-by-race-and-ethnicity.
21. "Child Population, by Race/Ethnicity." n.d. Kidsdata.Org. Accessed
    October 23, 2022. https://www.kidsdata.org/topic/33/child-population
    -race/table#fmt=144&loc=2,127,347,1763,331,348,336,171,321,345,
    357,332,324,369,358,362,360,337,327,364,356,217,353,328,354,323,
    352,320,339,334,365,343,330,367,344,355,366,368,265,349,361,4,273,
    59,370,326,333,322,341,338,350,342,329,325,359,351,363,340,335&tf
    =110&ch=7,11,10,72,9,73&sortColumnId=0&sortType=asc.
22. "Point in Time/In Care Report—California Child Welfare Indicators
    Project (CCWIP)." n.d. Accessed October 23, 2022. https://ccwip.berkeley
    .edu/childwelfare/reports/PIT/MTSG/r/ab636/s.
23. Fitzgerald, Michael. 2019. "New York City Confronts Overrepresentation of
    Black Children in Care." The Imprint. February 27, 2019. https://imprint
    news.org/featured/new-york-city-de-blasio-black-foster-care/33992.

24. Wildeman, Christopher, Frank R. Edwards, and Sara Wakefield. "The Cumulative Prevalence of Termination of Parental Rights for U.S. Children, 2000-2016." *Child Maltreatment* 25, no. 1 (February 2020): 32–42. https://doi.org/10.1177/1077559519848499.

25. U.S. Department of Health and Human Services, Administration for Children and Families, Administration on Children, Youth and Families, Children's Bureau. Preliminary Estimates for FY 2020 as of October 4, 2021(28). https://www.acf.hhs.gov/cb.

26. Harburger, Deborah S. 2004. "Reunifying Families, Cutting Costs: Housing-Child Welfare Partnerships for Permanent Supportive Housing." *Child Welfare* 83 (5): 493–508.

27. NAPW. 2022. From Complicity to Resistance: Demanding an Abolitionist and Ethical Model of Social Work in Reproductive Justice. Webinar. https://www.youtube.com/watch?v=Ko4YX4DtVOc.; Cloud, Erin Miles. n.d. "Toward the Abolition of the Foster System." S&F Online. Accessed October 9, 2021; "Rising Voices for 'Family Power' Seek to Abolish the Child Welfare System." 2020. The Imprint. July 9, 2020; Cilia, Ava. n.d. "The Family Regulation System: Why Those Committed to Racial Justice Must Interrogate It | Harvard Civil Rights-Civil Liberties Law Review." Accessed January 17, 2022; Roberts. *Torn Apart*, 66–70.

28. Cloud, Erin Miles. n.d. "Toward the Abolition of the Foster System." S&F Online. Accessed October 9, 2021.

29. Benedict, Mary I., Susan Zuravin, Mark Somerfield, and Diane Brandt. 1996. "The Reported Health and Functioning of Children Maltreated While in Family Foster Care." *Child Abuse & Neglect* 20 (7): 561–71. https://doi.org/10.1016/0145-2134(96)00044-0.

30. Feng, Huiling, Justin S Harty, Nathanael J. Okpych, and Mark E. Courtney. n.d. "Predictors of Homelessness at Age 2," 13.

31. Pilowsky, D. J., and Wu, L-T. 2006. "Psychiatric Symptoms and Substance Use Disorders in a Nationally Representative Sample of American Adolescents Involved with Foster Care." *Journal of Adolescent Health* 38(4): 351–58.

32. Courtney, Mark E., Sherri Terao, and Noel Bost. 2004. "Midwest Evaluation of the Adult Functioning of Former Foster Youth: Conditions of Youth Preparing to Leave State Care," Chapin Hall Center for Children at the University of Chicago:16.

33. Turney, Kristin, and Christopher Wildeman. 2016. "Mental and Physical Health of Children in Foster Care." *Pediatrics* 138 (5): e20161118. https://doi.org/10.1542/peds.2016-1118.

34. Doyle, Joseph J. 2007 "Child Protection and Child Outcomes: Measuring the Effects of Foster Care." *American Economic Review* 97, no. 5: 1583–610. https://doi.org/10.1257/aer.97.5.1583.

35. Doyle Jr., Joseph J. 2008. "Child Protection and Adult Crime: Using Investigator Assignment to Estimate Causal Effects of Foster Care." *Journal of Political Economy* 116, no. 4: 746–70. https://doi.org/10.1086/590216.

36. Arons, Anna. 2022. "An unintended abolition: Family regulation during the COVID-19 crisis." In *Columbia Journal of Race and Law Forum*, vol. 12, p. 1.

37. Roberts, Dorothy E. 1997. *Killing the Black Body: Race, Reproduction, and the Meaning of Liberty.* New York: Pantheon Books. 163–65.

38. Goodwin, Michele. 2020. *Policing the Womb: Invisible Women and the Criminalization of Motherhood.* Cambridge: Cambridge University Press. 81. doi:10.1017/9781139343244.

39. Goodwin. *Policing the Womb,* 110.

40. "Pregnancy & Substance Use—A Harm Reduction Toolkit by National Harm Reduction Coalition—Issuu." n.d. Accessed February 27, 2022.

41. Roberts. *Torn Apart,* 165.

42. "Opposition to Criminalization of Individuals During Pregnancy and the Postpartum Period." n.d. Accessed April 23, 2022. https://www.acog .org/en/clinical-information/policy-and-position-statements/statements -of-policy/2020/opposition-criminalization-of-individuals-pregnancy -and-postpartum-period; "Alcohol Abuse and Other Substance Use Disorders: Ethical Issues in Obstetric and Gynecologic Practice." n.d., no. 633: 9; "Substance Use." n.d. NPA. Accessed April 23, 2022. https:// www.nationalperinatal.org/substance-use.

43. "At-Risk Drinking and Alcohol Dependence: Obstetric and Gynecologic Implications." n.d. Accessed October 25, 2022. https://www.acog .org/en/clinical/clinical-guidance/committee-opinion/articles/2011/08 /at-risk-drinking-and-alcohol-dependence-obstetric-and-gynecologic -implications.

44. Cheng, Diana, Laurie Kettinger, Kelechi Uduhiri, and Lee Hurt. 2011. "Alcohol Consumption during Pregnancy: Prevalence and Provider Assessment." Obstetrics and Gynecology 117, no. 2 Pt 1: 212–17. https://doi.org/10.1097/AOG.0b013e3182078569.

45. "Substance Use during Pregnancy: Overview of Selected Drugs— UpToDate." n.d. Accessed October 27, 2022. https://www.uptodate.com /contents/substance-use-during-pregnancy-overview-of-selected-drugs ?search=cocaine%20use%20in%20pregnancy&source=search_result

&selectedTitle=1~150&usage_type=default&display_rank=1#H2459
602503.

46. "Neonatal Abstinence Syndrome—UpToDate." n.d. Accessed October 28, 2022. https://www.uptodate.com/contents/neonatal-abstinence -syndrome?search=opiod%20effect%20on%20pregnancy&topicRef =5010&source=see_link#H16.

47. Jaques, S. C., A. Kingsbury, P. Henshcke, C. Chomchai, S. Clews, J. Fal-coner, M. E. Abdel-Latif, J. M. Feller, and J. L. Oei. 2014. "Cannabis, the Pregnant Woman and Her Child: Weeding Out the Myths." *Journal of Perinatology: Official Journal of the California Perinatal Association* 34 (6): 417–24. https://doi.org/10.1038/jp.2013.180.

48. Roberts, S., and Nuru-Jeter, A. 2010. "Women's Perspectives on Screen-ing for Alcohol and Drug Use in Prenatal Care." *Women's Health Issues* 20(3): 193–200.

49. "Substance Use during Pregnancy." 2016. Guttmacher Institute. March 14, 2016. https://www.guttmacher.org/state-policy/explore/substance -use-during-pregnancy.

50. "Should Pregnant Women Addicted to Drugs Face Criminal Charges?" n.d. Accessed October 28, 2022. http://america.aljazeera.com/watch /shows/america-tonight/articles/2014/9/4/should-pregnant-women addictedtodrugsfacecriminalcharges.html.

51. Of note, *universal screening protocols* have **not** been found to reduce discriminatory screening—a literature review in 2010 reviewed the underlying logic behind universal surveillance providing for decreased reporting disparities based on the assumption that increased reporting comes from increased screening of Black women. Authors examined the assumptions underlying this logic and found that current evidence does not suggest that universal screening will result in more equitable report-ing. Roberts, Sarah C. M., and Amani Nuru-Jeter. 2011. "Universal Alco-hol/Drug Screening in Prenatal Care: A Strategy for Reducing Racial Disparities? Questioning the Assumptions." *Maternal and Child Health Journal* 15 (8): 1127–34. https://doi.org/10.1007/s10995-010-0720-6.

52. Chasnoff, I. J., H. J. Landress, and M. E. Barrett. 1990. "The Prevalence of Illicit-Drug or Alcohol Use during Pregnancy and Discrepancies in Mandatory Reporting in Pinellas County, Florida." *The New England Journal of Medicine* 322 (17): 1202–1206. https://doi.org/10.1056/NEJM 199004263221706.

53. Zellman, Gail L., C. Christine Fair, Jill Houbé, and Michael Wong. 2002. "A Search for Guidance: Examining Prenatal Substance Exposure

Protocols." *Maternal and Child Health Journal* 6 (3): 205–12. https://doi
.org/10.1023/A:1019734314414.

54. "Substance Use during Pregnancy." 2016. Guttmacher Institute. March
14, 2016. https://www.guttmacher.org/state-policy/explore/substance
-use-during-pregnancy.

55. "Substance Exposed Newborns Reporting and Notifications | Louisi-
ana Department of Children & Family Services." n.d. Accessed April 29,
2022. http://www.dcfs.louisiana.gov/page/substance-exposed-newborns
-reporting.

56. Zellman, Gail, Carol Fair, Jill Houbé, and Michael Wong. 2002. "A Search
for Guidance: Examining Prenatal Substance Exposure Protocols." *Maternal
and Child Health Journal* 6 (October): 205–12. https://doi.org/10.1023
/A:1019734314414.

57. "Alcohol Abuse and Other Substance Use Disorders: Ethical Issues
in Obstetric and Gynecologic Practice." n.d. Accessed April 5, 2022.
https://www.acog.org/en/clinical/clinical-guidance/committee-opinion
/articles/2015/06/alcohol-abuse-and-other-substance-use-disorders
-ethical-issues-in-obstetric-and-gynecologic-practice.

58. Khan, Yasmeen. 2020. "NYC Will End Practice of Drug Testing Pregnant Patients Without Written Consent." Gothamist. November 17,
2020.

59. "Active Campaigns." n.d. JMACForFamilies. Accessed April 30, 2022.
https://jmacforfamilies.org/active-campaigns.

60. "Demand 8 | Reimagine Child Safety." n.d. Reimagine Child Safety.
Accessed November 2, 2022. https://www.reimaginechildsafety.org
/demand8.

61. U.S. Department of Health and Human Services, Administration for
Children and Families, Administration on Children, Youth and Families,
Children's Bureau. 2021. "Child Maltreatment 2019: Summary of Key
Findings." https://cwlibrary.childwelfare.gov/permalink/01CWIG
_INST/10a03se/alma991000198129707651.

62. U.S. Department of Health and Human Services, Administration for
Children and Families, Administration on Children, Youth and Families,
Children's Bureau. 2021. "Child Maltreatment 2019: Summary of Key
Findings." https://cwlibrary.childwelfare.gov/permalink/01CWIG
_INST/10a03se/alma991000198129707651.

63. Doyle, Joseph J. 2007. "Child Protection and Child Outcomes: Measuring
the Effects of Foster Care." *American Economic Review* 97 (5): 1583–610.
https://doi.org/10.1257/aer.97.5.1583.

64. Young, N. K., Gardner, S., Otero, C., Dennis, K., Chang, R., Earle, K., & Amatetti, S. 2009. Substance-Exposed Infants: State Responses to the Problem. HHS Pub. No. (SMA) 09-4369. Rockville, MD: Substance Abuse and Mental Health Services Administration.

65. Roberts. *Torn Apart,* 168 (Italics added).

66. The Child Abuse Prevention and Treatment Act (CAPTA) with amendments made by the Substance Use – Disorder Prevention that Promotes Opioid Recovery and Treatment for Patients and Communities Act or the SUPPORT for Patients and Communities Act, Public Law (P.L.) 115-271, enacted October 24, 2018. Section 7065 (a) of P.L. 115-271 amended section 105 of CAPTA and section 7065(b) repealed the Abandoned Infants Assistance Act of 1988 (42 U.S.C. 5117aa et seq.).

67. Despite the clear federal position that evidence of prenatal drug use is not to be considered child abuse, as of 2022 twenty-four states consider substance use during pregnancy to be child abuse; three consider it grounds for civil commitment; and twenty-five states require health-care professionals to report suspected prenatal use ("Substance Use During Pregnancy." 2016. Guttmacher Institute. March 14, 2016. https://www .guttmacher.org/state-policy/explore/substance-use-during-pregnancy.)

68. Penal Code 11164-11174.3. Law Section. n.d. Accessed April 29, 2022. https://leginfo.legislature.ca.gov/faces/codes_displaySection.xhtml?law Code=PEN&sectionNum=11165.13.

69. "DCFS Child Welfare Policy Manual - 0070-521.10, Assessment of Drug Alcohol Abuse." n.d. Accessed April 23, 2022. http://policy.dcfs.lacounty .gov/#Assessment_of_Drug_Alc.htm.

70. Based on authors, conversations with hospital social workers as well as DCFS workers in Los Angeles County as well as review of available public protocol on LA DCFS website.

71. Chasnoff, I. J., H. J. Landress, and M. E. Barrett. 1990. "The Prevalence of Illicit-Drug or Alcohol Use during Pregnancy and Discrepancies in Mandatory Reporting in Pinellas County, Florida." *The New England Journal of Medicine* 322 (17): 1202–6. https://doi.org/10.1056/ NEJM199004263221706.

72. Kerker, Bonnie D., Sarah M. Horwitz, and John M. Leventhal. 2004. "Patients' Characteristics and Providers' Attitudes: Predictors of Screening Pregnant Women for Illicit Substance Use." *Child Abuse & Neglect* 28 (2): 209–23. https://doi.org/10.1016/j.chiabu.2003.07.004.

73. Ellsworth, Marc A., Timothy P. Stevens, and Carl T. D'Angio. 2010. "Infant Race Affects Application of Clinical Guidelines When Screening

for Drugs of Abuse in Newborns." *Pediatrics* 125 (6): e1379–85. https://doi.org/10.1542/peds.2008-3525.

74. Perlman, Nicola C., David E. Cantonwine, and Nicole A. Smith. 2022. "Racial Differences in Indications for Obstetrical Toxicology Testing and Relationship of Indications to Test Results." *American Journal of Obstetrics & Gynecology MFM* 4 (1). https://doi.org/10.1016/j.ajogmf.2021.100453.

75. NAPW. 2022. From Complicity to Resistance: Demanding an Abolitionist and Ethical Model of Social Work in Reproductive Justice. Webinar. https://www.youtube.com/watch?v=Ko4YX4DtVOc.

76. Interrupting Criminalization | Research in Action. "Beyond Do No Harm." Accessed December 17, 2023. https://www.interrupting criminalization.com/beyond-do-no-harm.

77. Albright, K., Gaines, M. Halvorson, J., Pearlman, J., Roy, W. 2022. "Creating a Child & Family Well-Being System: A Paradigm Shift from Mandated Reporting to Community Supporting. Safe & Sound. https://cwlibrary.childwelfare.gov/permalink/01CWIG_INST/10a03se/alma991001378328407651.

78. Loudenback, Jeremy. "Supporters, Not Reporters: Preventing Foster Care in California." The Imprint, May 16, 2023. https://imprintnews.org/top-stories/supporters-not-reporters-preventing-foster-care-in-california/241305.

79. "JMACforFamilies." n.d. JMACforFamilies. Accessed May 1, 2022. https://jmacforfamilies.org.

80. "Movement for Family Power." n.d. Movement for Family Power. Accessed February 21, 2022. https://www.movementforfamilypower.org.

81. "Resources." n.d. UpEND. Accessed May 1, 2022. https://upendmovement.org/resources/.

82. Interrupting Criminalization | Research in Action. "Beyond Do No Harm." Accessed December 17, 2023. https://www.interruptingcriminalization.com/beyond-do-no-harm.

83. "National Advocates for Pregnant Women - NAPW | Legal Advocacy Groups." n.d. Accessed November 2, 2022. https://www.nationaladvocatesforpregnantwomen.org/.

84. Movement for Family Power and National Advocates for Pregnant Women. (n.d.). *Violence against Women in the Medical Setting: An Examination of the US Foster Care System*. Retrieved June 1, 2022, from https://ccrjustice.org/sites/default/files/attach/2019/06/MFP_NAPW_UN_VAW_Submission-20190531-Final.pdf.

Figure 6.1: *Queer Youth, Medical Disparities, and School-to-Prison Pipeline* mini-zine
by Syan Rose and Ronica Mukerjee

BRANCHES

LGBTQ+ youth are disproportionately incarcerated in juvenile detention

- 15–20% of youth in juvenile detention are LGBTQ+ (and only 4–6% of gen pop)
- 40% of AFAB people in juvenile detention identify as LGBTQ+ &/or gender nonconforming

TRUNK

Policing systems impact the health of LGBTQ+ youth

- Over 40% of homeless LGBTQ+ youth have worse physical health than non-LGBTQ+, over 60% have worse mental health
- Over 60% of homeless gender-variant youth have worse physical health than non-gender variant youth, and ~80% have worse mental health

School exclusion and family lack of acceptance causes youth LGBTQ+ homelessness

- 20–40% of homeless youth in the United States are LGBTQ+
- 90% of transgender youth experience homelessness due to family rejection/harassment/bullying
- 70% of LGBTQ+ youth reported they are homeless resulting from family rejection/harassment/bullying

Figure 6.2

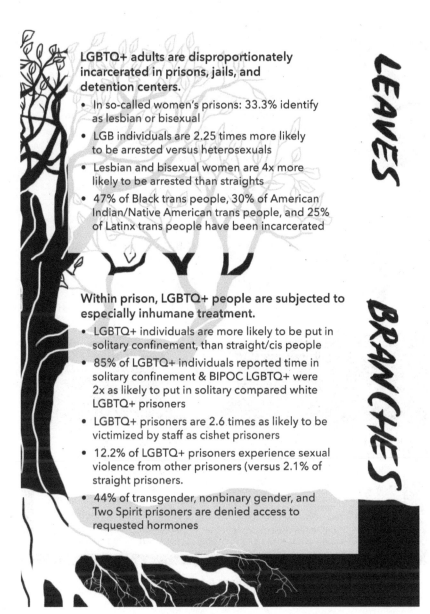

LGBTQ+ adults are disproportionately incarcerated in prisons, jails, and detention centers.

- In so-called women's prisons: 33.3% identify as lesbian or bisexual
- LGB individuals are 2.25 times more likely to be arrested versus heterosexuals
- Lesbian and bisexual women are 4x more likely to be arrested than straights
- 47% of Black trans people, 30% of American Indian/Native American trans people, and 25% of Latinx trans people have been incarcerated

Within prison, LGBTQ+ people are subjected to especially inhumane treatment.

- LGBTQ+ individuals are more likely to be put in solitary confinement, than straight/cis people
- 85% of LGBTQ+ individuals reported time in solitary confinement & BIPOC LGBTQ+ were 2x as likely to put in solitary compared white LGBTQ+ prisoners
- LGBTQ+ prisoners are 2.6 times as likely to be victimized by staff as cishet prisoners
- 12.2% of LGBTQ+ prisoners experience sexual violence from other prisoners (versus 2.1% of straight prisoners.
- 44% of transgender, nonbinary gender, and Two Spirit prisoners are denied access to requested hormones

LEAVES

BRANCHES

Figure 6.3

Once let out of prison, people have no access to drug treatment, LGBTQ+-inclusive socialization services. LGBTQ+ people are overrepresented in the community supervision population.

- People on probation/parole are almost 2x as likely to be LGB than people not on probation and parole—and again, lesbian and bisexual women are especially overrepresented
- Women on probation are nearly 3x as likely to be lesbian or bisexual (16.7%) as women not on probation (6.3%).
- Men on parole are nearly 2x as likely to be gay or bisexual (7.9%) as men not on parole (4.1%).
- Women on parole are nearly 3x as likely to be lesbian or bisexual (17.6%) as women not on parole (6.4%).
- During probation or parole, LGBTQ+ former prisoners' movements and choices are restricted

NEW FRUITS

People fall back through the cracks into the prison system. LGBTQ+ people are over-represented in sex offender registries, which creates huge barriers to housing and employment

- Many states require registration for HIV-related "crimes"
- Seventeen states ban name changes for people with some types of convictions, and a criminal record leads to additional scrutiny when it comes to name changes even if the state has no ban; this means gender-expansive people cannot apply for jobs with their true names

Figure 6.4

7

MEDICAL NEGLECT AS CARCERAL VIOLENCE

How Incarcerated Women Seek Health, Give Care, and Resist Violence behind Bars

BY AMINAH ELSTER, JENNIFER ELYSE JAMES,
GISELLE PEREZ-AGUILAR, AND LESLIE RIDDLE

I watched my friend have an asthma attack right in the middle of the fucking sidewalk. And her best friend carried her over to the clinic. When she got her there, she laid her on the floor, and she died right there because the motherfuckers acted like they didn't know she was having an asthma attack. Marva Hines was her name.

Patty Searles was standing in the med line because they didn't have an awning over it. It took us fifteen years to fight for an awning over the med line because you are standing in the middle of the fucking sun at twelve o'clock in the afternoon trying to get your meds because the bitch too fucking lazy to come and open it up on time. So, she comes at one o'clock. Patty passes out from a fucking heart attack. Guess what? She dies right there on the fucking sidewalk in front of us. Her name was Patty Searles.

Marge Tanner. Her pussy literally fell out of her body, but instead of them fixing her the correct way, you know what they did? They pulled it back up through her body, attached it to her spine, sent her back to her room, and she died in the hallway. Her name was Marge Tanner.

Candace Bennett. She got an ear infection. Something happened, but the shit went through her stomach. You think they knew what the fuck was going on? She died in the hallway at MTA. At seven o'clock at night. Her name was Candace Bennett.

Cheryl Morales, she was at VSP. Her stomach kept swelling and swelling and swelling. Oh well, you've got problems with your liver, so we are going to check you out. She sat in the motherfucking clinic on B yard and died on the bench because she was waiting for them to come and do something for her. I had just talked to her fifteen minutes before that.

These were my friends. These people were my family. They don't give a fuck. It's all about the fucking money. And you want to charge me a five-dollar co-pay to be seen and I ain't got five dollars? So you won't see me? Or I got to wait thirty days? Bullshit. Why I got to wait thirty days to be seen? I wasn't sick when I came in here. You motherfuckers didn't take care of me. Feed me bullshit, let mice and everything else run around, shit in the food, shit's all in the kitchen. Roaches. All this shit. You think they give a fuck? They don't care. We took better care of each other than the medical department did. We took better care of each other. If they did anything. And they got the taxpayers out here thinking that they are taking care of us. They ain't doing a motherfucking thing. That's it. Is this what you wanted to know?

When Sputnik shared her memories with us, her voice was full of emotion. She was crying, and we could hear her anger and anguish as she remembered and relived the deaths of her friends—her family—that occurred over her thirty-six years inside a California women's prison. Death is a part of life. Sputnik had seen people she cared for die before. But these deaths were different. For Sputnik, and many others who have survived mass incarceration, these deaths were caused by state violence. They were the result of medical neglect, correctional officers' contempt, and systems designed to punish rather than care. What Sputnik was describing went beyond loss; she was describing ongoing trauma following decades of enduring and witnessing violence inflicted by agents of the state.

Much of the discourse surrounding police and state violence has focused on overt acts of physical violence perpetrated against individuals. While it is critically important to shed light on the abuse inflicted by agents of the state, the everyday, insidious reality of systemic medical violence often remains hidden behind prison bars and barbed wire. In 2018 more than 4,500 people died in US prisons;[1] these numbers are only growing, with more than 2,600 deaths behind bars due to COVID-19 alone in 2020 and 2021.[2] While some attention is focused on deaths due to suicide, homicide, and drug overdose, less is focused on fatalities occurring at the hands of the state that result from subpar medical care, inadequate nutrition, unsanitary living conditions, and other harmful conditions of confinement.[3, 4] In addition to the lives lost to carceral medical violence, the punitive conditions of care lead many incarcerated people to experience fear and lack of trust in the medical system. Many people incarcerated in women's prisons report refusing or delaying care because of the poor quality of care and negative interactions with healthcare providers, leading to worsened health outcomes among an already marginalized population.

In this chapter, we will reflect on ethnography, activism, lived experiences, and interviews with dozens of formerly incarcerated women to describe the medical neglect and mismanagement of care experienced and witnessed inside California state women's prisons. Between 1980 and 2010 the number of women incarcerated in California increased 433 percent.[5] California is home to the world's largest women's prison and the nation's first prison hospital. Incarceration in the United States has always existed as a tool of violence. While the history of medical experimentation, torture, and extreme neglect in prisons has been explored,[6, 7] in this chapter we will advance theories of medical violence into carceral health care, highlighting the inherent contradiction of delivering care within institutions designed to punish. Importantly, we will describe how survivors make meaning of health, illness, and death while incarcerated and enact resistance to medical neglect through trauma healing, caregiving, and medical advocacy.

The Long Entanglement of Racism, Carcerality, and Health Care

Racism and structural violence in modern medicine are deeply rooted in the theft of and experimentation on enslaved Black people's bodies, as well as twentieth-century eugenics movements that led to the compulsory sterilization of tens of thousands of BIPOC people.[7, 8] These acts of violence are not only woven into the fabric of our medical system, but the US carceral system and its institutions, practices, and policies, which have "legitimized and even normalized the violation of people's bodily self-determination."[9] The embedment of health care into the carceral system consequently results in a carceral health system imbued with violence. Legislative efforts to address "cruel and unusual punishment" in these contexts have largely failed due to the emphasis on individual bad actors rather than larger structural harms.[10]

In 1976, *Estelle v. Gamble* established the right of people who are incarcerated to receive health care under the Eighth Amendment,[11] yet there is a long history of medical neglect, experimentation, and exploitation in US correctional institutions.[12, 13] In California, there has been repeated court oversight of health care administered by the California Department of Corrections and Rehabilitation (CDCR). In 2001 plaintiffs in *Plata v. Davis* claimed that inadequate medical care in California state prisons violated the Eighth Amendment prohibition against cruel and unusual punishment. In 2006, after failing to improve prison health care as ordered, the California state prison system was put under federal receivership. Despite this history and the eight-fold increase in the number of incarcerated women in the US over the late twentieth century, correctional institutions have struggled to provide adequate health-care services for people incarcerated in women's prisons.[14]

While people of all genders who are incarcerated are more likely to suffer from serious mental illnesses and infectious and chronic diseases than the general population,[15] women—who are more likely to enter incarceration with histories of trauma and abuse—have higher rates of medical and psychiatric conditions than incarcerated men.[16] Further, reproductive health care is compromised by the very nature of mass incarceration, which "undermines bodily autonomy and the capacity for incarcerated people to make decisions about their reproductive well-being and bodies . . . [violating] the most basic tenets of reproductive justice—the right to have a child, not to have a child, and to parent the children you have with dignity and in safety."[17] Such violations represent a "profound and persistent" form of gender-based violence,[18] which Heise describes as "any act of force or coercion that gravely jeopardizes the life, body, psychological integrity or freedom of women in service of perpetuating male power and control."[19] While this definition is perhaps overly essentialist, she explicitly notes medical violence as a form of gender-based violence and cites gender-based violence as "the most pervasive yet least recognized human rights abuse in the world." Prison itself is a critical form of gender-based violence as it limits freedom and causes bodily and psychological harm while perpetuating hegemonic power and control. Prison health care lies at the intersection of two forms of structural violence and oppression: the criminal legal system and the health-care system, which serve to "mutually create and reinforce each other."[20]

Dehumanization and Violence

Violence in prison is ubiquitous. It is a constant in the lives of people who are incarcerated, felt acutely in nearly all interactions with the staff and the institution. This violence is both allowed and perpetuated because, as a society, we have structurally and systematically dehumanized the people we incarcerate. We label them as "other" (criminal, felon, convict, inmate), strip them of their autonomy, and accept that they deserve poor treatment.[21] We separate them from their communities and hide them away in prisons, behind walls, bars, and barbed wire, then disregard their treatment inside due to the false notion that their imprisonment makes us safe.[22] We have given these institutions license to treat the people locked inside poorly, and this extends to their medical care.

People who work in prison health, many of whom may approach their work from an ethic of caring and compassion, are nonetheless working within a violent culture and one that acts with impunity. As one formerly incarcerated woman who asked to be called Optimus Prime described,

> *They're honestly, to me, they're a state-sanctioned gang and they kind of have carte blanche to do whatever they want because they are the state of California. And nobody's going to tell [them] what to do. . . . It's all the stigmas: You shouldn't be in jail, you did something wrong, you're bad for being in there so what does it matter anyways? You're already in state cus-tody. Basically, you're a society throwaway, so we don't care.*

She is describing the way in which incarcerated bodies are expend-able in our society. Once an individual is marked as a criminal, they no longer have a right to bodily autonomy and can be treated without compassion or respect. Prisons allow for the institutionalization of this expendability seen throughout our society,[23] almost demanding that pro-viders treat their patients as less than and encouraging patients to view themselves as unworthy of care.

When delivered within the structurally violent environment of the prison, even the most routine care can be dehumanizing, often failing to center or even acknowledge past trauma and leaving patients feeling further devalued. One formerly incarcerated patient, Monique, described the process of routine cervical cancer screenings and other preventive care, saying:

> *We were lined up like cattle to get our shots, to get a Pap smear. You should have seen Pap smear day . . . We'd all stand in line in these little dresses, they called them muumuus and would stand in line, and we get up to the bed and there would be just like blood, KY jelly, everything all over the floor. It was so gross. The guy was just like . . . they were doing them back-to-back. It was just horrible . . . He'll eat lunch and give a Pap smear*

at the same time, it's the truth. It's the truth. Doesn't use gloves, just . . . nothing. Back-to-back. And like everybody's in line, so like it's not like just one person he's like taking advantage of. Everybody is in line. There's a line clear down the hallway . . . We are told to take our underwear off and lift our muumuus up, get on the thing, and he does whatever. I mean, it's a line of people—line of women—already waiting for procedures . . . I look back and I think, how did I not know that shit wasn't normal? You know? It fucks me up.

In this dehumanizing narrative, Monique names the medical gaslighting[24] that incarcerated women face at the hands of correctional health providers and the internalized oppression when inhumane treatment becomes normal and "fucks them up." Medical gaslighting is a form of violence in which those with medical power cause people to question their reality and worthiness to receive adequate health care.[25] Through this repeated dehumanizing treatment and questioning of symptoms and motivations, incarcerated women are made to feel that they don't have value. They are made to feel that they don't deserve autonomy over their own body or quality medical care, that they are seeking care with ulterior motives, and that they deserve to be questioned and punished for expressing pain or asking questions in the medical setting.

Medical Neglect as Continued Abuse

Among women incarcerated in the US, an estimated 90–95 percent are survivors of physical, sexual, or emotional abuse.[26, 27]

Thus, many women arrive at prison with high levels of personal stress, trauma, and fear.[28, 29] The US criminal legal system targets survivors of violence; women are routinely convicted for crimes committed by their abusive partners, while others are incarcerated because they fought back against abuse. For most people incarcerated in women's prisons, violence is not new. Indeed, it has been a constant in many of their lives. This history of trauma and abuse has many implications for the delivery of health care inside prisons. Optimus describes the challenges that women, who are survivors, have in asserting their autonomy in medical encounters:

> *About 80 to 85 percent of the women in there have been survivors of some type of violence and/or have been traumatized and didn't have the tools to deal with what they've been through . . . .So it was, you know, typically people of color, people that didn't have the education there or just, honestly, as women who are incarcerated . . . So, no, I'm not going to stand up to authority when authority is telling me one thing, you know, or the other.*

Across dozens of interviews, we heard that choice and decision-making in health care are limited inside. Patients described often being given only one care plan option; while they do have the option to refuse care, this can be quite fraught. Standing up to a provider (especially a male provider) to ask for an alternative treatment plan or refuse care can evoke fear, particularly for women who are survivors of abuse. Monique, who "consented" to a hysterectomy while incarcerated, echoed Optimus's sentiment. She had been bleeding between periods, and a doctor told her that a hysterectomy was her only choice. In reflecting back on this, she said,

> *When I was taken out for the hysterectomy, there's no . . . The doctor didn't explain anything . . . I didn't know nothing. I grew up on the streets. I was on the streets at like twelve years old, so I didn't really understand . . . In fact, I didn't even know what a dang ovary was. Serious. I'm not an idiot, but I just never knew what all that stuff was. When it was explained to me later that what they did was wrong, I didn't know it was wrong. I trusted them. I mean who doesn't trust a doctor?*

For many women, the abuse and control they faced in relationships prior to incarceration were mirrored and replicated by the system, as was the case for Ruby. Ruby was in a horrifically abusive relationship before her incarceration, involving more than a decade of physical and sexual violence, humiliation, and having her every movement controlled. She came to prison as a result of fighting back against an abuser who was actively trying to kill her. She was inside for more than thirty years, and it took decades for her to begin to process her trauma. In describing being incarcerated, she said,

> *Being in prison was a daily reminder [of abuse] . . . .And I was still living under [my husband's] thumb. It didn't stop. The beatings stopped, but I'm still being controlled, I'm still being told what to do, when I can do it, how I can do it. Told where I have to work. When I can eat, when I can't eat. It's just more control, that's all. Except that the control in prison can control the rest of your life and how you live it.*

For many women like Ruby, the prison was an extension of the gender-based violence they endured throughout their lives, and health care inside was part of the punitive control exerted by the carceral system on their day-to-day lives. Ruby was in good health prior to her incarceration—she was young when she entered the system and progressed through middle age and into older adulthood while inside. Twenty years into her incarceration, she developed bronchitis. She'd had recurring bronchitis her whole life, so, as she said, "I know when I have bronchitis, I know when I don't." When she asked a doctor to treat her bronchitis, the doctor insisted she had a cold and refused to do further testing or prescribe medications. She suffered for three months before another doctor happened to pass by her as she was struggling to walk and breathe. She was finally sent for an x-ray, and her doctor called her in to go over the results. Ruby describes the encounter:

> *"Well, I have good news, I have bad news. Which do you want first?" I said, "Well I already know what the bad news is." She said, "What do you think the bad news is?" "That I have bronchitis." She said, "No, that's the good news." And I said, "What? What's the bad news?" She says, "You are in congestive heart failure; you are going to die." That was her bedside manner, I guess. But she said, "You are in congestive heart failure; you are going to die. You are going to die before Christmas." And every time I saw her it was always, "You cost the state so much money, you cost the state too much money."*

When she saw an outside cardiologist for the first time, he confirmed that the bronchitis contributed to her heart failure. Ruby experienced medical neglect inside prison. Her symptoms were dismissed, and she couldn't access care that she knew she needed. Her knowledge of her body was discounted, and she had no other options or avenues; she couldn't seek a second opinion as demanding additional tests or interventions could have resulted in disciplinary action. What should have been a routine illness became a disabling event because of poor care and the dismissal of her autonomy and humanity.

Carceral Patienthood: Inmate First, Patient Second

Dismissal and inadequate treatment of symptoms are common in the prison context. In prison health care, many women described being treated as an "inmate" first and a "patient" second. They are seen as criminal, deceitful, and manipulative, and their reports of symptoms or requests for intervention are viewed with skepticism. Katie described this phenomenon and her journey seeking care for what could have been a minor issue. It started very simply with a spider bite, but the cascade of neglect and poor care led to years of medical trauma. She said,

> I got a spider bite. They didn't want to take care of it, and so it got really bad and got staph infection. They finally were willing to see me and do something about it, but the antibiotics, because they had waited so long, the antibiotics didn't work. I got a tiny little nick on my stomach. A little scratch that turned into the second infection.

She was working at a job site that was dirty when she got the second infection. She was concerned that the infection wasn't healing properly or could worsen, but she said, "You still have to program." So she was expected to show up for work each day. She went on to describe her care, saying,

> This second site was on my stomach, and so they tried the third antibiotic. It wasn't working. They suggested taking me out to do an IV or something, but then changed their mind after discussing my sentence, in front

of me. The doctor and the chief medical officer, who basically is the one that decides who can go out of the institution and all that, they discussed it together, saying like, is there any way we can do something else before taking me back out? It's just at a quarter size, the size of a quarter. But it was deep. Still the infection didn't go away.

Katie was serving a "life without the possibility of parole" sentence, or LWOP. Because of this sentence, taking her to an outside hospital would require multiple correctional officer escorts and a chase car to follow behind her transport—it would be expensive and pull staff away from other work at the facility. Concerns about security and cost played a role in decisions about her care. In this case, they outweighed the concerns about her health. Katie continued her story, saying,

I ended up getting a tiny pimple on the corner of my lip, and that's where the infection landed last. My lip swelled up extremely huge. I could barely eat. And it went to my tonsil. They finally took me out then because I could barely talk. Took me out to an ear, nose, and throat [doctor], and they said, like, the tonsil is caving down my throat.

The doctor said she needed surgery immediately, but again security concerns overruled the recommendation. She was sent back to her cell to sleep, despite the surgeon cautioning that her airway could become obstructed at any time. Katie finally had her surgery, but security concerns continued to disrupt her care. An officer came in and woke her up in recovery to tell her it was time to go back to the prison. As Katie described it, "The nurse got really upset at the officer because [the officer] wanted to force me to do the squat and cough. She's like, 'She has stitches in her throat, she can't do that.' [The officer's] like, 'She has to.' So I basically ended up throwing up all over [the] officer."

Countless women we have interviewed describe being told again and again, "Nothing is wrong with you." Women described being mocked, kicked, shoved, and left alone in their cells after reporting that they were ill or injured. This abuse often comes from correctional officers, who serve as gatekeepers to medical care; people who are incarcerated are

expected to work every day to keep the prison running. Anyone expressing that they cannot work because of their symptoms is immediately a
target of suspicion and derision. If someone is able to access care, health-
care providers often make assumptions about their motivations: that they
want a "lay in" (permission not to work due to illness) or that they are
drug-seeking. These same types of assumptions are made of patients in
the free world—especially low-income patients and patients of color—
when they seek care in the emergency room or other safety-net settings.
However, both the inability to seek a second opinion or change facilities
and the inherently punitive nature of correctional health care make these
assumptions even more life-threatening for incarcerated patients.

One woman we interviewed described the experience of her roommate, Billie, a sixty-year-old "nice, insanely cool lady" who started experiencing debilitating symptoms to the point of "screeching" in pain. She
tried to convince Billie to seek medical care, but she resisted, saying, "I had
a bad experience, I'm not going over there; they are mean to me." Eventually, she was in too much pain to work and was threatened with a write-up,
which would come with loss of privileges, so she relented and went to
medical care. Billie's roommate walked her over, desperate for help, and
remembered, "They yelled instead. They were like, 'What do you want?
What do you want? Pain pills? What do you want?'" Billie had a family
member who was able to call and advocate for her, and eventually she was
seen by medical care. However, by that time her symptoms had progressed;
her toes had turned "black and fuzzy." Billie's roommate recalled seeing
her from across the yard coming back from medical, alone, attempting to
maneuver in a wheelchair. Billie had been told to come back to her room
and wait for her toes to fall off. She eventually had her foot amputated.

Enacting Resistance through Health

Many women we spoke with avoided or delayed seeking health care due to
systemic barriers and the punitive and stigmatizing nature of correctional
health care. In both carceral and free world health-care settings, refusing
medical care is labeled in stigmatizing, often pathologizing ways. Patients

are deemed "non-compliant" or told they must sign a form that they are leaving "against medical advice." This is done both to take the legal burden off the medical system and to label the patient as deviant from the patient role. Yet research has shown that patients of color are much more likely to receive labels like "non-compliant" or "non-adherent" or noted as "refusing" care, while white and wealthier patients are granted more agency and partnership in choosing alternative care paths.[30, 31] In the prison context, the avoidance of medical care is even more complex and, we assert, should be conceptualized as a tool of resistance in a carceral health system marked with violence and death. Incarcerated women cannot seek second opinions, bring friends or family with them to appointments, or do research on their condition—tools we encourage patients on the outside to utilize to take charge of their own health. The right they can assert is to remove themselves from a violent space. However, this prioritization of immediate safety comes at a high cost. As Fox, a fifty-one-year-old Black woman who was incarcerated for twenty-six years shared,

> I've seen people die in their rooms because they won't go to medical. [My friend] died in her room because she wouldn't take medical. She's like 'Why? They're not going to do nothing.' She died in the room three nights later.

Annie, who in describing her health as a formerly incarcerated older adult, explained this paradox, saying, "I think that I probably could be in better medical health if I had trusted them. But I may be in better medical health *because* I didn't trust them." Earlier interventions for her chronic health conditions may have been beneficial, but she intentionally avoided the potential for receiving damaging medical care as a form of self-protection.

Care and healing in prisons often occur within the community of incarcerated people formed inside—women didn't trust the system, but they came to trust each other deeply. This care work is another key form of resistance taken up by many women inside. In the absence of both a safe medical system and family support, the community formed inside assumed the roles of both health-care provider and caregiver. Loved ones inside cared for each other, providing support, nourishment, help with activities of daily living, medications, and advice, all of which is an affront to the carceral system. Some activities, like bringing food to a sick friend—so normal in free society—are expressly forbidden in prison. In general, finding ways to care within a violent environment is a tremendous act of resistance.[32] These acts of love and humanity are radical acts of standing up to a violent system to care for one another. The families and community formed inside are unrecognized, unsupported, and at times unallowed. Individuals can be isolated or removed from their families with no reason or notice. And yet, the system in many ways depends on these networks of care to fill its own gaps.

Sputnik described how incarcerated people often wait in line to receive medical care for hours when they are sick. Some of this is structural, the result of our culture of mass incarceration. But, for Sputnik, it often also felt like the people working inside didn't care or couldn't provide care, and it was up to the community to care for themselves and each other:

> We did more self-medicating and taking care of each other when shit happens than anybody else did. You know what I mean? You go over there for a triage; the nurse will give you a look. 'You know what? We've got a lot of people out here to see.' I was like, just give me what I need to take care of my damn self and let me go back to my room.

People with any medical training or background are often relied upon for advice and care. One woman who had been a nurse prior to incarceration described, "The number of times women would come to me with some pill in their hand and say, 'Birdy, what is this? Do you think I should take it? I have an ear infection.' And I would say, 'No, you shouldn't take it. And don't take someone else's antibiotics. Two or three doses is just going to create a resistant strain, don't do that.' But people would still come and ask." People incarcerated in women's prisons continually find ways to build a culture of caring in a violent system that attempts to strip away health, community, and love.

Building a community of care within a system designed for punishment is in and of itself a form of resistance to state-sanctioned violence.

Sputnik described how much she missed many of the people she came to know and love during her decades in prison and shared her pain and anguish remembering the loved ones she lost inside. She described the impact that her family inside had on her life, saying,

> I miss them. This is what you need to understand. I miss them. I wouldn't be the person that I changed to be if it wasn't for a lot of those ladies that's in there. Some of us made it out; some of us are still trying to get out; some of them ain't going to never get out. And then some of them died protecting us and teaching us and, you know, building a foundation for us in a prison. Who would've thought that people in prison could build a foundation where you can eventually come home and function as a human being?

Sputnik found healing—from the abuse and violence faced both before and during her incarceration—through the relationships she built inside. It was the community formed with other people who were incarcerated, not the health-care system, that allowed for her healing from trauma.

During, and perhaps especially after, incarceration, women described embarking on journeys to heal from trauma and reclaim their health-worthiness. Participants had to find ways to challenge internal and external notions that incarcerated bodies are deviant and thus not worth living. In our interviews, we learned that the structure of prison led incarcerated women to suppress their own needs and put their families—both inside and outside—first. This can be understood within the context of cultural frameworks like the Black Superwoman Schema,[33] which illuminates how Black women's wellness may be diminished as they care for others. This phenomenon extends into carceral spaces. As Kat shared, "Black women, we don't tell, we just keep going and holding this stuff on our back. And I'll tell you, the load for me was heavy." Kat is speaking to the burden that Black women hold, not only of their own trauma, but also in caring for others in their circles. She went on to say, "Being a Black woman, you know, there's already that stigma you are strong, you can do it, you just struggle through it, you don't get help, you help yourself." This reflection captures the loneliness that Black women and other women of color may be experiencing, feeling that they cannot ask for support from their loved ones or communities and that they must do this on their own. This is only heightened in the prison context where many relationships have been disrupted.

Part of reclaiming health worthiness is learning to self-advocate for quality care within a violent system and speaking up against medical negligence. Yet speaking up this way can be dangerous—an individual can receive a write-up and be subjected to further punishment for challenging the medical system. Patients are continually told "nothing is wrong with you" when they seek help. Many women described that it took them many years, or even decades, to be able to advocate for themselves within this system. System-impacted women endure and resist multiple layers of trauma with racialized and gendered bodies deemed not worth living,[34] living with fear that if they speak up, they are not staying in their place of oppression and will be pushed back to it via retaliation. It is through both healing from trauma and a commitment to resistance that women are able to reclaim their health worthiness and find avenues— through filing grievances or bringing lawsuits—to assert their right to care within the system. As incarcerated women transition home, they must relearn how to center their own health needs after often decades of caring for others and being uncared for by the system.

Conclusion

The punishment and structural violence embedded in the prison doesn't stop at the clinic or hospital doors. It is present in the dismissal of symptoms. It is pervasive in the assumptions of ulterior motives for seeking care. It is allowed to flourish through the prioritization of "security" over the health and well-being of the patients seeking care. Incarcerated patients are expected to avail themselves of medicine; to be vulnerable and trusting in a system that continually abuses them. While there are health-care providers working in carceral settings who are passionate about providing quality care and who treat their patients with respect, even their efforts are overshadowed by the structural violence that defines each encounter.

As described, most incarcerated women have experienced trauma and abuse prior to incarceration, which is perpetuated by the violent prison industrial complex. By viewing trauma healing as resistance, we challenge limited beliefs that healing happens only in professional spaces. Instead, we found that women are in control of when, where, and how to heal from their traumatic experiences and do so within their communities, often despite the ongoing violence of the carceral state. System-impacted women described healing as a form of interpersonal, community, and systemic resistance and imagined new possibilities to break cycles of punishment and retraumatization.

For the women we interviewed, reclaiming health worthiness came in many shapes and forms. As with trauma healing, it was a choice they made on their own terms and by reconnecting to the sacredness of their bodies—from using their voice (in the form of self-advocacy) to giving themselves permission to rest, rather than "just pounding through." For most, reclaiming health worthiness took them on a journey of providing care and healing in community with other system-impacted women, sharing resources—including power and privilege—with each other. By holding space for each other and deepening the relationship with self, these women are on a path of liberation from the prison industrial health complex.

Prison is not and can never be the solution to trauma. Violent systems perpetuate harm and cannot promote healing. Instead, healing comes through community. Our findings call into question whether the idea of trauma-informed care is or can be truly possible in the prison system, though we would urge steps to be taken to prioritize models of patient-centered care. This is not a problem of bad-apple doctors but rather one of systemic violence. Routine medical care offered under the constant threat of punishment and violence will always be punitive in nature. We must invest in *community-based*, trauma-informed care and disinvest in prisons. Abolition medicine provides an antidote by questioning the systems that enable violence and create racial health inequities and reimagining medicine as an anti-racist practice.[35] As Pitts states,

"By building models for healthcare that eliminate structural oppressions, cycles of medicalized violence, and forms of criminalization, we can aim to effectively render prisons *and* correctional healthcare obsolete."[36]

CHAPTER 7 NOTES

1. Carson, E. A. (2021). Mortality in State and Federal Prisons, 2001–2018—Statistical Tables. *Statistical Tables*, 34.

2. Marquez, N., Ward, J. A., Parish, K., Saloner, B., and Dolovich, S. (2021). "COVID-19 Incidence and Mortality in Federal and State Prisons Compared with the US Population, April 5, 2020, to April 3, 2021." *JAMA*, *326*(18), 1865–67. https://doi.org/10.1001/jama.2021.17575.

3. Alohan, Daniel, and Michele Calvo. "COVID-19 Outbreaks at Correctional Facilities Demand a Health Equity Approach to Criminal Justice Reform." *Journal of Urban Health: Bulletin of the New York Academy of Medicine* 97, no. 3 (June 2020): 342–47. https://doi.org/10.1007/s11524-020-00459-1.

4. Bowleg, L. (2020). "Reframing Mass Incarceration as a Social-Structural Driver of Health Inequity." *American Journal of Public Health*, *110*(S1), S11–S12. https://doi.org/10.2105/AJPH.2019.305464.

5. Vera Institute of Justice. (n.d.). *Incarceration Trends in California*. https://www.vera.org/downloads/pdfdownloads/state-incarceration-trends-california.pdf.

6. Hornblum, A. M. (1999). *Acres of Skin: Human Experiments at Holmesburg Prison* (1st edition). Routledge.

7. Washington, H. A. (2008). *Medical Apartheid: The Dark History of Medical Experimentation on Black Americans from Colonial Times to the Present* (Illustrated edition). Anchor.

8. Cooper Owens, D. (2018). *Medical Bondage: Race, Gender, and the Origins of American Gynecology* (Paperback). University of Georgia Press. https://ugapress.org/book/9780820354750/medical-bondage/.

9. Hayes, C. M., and Gomez, A. M. (2022). "Alignment of Abolition Medicine with Reproductive Justice." *AMA Journal of Ethics*, *24*(3), E188–E193. https://doi.org/10.1001/amajethics.2022.188.

10. Pitts, A. (2019). "Carceral Medicine and Prison Abolition." In B. R. Sherman and S. Goguen (Eds.), *Overcoming Epistemic Injustice: Social and Psychological Perspectives* (p. 233). Rowman & Littlefield.

11. Niveau, G. (2007). "Relevance and Limits of the Principle of 'Equivalence of Care' in Prison Medicine." *Journal of Medical Ethics*, *33*(10), 610–13. https://doi.org/10.1136/jme.2006.018077.

12. Hornblum, *Acres of Skin*.

13. Washington, *Medical Apartheid*.

14. Aday, R., and Farney, L. (2014). "Malign Neglect: Assessing Older Women's Health Care Experiences in Prison." *Journal of Bioethical Inquiry*, *11*(3), 359–72. https://doi.org/10.1007/s11673-014-9561-0, 97(3), 342–47. https://doi.org/10.1007/s11524-020-00459-1.

15. Cloud, D. H., Parsons, J., and Delany-Brumsey, A. (2014). "Addressing Mass Incarceration: A Clarion Call for Public Health." *American Journal of Public Health*, *104*(3), 389–91. https://doi.org/10.2105/AJPH.2013.301741.

16. Swavola, E., Riley, K., and Subramanian, R. (2016). *Overlooked: Women and Jails in an Era of Reform*. Vera Institute of Justice.

17. Hayes, C. M., Sufrin, C., and Perritt, J. B. (2020). "Reproductive Justice Disrupted: Mass Incarceration as a Driver of Reproductive Oppression." *American Journal of Public Health*, *110*(S1), S21–S24. https://doi.org/10.2105/AJPH.2019.305407.

18. Richie, B. E., and Eife, E. (2020). "Black Bodies at the Dangerous Intersection of Gender Violence and Mass Criminalization." *Journal of Aggression, Maltreatment & Trauma*, *0*(0), 1–12. https://doi.org/10.1080/10926771.2019.1703063.

19. Heise, L. (1993). "Violence Against Women: The Missing Agenda." In M. Koblinsky, J. Timyan, and J. Gay. (Eds.), *The Health of Women: A Global Perspective*. (pp. 171-196). Routledge.

20. Richie, B. E., and Eife, E. (2020). "Black Bodies at the Dangerous Intersection of Gender Violence and Mass Criminalization."

21. Cacho, L. M. (2012). *Social Death: Racialized Rightlessness and the Criminalization of the Unprotected*. NYU Press.

22. Davis, A. Y. (2003). *Are Prisons Obsolete?* Seven Stories Press.

23. Rouse, C. M. (2021). "Necropolitics Versus Biopolitics: Spatialization, White Privilege, and Visibility during a Pandemic." *Cultural Anthropology*, *36*(3), 360–67. https://doi.org/10.14506/ca36.3.03.

24. Sebring, J. C. H. (2021). "Towards a Sociological Understanding of Medical Gaslighting in Western Health Care." *Sociology of Health & Illness*, *43*(9), 1951–64. https://doi.org/10.1111/1467-9566.13367.

25. Sebring, J. C. H. (2021). "Towards a Sociological Understanding of Medical Gaslighting in Western Health Care."

26. Goodmark, L. (2021). "Gender-Based Violence, Law Reform, and the Criminalization of Survivors of Violence." *International Journal for Crime, Justice and Social Democracy*, *10*(4), 13–25. https://doi.org/10.5204/ijcjsd.1994.

27. Owen, B., Wells, J., and Pollock, J. (2017). *In Search of Safety: Confronting Inequality in Women's Imprisonment*. University of California Press. https://doi.org/10.1525/california/9780520288713.001.0001.

28. Aday and Farney. (2014). "Malign Neglect."

29. Sufrin, C. (2017). *Jailcare: Finding the Safety Net for Women Behind Bars*. University of California Press.

30. Beach, M. C., Saha, S., Park, J., Taylor, J., Drew, P., Plank, E., Cooper, L. A., and Chee, B. (2021). "Testimonial Injustice: Linguistic Bias in the Medical Records of Black Patients and Women." *Journal of General Internal Medicine*, *36*(6), 1708–14. https://doi.org/10.1007/s11606-021-06682-z.

31. Sun, M., Oliwa, T., Peek, M. E., and Tung, E. L. (2022). "Negative Patient Descriptors: Documenting Racial Bias in the Electronic Health Record." *Health Affairs*, *41*(2), 203–11. https://doi.org/10.1377/hlthaff.2021.01423.

32. Callahan, M., and Paradise, A. (2019). "Fierce Care Politics of Care in the Zapatista Conjuncture." *Transversal*. https://transversal.at/blog/Fierce-Care.

33. Woods-Giscombé, C. L. (2010). "Superwoman Schema: African American Women's Views on Stress, Strength, and Health." *Qualitative Health Research*, *20*(5), 668–83. https://doi.org/10.1177/1049732310361892.

34. Cacho, L. M. (2012). *Social Death: Racialized Rightlessness and the Criminalization of the Unprotected*. NYU Press.

35. Iwai, Y., Khan, Z. H., and DasGupta, S. (2020). "Abolition Medicine." *Lancet (London, England)*, *396*(10245), 158–159. https://doi.org/10.1016/S0140-6736(20)31566-X.

36. Pitts. "Carceral Medicine and Prison Abolition."

Figure 7.1: Artwork by Glenn "Kinoko" Tucker

8

ABOLISH ICE TRANSFERS

BY TIEN PHAM, AMBER AKEMI PIATT, AND NATE TAN

Policing[1] and incarceration[2] are harmful to individual, family, and community health. They are death-making institutions.[3] This was true before the onset of the COVID-19 pandemic and has continued to be glaringly true since. For example, ICE detention facilities have reported a COVID-19 case rate thirteen times higher than that of the general US population. This is devastating, and, at the same time, public health crises in carceral facilities have wide-reaching impacts. More cases inside prisons and jails have meant more outside of them too. A statistical analysis by the Prison Policy Initiative estimated that United States incarceration added about 566,800 cases—among people both inside and outside of carceral facilities—between May 1 and August 1, 2020, alone.[4] That's roughly 13 percent of all new US cases for the same time period.

One way that systems of criminalization grow power, expand reach, and diversify their tools is by collaborating with adjacent systems, including child welfare systems,[5] public health systems,[6] and immigration systems. Specifically, people who are not US citizens—or who are perceived to not be US citizens—are subjected to further surveillance, policing, and too often incarceration, and ultimately deportation under immigration law. Collaborations between Immigrants and Customs Enforcement (ICE) and local jails or state prisons create a pipeline that enables the immediate immigration detention of someone who was deemed suitable for parole—a process that deems an individual rehabilitated and fit to reenter society. After many immigrants and refugees have served their time, they are transferred to immigration detention to await their deportation. This pipeline is the main way people end up in ICE detention centers.

Millions of people are incarcerated every day nationally,[7] and hundreds of thousands are deported annually.[8] Because of structural racism and classism, the prison system disproportionately impacts low-income people of color, and low-income immigrants and refugees are no exception.

In this chapter, we explore how ICE transfers specifically impact Southeast Asian refugees in California and the broad—as well as health-specific—efforts to stop this vicious form of state violence. We start with firsthand testimony from Tien—one of the coauthors of this chapter who was incarcerated, transferred to ICE, and ultimately deported. We then describe some of the community organizing efforts—led by grassroots groups like the Asian Prisoner Support Committee (APSC), where one of the coauthors (Nate Tan) works—to change policy, build people power, and bring our loved ones (including Tien) home. Finally, we discuss how one public health organization—Human Impact Partners (HIP), where another coauthor (Amber Akemi Piatt) worked—supported the campaign through community-driven, health-focused research and an ongoing partnership to shift policies and narratives. While HIP is not a central campaign leader, we describe their role in greater detail to shine a light on the intersections between public health, incarceration, and immigration.

Tien's Story

On July 17, 2000, I was at home with my mom when two detectives knocked on the door. I knew immediately that they came to arrest me. I was involved in the stabbing of three people on the previous Saturday evening. After searching my room and interrogating me, the detectives took me into juvenile custody and charged me with attempted murder. I was seventeen years old.

My mom came to visit the next day. As I walked into the visiting room, she was already tearing up. She didn't talk much, unlike her usual self. I could sense her worries, sorrows, embarrassment, and disappointment.

For a moment, I felt sorry for her but immediately numbed my pain—my false pride didn't allow me to show any weaknesses.

The next day, the same detectives came and took me to a Santa Clara County jail. Once inside, I noticed people around me were adults and started to feel afraid. I really thought that somebody had died in my crime. "I'm underage. What am I doing here?" The detectives told me that since my crime was serious, I would be charged as an adult. I felt overwhelmed. I was taken back to juvenile hall. Although scared, I showed an "I don't care attitude" in front of my peers.

The rest of my family found out about my arrest soon after. Having been in the United States for less than four years, none of us knew much English, let alone criminal law. A public attorney was assigned to me, but my family decided to hire a private lawyer because we didn't trust the authority. It cost $10,000—a huge amount of my family's hard-earned money.

After three years in juvenile hall, I was transferred to adult county jail while going through court proceedings. During these times, I spent most of my time locked inside a cell. We were allowed one hour every other day to shower and make phone calls. I spent a lot of time reading, writing, and imagining. These were the only tools that could help me escape my mental distress.

Most of my peers in juvenile hall were sentenced to long sentences or life in prison. I started to accept that I would be in prison for a long time; my attorney estimated twelve to fifteen years. That reality changed when the sentencing day came: the judge announced a sentence of twenty-eight years and four months. I felt discombobulated and didn't hear anything else afterward. I turned around and looked for my family in the courtroom for support. I saw my dad tearing up, and my younger sisters were sobbing aloud. I wondered where my mom was. At that moment, I felt regretful and sorry for my family more than ever. I couldn't even imagine the pain, embarrassment, and disappointment I had put them through. Once again, I numbed my pain. I was twenty-one years old.

I was transferred to San Quentin Prison's reception a few days later. I wasn't prepared for a twenty-eight-plus-year sentence, but I was prepared for prison. Well, at least I thought I was. Because of the seriousness of my crime and sentence, I was immediately placed in a maximum-security unit.

The first incident happened when I was released for dinner. As I was walking with the crowd, all of a sudden, an inmate was attacked by two others. They sliced his throat with a manufactured razor. Blood was oozing out of his throat while he was running away. The incident left me shaky and traumatized. I knew there were unspoken rules within the prison that each inmate must follow, and I had just witnessed what happens if you don't.

After classification, I was transferred to High Desert State Prison, a level four facility where inmates were placed for the most heinous crimes. I arrived on December 17, 2004, on a cold and snowy night. The whole prison was on lockdown for an incident that involved a staff member being assaulted. I was already familiar with lockdowns. What I wasn't used to, however, was the loneliness of being so far away from loved ones and friends.

In the years that followed, I served time in High Desert State Prison, Old Folsom State Prison, California Men's Colony, and eventually San Quentin State Prison. Things got worse before they got better. I got into multiple fights and turned into an alcoholic and a hustler. I got involved in gambling, as well as dealing drugs and other illegal products. I got caught with marijuana and received a consecutive four-year term. Once again, I went through the stress of court procedures. How would I explain putting my family through disappointment all over again? I decided to not tell them, even to this day.

After receiving the additional four years, I was more careful. Proposition 21 passed and had allowed youth offenders like me to seek earlier release. I went to the board of parole hearing (BPH) and was denied for three years. However, for the first time in fifteen years, I finally felt motivated and hopeful. I told myself to stay disciplined and earn as many certifications from self-help programs, vocation, and education as possible. Freedom was finally near.

To better my chances at the BPH, I asked to be transferred to San Quentin State Prison because of their self-help programs. It took me three years to finally get my wish. I arrived in San Quentin in 2018, the same year as my second BPH. To my and my family's disappointment, I received another three years' worth of denial. It didn't discourage me though, for I had found a new purpose in life: bettering myself. The journey of self-improvement was a blessing—I'd discovered so much about myself, and I met many wonderful people inside and outside of San Quentin.

I went back to the BPH in 2020 and was found suitable for parole. I was excited yet concerned at the same time. I was one step closer to freedom, but I knew I had to face ICE, who sought to deport me.

The day came when my family and friends were waiting outside of San Quentin's gate for my release. However, instead of being joyously reunited, I saw a white van come to take me to ICE detention from the holding cage. As I left San Quentin, I looked everywhere for my loved ones. I asked gate security if they saw them, and he said they had already left; they were meeting me at the San Francisco ICE processing center. Once I arrived there, my lawyer arranged a visit. I was able to spend an hour with them, and I stayed in the processing center until nighttime.

Eventually, two ICE officers escorted me to a plane, and I was flown to Aurora ICE Detention Center in Colorado. Despite my hard work, the nightmare of being incarcerated still wasn't over. But this time was different: my release day was unknown, and the fear of being deported to a country I no longer knew and being so far away from family and friends—including those I had met in San Quentin—was extremely stressful. Despite access to video visits, ICE detention was extremely lonely.

My worst fears became a reality when they put me on a flight to Vietnam with thirty other deportees. Although scared, I told myself to be strong, to look forward, and to be grateful for the journey I had gone through. I still have hope: I plan to request a pardon from the California governor in a few years so that I can return to the United States and reunite with my family. So many people helped fight my ICE transfer, and our struggle is not over yet.

Beyond Criminalization: Moving toward Critical Connections in Immigrant Rights Movements

Tien's story is astounding, but not unusual. Policy decisions in the United States and abroad have long shaped people's—like Tien's—life conditions, social environments, and future trajectories. Telling our stories and building relationships across our shared experiences and our differences allows us to make meaning of what we have been through and to build the collective power needed to make social change.

One organization doing this type of work is the APSC, which provides direct support to Asian and Pacific Islander (API) prisoners and raises awareness about the growing number of APIs being imprisoned, detained, and deported. APSC and many other groups lead and support work within immigrant rights movements in California and beyond. This work has yielded powerful results, including passing the California Values Act (SB 54) in 2017. This bill limited local law enforcement from collaborating with ICE, including in county jails. This and other policies like it have been part of the larger organizing effort to protect immigrants and refugees from compounding years of xenophobic and anti-immigrant policies at various levels of government.

However, the immigrant rights movement has also been at a crossroads. We are being forced to reckon with false dichotomies—namely, the idea of a deserving and undeserving immigrant—and how that shapes our advocacy priorities. These long-standing binaries became more deeply entrenched and operationalized during the Obama administration, which emphasized deporting "felons, not families."[9] That is, his administration—and its policies and practices—asserted that some immigrants deserve to stay in the United States and others do not, subjecting immigrants with criminal records to double punishment via immigration detention and deportation. The resistance to these assertions has led to a critical narrative question over the last decade: don't all immigrants deserve basic human rights?

Deportation is no small punishment. It is devastatingly harmful to individual, family, and community health[10]—even the threat of deportation harms health.[11, 12] Given its deleterious effects, organizers and advocates argue that it is an inhumane and unjustified policy, even for people who have criminal records.

For Tien, for example, his incarceration, ICE detention, and deportation have tremendously impacted him and his family physically, financially, mentally, emotionally, and spiritually. After twenty years of being rehabilitated, they expected to be reunited but instead faced yet another challenge, another hardship, another punishment. They are frustrated and disappointed with the legal system.

In recent years, a movement has taken place to advocate for immigrants and refugees with criminal convictions. Immigration policy at the national level has had tremendous impacts on what occurs at the state level. With its historic reputation of scapegoating immigrants for this country's social ills, the United States has taken a punitive approach to immigration enforcement. Examples of this include the expansion of border patrol staff, power, and resources; the proliferation of ICE detention centers;[13] and the ever-growing budgets for immigration enforcement[14] since these agencies' inceptions.

One specific federal policy that has wreaked havoc on the immigrant and refugee population is the 1996 Illegal Immigration Reform and Immigrant Responsibility Act (IIRAIRA). Due to IIRAIRA, immigrants and refugees with convictions or "crimes of moral turpitude" were deemed deportable.[15] This has subjected thousands to a system of double punishment: once going through the criminal legal system in the United States they are forced into the immigration system. Even minor crimes, such as shoplifting or possessing drugs, became deportable offenses under IIRAIRA.[16] While there has been significant organizing to protect immigrants in California, very little has been done to protect immigrants who fall into the crosshairs of both the immigration and the criminal legal systems.

Advancing Policies That Stop ICE Transfers

In recent years, organizing and advocacy efforts have sought to disrupt this prison-to-ICE pipeline. Advocacy groups like APSC are demanding that all people, regardless of citizenship status, should have the right to be with their families and are organizing for incarcerated people to be released to their families instead of ICE. Campaigns such as #FreeNy, #Keep-PJHome, #HomeNotHeartbreak, and other freedom campaigns have brought to the forefront a more expansive and inclusive immigrant rights movement—one that demands humanity and dignity for immigrants and refugees in the criminal legal system. Individual freedom campaigns highlight the impact of the prison-to-ICE pipeline and the traumas of this double-punishment system. Because of how storytelling can shift people's hearts and minds, these freedom campaigns are creating a narrative shift toward seeing the humanity and worthiness of all people, including immigrants who have criminal records. Through sharing their individual experience, they paint a picture of how systems and structures failed them and constrained their choices. They demand accountability from incarceration and immigration enforcement institutions that enable and commit systemic violence and advocate for people impacted by them.

Many immigrants arrive to the United States as young children impacted by wars—including Tien, whose family fled the US-backed war in Vietnam—and resettle in impoverished communities. While resettling, these children face a wide range of social challenges—including poverty, bullying, overpoliced neighborhoods, gangs, and violence—that funnel them into the prison system. Tien and his family, for example, emigrated to the US and had to deal with financial problems, cultural shock, language barriers, fitting in, and past traumas. They could only afford to locate in an area in East San Jose, where poverty, gangs, and violence were normalized. His grades were dropping, and he joined a gang to fulfill his social needs. This path led to twenty years of imprisonment and now deportation. As Tien's story shows, the school-to-prison pipeline doesn't start with school and end at prison for immigrants. It would more accurately be described as the migration-to-school-to-prison-to-deportation pipeline.

At the policy level, much work remains to ensure that all immigrants and refugees, including those with criminal records, are protected in the state of California. Freedom campaigns and narrative shifts have enabled advocates to attempt to pass the VISION (Voiding Inequality and Seeking Inclusion for Our Immigrant Neighbors) Act, a bill that would prohibit California prisons and jails from carrying out direct ICE transfers.[17] If passed, the VISION Act would ensure that those who are released from prison get to reunite with their families and have a better chance at fighting their deportation case.

Organizers, advocates, and people impacted by the jail/prison-to-ICE pipeline argue that our current system treats immigrants and refugees as second-class citizens—from the additional level of punishment to the poor conditions they face while in ICE. Individuals who have been funneled through the pipeline and managed to return home to their families have spoken out about the inhumane experiences they had to endure and demand an end to these injustices. Powerful storytelling along with fierce advocacy have moved politicians to place themselves on the side of justice—seeing immigrants and refugees in prison and jails as deserving to be reunited with their families.

Using Public Health Research for Good

Recognizing both the opportunities and challenges of research, HIP—a national public health organization headquartered in California—works to align our research ethics,[18] process, and products with our broader mission: to transform the field of public health and build collective power with social justice movements. While we collaborate with community organizers, public health professionals, governmental public health departments, and other parties on all of our efforts to carry out our purpose, one of our more extensive types of cooperation is through research projects. We take care to approach research partnerships in ways that attend to power dynamics, center our community partners' goals, and build sustainable relationships.

Though research alone will not solve social injustices, it can be a powerful tool in the struggle for structural change. At its best, research builds people's power, enumerates, and elucidates problems facing communities, and provides clues as to what solutions will help repair problems and advance justice. Furthermore, for research participants, it can be healing to have your experience heard and validated and to see the ways that you are not alone. However, research is not inherently good or just.

Beyond academic issues related to research rigor and validity, research processes, as well as their subsequent data, have also long been used to harm. At its worst, research retraumatizes vulnerable populations, calcifies social stigma, and places blame on individuals for structural problems. Masquerading as objective truth, research has been used to double down on stereotypes and to justify oppression.

Research—and its interpretation and application—is fundamentally political. The process and outcomes of research can both be consequential. Indeed, decisions around the framing, conducting, and disseminating of research can impact what is discovered, undiscovered, and ignored; how participants experience the research process; and how audiences understand the research findings, as well as the limitations. Furthermore, because political conditions shape our daily lives—from how our schools are funded to what is criminalized to who is deported—research findings cannot be understood in a vacuum. Political and social contexts must stay within view.

These issues notwithstanding, research continues to be an important strategy for advancing public health broadly. We can see how community-based, policy-driven research is reflected in several of the updated 10 Essential Public Health Services, including:

- ▸ Assess and monitor population health status, factors that influence health, and community needs and assets.

- ▸ Investigate, diagnose, and address health problems and hazards affecting the population.

- ▸ Strengthen, support, and mobilize communities and partnerships to improve health.

- ▸ Create, champion, and implement policies, plans, and laws that impact health.

Public Health Partnership to Stop ICE Transfers

HIP initially met with staff from APSC in 2019 to learn more about their current priorities and explore ripe opportunities for collaboration. Once we decided to conduct a research project together on the campaign to end ICE transfers, we found points of alignment and discussed our hopes, dreams, and fears for our partnership. We also decided to recruit Asian Americans Advancing Justice - Asian Law Caucus (ALC) to join us, given their work advocating to end ICE transfers legislatively, as well as providing direct legal services to Asian American and Pacific Islander clients facing incarceration or deportation, including Tien.

We spent several weeks discussing possible research directions and building consensus on what would be most valuable, relevant, and appropriate. Given that both APSC and ALC work primarily (if not exclusively) with Asian American and Pacific Islander communities, we decided to narrow the research project's focus to Asian American and Pacific Islander communities. This is who we have close relationships with, and our work could fill a gap in research materials exploring how criminalization, incarceration, and immigration enforcement affect these communities. We ultimately narrowed even further to focus the research project on Southeast Asian communities—that is, those who immigrated or fled from Brunei, Burma (Myanmar), Cambodia, Timor-Leste, Indonesia, Laos, Malaysia, the Philippines, Singapore, Thailand, or Vietnam—for several key reasons:

▶ Southeast Asian refugees and immigrants make up an important part of the broader California community yet are often left out of mainstream immigration narratives.

▶ California has the largest Southeast Asian population of any state in the United States by far, with 992,257 Californians identifying as Southeast Asian.[19]

▶ In the US, Southeast Asian communities are three to four times more likely to be deported for past convictions when compared with other immigrant communities.[20]

Thus, we ultimately agreed to explore a set of three key research questions:

1. What is the disaggregated data on Southeast Asian communities being affected by direct transfers from CA prisons and jails to ICE custody?

2. What health factors, including trauma, are criminalized, especially in Southeast Asian communities?

3. What is the health impact of direct transfers from prisons/jails to ICE custody on Southeast API individuals in the system?

   a. Health impact of releasing people from jails and prisons with various levels of restrictions (e.g., electronic monitoring, community supervision, on one's own recognizance, etc.)

   b. Health impact of family reunification

   c. Health impact of sanctuary city policies with no caveats

   d. Health impact of deportation, especially for refugees

To answer these questions, we conducted a literature review exploring the preceding research questions and interviewed Southeast Asian people directly impacted by ICE transfers between May and June 2020. Initially, we had hoped to interview people currently incarcerated or detained by ICE and distribute a mass survey to currently incarcerated people, but we were unable to because of the COVID-19 pandemic. Ultimately, we interviewed seven people who were formerly incarcerated, people who were deported after an ICE transfer, and their family members. Each interview involved a pair of HIP research staff and our community partners, who had long-term relationships with the interviewees. Each interview involved an informed consent process that reassured interviewees that they were free to share as much or as little as felt comfortable.

Through our literature review, we found that the pipeline from prison or jail to ICE detention and deportation feeds a cycle of trauma that has adverse health impacts for those who experience it, as well as their loved ones and the broader community. For example, we found that Southeast Asian adults have some of the highest rates of post-traumatic stress disorder (PTSD), depression, and anxiety compared with the general population.[21] Furthermore, one study demonstrated that parental refugee status was a predictor of young people's engagement in violence, which was compounded by contact with peers involved in criminalized activities and by limited parental engagement (likely due to parents' challenges managing their own trauma around their refugee status).[22] This pre-existing trauma is compounded by the harm inflicted by the legal system. When faced with the looming threat of deportation, studies have found adults experience exacerbated existing health conditions, such as high blood pressure, and self-report their health to be poor.[23] We also have found that when worried about their parents' deportation, children often experience stress, anxiety, and fear and have trouble keeping their grades up at school.[24]

Our literature review findings are echoed in Tien's story, as well as the stories of those we interviewed, which brought profound nuance and irreversible urgency to what we learned. We heard devastating firsthand stories about the weight of intergenerational trauma from US-backed wars in Southeast Asia, the physical abuse women experience in immigration detention, the debilitating fear of deportation after being released from prison, the untenable burden children face when their parents are incarcerated, and the devastation of ongoing separation from one's family after being deported. The interviews were heart-wrenching. We also heard about the desperate desire to be given a second chance, to be able to reunite with their families, and to be able to give back to their communities.

While we were not able to fully answer every question—because of the criminal legal system's poor data collection, the barriers the criminal legal system creates to communicate with currently incarcerated people, and the rapidly shifting pandemic conditions—our research was conclusive. Criminalization, incarceration, and deportation are not a justified or healthy way to deal with social, political, or economic issues, including the incident described by Tien previously. These systems of punishment simply exacerbate and compound harm and violence.

We discussed all findings with our community partners and decided collectively what parts of the research we would share publicly—and, crucially, not share publicly. Our top priorities were to honor people's stories and to create research products that would support the campaign to end ICE transfers in California and advance narratives that center people's dignity. We wanted to be sure that the findings would be put to good use, not sit on a shelf. To that end, we created advocacy materials that were tailored toward specific audiences: the governor of California and California legislators who could change the laws governing ICE transfers; people directly impacted by ICE transfers who could share their stories to affect change; and public health practitioners who could speak from their authority to support the effort.[25]

With our research materials in hand, we met with the governor's staff and lobbied state legislators to discuss why ending ICE transfers—by passing the VISION Act—is important to advancing individual, family, and community health and promoting health equity. These meetings often included a cross-section of representatives, including public health practitioners, directly impacted people, faith leaders, and more. Furthermore, we educated public health workers and organizations on the issue through webinars, classroom lectures, blogs, social media, and op-eds, and we mobilized our networks to support the campaign.

Conclusion

Whether you take a pragmatic, moral, or scientific lens to the issue, health workers and organizations must do more to focus on the public health crisis that is incarceration. For one, the "public" in public health necessarily includes incarcerated people. Furthermore, because structural racism guides both what is criminalized and who is policed, Black people, Indigenous people, and other people of color are disproportionately incarcerated. Failing to act against the incarceration system is complicity with structural racism—we have an ethical and anti-racist obligation to act.

The evidence was striking prepandemic and is now ever more unambiguous. Thankfully, the field of public health is catching up. In 2021, the American Public Health Association passed a policy statement on carceral systems that specifically summarizes the public health evidence demonstrating why we must "move toward the abolition of jails, prisons, and detention centers."

They catalog action steps, including releasing incarcerated people and providing reentry support, that echo the specific recommendations put forward through our research project and the advocacy efforts overall.

Organizing for abolition is a fundamentally hopeful endeavor.[26] This campaign is not asking for something outlandish; it seeks fair treatment for immigrants, refugees, and asylum seekers. In an interview with Tien's sister, Lien, she describes her hopes: "In the ideal world, when someone is released from prison, he or she would get to have a reset button in their life. He's granted rights like any other citizen. He goes back out to his community, earns a degree he desires, [and] works in a job where he can give back to his community."[27] Isn't that a cause we can all get behind?

CHAPTER 8 NOTES

1. American Public Health Association, "Addressing Law Enforcement Violence as a Public Health Issue." (2018). https://www.apha.org/policies -and-advocacy/public-health-policy-statements/policy-database/2019 /01/29/law-enforcement-violence.
2. American Public Health Association, "Advancing Public Health Interventions to Address the Harms of the Carceral System." (2020). https:// www.apha.org/Policies-and-Advocacy/Public-Health-Policy-Statements /Policy-Database/2022/01/07/Advancing-Public-Health-Interventions -to-Address-the-Harms-of-the-Carceral-System.

3. Widra, Emily. "State prisons and local jails appear indifferent to COVID outbreaks, refuse to depopulate dangerous facilities," Prison Policy Initiative, February 10, 2022. https://www.prisonpolicy.org/blog/2022/02/10/february2022_population/.

4. Hooks, Gregory and Wendy Sawyer. "Mass Incarceration, COVID-19, and Community Spread," *Prison Policy Initiative*, December 2020.

5. Roberts, Dorothy. *Torn Apart: How the Child Welfare System Destroys Black Families—and How Abolition Can Build a Safer World*. Basic Books, 2022.

6. Mitchell, Christine. "Blog: How to Protect Privacy & Public Health in Covid-19." Othering and Belonging Institute, 2021. https://belonging.berkeley.edu/blog-how-protect-privacy-public-health-covid-19.

7. Sawyer, Wendy and Peter Wagner. "Mass Incarceration: The Whole Pie 2022." Prison Policy Initiative, 2022. https://www.prisonpolicy.org/reports/pie2022.html.

8. U.S. Department of Homeland Security, "Table 39. Aliens Removed or Returned: Fiscal Years 1893 to 2019." Office of Homeland Security, Statistics, 2023. https://www.dhs.gov/immigration-statistics/yearbook/2019/table39.

9. Stevenson, Kathryn K. "'Felons, Not Families': U.S. Immigration Policies and the Construction of an American Underclass." *Pacific Coast Philology* 53, no. 2 (2018): 155–74. https://doi.org/10.5325/pacicoasphil.53.2.0155.

10. Lopez, William D. *Separated: Family and Community in the Aftermath of an Immigration Raid*. JHU Press, 2019.

11. Johnson, Amy L., Christopher Levesque, Neil A. Lewis, and Asad L. Asad. "Deportation Threat Predicts Latino US Citizens and Noncitizens' Psychological Distress, 2011 to 2018." Proceedings of the National Academy of Sciences 121, no. 9 (February 27, 2024): e2306554121. https://doi.org/10.1073/pnas.2306554121.

12. Torres, Jacqueline M., Julianna Deardorff, Robert B. Gunier, Kim G. Harley, Abbey Alkon, Katherine Kogut, and Brenda Eskenazi. "Worry About Deportation and Cardiovascular Disease Risk Factors Among Adult Women: The Center for the Health Assessment of Mothers and Children of Salinas Study." *Annals of Behavioral Medicine* 52, no. 2 (February 5, 2018): 186–93. https://doi.org/10.1093/abm/kax007.

13. Detention Watch Network and Immigrant Legal Resource Center, "If You Build It ICE Will Fill It: The Link between Detention Capacity and ICE Arrests." Ceres Policy Research Institute, 2022. https://www

.detentionwatchnetwork.org/sites/default/files/reports/If%20You%20
Build%20It%2C%20ICE%20Will%20Fill%20IT_Report_2022.pdf.

14. Defund Hate Now. "Understanding the Finances behind ICE and CBP,"
n.d. https://defundhatenow.org/how-to/#ICE-and-CBP-budget.

15. Warner, Judith Ann. "The social construction of the criminal alien in
immigration law, enforcement practice and statistical enumeration: Consequences for immigrant stereotyping." *Journal of Social and Ecological
Boundaries* 1, no. 2 (2005): 56-80.

16. Matos, Kica and Erica Bryant. "25 Years of IIRIRA Shows Immigration
Law Gone Wrong," *Vera Institute,* June 28, 2022. https://www.vera.org
/news/25-years-of-iirira-shows-immigration-law-gone-wrong.

17. Bierria, Alisa and Lee Ann S. Wang. "Prison-to-Detention Pipeline for
Migrants Must End," Cal Matters, August 26, 2022. https://calmatters
.org/commentary/2022/08/prison-to-detention-pipeline-for-migrants
-must-end/.

18. Health Impact Partners. *Human Impact Partners Research Code of Ethics.*
(January 2023). https://humanimpact.org/hipprojects/research-code
-of-ethics/.

19. Southeast Asia Resource Action Center. States with the Largest Southeast
Asian American Populations. Accessed August 10, 2020. https://www
.searac.org/wp-content/uploads/2018/04/Top-SEAA-states-factsheet
.116th-Congress.jpg.

20. Southeast Asia Resource Action Center. Asian Americans & Pacific
Islanders Behind Bars: Exposing the School to Prison to Deportation
Timeline. SEARAC; December 2015. Accessed August 10, 2020. https://
www.searac.org/wp-content/uploads/2018/04/18877-AAPIs-Behind
-Bars_web.pdf.

21. Spencer, J. H., and T. N. Le. "Parent Refugee Status, Immigration Stressors, and Southeast Asian Youth Violence." *Journal of Immigrant and Minority
Health* 8, no. 4 (November 2006): 359–68. doi: 10.1007/s10903-006
-9006-x.

22. Spencer et al. "Parent Refugee Status, Immigration Stressors, and Southeast Asian Youth Violence." 359–68.

23. Cavazos-Rehg, P., L. Zayas, and E. L. Spitznagel. "Legal Status, Emotional Well-Being and Subjective Health Status of Latino Immigrants."
JAMA 99, no. 10. (November 2007): 1126–31. Accessed August 10, 2020.
https://www.ncbi.nlm.nih.gov/pmc/articles/PMC2574408/pdf
/jnma00209-0050.pdf.

24. Ockenfels-Martinez, Martha, Sara Satinsky, and Jonathan Heller. "The Effects of Forced Family Separation in the Rio Grande Valley—A Family Unity, Family Health Research Update" (October 2018). https://familyunityfamilyhealth.org/wp- content/uploads/2018/10/HIP-LUPE _FUFH2018-RGV-FullReport.pdf.

25. Human Impact Partners. "Stop ICE Transfers: Promoting Health, Unifying Families, Healing Communities." (August 2020). https:// humanimpact.org/HealthNotTransfers.

26. Kaba, Mariame. "Hope Is a Discipline: Mariame Kaba on Dismantling the Carceral State," *The Intercept* (March 17, 2021). https://theintercept .com/2021/03/17/intercepted-mariame-kaba-abolitionist-organizing/.

27. Mitchell, Christine, Lien Pham, and Narissa Pham. "Fear of the Unknown: How ICE Transfers Impact the Health of Immigrants and Their Families," *Human Impact Partners* (September 29, 2020). https:// humanimpact-hip.medium.com/fear-of-the-unknown-how-ice-transfers -impact-the-health-of-immigrants-and-their-families-bca62c9b3d46.

Figure 8.1: Artwork by Fritz Aragon

Figure 8.2: Artwork by Fritz Aragon

9
CARE, NOT CAGES

A Call to End the Global War on Drugs

BY ONYỊNYE ALHERI

For William Miller Sr., and everyone who did not survive.

On June 17, 1971, United States President Richard Nixon announced the commencement of the War on Drugs (WoD) during a press conference that would mark the start of, now, an over fifty-year failure of epic proportions. This announcement—meant to assuage the manufactured moral panic of middle-, upper-, and ruling-class Americans—would lead to a futile movement orchestrated by one of the most dominant nation-states in human history. Two years later, via an executive order, Nixon created the Drug Enforcement Agency (DEA) to establish "a single unified command to combat an all-out global war on the drug menace."[1] When it was created, the DEA had 1,470 special agents and an annual budget of under $75 million. It now has about 5,235 special agents, 227 US-based field offices, 62 international offices, and a budget of almost $2.5 billion.

The US WoD has negatively impacted communities and economies around the world, leaving many dead and traumatized in its wake. All the while, the global drug supply and potency levels have increased,[2] fatal overdose continues to rise, and many poor people, mostly people of color, continue to be criminalized and killed through direct and indirect forms of violence.

This campaign has been called an "unmitigated human rights disaster" by the Open Society Foundation. Though the United Nations first

supported the WoD at an international level in 1988 with their conference "A Drug-Free World: We Can Do It," the UN Office on Drugs and
Crime (UNODC) has explicitly written of its negative consequences on
health, violence, and human rights. Earlier in the century, the 1912 Hague
Convention, the passage of the Harrison Narcotics Act in 1914, and the
formation of the League of Nations in 1919 all provided a codified foundation for the United States' and Europe's involvement in global anti-
drug efforts.[3] All three were formed amid global pressure to curb opium
production in Asia.[4]

After five decades of a militarized approach to a social and public
health problem, studies continue to demonstrate ever-higher records of
drug production in the Majority World* and rising rates of consumption
and overdose in the Global North, particularly the United States of
America. Furthermore, as Majority World nations industrialize and
expand their cities, drug consumption in these regions, particularly the
African continent, is projected to rise.[5]

Though government representatives and agencies have argued that
the WoD is meant to combat the "drug menace" wreaking havoc in
communities, US drug policy has historically been contradictory. Notably, between May and August 1986, Ronald Reagan provided funding
to the Nicaraguan right-wing paramilitary group the Contras, known
for funding their operations with drug money, in their assault against
the leftist Sandinista Revolutionary government. It is also clear that the
US has had close relationships with drug traffickers in Latin America.
For example, after years of financially supporting the former president
of Honduras, Juan Orlando Hernández, the US government eventually
turned against him and then extradited him on charges of trafficking
cocaine and guns.[6]

---

* The term "Majority World," referring to those countries that together contain the
majority of the world's population, is used as an alternative to "Third World," which
implies a civilizational and racial hierarchy.

The Global War on Drugs Today

The racist WoD is now a fifty-plus-year-old expansionist campaign of conflict and violence created by the enforcement of prohibitionist policies related to the manufacturing, distribution, and consumption of banned substances commonly known as "illegal drugs."[7] It is a tactic to control, displace, and police poor communities of color globally and in the US, through the prohibition of illicit drugs and criminalization of people engaged in drug selling or use. The WoD is an arm of the prison industrial complex (PIC), which contributes to negative health impacts for individuals, communities, and generations. The US-based abolitionist organization Critical Resistance describes the prison industrial complex as the "overlapping interests of government and industry that use surveillance, policing, and imprisonment as solutions to economic, social, and political problems."[8] The PIC serves to uphold white supremacy, imperialism, and cisheteropatriarchy and is used to maintain social and economic inequities, which have devastating health impacts on poor and working communities of color.

The War on Drugs' prohibitionist foundation is rooted in racist, anti-immigrant sentiments and functions using three main methods: (1) interruption of drug-trafficking networks and routes, otherwise known as interdiction, (2) destruction of drug crops, and (3) alternative crop development programs. All three place responsibility on the supply side and do little to address the demand, which was and is largely US-based.[9] They all have resulted in diminished revenue for already poor people and nations, which only further encourages participation in the illicit drug trade. Since prohibition does not reduce demand, the aim is to limit supply, a strategy that has continuously failed given the highly adaptable nature of the trade.[10]

Furthermore, the rhetoric of the drug war relies on a model that views drug misuse as an individual disease to be eradicated by any means necessary, often through violence.[11] Such a model has been used to justify harmful campaigns against marginalized people. Though US government officials argue that drug trafficking threatens democracy in Latin America, it is the War on Drugs that contributes to the dissipation and destabilization of state structures as governments give in to US pressure and impart physical, economic, and environmental harm against their own denizens, some of whom resist through evasion and opposition. The WoD serves US economic and political interests first and foremost. In the words of scholar Dawn Paley, "[T]he war on drugs appears to be a bloody fix to US economic woes."[12] Contrary to the myth that the War on Drugs is being fought to eradicate illicit drugs and the harms that follow, there is evidence that indicates that the WoD in actuality serves to integrate other nations into global capitalism,[13] with the current emphasis being on the Americas, all the while displacing peasants and poor people from their lands and making them targets of state and (para)military violence.

According to the UNODC, eight of the world's ten countries with the highest murder rates in 2021 were located in Latin America and the Caribbean along major drug trafficking routes.[14] Additionally, the huge profits generated by illicit drug sales continue to fund the activities of violent cartel organizations, effectively undermining international efforts at peacebuilding. As Tom Wainwright writes, "the 'all-out war' approach has failed to cut the number of consumers, while it has driven up the price of a few cheap agricultural commodities to create a hideously violent, $300 billion global industry."[15] The WoD has severely aggravated political, economic, and social problems in developing countries, all the while justifying the expansion of defense budgets for the increased (para)militarization of narcotics-producing nations.

The Health Impacts of the Global War on Drugs

The global impacts of the War on Drugs are plentiful. Most notable are criminalization, environmental degradation, social isolation, physical harm, and the spread of misinformation. Mass criminalization, rooted in carceral and colonial logics, relies on the creation of a suspicious and malicious "other" who must be surveilled and punished to protect wealth under racial capitalism.[16] Given the low regard that drug users have in the social imaginary, they become an easy target for criminalization, which stigmatizes and encourages them to use in isolated and unsafe environments.[17] Furthermore, fear of judgment and arrest prevents people who use drugs from seeking support, treatment, and health services, including medication for opioid use disorder, supplies for safe use (such as sterile water and pipes), overdose-reversal medications, and voluntary substance use treatment. Criminalization can also prevent access to essential medicines and medical supplies necessary for the relief of psychological and physical ailments, such as pain relief medication and sterile syringes.[18] Paradoxically, it has been found that use of illicit drugs is generally higher within carceral environments (namely jails and prisons) compared to the general population,[19] further demonstrating the futility of the WoD.

Overwhelmingly, nation-states around the world have outlawed the use of many drugs, other than those manufactured by pharmaceutical companies and alcohol and tobacco industries. Global prohibitionist drug policies disproportionately affect marginalized people, including gender nonconforming people, cisgender women, people of color, and poor people.[20] Often, people who use, sell, and grow drugs face stigma, community/family separation, violence, incarceration, deportation, and even death, all consequences and aims of the prison industrial complex, which undermines individual and community health by maintaining social and economic inequities.

The decades-long War on Drugs has done nothing to prevent overdose occurrences and deaths. In fact, drug-related fatalities continue to climb each year, with deaths at an all-time high during the COVID-19 pandemic. In the US in 2021, 107,622 people died of a fatal drug overdose, mostly due to opioids.[21] Some advocates argue that the number is likely higher given that many fatal overdoses occur in isolation and may not be properly documented. When considering occurrences of nonfatal overdoses, these rates are even higher.

The harms of the War on Drugs reach all demographic groups yet are particularly devastating for communities of color.[22] This is partly due to the racist and xenophobic narratives of "urban predators" and "foreign menaces," which feed the trope of a dangerous outsider to the imaginaries of those with power, often white people in post-industrial nations, otherwise known as the West or Global North.[23] In communities throughout the Majority World, the enforcement of prohibitionist drug policy creates avenues for displacement, incarceration, policing, and killing of people of color while simultaneously generating profit for the prison and military industrial complexes and promoting the expansion of global corporate capitalism.

The War on Drugs has often gone hand in hand with political and cultural repression of historically marginalized communities. For example, throughout the 1990s and 2000s, Bolivian coca growers from the Chapare region, whose ancestors have been cultivating and safely using the coca plant for centuries, organized massive protests to demand that the government stop eradicating their crops—a policy that was promoted and funded by the United States in an effort to eliminate cocaine trafficking. The Bolivian government frequently sent thousands of soldiers and police into the Chapare, resulting in clashes that left many coca farmers dead, wounded, and incarcerated. In addition to this bodily harm, the punitive drug laws imposed by the United States on Bolivia cost the Andean nation millions in revenue annually, the impact of which was felt most by working-class communities and peasant farmers driven deeper into poverty.[24, 25]

Health is further undermined by the War on Drugs for those behind bars. The jails and prisons used to incarcerate people impacted by punitive drug policies are toxic environments that trap those inside in poor living conditions, often with limited access to health care.[26] Health-related atrocities are regularly imposed on detained migrants and incarcerated people, including forced sterilization, shackling of pregnant people, and denial of treatment for critical conditions.[27] Studies have shown that incarcerated people experience higher rates of asthma, high blood pressure, cancers, substance use disorder, HIV/AIDs, and other sexually transmitted infections (STIs) relative to those without histories of incarceration.[28] There is a long history of diseases and infections spreading throughout prisons and jail systems, often at higher rates than in the general population.[29] In prisons, poor response to infectious disease outbreaks is common.[30] Aside from physical ailments, the psychological impacts of imprisonment include paranoia, isolation, loss of autonomy, and a wide range of mental health ailments—all of which are associated with higher rates of drug use and overdose.[31]

The state violence created by the War on Drugs goes far beyond the prison cell. There are too many examples of people, whether involved with drugs or not, killed by police and military personnel in the name of the WoD. In one notorious incident, eighteen-year-old goatherder Esequiel Hernández was gunned down by a US Marine antidrug patrol in south Texas near the US-Mexico border, despite not being involved in the drug trade.[32] In 2001 Roni and Charity Bowers, a mother and her infant, were killed by the CIA, who shot down their plane after mistaking it for a drug trafficking plane.[33] Because they were white Christian missionaries, the story received massive media attention, yet other similar stories of the collateral consequences of the WoD have gone uncovered or presumably buried.

The Global Drug War in Latin America

When it comes to the War on Drugs, there are certain cases that stand out for their gruesomeness, amount of wasted taxpayer dollars, and sheer numbers of lives lost. Nation-states around the world that acquiesce to US prohibitionist demands have increased the presence of troops in their communities, which has resulted in great loss of life at the hands of military personnel. In Latin America, Mexico has been most heavily affected by this in recent years. The country has seen more than 360,000 homicides since 2006, the same year that the government declared war on the cartels and began receiving massive amounts of funding from the United

States government.[34] State representatives claim that those killed were involved in the drug trade, but such incidents are rarely investigated—nor would this justify such indiscriminate taking of life.

Mexico's Mérida Initiative, begun in 2008 by the US government under George W. Bush in collusion with Felipe Calderón, initially dedicated $1.4 billion with the stated purpose of "enhancing Mexico's ability to reduce crime, with overwhelming emphasis on the drug trade." A year later, an additional $300 million was spent to continue the project.[35] Yet the billions of dollars spent have not yielded the intended results. Instead, it has allowed for rampant killing, torture, and human rights violations and justified the deportation of Mexican and Central American nationals on the US side of the mythical border into unsafe conditions that they risked their lives to escape from. Between 2007 and 2014, during which the initiative was in place, 3,900 people were injured or killed by Mexican armed forces.[36]

Colombia is another such example. The US-sponsored effort, Plan Colombia, was launched in 2000 to quell the country's anti-government insurgencies and further advance capitalist globalization under the guise of antiterrorism and counternarcotics policy.[37, 38] Since the late 1980s, after giving in to US pressure to extradite leaders of the Medellín cartel, thousands of Colombian people have been killed in the crossfire of conflict between cartel members and police and military forces. Following Pablo Escobar's proclamation of a "blood feud" against then president Virgilio Barco's government, major bombing incidents occurred regularly.[39]

Rural communities have also been caught in the middle of ongoing battles between Colombian military and aligned paramilitary groups on the one hand and leftist insurgencies on the other. Even "peace communities" that have sought to maintain a neutral stance in this battle have been impacted. In 2005 one such community, San José de Apartadó, was targeted in a massacre led by Colombian military officials with a paramilitary unit, in which five adults and three children were killed. By the time Plan Colombia ended in 2015, over five thousand civilian lives had been taken by the Colombian military.[40]

In addition to its human toll, the global War on Drugs has had devastating impacts on ecosystems, diminishing the health of animals and plants. One of the most common methods used to eradicate coca crops under Plan Colombia was the aerial spraying of plants with herbicides, which contaminates the atmosphere, soil, and water—pollution that is then absorbed or consumed by living creatures. This fumigation campaign was associated with a wide range of health problems, including miscarriages and respiratory illnesses. Additionally, aerial spraying meant to destroy illicit crops also destroys licit food crops, such as bananas, corn, and yucca, that rural communities rely on.[41]

Given that 10 percent of the world's animal and plant species exist only in Colombia, aerial fumigation is an environmental conservation issue in addition to being a public health and human rights concern. Colombia's ecosystems are incredibly biodiverse, containing more wild bird species than any other country, and highly variable aquatic and terrestrial life.[42] These biological components have intrinsic value. Additionally, Indigenous people in the region generally have a symbiotic relationship with their ecosystems and rely on the region's biological diversity for air and water purification, climate moderation, energy, food, plant pollination, pest control, shelter, soil fertility, and waste decomposition. As one resident of a fumigated region in Colombia stated, "Our personal health and the health of our economy and human society, depends [sic] on the continuous supply of various ecological services that would be extremely costly or impossible to replace."[43]

Plan Colombia ruined whole ecosystems and displaced Indigenous peoples, effectively securing land and labor for private capital investments, and creating a landscape to support the ratification of free trade agreements between Canada, Colombia, and the US.[44] Armed paramilitary groups removed people from the land they had stewarded for centuries so that corporations could occupy it. Indigenous people's resistance was squashed through violent means, and the Colombian government allowed this to happen. The War on Drugs was used as a mechanism to promote a global capitalist regime, using paramilitary forces to seize and maintain control over people and land.[45]

The Global Drug War in Asia and Africa

While the global War on Drugs has had the most devastating effect on Latin America, its impact can be seen in other parts of the Majority World, including in African and Asian countries. In several countries, all drugs are illegal and those in possession of them are heavily persecuted, facing severe prison mandates, police torture, and death sentences. One of the world's most violent and repressive anti-drug campaigns in recent history has taken place in the Philippines, where former president Rodrigo Duterte made possession of any illicit substance punishable by death. Upon taking office in 2016, Duarte's War on Drugs led to the killing of over 12,000 Filipinos, including at least 2,555 people by the Philippine National Police.[46] Such policies have done little to address the greater social and economic issues faced by residents and have only driven drug use and distribution further underground, creating similar conditions as those seen in Latin America.

Across the African continent, drug policies remain repressive and punitive, resulting in the deep marginalization of people who use drugs. In recent years, there have been documented reports of police in Ghana, Liberia, Nigeria, and Sierra Leone killing people who use drugs with impunity.[47] Other human rights abuses—including detention, denial of due process and fair trials, extortion, sexual abuse, and torture—have occurred. People who use drugs are represented in mass media and political campaigns as criminal, morally weak, or demonic, which contributes to their incarceration, alienation, and the unavailability of services to meet their myriad needs. When arrested, people who use drugs often undergo forced detoxification and compulsory drug treatment, which can be life-threatening.[48]

Global Resistance to the WoD

Despite the pain and persistence of the War on Drugs, there are several examples of resistance that can and should be uplifted. Since the 1990s there have been an increasing number of individuals and organizations who have spoken out against the War on Drugs and provided rigorous analyses of the harms it has brought upon people, environments, and nations. In the US, organizations like the Drug Policy Alliance, the Drug Policy Foundation, and the National Harm Reduction Coalition have been dedicated to ending the War on Drugs, destigmatizing drug use, providing care for people who use drugs (PWUD), and advocating for policies that center health and well-being for PWUD.

Survived and Punished, a national coalition of abolitionist organizations, focuses on the defense of criminalized survivors and raises awareness of the symbiotic relationship between systems of punishment and gender-based violence. In 2015 Critical Resistance created the Oakland Power Projects to engage health-care workers in decoupling health care from policing through the provision of trainings and sharing of alternatives to calling 911 during mental and physical health emergencies. In Baltimore, which has one of the highest rates of drug use and fatal overdose per capita in the US, the BRIDGES Coalition has been advocating for nearly a decade to establish overdose prevention sites and save the lives of people who use drugs.

Around the world, several formations exist to counter the harmful rhetoric and practices of the War on Drugs. DeJusticia, also known as el Colectivo de Estudios de Drogas y Derechos (the Collective for the Study of Drugs and Rights), is a Colombia-based organization that illuminates the severe violence brought on by the WoD and offers platforms for creating lasting alternatives using a human-rights perspective.

In Africa, important political formations have emerged to halt abuses against drug users, including the "Support. Don't Punish" campaign, YouthRISE Nigeria, the International Drug Policy Consortium, and the West African Commission on Drugs. The ratification of the 1981 African Charter on Human and Peoples' Rights, otherwise known as the Banjul Charter, set a standard for the dignity and respect of people who use drugs on the African continent.[49] This list is not at all exhaustive, and I implore readers to seek out other organizations locally and abroad focused on harm reduction, abolition, and the provision of health services without collusion with law enforcement and military forces.

Alternatives to the Global War on Drugs

Paradigm Shifts

In recent years, dehumanizing narratives about people who use drugs have lessened such that substance use is now considered by some as a public health issue instead of a moral deficiency. However, this varies greatly depending on the cultural and social contexts within which one finds themself. Around the world, many people still face social isolation, prison time, and death sentences for their involvement with illicit substances. Even among the most progressive of circles, the consensus is that drug use is negative. If we are to adequately address the potential harms associated with substance use, we must first address the stigmatization of substance use. For as long as humans have existed, we have used substances to alter our physical, mental, and emotional states.[50] This phenomenon is not just prevalent in humans. It has been documented that elephants in southern Africa will drink the fermented fluid of the rotten marula fruit for pleasure. Reindeer in Siberia are known to indulge in psilocybin, commonly referred to as magic mushrooms. Wallabies consume poppy plants, and domestic cats love catnip.[51] What is legal versus what is not has little to do with current scientific understandings of substance use and its centrality to human cultures.

This author calls for a radical acceptance of drug and substance use as normal behavior. Drugs have been used by people all over the world for several reasons, including but not limited to spiritual initiation, pain relief, mental expansion, emotional healing, community building, and physical repair. This is not to deny the immense suffering and loss that results from alcohol abuse and substance use disorder. The compulsion to engage in harmful substance use is a terrible condition that deteriorates one's physical, mental, and social health. However, the level of stigma that one attaches to a particular substance and the person using it contributes greatly to physical, social, economic, and political harm. People living with addiction and dependency need care, not punishment.

Part of the paradigm shift this author calls for includes transitioning from the rehab model to the habit model for understanding drug use. Unlike the rehab model, which views drug use as a disease, the habit model recognizes that all habits, including drug use, are functions of normal psychological and physiological processes.[52] Habits are learned behaviors that generally are practiced if they bring pleasure or ease and are often discarded when they cause discomfort or pain. For some, rehab is not effective because it does not address the social and material conditions that lead to drug use. It is also expensive and often inaccessible due to lack of governmental support for publicly available voluntary drug treatment.[53] Under the abstinence-based rehab model, relapse is common because once people complete their 30-/60-/90-/120-day stint, they tend to return to the environments and social situations that encourage harmful substance use. Abstinence-only methods deny the basic human drive toward reward-seeking behavior and create mental conditions of shame that can contribute to the misuse of drugs.

Policy Shifts

From an economic perspective, we must contend with the fact that the demand for drugs is largely inelastic, meaning that even as the price of a good increases, the desire to consume it does not change significantly.[54] The War on Drugs supposes that if supply is diminished or made expensive, demand will decrease, but this is simply not true. Failing to address and reduce demand, the WoD has targeted supply, which has significantly inflated the price of illicit drugs, increasing their market value and incentivizing participation in drug selling, arms trafficking, labor exploitation, and the growth of cartels, ultimately producing immense suffering, violence, and death.

To end the racist War on Drugs, we must abolish borders and the prison industrial complex. Border enforcement has long been touted as a necessary measure in stopping the flow of drugs into the United States, giving way to policies that unjustly target migrants from Central and South America.[55] For example, during the Nixon presidency,

Operation Intercept was launched with the aim of stopping marijuana from Mexico from entering the US. The operation instructed border, customs, and immigrations agents to stop and inspect all movement by foot, vehicle, or plane, effectively targeting all migration from Mexico into the southern US.[56]

In reality, border enforcement efforts to stop the supply of drugs have simply led to the increased trafficking of increasingly potent and deadly drugs. Historically, drug interdiction has incentivized drug sellers to produce substances that are more potent but smaller in size to avoid detection—a phenomenon referred to as the "iron law of prohibition."[57] This occurred with alcohol during the Prohibition era in the United States, and we are seeing this in our current era with the introduction of increasingly potent illicit opioids, such as fentanyl, into the drug market.

As in the past, migrants are being falsely targeted and scapegoated for drug trafficking and substance use in the United States, which is being used to justify increased border enforcement and deportations—neither of which will resolve our current overdose crisis.[58] Borders, military, police, sanctions, and capitalist regimes do not keep people healthy or safe. They instead result in family separation, community disruption, forced removal, detention, and unsafe border crossings, which can cause psycho-physiological ailments and create conditions ripe for labor exploitation and human trafficking.[59]

Some states and nations have realized the harm of the drug war and made efforts toward legalization, which has the potential to reduce drug costs and thus the incentive for participation in the illicit drug trade. However, to bring greater benefits to societies, full decriminalization is a must. This will not only reap the benefits of legalization but also erase the harms that carceral systems have brought upon marginalized people and communities. The hundreds of thousands of people incarcerated for their use or sale of drugs face material consequences long after they are released, including lack of access to affordable health care and housing, few employment prospects, and restricted mobility across geographies.

This impacts their ability to rebuild their lives after the trauma of incarceration, which often leads them to continued misuse of drugs and engagement in criminalized activities that send them back to jail or prison.

The current popular trend is toward the legalization of marijuana—at the time of writing, over half of the states in the US have decriminalized recreational marijuana use. However, the world's drug violence is not largely due to marijuana distribution and use but instead to the prohibition of other drugs, namely cocaine, opioids, and methamphetamines. If we are to create healthy systems for the people and the planet, we must decriminalize all drugs, not just marijuana. As the push for legalization continues, we must also ensure the retroactive release and erasure of criminal records for people with drug convictions.

Another means of promoting health for communities and people impacted by the War on Drugs is by abundantly funding comprehensive health and social services to address conditions that lead to addiction and fatal overdose, including counseling and medication like buprenorphine and methadone. Availability of universal health care can help those suffering from abscesses, hepatitis C, and other medical ailments related to excessive, prolonged, and unsafe drug use seek treatment.

Grassroots organizing, participatory defense, and mutual aid networks are some tactics we can use to push back against the violence of the prison and military-industrial complexes. Through these means and others, we are able to diminish the PIC's reach and scope while creating new ways of caring for one another. We must commit to building solid alliances, formations, syndicates, and networks that increase our trust in one another in order to achieve and maintain our health and well-being.

Shifts in Health-Care Practice

Those in service provider roles can honor a client's dignity by decoupling service provision from punitive systems and using a person-first approach, wherein a person's substance use is not considered as the primary trait that defines them. Furthermore, medical care providers can

attend continuing education courses on topics including harm reduction, addiction medicine, opioid agonist therapy, and pain management
to deepen their understanding of how drug use impacts patients and how
best to provide care without stigma.

A truly effective way to ensure health and safety for people who use
drugs is through the creation of overdose prevention sites (OPS), sometimes called supervised injection facilities or safe consumption sites, where
people can safely use drugs and have an overdose reversed, if necessary.[60]
In 2003 Canadian drug user activists launched Insite in Vancouver—the
first OPS in North America.[61] There are now over 200 safe consumption
sites operating in fourteen countries throughout the world.[62]

In all those legal safe consumption sites, not a single death has occurred
in the past thirty-one years.[63] Due to the federal "crackhouse" statute
introduced in 1986 under Ronald Reagan's presidency, which makes
it a crime to maintain drug-involved premises, these sites are currently
illegal everywhere in the United States except for New York City.[64] As
someone who has lost loved ones to fatal overdose, I often wonder what
would have happened if they were able to use drugs in a safe environment instead of dying alone out of fear of being criticized or persecuted.
We can and must do better by advocating for the establishment of more
OPS and learning from existing sites.

Countless activists have done the hard work of community outreach,
network building, and abolitionist visioning to understand what fosters
true health. Using a nonjudgmental harm reduction approach, health-
care workers can eliminate stigma in service provision and client interaction. By meeting our clients where they are and connecting them to
wraparound services, we can support them in accessing counseling, stable
housing, nutritious food, space for leisure and rest, and fulfilling activities. To do so, health workers must first examine and change our carceral
behaviors and practices to provide the best quality care to the people
and communities we serve. To that end, I close this chapter with a set
of questions for health-care workers to reflect upon in considering how
they provide care to people who use substances.

SELF-REFLECTION QUESTIONS FOR
HEALTH-CARE AND SOCIAL SERVICE PROVIDERS

▶ What barriers do you face in providing quality care to your clients?

▶ What are some methods of care delivery that can honor the agency of those you serve?

▶ How have you perpetuated or sustained the PIC, either intentionally or unintentionally?

▶ What local healing justice efforts exist for you to engage in? If none, what would you need to start one?

▶ What is one concrete way you can disrupt carceral logic and practice in your care work?

CHAPTER 9 NOTES

1. Elon, Rebecca D, Claudia Schlosberg, Steven Levenson, and Nicole Brandt. 2011. "DEA Enforcement in Long-Term Care: Is a Collaborative Correction Feasible?" *Journal of the American Medical Directors Association* 12 (4): 263–69. https://doi.org/10.1016/j.jamda.2011.01.013.

2. Beletsky, L., and Davis, C. S. (2017). "Today's Fentanyl Crisis: Prohibition's Iron Law, Revisited." *The International Journal on Drug Policy*, 46, 156–59. Accessed: 28 October 2022, from https://doi.org/10.1016/j.drugpo.2017.05.050.

3. Musto, D. F. (1999). "The Impact of Public Attitudes on Drug Abuse Research in the Twentieth Century." In M. D. Glantz and C. R. Hartel (Eds.), *Drug Abuse: Origins & Interventions* (pp. 63–78). American Psychological Association. https://doi.org/10.1037/10341-003.

4. Canadian Senate Special Committee on Illegal Drugs Volume 3 - Public Policy Options. (n.d.). *Major Studies of Drugs and Drug Policy: Chapter 19 - The International Legal Environment.* The 1912 Hague International Opium Convention. https://druglibrary.org/schaffer/library/studies/canadasenate/vol3/chapter19_hague.htm#_ftnref7.

5. World Drug Report 2021. (2021). Accessed 17 May 2022, from: https://www.unodc.org/unodc/en/data-and-analysis/wdr2021.html.

6. Norton, B. (2022, February 22). "US Turns on Honduran Narco-Dictator Juan Orlando Hernández." PopularResistance.Org. Accessed 1 November 2022, from: https://popularresistance.org/us-turns-on-honduran-narco-dictator-juan-orlando-hernandez/.

7. Esquivel-Suárez, Fernando. (August 23, 2018). *The Global War on Drugs.* Majority World Studies: A Collective Publication with the Majority World. Accessed 14 May 2022. https://globalsouthstudies.as.virginia.edu/key-issues/global-war-drugs.

8. Critical Resistance. "What Is the PIC? What Is Abolition?," https://criticalresistance.org/mission-vision/not-so-common-language/.

9. United Nations Office on Drugs and Crime (UNODC). (2022, June). "World Drug Report 2022." Global Overview on Drug Demand and Drug Supply. https://www.unodc.org/res/wdr2022/MS/WDR22_Booklet_2.pdf.

10. Wodak, A. (2018, June 7). From Failed Global Drug Prohibition to Regulating the Drug Market. https://onlinelibrary.wiley.com/doi/full/10.1111/add.14111.

11. Reznicek, M. (2012). *Blowing Smoke: Rethinking the War on Drugs Without Prohibition and Rehab.* Lanham: Rowman & Littlefield Publishers.

12. Paley, Dawn. (2014). *Drug War Capitalism.* Oakland, CA: AK Press.

13. Aviles, W. (2018). *The Drug War in Latin America: Hegemony and Global Capitalism.* Abingdon and New York: Routledge.

14. United Nations Office on Drugs and Crime. *The Global Study on Homicide 2023.* https://www.unodc.org/documents/data-and-analysis/gsh/2023/GSH_2023_LAC_web.pdf.

15. Wainwright, Tom. 2016. *Narconomics: How to Run a Drug Cartel.* New York, Public Affairs.

16. Jordan, I. M., Bradley, G., and McBean, S. (2021, September 8). *Intersecting Drug Policy and Abolition: A Conversation.* TalkingDrugs. Accessed 1 November 2022, from: https://www.talkingdrugs.org/intersecting-drug-policy-and-abolition-a-conversation.

17. Transform Drug Policy Foundation. 2017. *Decriminalisation of People Who Use Drugs: Reducing Harm, Improving Health, Helping the Vulnerable and Releasing Resources.* https://transformdrugs.org/assets/files/PDFs/decriminalisation-briefing-2018.pdf.

18. Walsh, John. 2023. "Challenges of an Integral Approach and a Human Rights Perspective to the Drugs Issue: A Civil Society Perspective." Washington Office on Latin America. https://www.wola.org/2023/12/challenges-of-an-integral-approach-and-a-human-rights-perspective-to-the-drugs-issue-a-civil-society-perspective/.

19. Norman, C. (2022, November 1). "A Global Review of Prison Drug Smuggling Routes and Trends in the Usage of Drugs in Prisons." https://wires.onlinelibrary.wiley.com/doi/full/10.1002/wfs2.1473.

20. Koram, K. (2019). *The War on Drugs and the Global Color Line*. London: Pluto Press.

21. CDC, National Center for Health Statistics. (2022) *U.S. Overdose Deaths in 2021 Increased Half as Much as in 2020—But Are Still Up 15%*. Accessed 11 May 2022, from https://bit.ly/3xSMS5H.

22. Levenson, J., Textor, L., Bluthenthal, R., Darby, A., Wabhi, R., and Clayton-Johnson, M.-A. (2023, September 16). "Abolition and Harm Reduction in the Struggle for 'Care, Not Cages.'" ScienceDirect. https://doi.org/10.1016/j.drugpo.2023.104163.

23. Musto, David F. (1999). *The American Disease: Origins of Narcotic Control*. 3rd ed. New York: Oxford University Press.

24. Grisaffi, T. (2018). *Coca Yes, Cocaine No: How Bolivia's Coca Growers Reshaped Democracy*. Duke University Press.

25. Kohl, Ben, and Linda Farthing. "The Price of Success: Bolivia's War Against Drugs and the Poor." *NACLA Report*. September 25, 2007.

26. Massoglia, Michael, and William Alex Pridemore. "Incarceration and Health." *Annual Review of Sociology* 41, no. 1 (2015): 291–310.

27. Kuhlik, Lauren, and Carolyn Sufrin. (2019). "Pregnancy, Systematic Disregard and Degradation, and Carceral Institutions." *Harvard Law & Policy Review* 14: 417.

28. Critical Resistance, *PIC and Health, OPP Presentation*. (2015) Oakland, CA. Accessed 29 April 2022, from https://bit.ly/3btE0fw.

29. Maner, Morgan, Marisa Omori, Lauren Brinkley-Rubinstein, Curt G. Beckwith, and Kathryn Nowotny. "Infectious Disease Surveillance in U.S. Jails: Findings from a National Survey." *PLoS ONE* 17, no. 8 (August 25, 2022): e0272374.

30. Franco-Paredes, C., Jankousky, K., Schultz, J., Bernfeld, J., Cullen, K., Quan, N. G., Kon, S., Hotez, P., et al. (2020). "COVID-19 in Jails and Prisons: A Neglected Infection in a Marginalized Population." *PLoS Neglected Tropical Diseases* 14, no. 6: e0008409.

31. Baranyi, Gergő, Seena Fazel, Sabine Delhey Langerfeldt, and Adrian P. Mundt. (June 1, 2022). "The Prevalence of Comorbid Serious Mental Illnesses and Substance Use Disorders in Prison Populations: A Systematic Review and Meta-Analysis." *The Lancet Public Health* 7, no. 6: e557–68.

32. Fernandez, Manny. "U.S. Troops Went to the Border in 1997. They Killed an American Boy," *The New York Times.* (November 27, 2018).

33. ABC News. "'Justice Denied' in CIA Shootdown of Missionaries." *ABC News.* (February 3, 2010).

34. Beittel, J. S. (2022). *Mexico: Organized Crime and Drug Trafficking Organizations.* Available at https://sgp.fas.org/crs/row/R41576.pdf.

35. Brewer, Stephanie Erin. "Rethinking the Mérida Initiative: Why the U.S. Must Change Course in Its Approach to Mexico's Drug War." Human Rights Brief 16, no.3 (2009): 9-14.

36. Brewer, Stephanie Erin. "Rethinking the Mérida Initiative: Why the U.S. Must Change Course in Its Approach to Mexico's Drug War."

37. Paley. *Drug War Capitalism.*

38. Lindsay-Poland, J. (2018). *Plan Colombia: U.S. Ally Atrocities and Community Activism.* Duke University Press.

39. Carpenter, Ted Galen. 2003. *Bad Neighbor Policy: Washington's Futile War on Drugs in Latin America.* New York: Palgrave Macmillan.

40. Lindsay-Poland, J. (2018). *Plan Colombia.*

41. Camacho, A., and Mejia, D. (2017). "The Health Consequences of Aerial Spraying of Illicit Crops: The Case of Colombia." *SSRN Electronic Journal,* (54), 147–60. doi: 10.2139/ssrn.2623145.

42. Camacho and Mejia. "The Health Consequences of Aerial Spraying of Illicit Crops: The Case of Colombia."

43. Peterson, S. (2002). "People and Ecosystems in Colombia: Casualties of the Drug War." *The Independent Review* 6, no. 3: 427–40.

44. Gould, Jens. (2007). "The Failure of Plan Colombia." *The American Prospect.* https://prospect.org/article/failure-plan-colombia/.

45. Paley. *Drug War Capitalism.*

46. Conde, C. *Philippines' "War on Drugs."* Human Rights Watch. Retrieved 2 June 2022, from https://www.hrw.org/tag/philippines-war-drugs.

47. International Drug Policy Consortium. (2017). *Drug Policy in Africa: Towards a Human Rights-Based Approach.* file:///Users/cmart195/Downloads/IDPC-advocacy-note_Human-rights-in-Africa.pdf.

48. Darke, Shane, Sarah Larney, and Michael Farrell. "Yes, People Can Die from Opiate Withdrawal." *Addiction* 112, no. 2 (2017): 199–200. https://doi.org/10.1111/add.13512.

49. International Drug Policy Consortium. *Drug Policy in Africa.*

50. Anderson, Peter. "Global Use of Alcohol, Drugs and Tobacco." *Drug and Alcohol Review* 25, no. 6 (2006): 489–502.

51. Pachniewska, A. (2016, October 29). "The Animals That Love Doing Drugs." Animal Cognition. Accessed 1 November 2022, from: http://www.animalcognition.org/2015/05/16/animal-drug-use/.

52. National Institute on Drug Abuse - NIDA. 2018, June 6. *Understanding Drug Use and Addiction.* Accessed 11 May 22, from https://nida.nih.gov/publications/drugfacts/understanding-drug-use-addiction.

53. Aviles. *The Drug War in Latin America.*

54. Cunningham, Scott, and Keith Finlay. "Identifying Demand Responses to Illegal Drug Supply Interdictions." *Health Economics* 25, no. 10 (2016): 1268–90.

55. Siegel, Loren. (2021). *Report: The War on Drugs Meets Immigration - Uprooting the Drug War.* Drug Policy Alliance. https://uprootingthedrugwar.org/wp-content/uploads/2021/02/uprooting_report_PDF_immigration_02.11.21.pdf.

56. Kate Doyle (2003). *Operation Intercept: The Perils of Unilateralism.* National Security Archive.

57. Beletsky and Davis. "Today's Fentanyl Crisis."

58. Guzman, Laura, Carlos Martinez, and Jorge Zepeda. "No, Deporting Undocumented Immigrants Won't Solve the Fentanyl Crisis" *San Francisco Chronicle* (March 30, 2023). https://www.sfchronicle.com/opinion/openforum/article/immigration-fentanyl-drugs-deportation-17850457.php.

59. Hales, Anna. (2021). "Beyond Borders: How Principles of Prison Abolition Can Shape the Future of Immigration Reform." *U.C. IRVINE Law Review* 11, no. 5: 1415. Accessed: 28 October 2022, from https://scholarship.law.uci.edu/ucilr/vol11/iss5/9.

60. Yoon, Grace H., Timothy W. Levengood, Melissa J. Davoust, Shannon N. Ogden, Alex H. Kral, Sean R. Cahill, and Angela R. Bazzi. "Implementation and Sustainability of Safe Consumption Sites: A Qualitative Systematic Review and Thematic Synthesis." *Harm Reduction Journal* 19, no. 1 (July 5, 2022): 73. https://doi.org/10.1186/s12954-022-00655-z.

61. Doberstein, Carey. "Insite in Vancouver: North America's First Supervised Injection Site." In *Policy Success in Canada: Cases, Lessons, Challenges*, edited by Evert Lindquist, Michael Howlett, Grace Skogstad, Geneviève Tellier, and Paul 't Hart. Oxford University Press, 2022.

62. Yoon et al. "Implementation and Sustainability of Safe Consumption Sites."

63. City of New York. (2022, April). *Overdose Prevention Centers: Frequently Asked Questions—New York City*. NYC Health. Accessed: 28 October, 2022, from: https://www1.nyc.gov/assets/doh/downloads/pdf/basas/overdose-prevention-centers-faq.pdf.

64. Kreit, Alex. "Safe Injection Sites and the Federal Crack House Statute." *BCL Rev.* 60 (2019): 413.

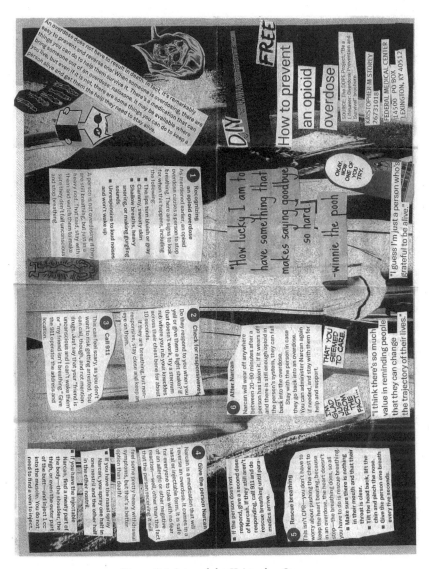

Figure 9.1: Artwork by Kristopher Storey

10

SURVIVAL PENDING REVOLUTION

Toward an Abolitionist Harm Reduction Praxis

BY RAFIK NADER WAHBI, CARLOS MARTINEZ, AND LAUREN TEXTOR

Disaster Care

Since the beginning of this century, the United States has been experiencing a prolonged and increasingly deadly drug overdose epidemic. Between 1999 and 2021 nearly 645,000 people died from an opioid overdose.[1] This public health disaster has grown precipitously during these years, with drug overdose deaths quadrupling between 2002 and 2022.[2] The introduction of increasingly potent forms of fentanyl, a synthetically synthesized opiate, into informal drug markets and the COVID-19 pandemic converged to make this catastrophe even more lethal.[3] The national increase in homelessness, particularly since the beginning of the pandemic, has only exacerbated this trend by placing more people in desperate social and economic conditions with little access to substance use care.[4]

Predictably, the overdose epidemic has been prejudicially reframed and exploited by drug war hawks advocating for carceral and militarized responses to substance use. Despite their previous failures, they are calling for more of the same: increased penalties for drug possession and dealing, police crackdowns, coerced drug treatment, border enforcement, deportation, and even calls to bomb Mexico.[5] As the historical record overwhelmingly demonstrates, such strategies do nothing to reduce drug consumption or overdose-related deaths.[6, 7, 8]

Meanwhile, the harm reduction movement has found itself in a strange place two decades into the opioid overdose crisis, maneuvering between recognition and repudiation. Since at least the rise of the HIV/AIDS pandemic in the 1980s, harm reduction activists in the United States have exposed the brutality of punitive approaches to substance use and placed themselves at risk of imprisonment by offering people who use drugs sterile syringes and other lifesaving practices.[9] Harm reduction, as Shira Hassan emphasizes, emerged as a liberatory strategy "by Black, Indigenous, and People of Color (BIPOC) who were sex workers, queer, transgender, using drugs, young people, people with disabilities and chronic illness, street-based, and sometimes houseless."[10]

As in earlier drug panics, harm reduction activists and service providers have worked to navigate the current landscape of punitive drug policies and fill the devastating void left in its wake. Where abstinence or risk of imprisonment often are still the only options in many parts of the country, harm reductionists have slowly built non-coercive networks of support, trust, and care to help people who use drugs stay alive while defending their autonomy.

Thanks to the persistent efforts of both grassroots organizations and researchers, harm reduction practices—such as syringe exchange and the distribution of naloxone, a lifesaving opioid reversal medication—have now been recognized as evidence-based forms of overdose prevention. All fifty states and the District of Columbia have passed legislation in recent years aimed at increasing access to naloxone.[11] As of 2023 nearly forty states have legalized the distribution and possession of fentanyl testing strips, previously viewed widely as illegal drug paraphernalia.[12] Syringe service providers have even received acknowledgment and some support under the Biden administration's National Drug Control Strategy.[13]

At the same time, harm reduction organizations have continued to withstand attacks and efforts at rolling back their operations, even in purportedly liberal states, including California and Oregon.[14, 15] The attempt to establish safe consumption sites, where people can use preobtained drugs under the supervision of trained personnel, has been stymied in several states, including California, Colorado, and Pennsylvania.[16, 17, 18] Harm reduction has been falsely cast as a culprit and perpetrator of the overdose crisis by critics from across the political spectrum.[19, 20]

Some on the left contend that harm reduction activism is not confronting the root causes of drug use and addiction—political and social inequalities.[21] This line of argument is often tied to a broader critique of mutual aid efforts, suggesting that such forms of political activity merely enable the neoliberal retreat from social welfare provision.[22] Without a doubt, the recent political and institutional tolerance for harm reduction has risked reducing the independence of the movement and its radical demand to transform care for people who use drugs. As harm reduction is increasingly being incorporated into governing strategies up to the federal level and into state-driven social services, its official meaning has gradually narrowed to focus on the dissemination of naloxone and substance overuse treatment.[23]

This form of harm reduction, often carried out by professional service providers within health departments or even law enforcement organizations conducting "outreach work," *can* certainly lead to depoliticization. This professionalization has the potential to convert harm reduction into a form of charity or a commodity billed to insurance, reinforcing the priorities of a privatized health-care system.[24] Moreover, in reducing the harm reduction movement into the mere provision of material goods and services, carceral approaches to our contemporary overdose crisis can easily remain intact and left unchallenged.

Today's harm reduction activists must navigate between ever-present attacks from prohibitionists and the co-optation of the movement into a depoliticized and narrowly medicalized practice. Theorist Ivan Illich argues that medicalization can lead to a loss of self-determination: the harmful institutionalization not only of knowledge and expertise but of the ability to define what well-being and care mean for oneself.[25] This institutionalization of knowledge and care, we contend, is not simply of potential harm for individuals, but also for social movements aimed at decentralizing and destabilizing broader power structures.

Yet most harm reduction organizations remain connected to the ideological principles of the movement's founders, including mutual aid, the radicalization of health, the empowerment of individuals and communities, the practice of nonjudgment, and the disruption of harmful discourses about people who use drugs. Grounded in a politics of solidarity, these grassroots and liberatory harm reduction organizations challenge hegemonic discourses of individual responsibility for one's health. In contrast to privatized care, the harm reduction movement relies on collaboration, autonomous direct action, and nonpaternalistic forms of care.[26]

Harm Reduction Grounded in Mutual Aid

The radical care provided by mutual aid is often essential for survival in times of disaster. This has become most evident in the context of climate-related disasters, where mutual aid collectives have emerged from the wreckage to establish critical networks of relief as seen, for example, in the northeastern United States in the aftermath of Hurricane Sandy in 2012 and in Puerto Rico following Hurricane Maria in 2017.[27, 28] In the wake of the COVID-19 pandemic, hundreds of mutual aid collectives sprang into action across the country to help communities meet basic food needs, distribute personal protective equipment, and provide various other forms of assistance.[29] In the context of our contemporary overdose disaster, harm reductionist mutual aid projects demonstrate the urgency and efficacy of creating nonauthoritarian and peer-to-peer models of care that break away from the failed politics of punishment, coercion, and incarceration.

But beyond simply supporting survival in the immediate moment, mutual aid projects have the potential for developing new political networks and forms of activity. Through training communities in practices of communal care, mutual aid projects help participants to experience and imagine alternatives to capitalist social relations.[30] Liberatory harm reduction holds the potential not only to support the most marginalized and criminalized communities with surviving, but also with providing the foundation for alternative visions of health and society. Because of this, we believe that harm reduction, as a form of political practice rather than mere health service, has an important role to play in the abolitionist project.

Building systems of lifesaving mutual aid is a baseline, we contend, for generating effective movements over the long term. Any abolitionist or anti-capitalist movement worth its salt cannot afford to forsake short-term practices of mutual care. This is particularly true when the lives of those being marginalized and criminalized are under profound threat. At the same time, harm reductionists, like all mutual aid activists, are confronted by the predicament of establishing structures for survival amid the present disaster while seeking to create what theorists André Gorz and Ruth Wilson Gilmore have referred to as non-reformist reforms—challenges to contemporary power relations that can ultimately lead to more radical transformations.[31, 32] This requires resisting co-optation into professionalized structures and staying tied to social movements and wider organizing against carceral systems. As Dean Spade reminds us, mutual aid efforts that devolve into mere volunteerism without political demands run the risk of becoming projects that "barely hold the threads of a survivable world together while the one percent extracts more and more while heroizing individual volunteers."[33]

Transitioning from a movement that hinges on the fight for daily survival to organizing for radical transformation is a tall order. But both historical and contemporary examples demonstrate that overcoming the chasm between strategies aimed at short-term survival and longer-term social change is not only possible but essential to organizing for abolition. In this chapter, we seek to describe what an *abolitionist harm reduction praxis* can look like by drawing on these examples.

First, we look at how this dual task was a central component of the theoretical and organizing frameworks of the Black Panther Party and the Young Lords Party in the 1960s and '70s. Then we turn to contemporary organizing among unhoused and drug-using communities that has occurred in Los Angeles in recent years, which provides glimpses into the strengths and challenges of building an abolitionist harm reduction movement. These examples show that efforts to build radical models of care will always be met by both repression and co-optation. Our goal in this chapter is not to be prescriptive or formulaic, and we are not suggesting that engaging in an abolitionist harm reduction praxis is an easy task. But, as we hope to make clear, it is an urgent one.

Serving the People

The tension between responding to urgent material needs in the present and the longer-term task of disassembling and replacing unjust systems with radical alternatives is not a new phenomenon facing activist movements. This same tension animated many of the theoretical debates and programmatic pivots among radical organizations during the political upheavals of the 1960s and '70s Black Power era. Most emblematically, amid its growth and evolution, the Black Panther Party (BPP) shifted from a theoretical and political strategy focused on direct militant struggle against the state toward the development of so-called survival programs.[34, 35] These programs included free breakfast for children, free medical clinics, and employment centers, among a multitude of other small-scale and often unrecognized efforts to improve conditions in Black communities.[36]

Other militant organizations led by "Third Worldist" activists from racialized communities, such as the Young Lords Party (YLP), the Red Guards, and I Wor Kuen, followed suit and launched similar survival programs in neighborhoods throughout the US.[37, 38, 39] In 1970, the YLP combined service provision with their militant political activities by occupying Lincoln Hospital, a public hospital in the South Bronx, to protest the deplorable conditions there. During their brief occupation, which garnered widespread media attention and a heavy police response, they provided free health screenings, political education, and other services to the local Black and Puerto Rican communities in collaboration with radicalized public health workers and doctors.[40]

BPP leaders, such as Huey P. Newton, used the concept of "survival pending revolution" to describe the ideological and strategic value of such programs. For Newton, survival programs were an insufficient but necessary part of the BPP's work toward building a movement for Black liberation.[41] The BPP and similar organizations viewed survival programs as important sites for building ties with, organizing, and politically educating their communities. Moreover, they were critical for meeting the needs of marginalized communities that were systematically excluded from and underserved by existing social welfare programs. As Newton articulated,

> All these programs satisfy the deep needs of the community, but they are not solutions to our problems. That is why we call them survival programs, meaning survival pending revolution. We say that the survival program of the Black Panther Party is like the survival kit of a sailor stranded on a raft. It helps him to sustain himself until he can get completely out of that situation. So, the survival programs are not answers or solutions, but they will help us to organize the community around a true analysis and understanding of their situation. When consciousness and understanding is raised to a high level then the community will seize the time and deliver themselves from the boot of their oppressor.[42]

Thus, survival programs were aimed at responding to some of the most immediate needs of marginalized communities as a means to prepare and organize them for engaging in a revolutionary transformation of society. What lessons can we draw from this "survival pending revolution" framework, and how might this apply to harm reduction activists today? There are many differences between the organizing that the BPP and similar organizations were engaged in and the activities of most harm reduction activists today. But we can also find instructive examples of how radical organizing was done among drug-using communities in the 1970s.

In 1971 the YLP led a second occupation of Lincoln Hospital in collaboration with a recently formed group called the South Bronx

Drug Coalition. During this period, the rate of heroin use had markedly increased in the South Bronx, and services for people using drugs were largely nonexistent. Together, the YLP and the South Bronx Drug Coalition called upon Lincoln Hospital administrators to establish a drug rehabilitation program. After holding a number of unproductive meetings with the hospital administration, they occupied one floor of the hospital's nurses' residence, and fifteen activists were arrested. After days of negotiation, the coalition won the right to use the hospital auditorium to establish what they referred to as the Lincoln Detoxification Program, or Lincoln Detox for short.[43]

One of the organizations in the coalition, the Spirit of Logos (SOL), consisted of a group of self-identified active and recovering drug users. The organization was born out of a residential therapeutic community under Lincoln Hospital called Logos, after several of the residents rebelled against the program's conversion from a community reintegration program to a lifelong "utopian" community. Many former members of SOL became counselors at Lincoln Detox. Strongly influenced by the Black Panthers' analysis of drug addiction, summed up by the slogan, "Capitalism + Dope = Genocide," the SOL developed a ten-point revolutionary platform.[44, 45] They argued that drug use was simultaneously the result of the deprivation brought about by capitalism and an imperialist strategy for control of colonized communities. A key component of Lincoln Detox's drug rehabilitation strategy was to provide political education classes indicting capitalism and imperialism for creating acute levels of drug use. For them, the ultimate goal of drug rehabilitation was to get people into the movement for radical social change.[46]

While today's harm reduction movement might not share the same analysis of drug use as Lincoln Detox workers, this history does provide us with one example of how service provision and radical organizing have intersected. As Gil Fagiani, a founding member of Spirit of Logos, has noted, this period "represented perhaps the most serious and sustained effort the US left has ever undertaken to specifically deal with drug addiction." Perhaps most importantly, Lincoln Detox workers promoted an analysis of drug use that placed a spotlight on the oppression that Black and Puerto Rican communities experience as an alternative to treating drug use as an individual shortcoming.[47] Ultimately, Lincoln Detox's more radical elements were purged from the organization while the innovative techniques developed by its practitioners, such as auricular acupuncture as a substance use therapy, were incorporated into a less overtly political reformulation of the program.[48] Despite this, Lincoln Detox continues to stand as an inspiring, if short-lived, example of radical care in pursuit of revolutionary change.

Mutual Aid Sketches toward an Abolitionist Harm Reduction Praxis

Across the country, cities and counties have responded to the contemporary overdose and homelessness crises by creating and expanding various forms of carceral "care." In the remainder of this chapter, we emphasize how people in Los Angeles, California have formed mutual aid communities of care and struggle against these oppressive forces that, in many ways, are an extension of the community health organizing that the Young Lords and Black Panthers engaged in during the 1970s. The mutual aid organizations we describe have moved toward building a people's public health infrastructure grounded in abolitionist harm reduction praxis that doesn't exclude drug users and people with mental health disabilities. We focus on these examples to draw lessons for health workers and activists today who are involved in parallel struggles or who seek to join similar movements. We don't aim to give a comprehensive description of all the mutual aid groups in LA, but rather to politically and historically contextualize this work through the framework of abolitionist harm reduction.

California, and specifically Los Angeles, is a carceral capital of the United States, constantly experimenting, reconfiguring, and rebranding the ways in which marginalized communities, including unhoused people, those with mental health disabilities, and drug users, are confined, displaced, abandoned, and in the end, killed.[49,50] In 2022 Los Angeles also became the county with the largest population of unhoused people in the nation.[51] While in recent years social movements in California and elsewhere have successfully organized for decarceration and for releasing people serving life without parole, new carceral systems are being constructed under the auspices of providing health care to the unhoused and substance users. Often this is done behind a veneer of liberal care for the disadvantaged that seeks to hide the suffering experienced by these communities.[52]

In July 2021 the Los Angeles City Council passed an amended version of Los Angeles Municipal Code 41.18, which further criminalized homelessness in Los Angeles by banning sitting, lying, and sleeping next to underpasses, schools, parks, and other public facilities.[53] This supposed public health and safety measure heralded the era of regularly scheduled sweeps of unhoused encampments under the city's recently established CARE (Cleaning and Rapid Engagement) Program. Though public officials claim that people are offered temporary housing or placed on waitlists, sweeps very rarely ever lead to permanent housing for those affected.[54, 55]

Homeless sweeps are harmful and even deadly to unhoused individuals, who experience severe disruption to their lives and are placed at increased risk of hospitalization and overdose death.[56, 57] Knowing the harm that was going to be unleashed by the city, communities across Los Angeles began coming together to ask: What is needed, what resources do we have, and how can we mobilize others to distribute immediate material aid to unhoused Angelenos, as they were being displaced, criminalized, and potentially placed into forced psychiatric treatment holds? Over the past few years, this has resulted in the building and organizing of several mutual aid groups across Los Angeles.

Palms Unhoused Mutual Aid and South Bay Mutual Aid Care Club

Palms Unhoused Mutual Aid (PUMA) was founded in March 2020 by Ndindi Kitonga, a Kenyan American educator and organizer, on the west side of Los Angeles.[58] The South Bay Mutual Aid Care Club (SBMCC), was founded by organizer Bunny Mitchell and serves the South Bay area of Los Angeles.[59] Like many of the other mutual aid groups in Los Angeles, harm reduction is a central part of both of these organizations' values, principles, and organizational structures. On a material level, these groups provide needles, pipes, naloxone, and information about health services in the area. They communicate to unhoused residents who use drugs in their community that they will meet them where they are rather than further isolating them.

The distribution of harm reduction materials is where most medicalized models of harm reduction begin and end—with mere service provision because it is often sorely needed. But this doesn't capture the essence of what PUMA and SBMCC are seeking to build. Undoubtedly, there remain many health service gaps for those who are unhoused, who use drugs, or who have a mental health disability that needs immediate addressing. However, many of these gaps are manufactured and maintained by the state's organized violence and abandonment of these communities. Unhoused residents regularly explain that they lose important belongings during sweeps, not limited to but including life-sustaining medicines like naloxone and buprenorphine (an opioid overuse treatment).

To address the root causes of overdose fatalities, PUMA and SBMCC work in collaboration with individuals who use drugs, who are seen as teachers and leaders in what Ndindi refers to as their "network of care." One of the ways that PUMA and SMBCC are building power with unhoused drug users in their encampments is through organizing public and popular education led by those who are normally excluded from thinking about how care is administered, practiced, and valued. In this way they are redefining who is considered a public health expert.

For example, in October 2022 PUMA and SBMCC organized a harm-reduction workshop hosted at Ndindi's school. About twenty-five people joined, ready to learn about harm reduction, drug use, and community-determined health rights and demands. The last section of the workshop introduced three unhoused residents from the South Bay encampment who were either current drug users or had used in the past. As each unhoused resident shared insight into how best to care for drug users, they were given the opportunity to define the terms of care and shape how both PUMA and SBMCC engage with drug users at encampments amid the ongoing CARE sweeps.

For decades, the city of Los Angeles, like other cities throughout the country, has systematically dehumanized, criminalized, and disempowered drug users and unhoused people. In the face of such dire systemic exclusion, the first step is to ensure that people who use drugs and are forced to rely on an unpredictable drug supply can stay alive. But abolition and harm reduction, in stark contrast to the carceral systems, laws, and policies they confront, also seek to create space for drug users to empower themselves.

An abolitionist harm reduction praxis builds and organizes with those most impacted and excluded from determining what care means and looks like. PUMA and SBMCC aren't simply harm reduction service providers. They are community health organizers and educators. They don't see themselves as experts in the health-care field, but instead view their role as building power to achieve things like housing for all, free and community drug user health care, and non-carceral responses to mental health crises. In their workshops and broader organizing work, dehumanizing power dynamics are shifted, and those who are typically demeaned as "dirty," "unhealthy," and "addicts" are provided with space to be teachers and architects of community care, health, and safety.

LA Street CARE and the Housing for Juanita Campaign

Los Angeles Street CARE & Mutual Aid is another mutual aid organization that services Historic Filipinotown, Echo Park, Silver Lake, and Rampart Village, founded by two Angelenos, Kris and Marcy.[60]

They provide harm reduction materials, meals, sleeping bags, and other essential supplies to unhoused people across Los Angeles's City Council District 13. LA Street CARE has developed some of its deepest relationships and connections with an encampment on one street in Historic Filipinotown—Juanita Avenue. This encampment was mostly made up of unhoused Filipino immigrants, many of whom were health-care or home-care workers, who had only become homeless since the beginning of the pandemic.

The Juanita Avenue encampment stretched down a block that had an elementary school at one end and a large housing development all along the street. About half of the residents lived in tents, but the rest lived in shelters they had built. It didn't take two visits before one of this chapter's authors, Rafik, was playing darts with the residents and being greeted in his native language, Arabic, by Filipinos who had worked overseas in the Middle East. The Juanita residents had created a community for the last two years that had rules, friendships, conflict, disagreement, and reconciliation. Kris, Marcy, and the rest of the LA Street CARE & Mutual Aid have played an important role in the building and sustaining of that community.

Municipal Code 41.18 was in full effect by 2023: encampments were swept with no follow-up, housing, or services offered. Every week, the city of Los Angeles releases a new schedule of the locations they will conduct sweeps in and post signs to warn people living in the encampments. In April 2023 one of those signs was posted on Juanita Avenue, giving residents forty-eight hours before a massive sweep would be conducted to uproot the community. LA Street CARE members were present for the entire duration of the sweep and witnessed its traumatic nature. The residents were placed under extreme stress and anxiety, having to move as many of their personal belongings out of the street so that the city could clean the sidewalk. Residents were told they could return to the street, and after a hard day, they returned to Juanita Avenue.

In the fall of 2023 Karen Bass was elected as the new mayor of Los Angeles. In response to the clear failures of the 41.18 sweeps, she launched a new citywide initiative called Inside Safe, which was touted as a "voluntary program" for unhoused people to get off the streets.[61] Unfortunately, this was to be accomplished by placing people inside temporary motels, not by providing them with a permanent path to housing. Mutual aid workers in Los Angeles are very aware of the harms that come to people who live on the streets, and none argue for residents to stay unhoused or discourage them from taking the offerings and services the city provides. But many mutual aid activists are aware that liberal "solutions" to homelessness are often also harmful to the unhoused. While being provided with housing in a motel seems to offer a solution, city officials have proven that the unhoused are simply political pawns, with the interests, health, and safety of the community rarely their main priority.

Inside Safe operations are intended to prevent residents from returning by destroying the structures that unhoused people build and erecting fences around the evacuated land. In November 2023, city officials visited Juanita Avenue residents and notified them that in a few days the city would conduct an Inside Safe operation and move all residents inside motels. However, this communication from city officials was unclear, and when LA Street CARE arrived to talk to residents about it, few realized the implications of the Inside Safe operation. Around fifty staff employed by the city showed up on the day of the operation, including teams of housing workers, social workers, and health-care providers. They provided a friendly face to what was, in effect, the forced displacement of an established community.

The city employees had little interest in talking with residents about their needs or concerns other than communicating the limited options they faced before their homes were going to be bulldozed. Undoubtedly, Juanita residents desired housing. But the uncertainty about where they were being taken, what conditions would be like at this unknown location, and the pressure to immediately decide how to face this dislocation and destruction of their homes and property made this a painful day for them and the mutual aid workers. After the street was fully cleared, the residents were allowed to bring two bags into the bus that would take them to the motel they were assigned to, about two miles away.

Five months later the Juanita residents were moved into a temporary Inside Safe hotel. Not a single person was moved into long-term or permanent housing. Some had not seen their case manager in three months or ever. Hotel residents continued to be highly surveilled, visitors were prohibited, and the health-care contractor that was supposed to provide care at the site had never visited. As a result, the physical and mental health of many of the Juanita residents worsened. Some hotel residents told mutual aid workers that "it's like being in prison."

In January 2024, Juanita residents, alongside a coalition of organizations, launched the Housing for Juanita Campaign.[62] The coalition has grown beyond LA Street CARE to include a larger contingent of aligned Filipino-led organizations such as GABRIELA, Anakbayan, Migrante International, Malaya Movement, Sining at Kultura Lab (SIKLAB), and the L.A. Kalusugan Collective, or LAKAS, a health-care worker/public health professional organization. The campaign aims to improve the Inside Safe program by ensuring that the promise of permanent housing is fulfilled.

The campaign began organizing meetings at a park next to the motel where they hosted political education sessions, shared meals, conducted phone banking, and grew their base of supporters. LAKAS, the organization that Rafik is a member of, began the process of developing a community health clinic after residents expressed the lack of health services and specifically the dire need for mental health care. The clinic is being organized alongside the unhoused members of the campaign, many of whom are currently or were previously health-care workers.

Harm reduction as a medicalized service typically uses language like "target population" to focus on a subgroup with a particular medical diagnosis and to deliver medication, treatment, or "intervention" prescribed by a health professional. It maintains that there is a divide between experts and service users. An abolitionist harm reduction praxis flips this narrative. Driven by abolitionist harm reduction principles, LA

Street CARE has planted the seeds for increased health service delivery to homeless people and substance users. They have also created the opportunity for community members most impacted by the city's carceral laws and policies to be the leaders in their struggle against displacement and confinement.

Building a Global Health Revolutionary Movement

At the height of the radical health movement of the late 1960s and early '70s, the YLP joined forces with Black and Puerto Rican hospital workers at Lincoln Hospital to form the Health Revolutionary Unity Movement (HRUM). HRUM grew to become a citywide organization that advocated for overcoming the unacceptable conditions in public hospitals by bringing them under community control. Before an action like the YLP's occupation of Lincoln Hospital could even be possible, they had to build a collective that included community members, health-care workers, physicians, and patients.

Similarly, following the implementation of Municipal Code 41.18, mutual aid organizers in Los Angeles began to coordinate campaigns in collaboration with a diversity of activists, health workers, and unhoused communities threatened by sweeps. The struggle that we have before us—in Los Angeles, across the US, and around the world—continues to be a struggle for community control over the terms and forms of care that marginalized communities are provided. This is not something that is fought and won in a single election cycle or even a generation but demands a commitment to building a people's public health infrastructure at the grassroots. Organizing broad coalitions of local health collectives that engage in both mutual aid and grassroots organizing campaigns will be central to this ongoing task.

As internationalists, the Young Lords and HRUM saw the struggles in their communities and hospitals as deeply connected to those of oppressed communities across the "Third World."

An abolitionist harm reduction praxis must also be rooted in an internationalist perspective.

Our contemporary overdose disaster, born out of the global War on Drugs and exacerbated by the displacement of vulnerable communities, is a phenomenon that necessitates both local and international organizing to break from carceral and militarized responses to drug use. International solidarity calls on us to see the resonances between our struggles against dehumanization and displacement across our nation's imagined borders. This is becoming particularly urgent and apparent amid the devastation of the Palestinian health-care system and violent displacement of Palestinian people, funded, and abetted by the United States. The only sustainable future for the people, for the land, is one guided by a global HRUM, from Los Angeles to Palestine to the Congo, the Philippines, Latin America, and beyond.

Aetna Street Solidarity Memorial—A Vision of a Restructured Society

Prison industrial complex (PIC) abolition is a political vision, a structural analysis of oppression, and a practical organizing strategy. While some people might think of abolition as primarily a negative project—"Let's tear everything down tomorrow and hope for the best"—PIC abolition is a vision of a restructured society in a world where we have everything we need: food, shelter, education, health, art, beauty, clean water, and more. Things that are foundational to our personal and community safety.

—*Mariame Kaba, We Do This 'Til We Free Us*

On March 16, 2024, a Los Angeles mutual aid collective in the San Fernando Valley named Aetna Street Solidarity organized a community memorial to honor lives that have been lost as a result of forced displacement, from Los Angeles to Palestine. The event, called "Without Community There Is No Life!," was held on Aetna Street in the Van Nuys neighborhood where unhoused people have been building a community and resisting street sweeps with the support of housed neighbors for several years. A memorial created by an organization called Eastside Café placed the names and pictures of Palestinian youth killed during the ongoing genocide perpetrated by the Israeli government. Healthcare Workers for

Palestine, an organization that formed in October 2023, was also present, sharing offerings and poems. The event was joined by poverty skolas with POOR Magazine, a collective that is "po', houseless, indigenous & resisting krapitalism by #unsellingmamaearth on stolen Land."

The All People's Power Clinic, a radical collective of health-care workers, was also present, distributing harm reduction supplies and conducting an overdose prevention and naloxone training for all in attendance. Several community members brought a truck that had a handmade clay pizza oven on wheels attached to it, making fresh pizzas for everyone. Perfumes and fragrances were made, songs were sung, and tears were shed, but for some time that evening, people had everything they needed: food, shelter, education, health, art, beauty, clean water, and more. In that moment we had everything that was foundational to our safety.

What if this configuration at the Aetna Street Solidarity Memorial—these practices and rejuvenating relationships with each other and the land, with the meanings of "health" and "care" self-determined by the community—was a vision for a restructured society? In her book *Take Care of Yourself: The Art and Cultures of Care and Liberation*, artist and cultural worker Sundus Abdul Hadi says about the struggle for care, "If, as Achille Mbembe says, in the context of Fanon, 'colonialism is a factory where madness is manufactured,' then imagination is a factory where hope is manufactured.[63] If the counternarrative to violence is care, then that's where you'll find me." While we may only be able to catch short glimpses of a restructured society where we move beyond mere survival in moments like those at Aetna Street, building both our political imaginations and our material infrastructures of care will be necessary to make these visions endure.

CHAPTER 10 NOTES

1. Centers for Disease Control. *Understanding the Opioid Overdose Epidemic.* Washington, DC: Centers for Disease Control (2022). https://www.cdc .gov/opioids/basics/epidemic.html.

2. Spencer, Merianne R., Matthew F. Garnett, and Arialdi M. Miniño. "Drug Overdose Deaths in the United States, 2002–2022." NCHS Data Brief, no 491. Hyattsville, MD: National Center for Health Statistics. 2024. https://www.cdc.gov/nchs/products/databriefs/db491.htm.

3. Imtiaz, Sameer, Frishta Nafeh, Cayley Russell, Farihah Ali, Tara Elton-Marshall, and Jürgen Rehm. "The Impact of the Novel Coronavirus Disease (COVID-19) Pandemic on Drug Overdose-Related Deaths in the United States and Canada: A Systematic Review of Observational Studies and Analysis of Public Health Surveillance Data." *Substance Abuse Treatment, Prevention, and Policy* 16, no. 1 (November 29, 2021): 87.

4. Bradford, W. David, and Felipe Lozano-Rojas. "Higher Rates of Homelessness Are Associated with Increases in Mortality from Accidental Drug and Alcohol Poisonings." *Health Affairs* 43, no. 2 (February 2024): 242–49.

5. Grandin, Greg. "The Republicans Who Want to Invade Mexico." *New York Times.* Nov 1, 2023.

6. Godlee, Fiona, and Richard Hurley. "The War on Drugs Has Failed: Doctors Should Lead Calls for Drug Policy Reform." *BMJ.* November 14, 2016. i6067.

7. Tosh, Sarah. "Drug Prohibition and the Criminalization of Immigrants: The Compounding of Drug War Disparities in the United States Deportation Regime." *International Journal of Drug Policy* 87 (January 1, 2021): 102846.

8. Werb, D., A. Kamarulzaman, M. C. Meacham, C. Rafful, B. Fischer, S. A. Strathdee, and E. Wood. "The Effectiveness of Compulsory Drug Treatment: A Systematic Review." *International Journal of Drug Policy* 28 (February 1, 2016): 1–9.

9. Szalavitz, Maia. *Undoing Drugs: How Harm Reduction Is Changing the Future of Drugs and Addiction.* New York: Hachette Book Group, 2021.

10. Hassan, Shira. *Saving Our Own Lives: A Liberatory Practice of Harm Reduction.* Chicago: Haymarket Books, 2022.

11. Bohler, Robert M., Dominic Hodgkin, Peter W. Kreiner, and Traci C. Green. "Predictors of US States' Adoption of Naloxone Access Laws, 2001–2017." *Drug and Alcohol Dependence* 225 (August 1, 2021): 108772.

12. Davis, Corey. *Legality of Drug Checking Equipment in the United States.* Edina, MN: Network for Public Health Law. August 2023. https://www.networkforphl.org/resources/legality-of-drug-checking-equipment-in-the-united-states/.

13. Walsh, John. "Biden's New Drug Control Strategy: Long Overdue Focus on Harm Reduction and Other Takeaways." Washington D.C.: The Washington Office on Latin America. 2022. https://www.wola.org /analysis/bidens-new-drug-control-strategy-long-overdue-focus-harm -reduction-other-takeaways/.

14. Alpert Reyes, Emily. "California Communities Are Banning Syringe Programs. Now the State Is Fighting Back in Court," *The Los Angeles Times*. March 19, 2024.

15. Sierra, Antonio. "With Measure 110 Gutted, Eastern Oregon Harm Reduction Group Remains Undeterred." *Oregon Public Broadcasting*. April 23, 2024.

16. Chabria, Anita, and Paul Kuroda. "I Went to an Overdose Prevention Site. Biden and Newsom Need to Stop Blocking Them," *The Los Angeles Times*. September 1, 2023.

17. Klamann, Seth. "Facing Veto Threat by Gov. Jared Polis, Colorado Lawmakers Kill Supervised Drug-Use Sites Bill," *The Denver Post*. October 31, 2023.

18. Ovalle, David. "Philadelphia Council Bans Safe-Injection Sites in Most of the City," *The Washington Post*. September 14, 2023.

19. Greschler, Gabe. "Breed Blames Harm Reduction Strategy for Surging Drug Overdose Deaths." *The San Francisco Standard*. February 26, 2024.

20. Smith, Mitch. "Nebraska Lawmakers Sustain Veto of Needle Exchange," *The New York Times*. March 12, 2024.

21. Mechoui, Leila. "The Harms of 'Harm Reduction.'" *Compact Magazine*. Oct 4, 2023.

22. Illner, Peer. *Disasters and Social Reproduction: Crisis Response between the State and Community*. London: Pluto Press, 2020.

23. Goodyear, Trevor. "(Re) Politicizing Harm Reduction: Poststructuralist Thinking to Challenge the Medicalization of Harms among People Who Use Drugs." *Aporia* 13, no. 1 (2021).

24. Hassan. *Saving Our Own Lives*.

25. Whitehead, Patrick M. "Medicalization." *Existential Health Psychology: The Blind-Spot in Healthcare*. London: Palgrave Pivot, 2019.

26. Hassan. *Saving Our Own Lives*.

27. Firth, Rhiannon. *Disaster Anarchy: Mutual Aid and Radical Action*, London: Pluto Press, 2022.

28. Rodríguez Soto, Isa. "Mutual Aid and Survival as Resistance in Puerto Rico," *NACLA Report on the Americas* 52, no. 3 (2020): 303–8.

29. Mould, Oli, Jennifer Cole, Adam Badger, and Philip Brown. "Solidarity, Not Charity: Learning the Lessons of the COVID-19 Pandemic to Reconceptualise the Radicality of Mutual Aid." *Transactions of the Institute of British Geographers* 47, no. 4 (December 1, 2022): 866–79.

30. Spade, Dean. *Mutual Aid: Building Solidarity During This Crisis (and the Next)*. New York: Verso Books, 2020.

31. Gilmore, Ruth Wilson. *Golden Gulag: Prisons, Surplus, Crisis, and Opposition in Globalizing California*. Berkeley: University of California Press, 2007.

32. Gorz, André. "Strategy for Labor. A Radical Proposal." *Science and Society* 32, no. 4 (1968).

33. Spade. *Mutual Aid*.

34. Burke, Lucas N. N., and Judson L. Jeffries. *The Portland Black Panthers: Empowering Albina and Remaking a City*. Seattle: University of Washington Press, 2016.

35. Narayan, John. "Huey P. Newton's Intercommunalism: An Unacknowledged Theory of Empire." *Theory, Culture & Society* 36, no. 3 (May 1, 2019): 57–85.

36. Jeffries, Judson L., ed. *On the Ground: The Black Panther Party in Communities across America*. Jackson: University Press of Mississippi, 2010.

37. Fernández, Johanna. *The Young Lords: A Radical History*. Chapel Hill: University of North Carolina Press, 2020.

38. Maeda, Daryl J. "Black Panthers, Red Guards, and Chinamen." *Contemporary Asian America: A Multidisciplinary Reader* (2007): 89.

39. Pulido, Laura. *Black, Brown, Yellow, and Left: Radical Activism in Los Angeles*. Berkeley: University of California Press, 2006.

40. Fernández. *The Young Lords*.

41. Newton, Huey P. *To Die for the People: The Writings of Huey P. Newton*. New York: Random House, 1972.

42. Newton. *To Die for the People*.

43. Fernández. *The Young Lords*.

44. Tabor, Michael C. *Capitalism plus Dope Equals Genocide*. San Francisco, CA: Freedom Archives, 1970. https://freedomarchives.org/Documents/Finder/DOC513_scans/Michael_Cetewayo_Tabor/513.Michael.Tabor.Capitalism.Dope.Genocide.pdf.

45. Tracy, James. "Rising Up: Poor, White, and Angry in the New Left," In *The Hidden 1970s: Histories of Radicalism*, ed. Dan Berger. Ithaca, NY: Rutgers University Press, 2010. 214–30.

46. Fernández. *The Young Lords*.

47. Fagiani, G. "White Lightning: Organizing the White Working Class in the Bronx, 1971–1975." Lecture, John D. Calandra Italian American Institute, New York, NY, April 27–28, 2012.

48. Meng, Eana. "Use of Acupuncture by 1970s Revolutionaries of Color: The South Bronx 'Toolkit Care' Concept." *American Journal of Public Health* 111, no. 5 (May 2021): 896–906.

49. After Echo Park Lake Research Collective. "Continuum of Carcerality: How Liberal Urbanism Governs Homelessness." *Radical Housing Journal* 4, no. 1 (2022): 71–94.

50. Hernández, Kelly Lytle. *City of Inmates: Conquest, Rebellion, and the Rise of Human Caging in Los Angeles, 1771–1965.* University of North Carolina Press, 2017.

51. Gong, Neil. *Sons, Daughters, and Sidewalk Psychotics: Mental Illness and Homelessness in Los Angeles.* Chicago: The University of Chicago Press, 2024.

52. Roy, Ananya. "A Political Autopsy of Liberal Los Angeles." *Human Geography* 17, no. 1 (March 1, 2024): 117–21.

53. Oppenheimer, Peer. "The Illusion of Public Space: Enforcement of Anti-Camping Ordinances Against Individuals Experiencing Homelessness." *University of Chicago Legal Forum* 2023, no. 1 (January 22, 2024).

54. Deloso, Katrina, and Audrey Jang. *Centering Unhoused Communities in Transit-Oriented Development.* Los Angeles, CA: UCLA Institute of Transportation Studies, 2023. https://escholarship.org/content/qt6tx8h19r/qt6tx8h19r_noSplash_3c04a1d7af5afc9100bfbb9d60ceea7f.pdf.

55. Smith, Doug, Ruben Vives, and David Zahniser. "Are L.A.'s Anti-camping Laws Failing? We Went to 25 Sites to Find the Truth," *The Los Angeles.* March 7, 2024.

56. Barocas, Joshua A., Samantha K. Nall, Sarah Axelrath, Courtney Pladsen, Alaina Boyer, Alex H. Kral, Ashley A. Meehan, et al. "Population-Level Health Effects of Involuntary Displacement of People Experiencing Unsheltered Homelessness Who Inject Drugs in US Cities." *JAMA* 329, no. 17 (May 2, 2023): 1478–86.

57. Goldshear, J. L., N. Kitonga, N. Angelo, A. Cowan, B. F. Henwood, and R. N. Bluthenthal. "'Notice of Major Cleaning': A Qualitative Study of the Negative Impact of Encampment Sweeps on the Ontological Security of Unhoused People Who Use Drugs." *Social Science & Medicine* 339 (December 1, 2023): 116408.

58. Jacoby, Evan. "How Mutual Aid Works." *LAist.* Dec 5, 2023.

59. Burley, Shane. "Where Mutual Aid Comes to Its Own Assistance." *Yes! Magazine*. Mar 20, 2023.

60. Kendall, Marisa. "L.A.'s New Homeless Solution Clears Camps but Struggles to House People," *Cal Matters*. July 24, 2023.

61. Beckner-Carmitchel, Sean. "Inside Safe: More Than a Year of Limited Success and Ongoing Controversy." *Knock LA*. March 27, 2024.

62. Haskell, Josh. "Group of Inside Safe Participants in Historic Filipinotown Says City Program Lacks Services," *KABC*. April 16, 2024.

63. Abdul Hadi, S. *Take Care of Yourself: The Art and Cultures of Care and Liberation*. New York: Common Notions, 2020.

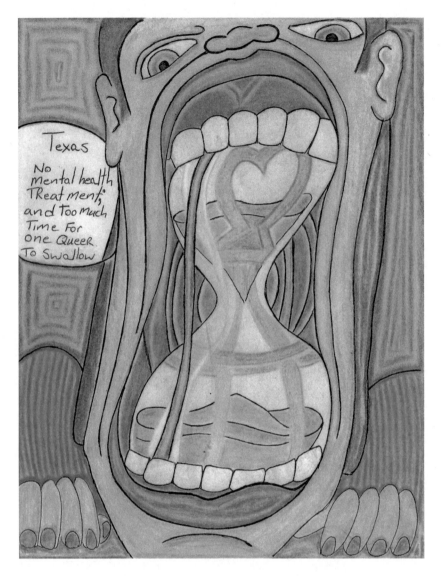

Figure 10.1: Artwork by Billy Thomas on having recurring
psychosis within the Texas prison system

11

INTERVIEW WITH LIAT BEN-MOSHE

BY RONICA MUKERJEE

Ronica Mukerjee (R): *You mentioned in your book* Decarcerating Disability *that decarceration has already happened with deinstitutionalization. Can you speak to how deinstitutionalization can be a jumping-off point, or even an inspiration, for abolition activists?*

Liat Ben-Moshe: *Sure. To start with, what I mean by "deinstitutionalization" is three things. The first is the exodus of people with psychiatric, or intellectual and developmental disabilities, out of psychiatric hospitals and residential facilities. Already, now you can see that there were two kinds of deinstitutionalizations, and we don't always talk about both of them. One is psychiatric, and the other is in the field of intellectual developmental disabilities.*

The second thing deinstitutionalization represents is the actual closure of the facilities. It's not just moving people from institutional living into community living, but it's also the closure of these large residential facilities, psychiatric hospitals, and so on. That's the usual kind of definition for deinstitutionalization.

To me, thirdly, deinstitutionalization is also a mindset, a framework, a kind of anti-carceral framework and a logic. And so if we understand it as a logic, then we can see it as a precedent for contemporary prison and police abolition movements. And this is because psychiatric hospitals, and residential institutions for people with intellectual and developmental disabilities, and other disability institutions are carceral. That's just the baseline for people who are kind of entering the conversation. They're not like *carceral, they* are *carceral.*

So when we talk about carceral abolition, we absolutely should be talking about the abolition of psychiatric confinement and confinement of people with disabilities in residential institutions. We are also talking about boarding schools for Indigenous people, which it's not like carceral. It is carceral. It's very important to understand that. I don't mean that it's a prison—it's not a prison—it's something else. It's a residential institution or a boarding school, but it's a place you don't leave.

Those of us who are abolitionists often get a certain kind of pushback. Let's say people are very on board with the abolitionist critique and mindset, and these people considering abolition are like, okay, we know people languish in prisons and in these psychiatric hospitals, and maybe we don't need these systems and these places. They can consider that perhaps this logic of incarceration doesn't make sense in 2024; in this way, people considering abolition are with you . . . but then they think, "Surely it's not realistic, right?" They think, "You don't mean right now abolish these things? And you don't mean abolish all of them, right? It's just unrealistic. It can't happen right now. And surely you don't mean in the United States, right? This is something we can do in like Sweden or something, but surely you don't mean here?"

Deinstitutionalization is then very helpful with these doubting people because it has been here. It is here. I mean, the closure of psychiatric hospitals and institutions for people with intellectual, and/or developmental disabilities has happened in the US and in Canada, on Turtle Island. It has happened already. So I think we should learn from this about what to do—also probably what not to do as well. But it was the largest decarceration movement in US history, without a doubt.

R: *So many things you said resonated, including how normal we think it is to put people away. We have this idea that we're putting people away because they're criminals or we're deporting people because they're criminals, but we've also normalized the concept that people's differences are the reason they should be put away. I think about my patients who spend so much time in and out of psychiatric facilities and how those are punishment-based facilities. A person fucks up the norms, and medication or punishment is used. We have a moralization around people's mental health and a normalization of carceral culture, and everyone fails as a result of this construct. It's also such a failure for people with disabilities. I would love to know what you think about specifically carceral culture and how it's affected people who have disabilities and/or mental health diagnoses.*

Liat: *Yeah. That's really the core: to understand that as a carceral logic. I call it carceral sanism and carceral ableism. Sanism itself is the oppression that particularly people with psychiatric diagnoses, people who are psychiatrized, or that all/many people experience from the imperative to be sane and to be rational.*

Carceral sanism is a belief system and also a practice that builds on the idea that people with disabilities need special or extra protections. In terms of carceral sanism and ableism, it means to protect people with disabilities in ways that often leads to their marginalization, and further incarceration. Sometimes even abolitionists, including prison abolitionists who are saying that we gotta get people with mental health differences out of solitary confinement, are part of carceral sanism. That has been a big, big battle of abolitionists and reformers and policy people. It is this process of chipping away at the system because, at the very least, we know that solitary confinement is very harmful for people's mental health.

> ... abolitionists may defer and say that the very least we could do is not put people with mental health differences or people who experience psychotic breaks or people who are suicidal at least in solitary confinement, and it's a harm reduction approach. However, why this is really carceral sanism and not actual abolition, is that, first of all, chipping away at the system doesn't get to the core of the system. When you play with the margins, the core does not fall. What it does is justify the incarceration of other people in solitary.

So these abolitionists may defer and say that the very least we could do is not put people with mental health differences or people who experience psychotic breaks or people who are suicidal at least in solitary confinement, and it's a harm reduction approach. However, why this is really carceral sanism and not actual abolition is that, first of all, chipping away at the system doesn't get to the core of the system. When you play with the margins, the core does not fall. What it does is justify the incarceration of other people in solitary. This construction purports that solitary can't be used for people with mental health differences, but then it means that other people can or should be in solitary, just not these people. So it becomes carceral sanism exactly for a mechanism, solitary confinement, that, by the way, makes people crazy.

It's an ableist sanist mechanism on its own, but saying that we just can't put particular people like our people in there—to me that is not disability activism. That is of course not disability justice; I don't even think it's disability anything. It's not liberatory. And yes, getting anybody out is better than getting nobody out. But I don't think getting people out of solitary is the same as getting them out of prisons. That's what I mean by carceral sanism and carceral ableism—we end up with these things as our solutions or alternatives, like instead of putting people in solitary confinement, we'll put them in a psych ward on psych watch in the prison, or maybe we get them out of the prison with them in a psych facility as an alternative. And people think that that's somehow better, like that psych confinement is somehow not confinement. I don't know what people think to be honest. People don't understand that psychiatrization is a carceral modality.

People don't understand that psychiatrization is a carceral modality.

R: *Part of what you talk about in your book* Decarcerating Disability *is that linking of disability and racism. If you wouldn't mind talking more about that.*

Liat: *Sure. So "DisCrit" means disability with critical race theory, and that doesn't come from me. That's from Subini Annama, Beth Ferry, and David Connor. They coined this term "DisCrit": disability and critical race theory. All* three are education scholars, so they got to this framework through looking at the extreme "overrepresentation" of kids of color in special education. But what we all know is that it's not overrepresentation. It's the system not failing. The system is working, and the system is ableist and racist. So, this great framework critiques all of that. People should look at their writing and their book to see more examples of that, especially in the field of education. What I take from that and talk about in the work is the framework of racialization, criminalization, and pathologization ("pathologization" meaning making something pathological or psychiatric, whether it's psychiatric disabilities or maybe things that don't even have a label, like a medical label, but we pathologize). All three of those things are completely connected to each other. We can't understand the way people are pathologized, for example, like called crazy, without understanding race—it is just not possible.

[We] can't understand race and pathologization without understanding how that leads to criminalization.

And we can't understand race and pathologization without understanding how that leads to criminalization. So those three things to me are completely interrelated in these carceral logics that we're talking about and discussing the abolition of. It's really hard for me to understand how one works without the other two. And it's not just a framework of analysis; that's how I see it operating in people's lives and in the consequences of people's lives, like where they end up, or are captured into. I know you talked to Leroy (Moore), so you could see that in the cases of police brutality and people with disabilities, and very obviously how those three things are linked. You can see also how racialization and pathologization are completely related to criminalization—like when young Black men are seen as "abnormal giants" and always older than what they really are.

This was the case with Tamir Rice . . . and I don't need to mention all the people, because it's very triggering. There are so many cases with Black men that demonstrate how pathologization facilitates criminalization of a person and how there are very severe consequences of this pathologization, including death by police or murder by police. This pathologization works in the cases of Black and Brown women who are deemed crazy. There are so many names that we can mention in terms of the adverse consequences. Those three processes really work together.

So then our collective resistance has to be about those three things together. It's the most important thing to take away here. This is not just about analysis. It's also about how we resist. So the frameworks of "disability rights" that don't see race are completely ludicrous and could never address something like I just discussed—state violence, or so-called police brutality, because what is policing, but brutality. So I'm just gonna say policing, but policing and any kind of state violence, including what I mentioned earlier around education, these all have to be addressed at the core. And the core is intersectional about those three things together—racialization, criminalization, and pathologization.

> **Policing and any kind of state violence . . . these all have to be addressed at the core. And the core is intersectional about those three things together—racialization, criminalization, and pathologization.**

R: *Yes, and resisting slavery was a diagnosis, right? Like those sort of basic diagnoses that have been used to pathologize Black communities, Indigenous communities, Latinx communities—*

Liat: *Well, what you're referring to is drapetomania, but now we have excited delirium, and excited delirium is now the new category mostly talked about in relation to people of color, and mostly in relation to disabled people of color who resist arrest. And so excited delirium is like the new kind of drapetomania.*

R: *Kids also get these diagnoses of conduct disorder, oppositional defiant disorder, and borderline personality that lead them down this pathway of the school to prison pipeline. I do not know how anyone sees these diagnoses in a kid's file and thinks to themselves, this kid's gonna be easy to deal with. You see at least these first two diagnoses in kids of color much more often.*

Liat: *Well, let's be frank, all three of those diagnoses that you just mentioned— borderline, oppositional defiant disorder, and conduct disorder—are racist to begin with. If you look at the percentage of who's given these diagnoses, it's the same with emotionally disturbed. These are all racist. Those of us who are anti-psychiatry and are interested in the abolition of not just carcerality, but also psychiatry, bio-psychiatry (what psychiatry is today), see all of these psychiatric labels as socially constructed. Those diagnoses we discussed specifically are racist, and borderline also sexist, and very much about sexuality as well. There are so many people—particularly women or nonbinary, trans people—who are caught in the borderline world of diagnosis. Yes, that's another example of how these things are so intertwined. How can you detach racism from psychiatry?*

R: *I also think about the targeting of Black women and the 700 percent increase since the 1980s of Black women in prison. And the perception of what is a woman, the societal masculinization and aging of Black women—when most people conceptualize "women" as a cis, nondisabled white woman, that default gendering just brings somebody into the focus of police, CPS, and all these harms, as you know.*

Liat: *Yes, and also leads to detrimental health-care consequences. I'm sure I don't have to tell you, but, like you just said, masculine also means stronger. So then there is an increased likelihood of heart attacks in Black women and of post-labor detrimental consequences because Black women are perceived as "stronger" or "malingering."*

R: *Or more normalized as single parents, just more suited to be fine single mothers without any public resources.*

Liat: *I really recommend Dorothy Roberts's work for more information about this and the origins of those family courts. They have always been just racist and ableist; people don't talk about the ableism aspect. I don't see that in the historical stuff, but you know, we see kids taken away from Black disabled women all the* *time. That's a very common thing to happen. And where is that history? Hopefully somebody has it, but I don't see it very commonly spoken or written about.*

R: Decarcerating Disability *talks about how the closing of psych hospitals does not necessarily mean more people in prison. Can you talk about strategies and also the connected logics and the argument against the idea that we need good psych hospitals, which many abolitionists do believe in.*

Liat: *When I talk about deinstitutionalization, a lot of people have this idea of what deinstitutionalization was and is. Many people have the idea that dein-stitutionalization failed and that people ended up either homeless or housing insecure, in the streets mostly, and then a lot of them ended up in prisons and jails coinciding with the rise of incarceration in the eighties and nineties. And in a lot of people's minds, including scholars, deinstitutionalization was one of the factors that led to the rise of incarceration. There was also this claim that it led to the rise of people with disabilities, especially psychiatric disabilities, in jails and prisons. For anybody who's an abolitionist or has a family member or been incarcerated themselves and goes into a jail and prison, it's very obvious that there are a lot of people with mental health differences and people who are really struggling in terms of mental health and disability that are in prisons and jails, without dispute, even though we don't have good statistics to show this. I think if you go in, it's very obvious what's happening. And for a lot of people post-incarceration too.*

R: *And post-incarceration also, when people are in community, there is untreated mental illness that has never been properly addressed.*

Liat: *Absolutely. The assumption is that these people need to be in psychiatric hospitals, and deinstitutionalization had good ideals but it was irresponsible. And then when the psych facilities and institutions closed, people ended up in the streets and then they ended up in prison. And now we have a lot of people with mental health differences in prison. And what I try to do in the book, and in a lot of my work, is to critique all of these assumptions. As a scholar, I'm happy that I can do that. For some people they're swayed by statistics or demo-graphics, but my claim is really about how we understand disability and how we understand incarceration.*

The claim that people ended up in the streets and then in prisons and jails and the claim that deinstitutionalization led to the rising incarceration doesn't really add up . . . In terms of the demographics . . . we know that the rise in incarceration exploded, especially in the '80s or '90s for particularly men of color. This was not the population that exited institutions and psychiatric facilities.

If we would've had—I'm just simplifying it—buses leaving psychiatric hospitals that closed down, starting in the '50s, buses waiting for people all through the '60 and '70s, that just led them into the prison? We would see way more white women in prisons, which is *not* what we see.

The claim that people ended up in the streets and then in prisons and jails and the claim that deinstitutionalization led to rising incarceration doesn't really add up in terms of the demographic of the people, specifically in terms of the time in which it happened. We know that the rise in incarceration exploded, especially in the '80 or '90s, for particularly men of color. This was not the population that exited institutions and psychiatric facilities.

If we would've had—I'm just simplifying it—buses leaving psychiatric hospitals that closed down, starting in the '50s, buses waiting for people all through the '60s and '70s, that just led them into the prison? We would see way more white women in prisons, which is not what we see.

Then we have the issue of temporality, which is that the population in psychiatric hospitals in the US started to decline from the highest population around 1955 and every day since it's been declining. Definitely by the '60s, there's deinstitutionalization on a mass level, but the rise of incarceration came much later.

And if we're talking about homelessness, which is the other thing people say, we didn't see homelessness on this mass scale until the '80s, and guess what else happened in the '80s? Yes, everything, pretty much, but just to give a few examples, Reagan happened, and the decimation of welfare, of any kind of affordable housing, all of those structural things happened. But deinstitutionalization actually happened fifteen years before.

So these claims [of increased prison populations, increased homelessness in response to deinstitutionalization] do not make a lot of sense. My question throughout is why? Why do we vilify deinstitutionalization? Why is the story told that deinstitutionalization failed and that it left people in the streets and in prison? I'm not saying deinstitutionalization was a huge success and everybody was liberated and living in a castle on the ocean. Of course it didn't happen like that, because of what I just said: welfare was decimated at the same time housing was decimated. So of course, it didn't lead to the kind of liberation that a lot of people were looking for. But our story about the failure of deinstitutionalization is also a story of the failure of our imagination of radical organizing and what it was able to do, which is to close down psychiatric facilities.

And they didn't close just because of organizing. Of course they closed because people like Reagan didn't want to put more money into any kind of mental health, whether it's community mental health or hospitals, which also led to adverse consequences. So what I'm trying to say is two things happened at the same time, but it doesn't mean one led to the other.

There was actually a third factor, neoliberalism, which led to the decimation of the welfare system and housing, and also the closure of psychiatric hospitals and other facilities. But, lo and behold, money was found to be put into corrections. So neoliberalism also signaled this rise in corrections, in incarceration, and ever since then money goes into corrections and not into welfare. That has nothing to do with deinstitutionalization whatsoever.

So this whole idea of the failure of deinstitutionalization is about blaming very easy targets, which is disability and people with disabilities and disability activists, for something that was structural and completely outside of disability.

Let's say that you followed me on my journey so far. And you're thinking that I started this whole thing saying that there are a lot of people with mental health differences and they are really struggling in prison and also outside of prisons. So you may be wondering, well, what do you want? If deinstitutionalization didn't fix things, and prisons don't work, what are we supposed to do with all these problem people?

To me, that is the wrong question, because that means that it's a population that's outside us, that it's a population we need to "do something about." And that we need something like a different kind of carceral system. Like let's bring back psychiatric hospitals. And that's where a lot of policy people are now; they're like, deinstitutionalization failed. That's why we have a lot of people with mental health differences in prison, but prison is disabling and it's stress inducing, it's trauma inducing, and it induces mental health issues. And so the problem is intrinsic in the prison.

R: *And how prison disables people is poorly understood. There's starting to be more research around post-incarceration syndrome, for example. Can you speak to how prison is disabling?*

Liat: *When I taught in prison, in that particular facility, the only way to access the classroom was in the visiting area when the visiting area was closed. The only way to go to the visiting area, and I think that's why they put it there, was to get strip searched. So if people wanted to access classes in that facility, they needed to be strip searched. I don't think people understand—that's sexual assault that happens to people every day. So in terms of my class, that happened before the class and after the class.*

So basically, people are assaulted daily. We know that in women's facilities (and not only women are in women's facilities), but particularly in what the carceral system calls women's prisons, there's a very high population of people who have experienced sexual assault. So think about the retraumatizing effect of something that we innocuously call strip search, which is, in essence, sexual assault. And then think about how could somebody come out of this and not be traumatized?

R: *Right. "Having done their time." That concept in and of itself is so troubling because what is actually happening is the damage of communities further. Prisons were never meant to rehabilitate, just like psychiatric institutions were never really meant to "normalize"; they were both meant to contain people who were inconvenient and/or poor.*

Liat: *If you think about rehabilitation, and this is a framework we get from particularly Indigenous thinkers—I'm thinking of Luanna Ross, for example— rehabilitation is a colonial apparatus that's about assimilating people. And this is something that has been done to Indigenous people in "boarding schools" as they are euphemistically called, and in carceral settings and continuing on into prisons today. So even the word and the impetus of rehabilitation is really about state violence.*

R: *And what you brought up before about what community means, that somehow we have incorporated this idea of community as the people who are so-called sane and people who are so-called able-bodied. And that everybody else is a burden and/or an outlier that we have to care for as a community, as opposed to recognizing all the ways that people who aren't defined as sane or able-bodied do care within those communities.*

Liat: *Exactly. In the book I talk about the practice of neighborhood notification that is often done in order to prevent that kind of NIMBY [not in my backyard] resistance that comes with the establishment of a group home, a halfway house, or a drug rehab program in a specific neighborhood. And to me, that is such a damaging practice because it builds an us-versus-them mindset. Like when we move to a neighborhood, do people really need to be notified? And who are these people, right? We've been a part of every neighborhood already.*

R: *Throughout* Decarcerating Disability, *you discuss the way that disability rights and the ADA and governmental policy and institutions interact with neoliberalism and are decidedly different in intention and direction from disability justice. This made me think about domestic worker rights issues and how domestic workers are pitted against people with disabilities who need more services than the government metes out. So why doesn't the government just pay for these things? I'd love to hear your perspective about that.*

Liat: *Disability rights, by my definition, are really about incorporating people into the status quo, right? So it's, "let's give people the right to education." Everybody has the right to education, including disabled people. To employment. Everybody should have the right to employment, including disabled people and so on. But then there's disability justice, or more radical imaginings that are like, the status quo sucks. We want to live in a society that's not just nonableist, but also not* *capitalist and that critiques transnational empire and critiques people as exchange value because a lot of the domestic workers are part of this multinational transnational capitalism, which of course is racial capitalism. And the whole thing's super gendered as well.*

It's really important to understand the difference between the frameworks of disability rights and disability justice. We're talking about two different visions of the world. One is about incorporating into the world as is, and just working towards having people with disabilities in it. A lot of disability rights activism is against the literal death of people with disabilities. Like, when I say "included in the world," I mean, like, absolutely literally, anti-eugenics, neo-eugenics, all eugenics, all of those things. Great.

But then there are a lot of us who are more interested in breaking the world and in creating openings that are not just about, let's have people with disabilities also exploited under capitalism. Or, you know, let's have people with disabilities have access to this educational system that is completely inadequate for anybody. And of course, would be completely inadequate for people with particular disabilities. And so, even in the field of education, like we just talked about DisCrit earlier, people are trying to create openings that implode systems like special education and that implode the whole system of education.

> **Sometimes, the alignment between disability rights and disability justice is a little bit more fluid, but sometimes it's very clear that we're talking about different visions of what we want and how we want the world to be. And I think that state violence, and the way we understand it under the rubric of abolition, is a very clear example of how disability rights are a very inadequate and sometimes harmful heteropatriarchal capitalist white framework.**

Sometimes, the alignment between disability rights and disability justice is a little bit more fluid, but sometimes it's very clear that we're talking about different visions of what we want and how we want the world to be. And I think that state violence, and the way we understand it under the rubric of abolition, is a very clear example of how disability rights are a very inadequate and sometimes harmful framework and a sometimes very white framework. And I mean, white—not just the way that some people talk about it—which I totally understand that disability rights are very often done by white people. That is also true, but I don't think it gives us the kind of analysis that I'm talking about, which is that it's a white framework and it's a heteropatriarchal framework, because it clings to the status quo. So, you know, when we try to push this (some people call it) "queer agenda," but really queer of color critiques, critiques of state violence that come from the framework of racial capitalism, those are not compatible with disability rights as a system of thought.

What I mean by, like, "queer of color critique" is, for example, critiques of gay marriage. Or gays in the military. So there's the agenda of rights that says gay people should also have access to the military. And then there's the queer of color critique, which is, no, we shouldn't have a military, and, in fact, we have an anti-imperialist critique and we have a critique of war and we have a critique of where the budget is going and we have . . . so on and so on. So that is part of where, some people call it a disability justice critique, I call it a crip and mad of color critique. That's where it comes from. It's a critique of the state and it's a critique of state violence and it's a critique that sees something like the military as an oppressive force and not a liberatory force. And so the framework of disability rights cannot hold that kind of critique, because rights as a frame is about inclusion.

R: And also coming up to a level that is kind of owned by white supremacy. So then what are we aspiring to?

Liat: Exactly. So that's what I mean by the framework is white. It's not just about the color of the people doing it, although that's important, but it's a heteropatriarchal capitalist white framework.

R: When we're talking about decarceration and deinstitutionalization, how can people who have not been thinking about the disability justice perspective on it before—people who are doing parallel kinds of work, like stopping new jails—really include these deinstitutionalized logics into the work that they're doing?

> ... the most important thing is to be in community with people who are politicized as disabled, with people who do disability justice, with people who are part of anti-psychiatry, mad pride, consumer survivor ex-patient movements, people who are part of self-advocacy movements; you have to be onboarded with community.

Liat: *So I'm politicized as disabled, and in some ways it's a framework I got into because I had to. And I wasn't always politicized, like I was disabled, but I wasn't politicized until I was older, and it came from community. I think the most important thing is to be in community with people who are politicized as disabled, with people who do disability justice, with people who are part of anti-psychiatry, mad pride, consumer survivor ex-patient movements, people who are part of self-advocacy movements; you have to be onboarded with community. I think it's really important, especially people who are newly disabled or newly mad or newly medicalized or diagnosed or literally fell, you know, into this universe. I think that that's really important. Everything that I write about in the book I learned from community. I learned from activists, I learned from movements. I learned from people that were very generous with their wisdom and their kind of knowledge. This is true to all of us who were politicized by something. I don't think disability is different than any other form of politicization. It's only different in the sense that a lot of people don't see it as political. Maybe the only difference. So that's one on-ramp.*

The second one that I offer particularly in the book is that if people understand, even just analytically, that deinstitutionalization was about literally closing down carceral facilities and the attempt to abolish the logic of incarceration for a whole population of people, people with disabilities, then surely people will have some interest in learning about it. This could be intellectual curiosity. What did we do? How did we do it? What can we do better? What can we do different? What should we do different? What are the lessons? And that would be another point of entry.

Figure 11.1: *The Policing of Psychiatric Care* mini-zine by Clio Sady

Figure 11.2

Figure 11.3

Figure 11.4

Figure 11.5

12

CRISIS LIMITS

Toward Abolitionist Behavioral Health Infrastructures

BY NAOMI SCHOENFELD AND JENNIFER ESTEEN

Dedicated to the memory of Sam Dubal, MD, PhD. May his memories continue to be a blessing, inspiring radical acts of justice, kindness, and the radical transformation of our health-care systems Sam envisioned.

> Someone called 911 about a young woman lying face down on the ground outside the Starbucks in an upscale neighborhood known for multimillion-dollar homes in San Francisco. She wore a dirty white sweater and a denim skirt visibly soiled with feces. Breathing normally without signs of obvious injury, she looked like she had been outside for a few days, not months or years. I introduced myself and asked if she needed any help or medical care. She replied, "Get me a toilet." "OK I'll look into it, but I don't think I can do anything like that right now. You look like you might not be feeling well. Would you like to go to the hospital?" "No, but I need to clean up. Can you get me some wipes and clothes?" She refused other offers of help, so we eventually left. Later in the day, we are dispatched to the same location and, on arrival, find both an ambulance and a police car at the scene. Apparently, her unkempt presence in the upscale neighborhood triggered an escalation. This time she was transported to the ED [emergency department] where she was held for several hours before being released.

Crisis conveys urgency, implying life and death situations. Most countries across the globe have developed a three-digit phone number dispatch system to be used for acute crises or emergencies, like 911. In some cases, calling this three-digit number hails first responders, including police, paramedics, and firefighters, to respond to a situation. These calls might relate to urgent medical conditions like cardiac arrest, car accidents, fires, disaster, or active shooters. For some, especially those in whiter, wealthier communities, emergencies and crises are associated with the possibility of dialing 911 to hail emergency responders without fear. In contrast, for Black and Brown communities, hailing emergency responders via 911 is shaped by conditions of racial capitalism and is often fraught with a high probability of violence, even including death at the hands of responders. Within the context of a broader abolitionist project, in this chapter we examine the limits of the concept of crisis as a focal point for investment and intervention. We further offer the beginnings of an alternative vision for an abolitionist behavioral health practice.*

We are nurses with over three decades of combined experience working in the public health "safety net" with patients experiencing severe mental illness (SMI) and substance use disorder (SUD) in San Francisco. This chapter draws on our experience working in mobile crisis teams and in psychiatric emergency services (PES) as a nurse practitioner (NP) and registered nurse (RN), respectively. As new non-police crisis and psychiatric emergency programs proliferate, they warrant careful consideration and examination of the foundational assumptions underlying the rationale for their existence. Further, we

---

* In this chapter we use the term "behavioral health," a definition that considers the full spectrum of impacts from both mental health and substance use from stress, anxiety, depression, bipolar disorder, schizophrenia, and the acute and chronic effects of substance abuse. As clinicians, we often speak about behavioral health with this spectrum in mind, recognizing that there are processes at play that are internal to the mind and body with organic and genetic origins and there are processes at play that have external origins like the use of legal and illegal substances, stress impacts related to housing, finances, trauma, work life, relationships, abuse, etc. We attempt to discuss substance use explicitly, and there are times that a scenario includes both organic disease and substance use issues. From a policy perspective, there are often distinct needs as well as distinct funding mechanisms for treatment, and these respond to different political pressures at the local, county, state, and federal level.

need to ask what success looks like and whether they may inadvertently reproduce harm and violence.

San Francisco's new crisis response programs, with whom Naomi worked, are based out of the San Francisco Fire Department (SFFD) and are staffed by community paramedics. Most of the teams partner with the San Francisco Department of Public Health (SFDPH) and community-based organizations (CBOs) focused on behavioral health and substance abuse treatment. The Transitions Division and Psychiatric Emergency Services, where Jennifer worked, is the city's only such unit and is in the county hospital. Drawing on our experience, we consider how the concept of crisis frames the types of responses available and what other forms of care may be foreclosed by the crisis model. We draw from economic anthropologist Janet Roitman's[1, 2] work to consider how crisis framing may serve to perpetuate the conditions of its own existence. We offer a vision for abolitionist modes of behavioral health response and systems of care more aligned with achieving health justice than crisis response.

The term and concept of "crisis" appears frequently in health care and social services. An estimated 20 percent of 911 calls are initiated in response to situations involving the behavior of an individual presumed to be related to underlying mental health or substance use.[3, 4] When these behaviors occur in public spaces, they are often taken to constitute a "crisis." One of many atrocities of racist policing of Black and Brown communities includes violence against and murder of individuals and families in the midst of what is often described as a mental health crisis. This can include the murder of a person in crisis who dialed an emergency number or whose family dialed an emergency number. Increasing evidence reveals a disproportionate number of 911 calls made in response to these types of crises end in the police murder/killing of the individual experiencing symptoms of distress, following the same patterns of racialized policing targeting Black and Brown bodies. Mario Woods, Ma'Khia Bryant, Daniel Prude, and Sonya Massey[5, 6] are but a few recent examples of police murdering a Black individual in distress.

In the summer of 2020, the uprisings following the murder of George Floyd and the growth of the Black Lives Matter movement accelerated the pace of abolitionist organizing, including an amplification of calls for non-police alternatives for persons experiencing substance use and mental health crises such as the Movement for Black Lives' (M4BL) People's Response Act, which calls for the creation of federal funding for non-carceral first responders.[7] A growing number of non–law enforcement crisis response outreach and patrol programs are emerging in response to the social problem of public mental health distress and substance intoxication.[8] The proliferation of crisis response teams has been one strategy of organizers seeking to make an impact on the violence of police against persons who are suffering from mental health challenges or who might be using substances. At face value, these programs seem aligned with calls to reduce police involvement in behavioral health struggles. Yet, behavioral health workers and professionals operate within systems governed by similar carceral logics and biases. The history and ongoing tragedy of medical racism and its attendant violence exacted on Black and Brown bodies means that programs of health worker–based crisis response are not exempt from exacting their own forms of violence on marginalized communities, sometimes with tragic consequences. The death of Elijah McClain in 2019 in Aurora, Colorado, injected with ketamine by paramedics in response to racial profiling and policing of mental illness, is a tragic example of the blurred lines between medicalized and carceral first-response programs.[9] In San Francisco, crisis programs recently received significantly increased funding from new taxes levied on the tech industry in response to political pressures around the visibility of homelessness.[10]

"Crisis Ordinary" Patrol

As of May 2022, San Francisco has five mental and behavioral crisis response teams, three of which are specifically dedicated to responding to crisis/ordinary events on the street.[11] One of these teams, the Mobile

Crisis Team, is based out of the San Francisco Department of Public Health.* The other four teams are based out of the San Francisco Fire Department, partnered with health and social service workers. The SFFD teams include the Street Crisis Response Team (SCRT), which responds to behavioral crises and is staffed by a paramedic, a peer advocate, and a mental health clinician; Street Wellness is staffed by paramedics who are tasked with checking in on people experiencing homelessness (PEH) who appear to have some level of distress but not have a medical or psychiatric emergency; the Street Overdose Response Team (SORT) responds to drug overdoses; and the original community paramedic program, EMS6, is designed for the highest utilizers of 911 to avert medically unnecessarily transports to the ED when possible.[12] These programs were not developed in response to existing evidence or best practices. Instead, they were created in response to political pressures and opportunities with the goal of cost savings. They were also able to capitalize on existing infrastructure of paramedic cars and trucks within the SFFD, as well as available 24/7 personnel.

The SFFD teams receive general 911 dispatch calls, as well as calls from a variety of clinicians and service providers ranging from ED social workers and physicians to substance use centers, unsheltered individuals, and even bystanders who report perceived emergencies and crises on the street. The teams are highly visible as they mobilize in firetruck-red SUVs and vans driving around the city or parked at hospitals or clinics. EMS6 has a rotating list of the top utilizers of 911 prehospital services, known as "high utilizers of medical services" (HUMS)—people with SUD or SMI about whom bystanders frequently call 911 or repeatedly call 911 for help. People who drink or use heavily, and are often publicly intoxicated and at risk, occupy the top slots on the HUMS list. The situations in which

---

* Mobile Crisis is an interprofessional clinician-run service for adults in San Francisco. Our experience over nearly two decades is that San Francisco's Mobile Crisis Team has had a significant decrease in availability and increase in response times. We do not have data but suspect that funding has not kept pace with demand. In San Francisco the SFFD programs seem to be supplanting these clinician-run teams.

EMS6 paramedics work with their clients are acute episodes within the context of chronic health and social suffering. Each engagement almost always involves something described as a mental health or substance-induced "crisis." Visible intoxication among PEH, which would otherwise go unnoticed behind closed doors by those with resources, and intensification of auditory hallucinations—"voices"—provoked by substances, hunger, stress, lack of access to care are among the spikes that draw attention and the resources of the crisis team. The programs were created to cut costs by circumventing possibly unnecessary and expensive ED visits from HUMS clients, to develop what they call a "prehospital" management plan. Mark Fleming and his colleagues argue that the HUMS designation for high-cost patients parallels racialized constructions of "users" of public services. They suggest that these patients are seen as both "objects for intervention" and "objects for containment,"[13] requiring intervention and cost control. Many of these calls and responses occur instead of a response by police officers. In other words, HUMS are people associated with high costs of care because they rely on crisis services to provide the majority of care, and sometimes housing, they need but are unable to access elsewhere. In turn, they are labeled as an expensive "drain on the system," which has failed to provide preventive and holistic long-term interventions instead of repetitive, expensive, and never-ending cycles of crisis care.

San Francisco's street crisis programs work closely with other clinics and centers charged with providing crisis care, including EDs, urgent care centers, and even an alcohol sobering center. The teams are typically activated for people experiencing symptoms associated with SMI or the effects of significant intoxication with alcohol or drugs. Most often, the range is between psychosis and intoxication, often both are present and difficult to distinguish. Services include dropping off clients, following up on existing clients, or finding new ones. Sometimes it involves a lot of driving around and waiting for things to happen; it often involves complex coordination between systems of care and services, de-escalation, and creative problem-solving, when it works well.

In what follows, Naomi describes a typical day with community paramedics:

Since 2020, I've worked alongside or in collaboration with all four SFFD crisis teams, but the bulk of my experience is with EMS6. On a typical day, our work revolves around treating people with SMI and SUD. Methamphetamines, opioids, alcohol, and benzodiazepines like Xanax and Klonopin are the most commonly involved substances in the scenarios to which we are called. On one day of driving around the streets of San Francisco, the "crisis" work includes de-escalation and providing basic first-aid provisions of ibuprofen or bandages and offering bottles of water. When resources allow, we offer army-style self-heating meals when available, used clothes we happen to have, and nutritional shakes. Here's what a day might look like, according to a typical crisis schedule.

08:30—My paramedic partner picks me up at the public health headquarters in his red SFFD SUV. We compare agendas and negotiate starting routes and timelines of who to check in on as we wait for calls to come in.

08:45—It's early in the pandemic; we go to follow up on COVID outbreaks in encampments. We talk to people and ask about COVID symptoms. Nobody has symptoms; a few people are interested in getting a supply of Narcan, the opioid overdose reversal drug.[14]

09:30—We respond to a call and go out to one of the local EDs about an intoxicated man with diabetes experiencing homelessness and decide to head over. This ED is in an affluent neighborhood where most patients have private insurance. They are less accustomed to caring for people experiencing homelessness than the county hospital or the downtown hospitals. They want to discharge the patient but don't know of any community resources that can help him. After interviewing him, we determine that he has a trailer at one of the COVID shelter-in-place (SIP) sites and he is amenable to returning there once he sobers up. We leave.

11:00—We are dispatched from 911 to find a young man masturbating in public. He exhibits signs of psychosis, including responding to internal stimuli and perseveration. I suspect he is high on methamphetamines. We engage him in conversation, asking where he's from, what he needs, and about connecting to shelter. He declines our offers of shelter or referrals and eventually pulls up his pants and walks away. Just then, a well-known, long-time HUMS client, Freddy [pseudonym], stumbles off the bus right in front of us. He is covered in urine, disoriented, surly, and smelling strongly of alcohol. Freddy hasn't been seen by our team for some time, so this is serendipitous. Our conversation starts off tense because he is irritable and generally angry. We're able to get him talking about music, and he gets expansive, regaling us with tales of past lives as a touring musician. But Freddy is completely disoriented, stumbling, and not safe. He wants to go inside. He has vague symptoms. Today, during the pandemic, we have few options besides sending him to the ED.

14:00—We arrive at a homeless shelter to respond to a young woman gesticulating enthusiastically and yelling about her work with NASA and "the grand conspiracy at play." She's on methamphetamines, and the shelter staff is concerned that, during the midst of the COVID-19 pandemic, she won't keep her mask on or adhere to social distance guidelines. They're attempting to continue offering her services and avoid discharging her or calling the police when her agitation increases. She's sitting down in the main area indoors, talking loudly, spitting due to her pressured speech (which is additionally risky during the current COVID outbreak). I ask her to walk and talk with me outside so we can problem-solve together. I'm hoping we can buy her some time to "metabolize"—parlance I learned from ED physicians—and regain self-control.

16:00—The county hospital calls us to come and engage a young man experiencing homelessness who is high on methamphetamine. He reportedly witnessed the murder of his friend (this is determined to be a paranoid delusion). We walk into the ED and join nurses, doctors, social workers, and other members of the team. This young man is literally covered in green and purple paint from his hair to his feet. The resident has no plan for the patient other than saying, "He just needs to metabolize for a few hours." In the midst of the busy, urban safety-net hospital, we were summoned in the hopes that we

*can help piece together some support or solution in the community so that
he can leave the ED and free up space and time for "real emergencies." The
notion that a roving NP and paramedic might have solutions not available to
the hospital is paradoxical and yet often true. We frequently act as a bridge
from the hospital to community settings and have a lot of connections. When
things work well, our motley crew comes together to create a solution; it often
feels like a miracle.*

While this "crisis schedule" is an amalgamation of visits, it's representative of a typical day I had with the crisis team. Over my one and
a half years with the program, I developed tremendous respect for the
community paramedics who make this work happen. These community
paramedics know their managed clients well. They are personally invested
in doing whatever is necessary to help get them stabilized, far beyond the
usual way of thinking about EMS stabilization. It may involve picking up
and dropping off medicines, bringing food, bringing cigarettes, finding
housing, calling a long-lost family member, working all the angles, and
even relying on connections to get clients readmitted to medical detox
facilities from which they were previously banned.

These public sector crisis teams have earned the trust of many community partners and, most importantly, they earned the trust of the
clients they work with over weeks or even years. The team members
respond to emergencies from multiple callers, including police, EMS providers, nurses, and doctors. They are trained and expected to respond
to life-threatening situations in accordance with established protocols.
Operating under the aegis of emergency affords SFFD paramedics a large
degree of latitude in problem-solving. Their official status and recognition as part of the SFFD affords them wide access, yet their role as
community paramedics demands a labor that is akin to case management.
The SFFD crisis teams are hailed most frequently by people who have no
other recourse for help other than calling 911. Yet the calls they receive
are usually not in response to an emergency, but in response to failures
or social voids. Street crisis response teams function as a technological
substitute for other forms of human social relations. As outlined in the

following section, the crisis mode can set off a cascade of events that often produce new and violent social responses, wreaking havoc on Black and Brown bodies.

Handcuffed for a Refill

Jennifer worked in the San Francisco County Hospital as a psychiatric RN in PES from 2010 to 2016, and then on a behavioral health placement team (now called Residential System of Care) from 2016 to today. The county hospital has the city's only dedicated 24/7 psychiatric emergency room; it is therefore almost always running over capacity.[15] Here Jenn describes a memorable but not unusual day.

While working in PES on a Tuesday morning, the bell rang, alerting us to the arrival of a patient. As usual, two uniformed San Francisco Police Department (SFPD) officers came through the door with a handcuffed young man in tow. This patient's presentation was calm, clean, and oriented to time, location, and purpose; he had no obvious psychosis and didn't seem to be in overt crisis, a much-needed relief after a frantic first few hours of the day. The stated reason for being placed on a 5150,* according to the police, was that he called 911, saying, "If I don't get meds, I'll kill myself or kill someone else." This kind of presentation appeared to be a mismatch. Here was a man that appeared cool and calm with a relatively clean exterior, but he was threatening suicide or homicide. I removed his handcuffs, asked a few standard clarifying questions of the officers, then sent them on their way. Once the police left, I assessed his vital signs all while doing my standard invisible nursing assessment with my senses on high alert. I touched his skin to check for pain, fever, and integrity; visually scanned his body, clothing, and gait to assess hygiene and for signs of injury; I smelled him, another hygiene

---

* *5150* refers to the California legal code that allows for the involuntary psychiatric commitment of someone who is deemed a danger to themselves or others due to a mental health crisis..

assessment; and I spoke with him to listen for the rhythm of his voice. All of this took place during the sixty seconds required to get his pulse, blood pressure, and respirations recorded.

Noting his continued calm, we entered the interview room. The man calmly explained that he is a client at a community clinic and needed a medication refill to avoid falling into a spiral of deep depression, which his meds have treated and prevented for many years. But he couldn't get access to the clinic because of a change in his housing status. He explained that he lost his housing three weeks prior, after breaking up with his boyfriend of several years. As a result, he slept in a shelter for two days, but after being threatened multiple times then having his belongings stolen while he was in the shower, he gave up on the shelter. He went to his mental health clinic to get an appointment to replace his meds but was told it was too soon for a refill and he could only get an emergency refill after seeing the psychiatrist, who had no appointments for another several weeks. Without a cell phone or address he had no way to follow up and had been struggling to keep his spirits up. He further shared that last night he was almost raped while walking around to stay awake. People have been offering him meth and cocaine to stay awake and heroin to sleep away his worries, but he isn't into drugs and doesn't want to develop an addiction. His work as a chef is in jeopardy because he's been sleeping during breaks and is so tired that he's also messed up people's food multiple times. The only clear request stated, aside from housing, which is a resource PES does not have to offer, is to get an emergency medication refill that can last him at least forty-five days until he sees his psychiatrist and/or help him secure an earlier appointment at the clinic.

Unfortunately, both of these reasonable requests fall outside the scope of what we offer in our crisis response system. The protocol for emergency meds is that we medicate while patients are in PES, and sometimes under dire circumstances we issue a five-day supply but almost never a full-month's refill. We also do not have a mechanism to schedule people for clinic appointments and cannot fast track people into the clinic system. I did have the ability to offer this patient a two-week stay in an acute diversion unit (ADU) where he can get respite from the street and sleep, but there are daily groups during the time he normally works. Having a job and staying in an ADU are not aligned and technically against the rules of the program. This means the only option my crisis services can offer my severely depressed client is a two-week program that will cause him to potentially lose his job and a five-day supply of medication even though he needs a forty-five-day supply.

Restrained for a Cigarette

"I want to smoke; I need a cigarette," repeated the fifty-seven-year-old woman banging on the locked door of the seclusion room in psychiatric emergency services (PES). Deborah [pseudonym] arrived at PES from the mental health rehabilitation center after staff told her she couldn't smoke in the locked unit, and she responded by banging on a table repeatedly. Now locked in PES, staff prepare restraints and injectable medications to be forcibly administered.

Ordinary Emergencies

Jennifer's experience as an RN in PES and Naomi's work as an NP with street crisis units highlight the limits of crisis and emergency as frameworks and infrastructures for addressing symptoms and impacts of SUD and SMI disproportionately impacting poor, Black, and Brown communities. Anthropologist Sharon Kaufman's *Ordinary Medicine* focused on the extraordinary measures to prolong the very end of life for geriatric patients on Medicare in intensive care units (ICUs), examining the ethical, cultural, and political influences and who benefits from the *standardization* of extraordinary medical intervention.[16] Kaufman's research shows how interventions conceived as responses to life-threatening events become ordinary, increasingly offered as life-prolonging interventions at the end of life.

Our work as safety-net nurses in behavioral crisis settings reveals a related logic. We see the materiality of crisis vehicles on patrol as a highly visible sign that something is being done, even if that something is intervening in a momentary way that is unlikely to have any long-term impact. That is not to say that the first responder crisis programs don't do good work. But the tools they have to work with are inadequate to the job at hand. In street crisis and PES, the mechanics and structures of emergency are marshaled in the service of addressing chronic problems of systemic and structural neglect and violence.

Our work in the safety net of street crisis and PES in San Francisco aligns with Armando Lara-Millan's archival and ethnographic research in Los Angeles. He argues that the county hospital and county jail are administratively linked through a continuum of budgetary machinations tasked with "redistributing the poor" out of jails and into hospitals, or vice versa, "disappearing" poverty and suffering through administrative channels.[17] Lara-Millan shows how police coordinate with sanitation and health workers to shuffle PEH between spaces like jails and hospitals. In our own clinical terrain, we see the exact same kind of shuffling, justified in the name of crisis response.

Our daily work in crisis and emergency response settings reveals the crisis/ordinary[*] consequence of systemic disinvestment in robust, community-oriented support for SMI and SUD, together with policies which further entrench the root causes, like poverty, lack of housing, and other impacts of racial capitalism. The framing of these ordinary events as crises, and the proliferation of a crisis and emergency apparatus, is another, flashier, form of "disappearing." Crisis response does not set out to transform the conditions of its creation. Instead, carceral logics wait in the wings for its inevitable failure.

---

[*] "Crisis ordinary" is a concept developed by Lauren Berlant in her book *Cruel Optimism*. She describes it as "not exceptional to history or consciousness but a process embedded in the ordinary that unfolds in stories about navigating what's overwhelming (2011:10).

Anti-Crisis

Anthropologist Janet Roitman developed a theorization of crisis following many years of fieldwork in central Africa, after noting the long-standing and persistent analyses of Africa in terms of crisis.[18,19] She argues,

> The claim to crisis is a political claim because it is a judgment about value as opposed to an observation of error. Despite the presumption that crisis does not imply, in itself, a definite direction of change—that it doesn't predict an outcome, partake of an ideology of progress or entail linear causality—it does imply a certain telos. That is, it is inevitably though most often implicitly directed towards a norm. Evoking crisis entails reference to a norm because it requires a comparative state for judgment: Crisis compared to what? Compared to what alternative state of affairs?[20]

Following Roitman, we are concerned about the framework of crisis as a focal point for intervention in mental health and substance abuse. While our experiences as nurses working in settings currently defined by crisis reveal some possibilities for creative interventions, crisis temporality demands short-term fixes, often foreclosing the possibility for more effective, long-term solutions. Programs designed to identify and intervene in behavioral health crises depend on a steady source of ongoing crises to continue justifying their existence.

> [T]he concept of crisis is an enabling blind spot for the production of knowledge . . . But if we take crisis to be a blind spot—or a distinction, which makes certain things visible and others invisible . . . it should be noted that this does not amount to denying crisis. The point is to take note of the effects of the claim to crisis, to be attentive to the effects of our very accession to that judgment . . . claims to crisis potentially serve to reestablish the status quo."[21]

Our experience suggests the framework of crisis renders "ordinary" the conditions undergirding the circumstances behind what gets framed as crisis: racial capitalism and systematic disinvestment in equitable and accessible behavioral health infrastructures. Our work in PES and street crisis teams leads us to question the prominent space occupied by crisis as both a focal point for increased public funding but also as an abolitionist organizing principle. Acute presentations of SMI and substance intoxication can elicit an emergent response under certain conditions determined by societal norms. The aim is to quell the crisis, to remove it temporarily from the public eye, while the longer-term structural problems underlying the acute exacerbations are left unaddressed.

The political demand to remove police from responding to situations framed as behavioral health crises, whether due to underlying psychiatric disorder or substance use, is urgent and necessary. Yet, the framework of crises emphasizes quick and temporary interventions that do nothing to address the urgent unmet needs of millions of persons suffering from un- or undertreated SMI and SUD, especially those without shelter or in abysmal housing conditions, without good jobs and social support. Teams designated as crisis responders, whether on the streets or in spaces like PES, often encounter situations that are not best responded to as crises/ emergencies. Chronically underfunded and inadequate mental health services across the country create the conditions in which police are often the first to respond to someone in a mental health or substance use crisis.

The framing of acute expressions of chronic conditions as crises could be thought of as a distraction or, to use Roitman's concept of crisis, as a "blind spot." The proliferation of street crisis programs is, on the one hand, clearly a significant improvement in comparison to any police response to people experiencing distress related to substance use or mental health challenges. The community paramedics of the SFFD offer an interesting model in contrast to other analyses of paramedics' roles at the border of security and health. Unlike the precariat workforce studied by sociologist Josh Seim working for private ambulance companies, SFFD paramedics enjoy relatively high wages, job stability, the possibility for career advancement, and pensions.[22] This structure of high-quality jobs with good benefits and opportunities for advancement offers an important counterpoint to the widespread problem of the private and nonprofit sector of behavioral health in maintaining adequate staffing in the face of low wages and high stress jobs resulting in high turnover, and an economically precarious workforce. These staffing challenges similarly impact non-professional or peer-led crisis response by some advocates who favor peer over professional responders.[23] Yet both the peer and the professional crisis response models focus attention on quick interventions, which do little to stem chronic suffering.

Toward Abolitionist Behavioral Health: Community-Based Care and Solidarity

Our experience of work in crisis and emergency settings shows that investing in crisis does not make us safer. Crisis response may appeal to politicians who want to publicly demonstrate a response. Crisis commands attention. Yet its urgent temporality casts a shadow and obscures the chronic suffering undergirding acute episodes. Following Roitman,[24,25] our experience suggests that crisis begets crisis. Abolitionist organizing for non-police alternatives to SMI and substance abuse can be strengthened by focusing on broad investment in community-based support and significant expansion of easily accessible and free mental health care and substance use treatment, with massive expansion of clinics, programs, and housing.

California has significant financial resources invested in mental health (MH) care and spends the most on behavioral health care in the nation, $6,762,808,997.[26] Yet despite this massive spending, we see an increase in the number of people visibly suffering on the street and cycling through crisis services. We need more pathways to exit crisis care. We have a shortage of providers in the public health system,[27] and behavioral health workers face chronic understaffing, overwork, and inadequate compensation.[28, 29, 30] Often, when providers have a choice between working in either a public or a private system that doesn't truly support their work, their patients, and prevention, many opt out of working within systems and instead branch out to work in private practice where they can offer patients care that is dignified and designed to benefit the people they serve over time. This leads to even greater inequity because a growing number of providers are not taking public or private insurance, offering care paid for in cash, out of reach for those without financial resources to pay out of pocket.[31, 32, 33] Those reliant on public health options and even private options covered by HMO and PPO insurers find themselves waiting for weeks or months for an intake or appointment to initiate care or see their regular provider. Weekly talk therapy, the gold standard in ongoing MH care, especially for those taking meds, is usually not available. When meds are prescribed, the insurer formulary forces prescribers to steer clients into medication trials that are based on financial formulas rather than client needs.

We envision supporting students and trainees who plan to work with historically marginalized communities, covering the cost of their education and offering them access to training that pays a living wage while working toward licensure, ensuring that clinicians have a job that continues to pay a living wage with supported working conditions and ongoing training and support. This is a baseline to create a healthy provider workforce that can provide dignified care. We need a massive expansion of care options to include fully funded acute interventions with options for telephone-based help, warm lines, suicide hotlines, and a teen support line with real people to talk with 24/7. These can be staffed by any number of people, including but not limited to, clinicians, seniors, youth, peers, and family members who have loved ones who are impacted by mental illness. Other supports like outreach teams can visit people where they live, even if that's on the street, and can respond to emergent and everyday calls.* We need to expand easily accessible psychiatric emergency rooms, urgent care, and same-day non-urgent care, fully staffed and open in every community. Preventive and ongoing care needs expansion with adequate staffing in community-based mental health and substance abuse clinics, primary care clinics, in schools, and in *resilience hubs* that act as a one-stop shop for myriad behavioral health care and community needs. This care will need to serve folks who have SMI and those who are considered to be in mild to moderate need. Funding mechanisms for these care options need to be reimagined so that systems are not

---

* The STAR Program in Denver, Colorado, is one such crisis response model.

incentivized to provide more care for those who can pay and less care for those without financial resources.

For both mental health, including SMI, and substance use, we envision robust multi-level systems of solidarity, harm reduction, and culturally appropriate, evidence-based treatment on demand designed by, accessible to, and prioritized for those who have been historically marginalized and excluded by medical racism and systemic exclusion. Instead of an army of red vans patrolling for crisis, we envision each neighborhood having fully staffed and easily accessible day programs where people can go to social-ize, take meds, and have human interactions in a safe, clean supervised healthy setting seven days a week. Treatment options must be made read-ily available on demand and should include residential living for terms as short as one day up to one year, so that people can stabilize and resume a regular daily schedule while also exploring options for work, job training, and permanent housing. Abolitionist behavioral health also includes mas-sive expansion of supported housing options that are permanent and do not have restrictions that hamper people's ability to work, attend school or training, and maintain healthy contact with family and friends.

Instead of focusing efforts on crisis response, we envision abolitionist behavioral health as an expansive network of care and solidarity. Crisis can be a rallying cry, but our experience shows that crisis is likely to fail as an organizing principle for a robust, community-oriented abolition-ist approach to mental illness and substance abuse. Instead, we need a radical remaking of behavioral health, centered around and designed by the very communities historically marginalized and victimized by the medico-carceral systems constituting our mainstream approach to behav-ioral health today.

CHAPTER 12 NOTES

1. Roitman, J. (2013). *Anti-Crisis*. Duke University Press.
2. Roitman, J., Angeli Aguiton, S., Cornilleau, L., and Cabane. L. (2020). "Anti-Crisis: Thinking with and against Crisis Excerpt from Interview

with Janet Roitman." *Journal of Cultural Economy* 13 (6),772–78. https://
doi.org/10.1080/17530350.2020.1807388.

3. Abramson, A. (2021), "Building Mental Health into Emergency
   Responses." *Forensics, Law and Public Safety*. https://www.apa.org/monitor
   /2021/07/emergency-responses.

4. Westervelt, E. (2020). "Mental Health and Police Violence: How Crisis
   Intervention Teams Are Failing." *NPR*, September 18, 2020, sec. National.
   https://www.npr.org/2020/09/18/913229469/mental-health-and
   -police-violence-how-crisis-intervention-teams-are-failing.

5. Mark, J. (2020). "Officers Who Killed Mario Woods Used 'Unnecessary
   Force'—but Will Face No Discipline." *Mission Local*, September 10, 2020.
   https://missionlocal.org/2020/09/officers-who-killed-mario-woods
   -used-unnecessary-force-but-will-face-no-discipline/ - :~:text=The
   Department of Police Accountability,no policies at the time.

6. Mubarak, Eman, Victoria Turner, Andrew G. Shuman, Janice Firn, and
   Daicia Price. "Promoting Antiracist Mental Health Crisis Responses."
   AMA Journal of Ethics 24, no. 8 (August 1, 2022): E788-794. https://doi
   .org/10.1001/amajethics.2022.788.

7. M4BL. "The Movement for Black Lives Announces Support for the
   People's Response Act." June 29, 2021. https://m4bl.org/press/support
   -for-the-peoples-response-act/.

8. Climer, B, and Gicker, B. (2021). "CAHOOTS: A Model for Prehospital
   Mental Health Crisis Intervention." *Psychiatric Times* 38, no. 1.

9. Lampen, C. (2021). "What We Know about the Killing of Elijah McClain."
   The Cut. Accessed May 14, 2022. https://www.thecut.com/2021/09
   /the-killing-of-elijah-mcclain-everything-we-know.html.

10. sfmayor.org, (2020). https://sfmayor.org/article/mayor-london-breed
    -announces-plan-create-behavioral-health-street-crisis-response-team.

11. Berlant, L. (2011). "Crisis Ordinary." *Cruel Optimism*. Duke University
    Press.

12. Tangherlini, N., Villar, J., Brown, J., Rodriguez, R. M., Yeh, C., Friedman,
    B. T., and Wada, P. (2016). "The HOME Team: Evaluating the Effect of
    an EMS-Based Outreach Team to the Frequency of 911 Use among
    High Utilizers of EMS." *Prehospital and Disaster Medicine* 31, no. 6, 603–7.
    https://doi.org/10.1017/S1049023X16000790.

13. Fleming, M. D., Shim, J. K., Yen, I., Dubbin, L., Thompson-Lastad, A.,
    Hanssmann, C., and Burke, N. J. (2021). "Managing the 'Hot Spots.'"

American Ethnologist 48, no. 4, 474–88. https://doi.org/10.1111/amet
.13032.

14. Campbell, Nancy D. (2020). *OD: Naloxone and the Politics of Overdose.*
    MIT Press.

15. Johnson, S. (2022). "S.F.'s Emergency Psych Unit Faces Dire Conditions."
    San Francisco Examiner, April 4, 2022. Accessed May 14, 2022. https://
    www.sfexaminer.com/archives/s-f-s-emergency-psych-unit-faces
    -dire-conditions/article_12878a56-e5aa-542c-8d3c-6ede94550311.html.

16. Kaufman, S. (2015). *Ordinary Medicine: Extraordinary Treatments, Longer
    Lives, and Where to Draw the Line.* Duke University Press.

17. Lara-Millan, A. (2021). *Redistributing the Poor: Jails, Hospitals, and the Crisis
    of Law and Fiscal Austerity.* Oxford, New York: Oxford University Press.

18. Roitman. *Anti-Crisis.*

19. Roitman, Angeli Aguiton, Cornilleau, and Cabane. "Anti-Crisis."

20. Roitman, Angeli Aguiton, Cornilleau, and Cabane. "Anti-Crisis."

21. Roitman, Angeli Aguiton, Cornilleau, and Cabane. "Anti-Crisis"

22. Seim, J. (2020). *Bandage, Sort, and Hustle: Ambulance Crews on the Front
    Lines of Urban Suffering.* University of California Press.

23. Carroll, J., Taleed El-Sabawi, T., Fichter, D., Pope, L., Rafia-Yuan, E.,
    Compton, M., and Watson, A. (2021). "The Workforce for Non-Police
    Behavioral Health Crisis Response Doesn't Exist—We Need to Create It."
    Health Affairs. https://www.healthaffairs.org/do/10.1377/forefront
    .20210903.856934/full/

24. Roitman. *Anti-Crisis.*

25. Roitman, Angeli Aguiton, Cornilleau, and Cabane. "Anti-Crisis."

26. SAMHSA. (2019). "Behavioral Health Spending & Use Accounts,
    2006–2015." SAMHSA Publications and Digital Products." Accessed
    May 14, 2022. https://store.samhsa.gov/product/Behavioral-Health
    -Spending-and-Use-Accounts-2006-2015/SMA19-5095.

27. Seim. *Bandage, Sort, and Hustle.*

28. Coffman, J, Bates, T., Geyn, I., and Spetz, J. "California's Current and
    Future Behavioral Health Workforce." (2018). *Healthforce Center at UCSF.*
    Accessed May 14, 2022. https://healthforce.ucsf.edu/publications
    /california-s-current-and-future-behavioral-health-workforce.

29. Phillips, Lindsey. (2023). "A Closer Look at the Mental Health Provider
    Shortage." *Counseling Today.* Accessed December 5, 2023. https://www
    .counseling.org/publications/counseling-today-magazine/article-archive
    /article/legacy/a-closer-look-at-the-mental-health-provider-shortage.

30. sfmayor.org. (2022). "San Francisco Hires 100 Public Health Workers under Streamlined Hiring Process." Office of the Mayor. Accessed May 14, 2022. https://sfmayor.org/article/san-francisco-hires-100-public -health-workers-under-streamlined-hiring-process.

31. ECRI. (2022). "ECRI Reports Staffing Shortages and Clinician Mental Health Are Top Threats to Patient Safety." Accessed May 14, 2022. https://home.ecri.org/blogs/ismp-news/ecri-reports-staffing-shortages -and-clinician-mental-health-are-top-threats-to-patient-safety.

32. Peterson, Andrea. (2021). "Why It's So Hard to Find a Therapist Who Takes Insurance - WSJ." *Wall Street Journal.* Accessed May 14, 2022. https://www.wsj.com/articles/why-its-so-hard-to-find-a-therapist -who-takes-insurance-11633442400.

33. LoCicero, A. (2019). "Can't Find a Psychologist Who Accepts Insurance? Here's Why." *Psychology Today.* Accessed May 14, 2022. https://www .psychologytoday.com/us/blog/paradigm-shift/201905/cant-find -psychologist-who-accepts-insurance-heres-why.

13
CONCLUSION
Abolitionism for Health-Care Workers

BY RONICA MUKERJEE AND CARLOS MARTINEZ

"When security culture prevails, are communities healthier?"

Part 1A: Suffering Is Linked with the Business of Health Care

As idealism-fueled clinicians know, once we leave school, we are not rewarded for the reduction of patient suffering. In truth, the alleviation of suffering may be the wrong goal to teach future health-care professionals working in the existing system. For several decades, health-care systems have been focusing on profit-making. This is managed through increasing volume, getting patients out of the building, and billing to the highest degree possible. When patients display behaviors or reveal histories that inconvenience health-care workers, relying on the powers of the carceral state seems like the easiest response to simply get them out of the hospital or clinic. It is not so much that clinicians think of the profit margins first, but clinic schedules are often packed in ways that ensure that patients are pushed out the door, one way or another, when they are perceived as bothersome or threatening. Medicine delivery is no longer synonymous with caring for the underserved or sick. No one asks what it means to be skillful in health care, as clinical staff are forced into the well-worn auto-pilot mode of the worker they replaced. Community health care has also become a series of Medicaid mills where clinicians are punished for not practicing fast enough and not seeing enough volume. Carceral methods are well suited to this type of environment, increasing the safety of the profit-making machine.

The wielding of suffering within prison, jail, and detention to teach a lesson through cruelty and discipline is a method to isolate and punish already marginalized groups of people because they have ostensibly violated a social contract. At times, poorly addressed mental health issues or physical issues like poorly treated chronic pain can be the reason that people become victims of carceral scrutiny. We know health-care workers are active in pushing people into police and detention officials' hands. But clinicians must question: How can suffering do anything but increase harm? When we induce suffering through incarceration, the impacts are exponential.

The carceral propagation of suffering produces wide community effects that have been well documented. In one study conducted in New York City, neighborhoods with high incarceration rates also had disproportionately high rates of diabetes, psychiatric hospitalizations, people with unmet medical needs, infant mortality, and early mortality.[1] The evidence provided by this and other studies make clear that individuals, families, and communities are often affected by repeated exposures to the trauma of incarceration, and poorer communities always experience a greater burden with these traumas with far fewer resources for dealing with the outcomes.

Part 1B: Race and the Business of Health

Even if our patients have not recently been incarcerated, we still must deal with carceral harms when their communities are burdened by high incarceration rates. We know that overall life expectancy in the United States is lowered by at least two years due to our country's high rate of incarceration.[2] We also know that the burden of this mortality is much greater in Black, Latinx, and Native communities while there are not enough Black, Latinx, and Native providing clinical care.

As Figure 13.1 demonstrates, in terms of prescribing clinicians, 66 percent of physicians are white,[3] 80 percent of nurse practitioners and nurse midwives are white,[4] and 76 percent of physician assistants are white.[5, 6] Though there is a higher percentage of non-white physicians, this largely consists of Chinese, Indian, and other Asian physicians, who make up approximately 22 percent of physicians and are not underrepresented in medicine.[7, 8] Additionally, most physicians come from the top-income quintile, while data on other clinicians is sparse but likely to reflect lower class background origin.[9] Physicians, who are often the best-paid clinicians, economically benefit from the punitive, expert-obsessed clinical culture and a castigatory environment that medicine has been historically steeped in. This punitive attitude is often passed down to nurses, medical assistants, and the people running the front desk. We clinicians lord over our patients but also enact this punitive culture on one another—replicating moralities that only very privileged people benefit from while punishing the people with the least access to resources and education. We have to challenge the cop in our clinician's heads.

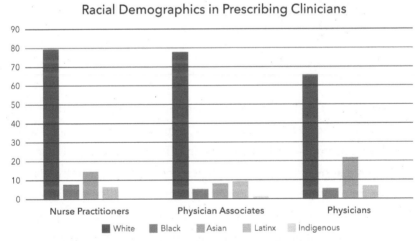

Figure 13.1: Racial demographics of prescribing clinicians[10, 11, 12, 13, 14]

Black, Latinx, and Native people are underrepresented as clinicians, particularly when contrasted with their numbers in the general population (Figure 13.2). While white people make up about three-quarters of the population, Black people constitute 14 percent. Asian people are 6 percent, Latinx people are 19 percent, and Indigenous people are slightly more than 1 percent of the population. In contrast, in the prescribing clinician population, Asians are overrepresented; white people are robustly represented; and Black, Latinx, and Native peoples are grossly underrepresented. It matters when the most-targeted racial groups are not providing health-care services because clinician solidarity with the patient does not reflect cultural understanding or even a clear understanding of racialized harms.

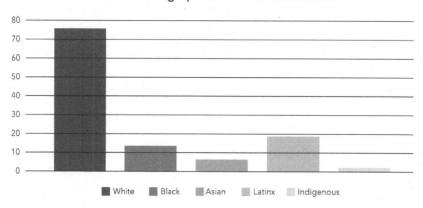

Figure 13.2: Racial demographics of the United States[15]

Unsurprisingly, the general population does not reflect the prison population either. Prisons are equally populated by Black and white peoples (about one-third each), although Black people are 14 percent of the population and whites are 76 percent of the population). Prisons contain more than triple the number of Latinx people than in the general population (Figure 13.2 and Figure 13.3). Queer and trans people, as well as people with disabilities, are wildly underrepresented in the provision of health care. The American Academy of Physicians estimates that 3 percent of physicians in family practice are LGBTQ+ (much lower than the general population),[16] while 12 percent of physician associates and nurse practitioners identify as LGBTQ+, higher than the general population.[17, 18]

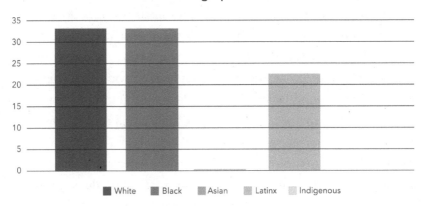

Figure 13.3: Racial demographics in prison[19]

Part 2A: Making the Case for Resisting Borders

The US health-care system must invest more in the health care of irregularly migrated people and workers. The inscrutable nature of borders makes immigrant-supporting abolitionist transformation difficult; however, most of us understand our clinical environments well enough to see what changes are needed to create borderless care in health-care centers that serve immigrant populations. This is especially true for clinics one hundred miles or less from the border.

The US-Mexico border affects the life expectancy of people living on the US side as much as it affects the health of migrants waiting in Mexico. A study published in 2021 found a clear connection between increased mortality and the border itself. On the US-Mexico border, where there are one and a half times more Latinx people than in other parts of the United States, Native and Latinx populations lived approximately two years less than Native and Latinx populations nationwide on average.[20] Could this be related to the stressors related to the border patrol's arrest and deportation reach, which occurs anywhere within one hundred miles of the external boundaries of the United States?[21] All of this American safety through border enforcement is killing us even within the borders of the United States.

Approximately half of hired farmworkers, 10 percent of all restaurant workers, and 40 percent of urban restaurant workers do not have authorization to work in the United States and are not legally eligible for Medicaid or other tax-related benefits. These workers often pay what is effectively a higher tax rate than restaurant workers with citizenship without those health-care benefits.[22] To practice social justice-informed care of these community members, we need to understand the ways that these health industries can affect people's health. These health-affecting variables include exposure to toxic chemicals; harsh environments (agricultural fields or food processing facilities); and employer harms, including harassment, threats, and coercion; as well as overworking without recourse.[23, 24]

In a 2021 article on the Harris Health System (HHS) in Houston, Texas, the author explored how HHS legally affected the lives of low-income undocumented migrants as they sought long-term care services. As a result of the 1986 Emergency Medical Treatment and Active Labor Act, hospitals are required to treat migrants; they are also incentivized to transfer undocumented patient care quickly, as they are not reimbursed for nonemergent care. Sometimes this results in medical deportation, and often it results in medical exploitation when poorly run long-term home-care agencies are the only options for chronic condition care. Just as lack of documentation pushes exploitation in workplace settings, that undocumented reality becomes an exploitable commodity in which privatized informal home-care agencies employ low-paid, often not as robustly trained health-care workers. Consequently, the care delivered through these agencies has been documented to worsen health conditions and even lead to death. This existing system sends migrants to private, medically unaccredited care homes that waylay the costs from the broader health industry and treat migrant illnesses as profit-making commodities.[25] Not only are the undocumented patients exploited, but undocumented workers are also paid substandard wages.

Cultural trauma, defined as ongoing social or physical harm caused by a group with dominant political power over marginalized groups, is also a clear outcome of forced and irregular migration. This is an often-unrecognized form and cause of health disparities.[26] Undocumented people have worse health outcomes that even spill over to their documented family members in cases of families with mixed documentation status.[27] While federal policies dictate access to citizenship status, the experience of being undocumented within a particular state and region can be affected by how immigrants have access to work and resources within that community. Finding and challenging migrant-exclusive policies for local businesses or health-care facilities, alongside increasing knowledge of nonexploitative employers, can decrease migration-associated stress. Access to employment doesn't always increase health-care access, but under the unfortunate actualities of American capitalism it can.

City dwellers often do not see the health effects that industrial agriculture has on the health of migrant communities. Of the more than five thousand crop workers surveyed between 2015 and 2016 in the National Agricultural Workers Survey (NAWS), half were undocumented, 83 percent were Latinx, and nearly 70 percent of those Latinx people were Mexican.[28] In American agriculture the health of workers rarely is as good as the people who own the business. Workers in agricultural settings are exposed to many health threats, including pesticide and pollutant exposure, workplace injury risks, extreme weather-related effects, lack of access to sanitation and water, and the risk of infection or animal- or insect-related injuries. Worries about facing deportation can force undocumented farmworkers to have even higher risks of unaddressed health hazards.[29] Understanding these health risks is important. Confronting industrial farming practices requires understanding the supposed worker protections that have so far been legislated and the regulations associated.

Part 2B: Clinicians Can Do Better Resisting Borders

Since people can so easily be arrested and deported in most parts of the United States for a border crossing offense, many undocumented immigrants do not seek out health care.[30] Over 90 percent of migrants report trauma exposures in their migration journeys, including sexual assault and violence to their loved ones.[31] The health-care system response has often been inadequate and has included a lack of access to mental health and clinical care that could even start to address these resultant emotional and mental health difficulties. Once here, there are new health-care stressors, including unhealthy workplaces and worries of deportation.

Being a migrant with irregular documentation produces workplace exploitation and potential carceral scrutiny in multiple settings, including hospitals. The exploitation of foreign-born nurses has also been part of the exploited worker landscape, specifically in hospital-based settings, where passports and large portions of income are withheld by contract agencies, producing a second and third class of clinical worker. Contractor companies arrange three-year contract hospital jobs with EB-3 visas in underresourced hospitals. Agencies like this often charge at least $2,500 to apply, with thousands of dollars in additional costs and hefty breach-of-contract fees—sometimes $30,000 or more.[32] Although these contracts and the threats within those contracts may breach human trafficking laws, who is monitoring them? This is another place where supporting migrant workers means trying to traverse a terrain of inscrutable trails of information. Supporting these workers means revising unethical hospital hiring policies so that fewer new workers are trapped in contracts, as well as understanding and supporting workers in their immigration concerns.

Hospitals and clinics are rife with violations against immigrant patients. Since 2017, there have been increased reports of ICE officials entering hospitals and forcibly taking patients and their visitors.[33] Involuntary medical repatriation of undocumented patients has been a sinister step in removing barely stabilized patients and sending them back to their country of origin, where appropriate subacute care may not be available. As of 2018, nearly one thousand patients had been repatriated, with no follow-up data about outcomes.[34] These hospital or clinic policies and practices must be challenged: medical deportations of sick and injured people in the name of border safety should never happen again. Engaging community support in changing an institution's policies around medical deportations sets precedents for bigger community shifts.

For migrants, entering most health-care facilities is not even possible without identification. If a clinician is living in one of the many states where clinics have dispensations for uninsured patients, they can advocate for any form of documentation to be accepted at their health-care facility. Facilities can also make identification cards with photos for patients who need them. This is common practice in places like New York, Los Angeles, and San Francisco within homeless shelters and syringe exchange facilities. Some cities and states also have identification cards that can be used like driver's licenses, without citizenship documentation, such as IDNYC in New York City. Connecting patients with these resources can mean that people are more able to access other resources, including libraries, museums, bulk-grocery-store memberships, prescription drug discounts, supermarket discounts, discounts on exercise classes and gyms, plus many other things that can just make life a little easier. Waiting rooms are places to inform patients of identification resources available and to display commitments to all people, regardless of citizenship.

Our waiting rooms should be places of learning and protection for any person who is receiving care, including people who are undocumented. The integration of "Know Your Rights" literature and teachings within federally qualified health center (FQHC) waiting rooms, emergency rooms, and urgent cares (where many people without documentation receive their care) ensures that immigrant patients not only receive information and resources but that they not see clinical settings as places of potential deportation or detention.[35] This is required for undocumented people to receive the care they need because fear of deportation has been demonstrated to decrease the likelihood that people without documentation will feel safe receiving medical and dental care.[36] Partnering with cultural centers, churches, mosques, and other faith-based organizations can demonstrably increase immigrant attendance within primary care settings.[37]

Part 3A: Prisons and Worse Health Outcomes

The targeting of Black and Brown people starts when they are young. Child incarceration has far-reaching health effects into adulthood, and we know that LGBTQ+ youth are incarcerated disproportionately. In 2017 almost 40 percent of people in girls' detention centers identified as LGB, and 20 percent of all incarcerated youth identified as LGB, with only about 8 percent of all youth in the United States identifying this way.[38] Unsurprisingly, 85 percent of incarcerated queer youth are people of color, particularly Black and Latinx youth. That is what the rest of the demographics of juvenile detention looks like as well. Forty-two percent of juvenile detention is Black youth even though Black young people are only 15 percent of our population.[39] These young people's health worsens as a result of incarceration.

Once youth are incarcerated, for many, adult physical limitations later manifest. Of the 14,689 adult participants in the National Longitudinal Study of Adolescent to Adult Health (Add Health) study, "the largest, most comprehensive longitudinal survey of adolescents ever undertaken," the data clearly shows that 16.5 percent of the adults that had been incarcerated either between the ages of seven to thirteen or fourteen to thirty-two had significantly worse health outcomes than adults who had never been incarcerated. Although the Add Health data is aging, it is unlikely that future research will show better outcomes. When children were first incarcerated between the ages of seven to thirteen, their adult general health was much more likely to be poor (21.2 percent versus 8.4 percent of the general population); their functional limitations—such as climbing stairs—were more likely to be poor (16.9 percent versus 5.9 percent—more than three times higher); they had more than double the rates of depression (37.7 percent versus 14.9 percent); and suicidal ideation was four times more likely (28.1 percent versus 6.5 percent).[40] While Black people are in prison for far fewer convictions than their white counterparts, they have an average of two and a half times more incarcerations and were 30 percent more likely to be incarcerated as a child.[41] These racialized health harms are erroneously disguised as measures for safety and security. Why do we settle for this depraved version of safety?

We also know that asthma prevalence in Black communities is related to incarceration. Asthma rates are 30 percent to 60 percent higher among prisoners,[42] and one of the reasons that asthma rates may be higher among Black populations in the United States is *because of* incarceration.[43] There has been a clear correlation between increased asthma-related mortality and incarceration.[44] Asthma is inadequately treated in prison settings, with asthmatic prisoners accounting for 0.85 percent of all asthmatic individuals and only 0.15 percent receiving needed asthma prescriptions.[45]

Strangely, other Black-white racial health disparities lessen when people are incarcerated, which is a result of short-term increases in health access only while incarcerated.[46] The correlation between lack of access to medical services outside of prison and increased carceral involvement has not been clearly studied. In the general population, a history of imprisonment is negatively associated with life expectancy, and there is an increased positive association with infant mortality in areas with higher rates of former incarceration.[47]

The mental health effects of incarceration are poorly understood, and one can partially blame the people who wrote the Diagnostic and Statistical Manual for Mental Disorders (DSM). The DSM, which has long been a source of marginalization and pathology for LGBTQ+ communities, has still never acknowledged the terribly unique traumas associated with post incarceration syndrome (PICS), even though this syndrome was coined in 2001. This lack of official acknowledgment in the DSM of the mental health outcomes of incarceration has cemented the idea that those traumas are intangible or incohesive. But when you look at those traits taken together, they are distinct. Habitualized institutionalization behaviors and sensory processing disorientation, as well as alienation from temporal and social norms, are all separate features. These traits are accompanied with the flashbacks and nightmares seen in post-traumatic stress disorder (PTSD). Like PTSD, PICS includes depressive and anxious symptoms and can be accompanied with isolating oneself and difficulty adjusting to life outside of carceral settings. PICS can be associated with challenges adjusting to the here and now of society and associated norms, possibly leading to greater targeting by police.[48] If you work in mental health, you may think to yourself, the diagnosis does not matter much if we can treat the person appropriately. As troubling as the aims of the research can be, it is fairly impossible to explore novel treatments for a syndrome that the DSM has yet to acknowledge, despite having more than twenty years to do it. For the institution of the DSM, where about forty years ago, homosexuality was considered a sociopathic personality trait,[49] this is an ongoing pattern of ignoring and allowing systemic marginalization. Overlooking diagnoses such as PICS, which illustrate the mental health harms of jails, prisons, and detention centers, means the consequences affect Black, Brown, queer, and trans people disproportionately.

Clinicians must also acknowledge and ask about the trauma of incarceration with our patients instead of treating incarceration as shameful. Hiding or diminishing the impact of traumatic experiences has been clearly proven to create distress linked with depression and anxiety, as well as post-traumatic stress disorder. It is also a likely exacerbating factor in PICS.[50]

Head injuries, common among prisoners, can also increase mental health consequences, and clinicians need a more thorough assessment process and treatment protocol to address them. Of the more than two million people in prisons and jails, between 25 percent and 87 percent of prisoners report a head injury or traumatic brain injury (TBI), as compared to approximately 9 percent of the general population.[51] We know that TBI predisposes people to mental health differences, including depression, anxiety, substance overuse, anger management issues, and suicidal ideation. For people in men's prisons, TBI has also been correlated with increased violent outbursts.[52] Screening for TBIs in intake visits can help inform the course of action, including physical therapy rehabilitation, which can decrease many of the symptoms associated with TBIs.

Part 3B: Abolition Through Disability Justice Movement Lessons and Harm Reduction

When people talk about the impossible problem of abolition of any sort, we have forgotten that decarceration via deinstitutionalization has already occurred in this country. Liat Ben-Moshe and Leroy F. Moore Jr. have both spoken and written eloquently on the reasons to further advance prison and police abolition. In her interview, Dr. Ben-Moshe details here and in her book, *Decarcerating Disability: Deinstitutionalization and Prison Abolition*,[53] how the misconception of deinstitutionalization in the eighties and nineties led to the misunderstanding that people with psychiatric illnesses were dumped into jails and prisons. But we need to stop believing in this myth; it was the Reagan regime drug policies of the eighties that drove the increase in prison populations and, of course, in prison profits.[54] From 1980 to 1998, the number of people arrested for drug offenses exceeded 1.5 million in total, with the rate of drug arrests per 100,000 residents more than doubling, from 288 to 661.[55] This increase in numbers, Ben-Moshe explains in her interview, was largely in populations of Black men, not reflective of the population of people who exited psychiatric institutions. This misapprehension of increased incarceration because of deinstitutionalization must be debunked because deinstitutionalization is an inspiring model for health justice abolitionists.

Destigmatization, normalization, and acceptance of underground drug use must increase. In the world of psychiatric psychedelics, somehow the barely legal use of ketamine for psychiatric care is praised as therapeutic (which it can be) and requires serene observation and support, while the nonprescribed use of MDMA, ketamine, heroin/fentanyl, cocaine, or methamphetamines is to be cautioned against and unsupported. Drug use has been normal since the beginning of time, and making the distinction between therapeutic and nontherapeutic use is only useful to cops, not clinicians. Some drugs are not better than others, and the idea of some substances being more addictive than others has been carefully debunked by the likes of Carl Hart, Bruce Alexander, Maia Szalavitz, Marc Lewis, Gabor Maté, and others. Addiction is a cultural alienation and dislocation issue. What if we could help socially locate people more within their communities?[56] What if we saw drug use of all types as part of a therapeutic continuum, and only sought to alleviate the harms that these usages can produce while offering free resources like safe, comfortable injection sites, therapy, and other creative supports? Clinicians can do that. These offerings can and should consist of helplines, including places that people can call to ask emergency drug questions, that are not exclusively Poison Control.

Part 3C: Social Welfare Is Needed; Families Are Better without Carceral Involvement

In 1996 the federal Personal Responsibility and Work Opportunity Reconciliation Act (PROWRA) was enacted, banning people with drug felony convictions from getting Supplemental Nutrition Assistance Program (SNAP) benefits. However, most states have lifted the bans on former prisoners accessing public assistance like SNAP, formerly food stamps, or cash assistance through Temporary Assistance for Needy Families (TANF).[57] There was a clear lack of benefit to families and individuals affected by incarceration, and since up to 36.5 million children have had one parent with a "criminal record," food insecurity issues were only exacerbated by the PROWRA ban.[58] Only South Carolina still has a ban on SNAP benefits for people with drug felony convictions, but about twenty states like Missouri have modified access to SNAP benefits for people with felony drug convictions. In Missouri, continuation in the SNAP program requires people with felony drug convictions to accept drug testing and treatment as part of their access to food for their families. Seven states withhold TANF financial assistance as well.[59] People with felony convictions who can access the SNAP- and TANF-associated job-readiness training services, health care, and day care are much more frequently employed, increasing overall access to resources, including financial assistance and food.[60]

In 2019 a study revealed that approximately 20 percent of formerly incarcerated people report suffering from food insecurity versus approximately 10 percent of the general population, with formerly incarcerated women and Black individuals demonstrating even higher levels of food insecurity.[61] The risks of food insecurity for adults and children are many and include higher risks of diabetes, hypertension, cardiovascular disease, back problems, arthritis, and chronic pain, to name a few. Other risks include higher risk of infectious diseases, chronic dental health issues, and higher risk of injuries, as well as depressive and anxious mental health diagnoses.[62] As abolitionists, we must work to address food insecurity with programs specifically for families who have one parent or guardian with recent incarceration. At the same time we have to increase other services, such as job training, without governmental intervention, giving formerly incarcerated people a much higher likelihood of receiving what they need without shame or recrimination. Free memberships to food co-ops with lower prices and free food for people with any kind of conviction record is a way to build both community and care for people who have been targeted by the so-called justice system while increasing access to health.

For clinicians who take care of children, the greatest health risks for kids can come from mandatory reporting, the often-biased practice of reporting child negligence, parental substance use, or other suspected issues. Yes, parental behavior can include abuse, neglect, and exposing kids to unsavory and dangerous elements, and yes, families are often filled with dangers. How do we support parents who are struggling, whether it be from anger management, working too many jobs, not having enough childcare resources, and regular drug use, among other things? Considering how mandated reporting is implemented by people within each institution is critical to child well-being. It is imperative for clinicians to search for resources for struggling parents. Mandated reporting laws vary from state to state, but in many cases, anyone in a school system or clinical-care system is a mandated reporter. Studies have shown us that nearly 50 percent of all children who have had a parent reported by a mandated reporter state that their lives worsened because of the reporting, and if kids end up in foster care and are shuffled around with five or more placements, 90 percent end up in prison.[63, 64] Mandated reporting is not as helpful as it has been purported to be, and creating alternative systems, including case workers and childcare workers, can alleviate many stressors that predispose people to reporting.

Mandatory reporting of pregnant people must also be avoided. As Heath, Hur, and Mitchell discuss in their chapter detailing the nonmandatory yet racialized nature of drug testing of pregnant people, white pregnant people are not being drug tested and reported in the same way that people of color are. This is why health-care workers must be instrumental in not reporting to authorities but instead referring parents and pregnant people to resources and the community. Parenting classes, substance overuse treatment, free daycare or childcare resources, and more financial resources like TANF are ways to increase the success possibilities for parents; figuring out the online or in-person resources available and completing a community resource evaluation are critical to creating ways to avoid carceral systems.

Part 3D: Consider the Diagnosis

Carceral system involvement can be preceded by diagnoses that predispose children and adults to carceral scrutiny. Clinicians must be cautious regarding the diagnoses that children are given. Giving a child a conduct disorder, intermittent explosive disorder, or an oppositional defiant disorder diagnosis is like casting a life-changing spell for their future interactions within the health-care and classroom settings, as school officials are also often provided with kids' diagnoses. These diagnoses affect the way that guidance counselors and teachers—who are not given enough support for kids with "disruptive" diagnoses—approach children. Conduct disorder specifically is often considered a preliminary diagnosis to antisocial personality disorder as children display violent and antisocial behaviors.[65] What we do know is that school nurses can be a part of interrupting the school-to-detention and eventually -prison pipeline common for kids with the behavior-related diagnoses as well as diagnoses of cognitive disability.[66, 67]

Cognitive disability diagnoses are very common in prisons, with nearly one in four of all prisoners having a diagnosed cognitive disability, attention deficit hyperactivity disorder, or a history of special education classes. Fourteen percent of prisoners are also diagnosed with a learning disability.[68, 69] Of course, childhood poverty means that kids are more likely to be diagnosed with both disruptive/impulse control disorders, which are closely followed by personality disorder diagnoses in adulthood; intellectual disabilities are also more common in poor kids.[70, 71] More funding is required for anti-carceral school nurses within school systems so that zero-tolerance school policies can be challenged, and health intervention plans can be created to support kids who are struggling or disruptive.[72] This kind of school nurse resource alone has been shown to decrease the likelihood of incarceration of children and the increase of resource allocation for children who are displaying behaviors that are more likely to be targeted by carceral systems later.[73] It is important for clinicians to recognize cognitive and neurological differences in children and adults so that people can receive resources. However, social norms are not adapted to most intellectual variances, and this increases the likelihood of social norm violation and resultant carceral scrutiny.

Part 4A: Policing Affects Health-Care Delivery

In the last three decades, policing has increased within health-care systems, including hospitals, as has the risk of medical deportation. Not only do at least two thousand people per year become hospitalized because of *documented* arrest-related injuries, but countless other arrest-related injuries and traumas remain undocumented. Although there is normalization of police inside and outside of many hospitals and clinics, health-care workers still call the police on Black and Brown patients and visitors at twice the rate of white patients.[74] Approximately 97 percent of all hospital systems have police officers present as security who can make arrests and facilitate deportations, over half of whom can shoot or pepper spray patients; in 1988 the number of hospitals with police as security officers was 35 percent less, a terrible tale pointing to security chasing in health-care settings.[75, 76] Leroy F. Moore Jr. discusses his own experiences of this in his interview, saying, "Krip-Hop (his music, history, art and more project) had this exhibit in the children's hospital, and we did an event there. I was shocked because, God! There were so many cops. This is a children's hospital! I was like, why are cops around in the freaking children's hospital? Wow! So that concept alone. Cops in hospitals? How did that become a reality?" This outrage should be our normal reaction to police in places of health and medicine.

Regrettably, medical staff often feel safer when there is a designated person in charge of security and responsible for the removal of people who are creating an uncomfortable or dangerous situation. Clinical staff are frequently not very good at knowing when patients are expressing aggression or frustration with no physical threat intended. Likely related, about 15 percent of hospital staff recommended increased access to weapons, including handguns, tasers, and pepper spray, for security personnel.[77] Sixty-two percent of public hospital security (over 20 percent of whom are police officers) had handguns as weapons, which is significantly higher than the number of security personnel with guns in private hospitals that often serve a wealthier and whiter clientele.[78] Hospital security culture has codified that poorer people are security risks. We all know that means wherever low-income BIPOC patients receive medical care in health-care settings with armed security, they are at greater risk of death. This increased likelihood of dying is not only because their pain won't be seen as significant or will be misinterpreted as med seeking. Not only might their symptoms be ignored, but they are also more likely to experience gun violence simply because guns are more likely to be present on security personnel in facilities where they are seeking care.[79, 80]

The nature of unfettered security and police activity within hospital systems is a risk to the physical and mental health of people seeking medical attention and presents both moral and ethical violations of clinician codes of conduct. This overarching moral violation is accompanied by, for example, the amoral nature of the shackling of pregnant and birthing prisoners—increasing their likelihoods of thromboembolic complications, worse pain, and increased laboring times.[81] Shackles, like those described by Mihir Chaudhary at the beginning of his chapter, are used in 20 percent of all jails during birth and may delay the ability of prisoners to receive surgical care promptly.[82] Although security may make some staff feel safer, what happens in the hours when security personnel are not available? Would it not make sense for all staff on the floor to consider the safety of patients and safety plan with each other as part of the collaborative effort of delivering health care when patients and their visitors are doing their worst?

Part 4B: Policing Leads to Medical Mistrust and Should Not Be Replicated by Clinicians

The data shows that police brutality, and negative police encounters, are experienced disproportionately by people who have unmet mental health-care needs.[83] As Liat Ben-Moshe discusses in her interview, "Carceral sanism is a belief system and also a practice that builds on the idea that people with disabilities need special or extra protections. In terms of carceral sanism and ableism, it means to protect people with disabilities in ways that often leads to their marginalization, and further incarceration." In this way, people with mental health disabilities are arrested to protect themselves and others and, before many other options, put into a jail cell, further cementing the likelihood of carcerally linked mental and physical health harms.

"White safety is cancer prevention. Black safety is all-day chemotherapy," wrote lawyer and journalist Josie Duffy Rice in *Vanity Fair*.[84] This illustrates well the backward nature of how clinicians view the health and safety of Black and Brown people in this country. A 2015 study in Akron and Cincinnati, Ohio, examining policing and safety asked 470 Black and white residents about their experiences with police and policing. Forty percent of Black residents stated that they were somewhat or very afraid of police, while only 15 percent of white residents stated they feared police somewhat or a lot. Twenty percent of the Black residents in this study reported they had been stopped by the police at least once a week, while only 3 percent of white residents had been stopped by police once a week.[85] And starkly, two-thirds of all Black respondents feared that they would be killed by police, while nearly two-thirds of white respondents never feared this same death threat.[86] The all-day chemotherapy tactic of stopping BIPOC people produces distrustful community members who, once they have experienced negative police encounters, trust medical providers less too.[87]

The mental health and health-care effects of police brutality are real. All the respondents in the 2018 Survey of the Health of Urban Residents (n=4,345) who had bad encounters with the police had higher levels of medical mistrust. Having experienced police brutality was additionally associated with having greater unmet need for health care.[88] In a separate analysis, the Survey of the Health of Urban Residents data set found that people who are exposed to police brutality are also likely to be those who experience unmet need for mental health care.[89]

When police brutality occurs and is known, particularly the police killing of unarmed Black people, Black mental health is affected. This is associated with increased depression-focused emergency room visits for Black people, demonstrated in five different states.[90] We also know that highly publicized killings of Black people do not affect white mental health much at all, but the number of days of poor mental health for Black people increased in the weeks with two or more racialized violence incidents, including police killings of Black people.[91] Black people are killed three times more than white people by the police.[92] Any factor that increases morbidity and mortality is something that health care is specifically tasked with alleviating. And since the mass incarceration of all people has also decreased our overall US life expectancy by at least two years,[93] what choice do we have but to see policing as a clinical harm that must be eradicated?

While mass incarceration's mental health effects might not be surprising, it does inform what clinicians should not say to patients in the clinical setting. Clinicians must never threaten a patient with policing, including mandatory reporting, and must do the work to create clinical policies that prohibit calling police, as much as an institution is willing to withstand. Clinicians need to learn how to treat the at-the-moment disruptive person as if being at their worst does not warrant a punishment that can force them into eventual poverty with the collapse of community and family as imminent threats. Mandated reporting is not inevitable either and, unless there is no other recourse, should not be used as a tool to control families.

Policing must not be seen as a safety-ensuring clinical tool to make health-care delivery more efficient or effective, and it must never be seen as a tool to make families healthier. It is rather a mechanism of control that further marginalizes the most marginalized people seeking access to medical care.

Health-care workers must always reconsider their reasons for calling the police. Is it out of inconvenience? Is it because this person reminds a clinician of a relative, friend, or television show character who is triggering? Is the clinician willing to follow through with the care and support that a person referred to carceral systems might need? Is the patient going through a mental health crisis that a mental health team could alleviate through calling 988, versus calling 911 with potential police intervention?

Teaching de-escalation techniques at all clinical settings is also part of creating the non-carceral atmosphere. If everyone is trained and on board with the idea that cops are not an option to call, this could be an important, culturally developed norm. That norm must also include urgent response algorithms where fellow clinical staff will respond when an employee is worried or distressed. This is so a supported environment can be created in a disruptive situation. To be clear, there is no anti-carceral health-care environment if a staff-support emergency response system is not deliberately constructed. When patients need emergency care, creating relationships with local ambulance companies can also mean an outpatient clinic calling for emergency services directly instead of using a dispatch service, who, dependent on locale, may be mandated to call the police. Also, clinicians must consider if calling the person's emergency contact would be helpful, which should be accompanied by regular updating of patient emergency contact information.

Police are not the answer to mental health crises, as the work of Naomi Schoenfeld and Jennifer Esteen clearly illustrates in their chapter on abolitionist behavioral health infrastructures. The authors question how being in crisis mode, particularly for health-care workers, can increase harm in Black and Brown communities. Alternatives to 911 must come from harm reduction-based models that are the least likely to create harm in people who are the most vulnerable to it in emergency care. This includes Black, Brown, queer, and trans people, as well as people with serious untreated mental illness, uncontrolled physiologic health conditions like diabetes, dementias, and hepatic encephalopathies, as well as intellectual disabilities or differences. There are too many reasons that people can be vulnerable in an emergency medical situation, and we can create safeguards on the days when people are not doing their best, whatever the reasons might be.

What's Next

Maybe tomorrow we will not yet be able to demolish prisons, aim sledgehammers at every border wall, or even take every funding source away from police departments. We may not yet be ready to finally dismantle big pharma and render insurance companies and privatized hospitals obsolete in the near future. While we assemble all of the tools and resources to do those things, we can be part of communities that are thriving and creating new resources and alternative routes to getting community, mental health, and medical care. This can help illuminate the path to eradicating punitive carceral health care and creating the abolitionist clinical-care systems that we deserve. Despite the inscrutable nature of carceral systems, we have so much clear data that points to resultant health harms that we really have no choice but to act against every single carceral system that exists. "Freedom to stay and freedom to move," as Harsha Walia has said,[94] is needed for all people, regardless of place of origin. These freedoms must be accompanied by the freedom to access medicine and clinical care without fear of punishment.

CHAPTER 13 NOTES

1. *Disorders and Disabilities among Low-Income Children.* The National Academies of Sciences, Engineering, and Medicine, Washington, DC. 2015.
2. Daza, Sebastian, Alberto Palloni, and Jerrett Jones. "The Consequences of Incarceration for Mortality in the United States." *Demography*, February 11, 2019. https://doi.org/10.31235/osf.io/b8xe6.

3. DATA USA. "Physicians." Data USA, 2023. https://datausa.io/profile/soc/physicians.

4. DATA USA. "Nurse Practitioners." Data USA, 2023. https://datausa.io/profile/soc/nurse-practitioners-nurse-midwives#demographics.

5. Blugis, Sarah. "New Data: PA Students Have Diverse Backgrounds, Life Experiences." AAPA, January 26, 2022. https://www.aapa.org/news-central/2022/01/new-data-pa-students-have-diverse-backgrounds-life-experiences/.

6. DATA USA. "Physician Associates." Data USA, 2023. https://datausa.io/profile/cip/physician-assistant#demographics.

7. DATA USA. "Physicians."

8. Association of Medical Colleges. "Figure 18. Percentage of All Active Physicians by Race/Ethnicity, 2018." AAMC, 2018. https://www.aamc.org/data-reports/workforce/data/figure-18-percentage-all-active-physicians-race/ethnicity-2018.

9. Le, Hai H. "The Socioeconomic Diversity Gap in Medical Education." *Academic Medicine* 92, no. 8 (August 2017): 1071. https://doi.org/10.1097/acm.0000000000001796.

10. AAMC. "Figure 18. Percentage of All Active Physicians by Race/Ethnicity, 2018."

11. Blugis, Sarah. "New Data: PA Students Have Diverse Backgrounds, Life Experiences."

12. DATA USA. "Physicians."

13. DATA USA. "Nurse Practitioners."

14. DATA USA. "Physician Associates."

15. United States Government. "U.S. Census Bureau Quickfacts: United States." Race and Hispanic Origin, 2022. https://www.census.gov/quickfacts/fact/table/US/RHI125222.

16. Leggott, Kyle. "Here's Why LGBTQ Physicians Should Self-Identify." AAFP, March 3, 2020. https://www.aafp.org/news/blogs/freshperspectives/entry/20200303fp-lgbtqphysicians.html.

17. "Nurse Practitioner Demographics and Statistics [2024]: Number of Nurse Practitioners in the US." Zippia, April 5, 2024. https://www.zippia.com/nurse-practitioner-jobs/demographics/.

18. "Physician Assistant Demographics and Statistics [2024]: Number of Physician Assistants in the US." Zippia, April 5, 2024. https://www.zippia.com/physician-assistant-jobs/demographics/.

19. Carson, E. Ann. "Prisons Report Series: Preliminary Data Release." Bureau of Justice Statistics, September 2023. https://bjs.ojp.gov/library /publications/prisons-report-series-preliminary-data-release.

20. Gennuso, K. P., E. A. Pollock, and A. M. Roubal. "Life Expectancy at the US-Mexico Border: Evidence of Disparities by Place, Race, and Ethnicity. *Health Affairs* 40, no. 7 (June 23, 2021), 1038–46. https://doi .org/10.1377/hlthaff.2021.00139.

21. American Immigration Council. "The Legacy of Racism within the U.S. Border Patrol." December 21, 2021. https://www.americanimmigration council.org/research/legacy-racism-within-us-border-patrol.

22. Tseng, Esther. "Undocumented Workers Hold the Restaurant Industry Together. Now, They Stand to Lose the Most." Eater, May 29, 2020. https://www.eater.com/2020/5/29/21273410/undocumented -workers-coronavirus-risks.

23. Castillo, Federico, Ana M. Mora, Georgia L. Kayser, Jennifer Vanos, Carly Hyland, Audrey R. Yang, and Brenda Eskenazi. "Environmental Health Threats to Latino Migrant Farmworkers." *Annual Review of Public Health* 42, no. 1 (April 1, 2021): 257–76. https://doi.org/10.1146/annurev -publhealth-012420-105014.

24. Tseng, Esther. "Undocumented Workers Hold the Restaurant Industry Together. Now, They Stand to Lose the Most."

25. Jimenez, Anthony M. "The Legal Violence of Care: Navigating the US Health Care System While Undocumented and Illegible." *Social Science & Medicine* 270 (January 2, 2021): 113676. https://doi.org/10.1016/j .socscimed.2021.113676.

26. Subica, Andrew M., and Bruce G. Link. "Cultural Trauma as a Fundamental Cause of Health Disparities." *Social Science & Medicine* 292 (January 2022): 114574. https://doi.org/10.1016/j.socscimed.2021.114574.

27. Subica, Andrew M., and Bruce G. Link. "Cultural Trauma as a Fundamental Cause of Health Disparities."

28. Castillo et al. "Environmental Health Threats to Latino Migrant Farmworkers."

29. Black, Julia, ed. "Migrant Workers Face Heightened Risk of Death and Injury: New IOM Report." International Organization for Migration, October 15, 2021. https://www.iom.int/news/migrant-workers-face -heightened-risk-death-and-injury-new-iom-report.

30. Walia, Harsha. *Border and Rule: Global Migration, Capitalism, and the Rise of Racist Nationalism*. Chicago, IL: Haymarket Books, 2021.

31. Weil, Alan R. "Borders, Immigrants, and Health." *Health Affairs* 40, no. 7 (July 1, 2021): 1023. https://doi.org/10.1377/hlthaff.2021.00998.

32. Almendral, Aurora. "A Hidden System of Exploitation Underpins US Hospitals' Employment of Foreign Nurses." Quartz, October 2, 2023. https://qz.com/a-hidden-system-of-exploitation-underpins-us -hospitals-1850888315.

33. Khullar, Dhruv, and Dave A Chokshi. "Challenges for Immigrant Health in the USA—the Road to Crisis." *The* Lancet 393, no. 10186 (April 10, 2019): 2168–74. https://doi.org/10.1016/s0140-6736(19)30035-2.

34. Franco-Vásquez, Andreé, Stephanie Lemus, Kevin Castillo, Martin Isaac, and Altaf Saadi. "Integration of Waiting Room 'Know Your Rights' Education into Medical Care of Immigrant Patients in a Federally Qualified Health Center: A Case Study." *Health Equity* 6, no. 1 (January 1, 2022): 13–20. https://doi.org/10.1089/heq.2020.0145.

35. López-Cevallos, Daniel F., Junghee Lee, and William Donlan. "Fear of Deportation Is Not Associated with Medical or Dental Care Use among Mexican-Origin Farmworkers Served by a Federally-Qualified Health Center—Faith-Based Partnership: An Exploratory Study." *Journal of Immigrant and Minority Health* 16, no. 4 (June 5, 2013): 706–11. https:// doi.org/10.1007/s10903-013-9845-1.

36. López-Cevallos et al. "Fear of Deportation Is Not Associated with Medical or Dental Care Use among Mexican-Origin Farmworkers."

37. López-Cevallos et al. "Fear of Deportation Is Not Associated with Medical or Dental Care Use among Mexican-Origin Farmworkers."

38. Center for American Progress, Movement Advancement Project, and Youth First. "Unjust: LGBTQ Youth Incarcerated in the Juvenile Justice System." Movement Advancement Project, June 2017. https://www .lgbtmap.org/policy-and-issue-analysis/criminal-justice-youth-detention.

39. Rovner, Joshua. "Black Disparities in Youth Incarceration—the Sentencing Project." The Sentencing Project, December 12, 2023. https://www .sentencingproject.org/wp-content/uploads/2017/09/Black-Disparities -in-Youth-Incarceration.pdf.

40. Barnert, Elizabeth S., Laura S. Abrams, Lello Tesema, Rebecca Dudovitz, Bergen B. Nelson, Tumaini Coker, Eraka Bath, Christopher Biely, Ning Li, and Paul J. Chung. "Child Incarceration and Long-Term Adult Health Outcomes: A Longitudinal Study." *International Journal of Prisoner Health* 14, no. 1 (March 12, 2018): 26–33. https://doi.org/10.1108/ijph-09 -2016-0052.

41. Blankenship, Kim M., Ana Maria del Rio Gonzalez, Danya E. Keene, Allison K. Groves, and Alana P. Rosenberg. "Mass Incarceration, Race Inequality, and Health: Expanding Concepts and Assessing Impacts on Well-Being." *Social Science & Medicine* 215 (October 2018): 45–52. https://doi.org/10.1016/j.socscimed.2018.08.042.

42. Viglianti, Elizabeth M., Theodore J. Iwashyna, and Tyler N. Winkelman. "Mass Incarceration and Pulmonary Health: Guidance for Clinicians." *Annals of the American Thoracic Society* 15, no. 4 (April 2018): 409–12. https://doi.org/10.1513/annalsats.201711-895ip.

43. Wang, Emily A, and Jeremy Green. "Incarceration as a Key Variable in Racial Disparities of Asthma Prevalence." *BMC Public Health* 10, no. 1 (May 28, 2010). https://doi.org/10.1186/1471-2458-10-290.

44. Forsyth, Simon, Rosa Alati, and Stuart A. Kinner. "Asthma-Related Mortality after Release from Prison: A Retrospective Data Linkage Study." *Journal of Asthma* 60, no. 1 (February 24, 2022): 167–73. https://doi.org/10.1080/02770903.2022.2039936.

45. Curran, Jill, Brendan Saloner, Tyler N.A. Winkelman, and G. Caleb Alexander. "Estimated Use of Prescription Medications among Individuals Incarcerated in Jails and State Prisons in the US." *JAMA Health Forum* 4, no. 4 (April 14, 2023). https://doi.org/10.1001/jamahealthforum.2023.0482.

46. Blankenship, Kim M., Ana Maria del Rio Gonzalez, Danya E. Keene, Allison K. Groves, and Alana P. Rosenberg. "Mass Incarceration, Race Inequality, and Health: Expanding Concepts and Assessing Impacts on Well-Being."

47. Blankenship, Kim M., Ana Maria del Rio Gonzalez, Danya E. Keene, Allison K. Groves, and Alana P. Rosenberg. "Mass Incarceration, Race Inequality, and Health: Expanding Concepts and Assessing Impacts on Well-Being."

48. National Incarceration Association. "The Definitive Guide on Post Incarceration Syndrome (PICS)." February 6, 2023. https://joinnia.com/post-incarceration-syndrome/#:~:text=PICS%20is%20characterized%20by%20a,productive%20members%20of%20the%20community.

49. Drescher, Jack. "Out of DSM: Depathologizing Homosexuality." Behavioral Sciences (Basel, Switzerland), December 4, 2015. https://www.ncbi.nlm.nih.gov/pmc/articles/PMC4695779/.

50. National Incarceration Association. "The Definitive Guide on Post Incarceration Syndrome (PICS)." February 6, 2023. https://joinnia.com/post

-incarceration-syndrome/#:~:text=PICS%20is%20characterized%20 by%20a,productive%20members%20of%20the%20community.

51. Centers for Disease Control and Prevention. (2024). *Traumatic Brain Injury & Concussion.* https://www.cdc.gov/traumatic-brain-injury/index.html.

52. Centers for Disease Control and Prevention. *Traumatic Brain Injury & Concussion.*

53. Ben-Moshe, Liat. *Decarcerating Disability: Deinstitutionalization and Prison Abolition.* Minneapolis, Minnesota: University of Minnesota Press, 2022.

54. Ben-Moshe, Liat. *Decarcerating Disability.*

55. Blumstein, Alfred, and Allen J. Beck. "Population Growth in U. S. Prisons, 1980–1996." *Crime and Justice* 26 (January 1999): 17–61. https://doi .org/10.1086/449294.

56. Alexander, Bruce. "Dislocation Theory of Addiction." April 19, 2017. https://www.brucekalexander.com/articles-speeches/dislocation -theory-addiction.

57. Thompson, Darrel, and Ashley Burnside. "No More Double Punishments: Lifting the Ban on SNAP and TANF for People with Prior Felony Drug Convictions." CLASP, April 19, 2023. https://www.clasp.org/publications /report/brief/no-more-double-punishments/.

58. Vallas, Rebecca, Melissa Boteach, Rachel West, and Jackie Odum. "Removing Barriers to Opportunity for Parents with Criminal Records and Their Children." Center for American Progress, December 10, 2015. https://www.americanprogress.org/article/removing-barriers-to -opportunity-for-parents-with-criminal-records-and-their-children/.

59. Thompson and Burnside. "No More Double Punishments."

60. Thompson and Burnside. "No More Double Punishments."

61. Testa, Alexander, and Dylan B. Jackson. "Food Insecurity among For-merly Incarcerated Adults." *Criminal Justice and Behavior* 46, no. 10 (June 19, 2019): 1493-1511. https://journals.sagepub.com/doi/pdf/10.1177 /0093854819856920.

62. Landon, Jenni, and Alexi Jones. "Food Insecurity Is Rising, and Incarcer-ation Puts Families at Risk." Prison Policy Initiative, February 10, 2021. https://www.prisonpolicy.org/blog/2021/02/10/food-insecurity/.

63. "Mandatory Reporting Is Not Neutral." Mandatory Reporting Is Not Neutral, 2024. https://www.mandatoryreportingisnotneutral.com/.

64. Perez, Jaxzia. "The Foster Care-to-Prison Pipeline: A Road to Incarcera-tion." The Criminal Law Practitioner, October 18, 2023. https://www

.crimlawpractitioner.org/post/the-foster-care-to-prison-pipeline-a-road
-to-incarceration.

65. Reading, Richard. "Recognition, Intervention, and Management of Antisocial Behaviour and Conduct Disorders in Children and Young People:
Summary of Nice-scie Guidance." *Child: Care, Health and Development* 39,
no. 4 (June 13, 2013): 615–16. https://doi.org/10.1111/cch.12074_5.

66. Aronowitz, Shoshana V., BoRam Kim, and Teri Aronowitz. "A Mixed-
Studies Review of the School-to-Prison Pipeline and a Call to Action
for School Nurses." *The Journal of School Nursing* 37, no. 1 (November 11,
2020): 51–60. https://doi.org/10.1177/1059840520972003.

67. Sarrett, Jennifer. "US Prisons Hold More than 550,000 People with
Intellectual Disabilities—They Face Exploitation, Harsh Treatment."
The Conversation, May 7, 2021. https://theconversation.com/us-prisons
-hold-more-than-550-000-people-with-intellectual-disabilities-they
-face-exploitation-harsh-treatment-158407.

68. Aronowitz et al. "A Mixed-Studies Review of the School-to-Prison
Pipeline."

69. Sarrett, Jennifer. "US Prisons Hold More than 550,000 People with
Intellectual Disabilities."

70. Sarrett, Jennifer. "US Prisons Hold More than 550,000 People with
Intellectual Disabilities."

71. Committee to Evaluate the Supplemental Security Income Disability Program for Children with Mental Disorders; Board on the Health of Select
Populations; Board on Children, Youth, and Families; Institute of Medicine;
Division of Behavioral and Social Sciences and Education; The National
Academies of Sciences, Engineering, and Medicine; Boat TF, Wu JT, editors. *Mental Disorders and Disabilities Among Low-Income Children.* Washington (DC): National Academies Press (US); 2015 Oct 28. https://www
.ncbi.nlm.nih.gov/books/NBK332882/ doi: 10.17226/21780

72. Aronowitz et al. "A Mixed-Studies Review of the School-to-Prison
Pipeline."

73. Aronowitz et al. "A Mixed-Studies Review of the School-to-Prison
Pipeline."

74. Gallen, Kate, Jake Sonnenberg, Carly Loughran, Michael J. Smith,
Mildred Sheppard, Kirsten Schuster, Elinore Kaufman, Ji Seon Song,
and Erin C. Hall. "Health Effects of Policing in Hospitals: A Narrative
Review." *Journal of Racial and Ethnic Health Disparities* 10, no. 2 (March
10, 2022): 870–82. https://doi.org/10.1007/s40615-022-01275-w.

75. Gallen et al. "Health Effects of Policing in Hospitals."

76. Schoenfisch, Ashley L., and Lisa A. Pompeii. "Security Personnel Practices and Policies in U.S. Hospitals." *Workplace Health & Safety* 64, no. 11 (July 9, 2016): 531–42. https://doi.org/10.1177/2165079916653971.

77. Schoenfisch and Pompeii. "Security Personnel Practices and Policies in U.S. Hospitals."

78. Schoenfisch and Pompeii. "Security Personnel Practices and Policies in U.S. Hospitals."

79. Schoenthaler, Antoinette, and Natasha Williams. "Looking beneath the Surface: Racial Bias in the Treatment and Management of Pain." *JAMA Network Open* 5, no. 6 (June 9, 2022). https://doi.org/10.1001/jamanetworkopen.2022.16281.

80. Gallen et al. "Health Effects of Policing in Hospitals."

81. Gallen et al. "Health Effects of Policing in Hospitals."

82. Alang, Sirry, Donna McAlpine, Malcolm McClain, and Rachel Hardeman. "Police Brutality, Medical Mistrust and Unmet Need for Medical Care." *Preventive Medicine Reports* 22 (June 2021): 101361. https://doi.org/10.1016/j.pmedr.2021.101361.

83. Alang, Sirry, Taylor B. Rogers, Lillie D. Williamson, Cherrell Green, and April J. Bell. "Police Brutality and Unmet Need for Mental Health Care." *Health Services Research* 56, no. 6 (August 5, 2021): 1104–13. https://doi.org/10.1111/1475-6773.13736.

84. Rice, Josie Duffy. "The Abolition Movement." Vanity Fair, August 25, 2020. https://www.vanityfair.com/culture/2020/08/the-abolition-movement.

85. Human Impact Partners. "Stress on the Streets (SOS): Race, Policing, Health, and Increasing Trust Not Trauma." January 23, 2018. https://humanimpact.org/hipprojects/trust-not-trauma/.

86. Human Impact Partners. "Stress on the Streets (SOS)."

87. Alang et al. "Police Brutality and Unmet Need for Mental Health Care."

88. Alang et al. "Police Brutality and Unmet Need for Mental Health Care."

89. Rice. "The Abolition Movement."

90. Das, Abhery, Parvati Singh, Anju K. Kulkarni, and Tim A. Bruckner. "Emergency Department Visits for Depression Following Police Killings of Unarmed African Americans." *Social Science & Medicine* 269 (November 28, 2021): 113561. https://doi.org/10.1016/j.socscimed.2020.113561.

91. Curtis, David S., Tessa Washburn, Hedwig Lee, Ken R. Smith, Jaewhan Kim, Connor D. Martz, Michael R. Kramer, and David H. Chae. "Highly Public Anti-Black Violence Is Associated with Poor Mental Health Days

for Black Americans." Proceedings of the National Academy of Sciences of the United States of America, April 27, 2021. https://pubmed.ncbi .nlm.nih.gov/33875593/.

92. Schwartz, Gabriel L., and Jaquelyn L. Jahn. "Mapping Fatal Police Violence across U.S. Metropolitan Areas: Overall Rates and Racial/Ethnic Inequities, 2013–2017." *PLOS ONE* 15, no. 6 (June 24, 2020). https:// doi.org/10.1371/journal.pone.0229686.

93. Daza et al. "The Consequences of Incarceration for Mortality in the United States."

94. Walia. *Border and Rule.*

RESOURCES

Balcazar, Fabricio E. "Policy Statement on the Incarceration of Undocumented Migrant Families." *American Journal of Community Psychology* 57, no. 1–2 (March 2016): 255–63. https://doi.org/10.1002/ajcp.12017.

Bleich, Sarah N., Mary G. Findling, Logan S. Casey, Robert J. Blendon, John M. Benson, Gillian K. SteelFisher, Justin M. Said, and Carolyn Miller. "Discrimination in the United States: Experiences of Black Americans." National Library of Medicine, October 29, 2019. https://onlinelibrary.wiley.com/doi/10.1111/1475-6773.13220.

Breyer, Shawn. "How Many Rapists Are Convicted?" The Hive Law, February 25, 2024. https://www.thehivelaw.com/blog/how-many-rapists-are-convicted/.

Burdge, Hilary, Adela Licona, and Zami Hyemingway. "LGBTQ Youth of Color: Discipline Disparities, School Push-Out, and the School-to-Prison Pipeline." National Center on Safe Supportive Learning Environments (NCSSLE). https://gsanetwork.org, 2014. https://nicic.gov/resources/nic-library/all-library-items/lgbtq-youth-color-discipline-disparities-school-push-out.

Giaritelli, Anna. "Hispanic Agents Make Up Majority of Border Patrol Yet White Men Dominate Leadership Posts." Washington Examiner, August 5, 2022. https://www.washingtonexaminer.com/policy/immigration/hispanic-agents-majority-border-patrol-white-men-dominate-leadership.

Lippy, C., C. Burke, and M. Hobart. "'There's No One I Can Trust': The Impact of Mandatory Reporting on the Help Seeking and Well Being." Issuu, November 8, 2016. https://issuu.com/thenwnetwork/docs/there_s_no_one_i_can_trust-_mandato/3.

National Academies of Sciences, Engineering, and Medicine; Health and Medicine Division; Board on Population Health and Public Health Practice; Roundtable on the Promotion of Health Equity. "Mass Incarceration as a Public Health Issue." The Effects of Incarceration and Reentry on Community Health and Well-Being: Proceedings of a Workshop., September 18, 2019. https://nap.nationalacademies.org /catalog/25471/the-effects-of-incarceration-and-reentry-on -community-health-and-well-being.

O'Carroll, Austin. "The Triple F★★k Syndrome: Medicine and the Systemic Oppression of People Born into Poverty." *The British Journal of General Practice* 72, no. 716 (February 24, 2022): 120–21. https:// www.ncbi.nlm.nih.gov/pmc/articles/PMC8884433/.

United States Sentencing Commission. "Quick Facts on Sexual Abuse Offenses." Quick Facts: Sexual Abuse Offenders, 2018. https://www .ussc.gov/sites/default/files/pdf/research-and-publications/quick -facts/Sexual_Abuse_FY18.pdf.

CONTRIBUTOR BIOGRAPHIES

Biographies are listed in alphabetical order:

Onyịnye Alheri, MSW, is an artist, curator, and scholar engaging with international movements that promote peace, justice, and wellness. Ọ believes in harm reduction and collective healing. Born in Èkó (aka Lagos, Nigeria), Onyịnye is blessed to have lived in many lands, connecting with beings across continents and realms. Ọ earned a bachelor of arts (BA) in international studies and philosophy from Macalester College and a master of social work (MSW) from the University of Maryland, Baltimore.

Alexia Arani, PhD, (she/they) is an assistant professor in the Department of Women's, Gender, and Queer Studies at California Polytechnic State University, San Luis Obispo. Her scholarship, activism, and teaching focus on the intersections of prison abolition, disability justice, and queer/trans liberation.

Hannah Michelle Brower, MS, is an abolitionist organizer. For several years, she has been organizing with the #DeeperThanWater Coalition to end medical neglect in Massachusetts state prisons. Hannah Michelle is close friends with Ronald Leftwich, and she supported him in editing his essay for this book. She lives on unceded Lenape land (Philadelphia, Pennsylvania) with her partner and pet pigeon.

Mihir Chaudhary, MD, MPH, (@mihirjaychaudh), a trauma surgery fellow at the University of Chicago and a researcher on policing, the carceral state, and violence, works with faculty across the disciplines of political science, African American studies, and trauma surgery. He has a BA in social studies from Harvard College, an MD from Harvard Medical School, and an MPH from Johns Hopkins, where he was a Sommer Scholar. His past work has explored how communities marginalized by race and class express abolitionism. He hopes to synergize his clinical work as a trauma surgeon, caring for those affected by (structural) violence with praxis and a scholarly focus on racial capitalism and resistance.

Aminah Elster is a Black feminist, prison abolitionist, legal/policy advocate, and researcher with years of experience leading policy advocacy work around criminal justice and driving participatory action research initiatives. Aminah is the cofounder and executive director of Unapologetically HERS, Healing Experiences through Research Solutions, and a co-organizer with the California Coalition for Women Prisoners and Survived and Punished. Aminah is committed to centering incarcerated and formerly incarcerated women of color in research and advocacy. She holds a bachelor's degree in legal studies from the University of California, Berkeley, and is the coauthor of "Criminal Record Stigma in the College-Educated Labor Market."

End Police Violence Collective is a growing group of public health researchers, teachers, students, nonprofit leaders, and community organizers that came together to draft and organize around passing the APHA statements "Addressing Law Enforcement Violence as a Public Health Issue" and "Advancing Public Health Interventions to Address the Harms of the Carceral System." These statements are rooted in the work of grassroots organizing against state-mediated violence. They recognize how structural racism and institutional oppression shape population patterns of criminalization, law enforcement violence, and incarceration and are firmly committed to a public health alternative, recommending preventive, community-based, and community-led solutions.

Jennifer Esteen, RN, is a registered nurse, mother, and community leader who has served as vice president of the Alameda Health System Board of Trustees and is currently a council member on the Eden Municipal Advisory Council. She has spent her career delivering care to the most vulnerable, working first as a nurse in the San Francisco General Hospital Psychiatric Emergency Room and now with San Francisco residents who have severe mental illness and need supportive housing and help managing activities of daily living. After Jennifer successfully led the fight to preserve funding for permanent housing for her clients, she was appointed to the role of vice president of organizing for SEIU 1021. In her work, Jennifer has helped clients navigate the vicious cycle that people experience from diminished funding for mental health care. Jennifer is a champion for working families and works to deliver policies that will keep our communities safe and healthy.

Vanessa K. Ferrel, MD, MPH, is a Black, queer HIV medicine and primary care physician, currently based out of Philadelphia. Vanessa has been on the frontlines of abolitionist medicine since 2014, organizing health-care workers for racial justice and striving to abolish carcerality from medical practice.

Jenna Heath is an OB-GYN resident working to decrease exposure of patients to child welfare systems in the perinatal period in Los Angeles, California. She grew up in Buffalo, New York, and studied anthropology prior to completing medical school at the University of Buffalo.

Rachel Herzing is coauthor, with Justin Piché, of *How to Abolish Prisons: Lessons from the Movement against Imprisonment* (2024). Herzing was executive director of Center for Political Education, a resource for political organizations on the left and progressive social movements; codirector of Critical Resistance, a national organization dedicated to abolishing the prison industrial complex; and director of research and training at Creative Interventions, a community resource that developed interventions to interpersonal harm that do not rely on policing, imprisonment, or traditional social services.

Elizabeth Hur is a Korean American woman who grew up in Wisconsin and experienced both privileges as well as microaggressions. She majored in sociology and learned the names of the many concepts she experienced in her childhood. She is currently an OB-GYN specializing in reproductive psychiatry in Sacramento, California, where she tries to apply the concept of "do no harm" daily.

Ronald Leftwich has been involved in the Restorative Justice group at MCI-Norfolk, where he has been incarcerated since 2014. In 2020 he became a member of the Restorative Justice Planning Team, and in 2021 he took on the role of internal coordinator. Ronald Leftwich earned his BA from Boston University in 2010 while incarcerated. Having committed very violent offenses, and having come to understand the impact of these offenses through restorative justice practices, Ronald has dedicated his life to nonviolence and restorative justice. Ronald has spent the majority of his life behind prison walls and is currently serving a life sentence without possibility of parole.

Jennifer James, PhD, MS, MSW, is an associate professor at the University of California, San Francisco. Jen is a sociologist, ethicist, and Black feminist scholar who conducts community-engaged qualitative research on health, racism, and structural violence. Her research interests include cancer, aging, patient-provider relationships, health decision-making, and reproductive justice. Her current work is focused on experiences of health and illness for people who are or have been incarcerated.

Carlos Martinez, MPH, PhD, is an assistant professor in the Department of Latin American and Latino Studies and core faculty member of the Global and Community Health program at the University of California, Santa Cruz. Trained in public health and medical anthropology, Carlos researches the health consequences and sociocultural implications of the deportation regime, asylum deterrence policies, the global drug war, and migrant captivity in the US-Mexico borderlands.

Nicole Mitchell Chadwick, MD, a Texas native, identifies as a biracial female person and throughout her life has often been the only woman of color in the room. During training, she developed a passion not only for medicine but for addressing inequities in health care and the health-care training process. She attended Texas Tech Medical School before OB-GYN residency training at Los Angeles County + University of Southern California (LAC+USC) Medical Center. As a senior resident, Dr. Mitchell Chadwick had the courage to speak up against disparities and injustices in the OB-GYN department and worked to educate and develop solutions. She currently is an assistant professor of clinical OB-GYN at USC and is a recognized Champion of Diversity, Equity, and Inclusion at the Keck School of Medicine (KSOM). She has developed a departmental program for DEI, which starts with IB training, and she strives to create a culture shift in OB-GYN. Her passions include addressing disparities in clinical care, especially for women and women of color, along with increasing the recruitment and retention of underrepresented providers.

Leroy F. Moore Jr. is the founder of the Krip-Hop Nation, a movement that uses hip-hop as a means of expression for people with disabilities. Moore is a writer, poet, community activist, and a hip-hop and music lover. He was born with cerebral palsy and has dedicated much of his writing and activism to disability rights. He is currently a doctoral student in linguistic anthropology at UCLA. He writes and delivers lectures and performances that reflect the intersections between racism and ableism in the United States and abroad. Moore's most recent book, *Black Disabled Ancestors*, came out in 2020.

Ronica Mukerjee, DNP, is a family and psychiatric mental health nurse practitioner and an acupuncturist. They are currently an assistant professor in Columbia University's School of Nursing. Dr. Mukerjee is passionate about racial, economic, and health-care justice among LGBTQIA+, refugee and migrant communities, people with substance use disorders, and people living with HIV. They were the program coordinator/creator of the Gender and Sexuality Health Justice concentration at Yale for nurse practitioner, medical, and physician assistant (PA) students. They maintain multiple practices in New York and Connecticut focused on substance use disorders, HIV, and LGBTQIA+-affirming care. Dr. Mukerjee codirects two organizations that they cofounded: Refugee Health Alliance in Tijuana, Mexico, as well as Healthcare for the People in Brooklyn, New York. They work closely with multiple community organizations in Connecticut focused on youth homelessness and support for former prisoners. They are first editor of and principal author of many chapters in their coedited textbook, *Clinicians Guide to LGBTQIA+ Care: Cultural*

Safety and Social Justice in Primary, Sexual, and Reproductive Healthcare, published by Springer in February 2021.

Giselle Pérez-Aguilar, LCSW, is a first-generation Mexicana Indigena doctoral student at the University of California, San Francisco. Giselle's main interest lies in bridging Indigenous healing practices with Western mental health, using psychoanalytic approaches, spirituality, and environmental justice to help undocumented women of color heal from complex trauma, reclaim their power, and become earth stewards. She was inspired by her Boyle Heights roots, Zapotec ancestors, and educational endeavors at UC Berkeley and the University of Michigan School of Social Work to give back to the communities that have uplifted her throughout the years and move health research in the direction of liberation.

Tien Pham is an online English teacher. He and his family immigrated to California as refugees in 1996, and shortly thereafter, at seventeen, he was sentenced to twenty-eight years in prison. He was granted parole in June 2020 but was transferred to Immigration and Customs Enforcement detention upon his release and subsequently deported. He is currently residing in Bien Hoa, Vietnam, with his wife.

Amber Akemi Piatt, MPH, is a public health practitioner and experienced advocate for justice. She has collaborated with grassroots groups on successful campaigns to curb militarism, incarceration, and policing. She is an alumnus of the Women's Foundation of California's Women's Policy Institute and completed her master's in public health at the University of California, Berkeley, and her bachelor of arts in psychology and Spanish at the University of California, Los Angeles.

Leslie Riddle, MPH, is a staff research associate in the Department of Humanities and Social Sciences at the University of California, San Francisco. Leslie has a background in public health and social sciences and has worked through direct clinical care and research to advance patient-centered reproductive health care.

Naomi C. Schoenfeld, PhD, FNP, is a medical anthropologist and nurse practitioner in San Francisco. She is currently faculty affiliate at the University of California San Francisco School of Nursing, Department of Social and Behavioral Sciences and in the Institute for Global Health Sciences. She serves as a social medicine clinician consultant for the Zuckerberg San Francisco General Hospital Emergency Department and works with the Whole Person Integrative Care Department of the San Francisco Department of Public Health. She has previously served as assistant clinical professor at the UCSF School of Nursing Family Health Care Nursing Department. She has worked as a nurse practitioner with marginalized populations for twenty years.

Nate Tan has been involved with Asian Prisoner Support Committee (ASPC) since 2014: first as a volunteer with ROOTS (Restoring Our Original True Selves), then core member, and now codirector. He brings over seven years of experience working with formerly incarcerated, incarcerated, ICE-detained individuals, and impacted families. He's excited to continue the work of APSC in bringing people home and reuniting families.

Ronni Tartlet is an editor and lives on a big rock in the Salish Sea, where they harvest fruit, build stuff, write Jewishly and anti-Zionistly, and respond to medical emergencies. Their lifelong goals include undermining structures of oppression and contributing to cultures of joy and liberation.

Lauren Textor, MD, PhD, is a physician resident in the department of psychiatry at the University of California, Los Angeles. She holds an MD and a PhD in anthropology from UCLA. Dr. Textor's research examines the downstream impacts of health-care and drug policies especially as they impact health-care providers and people seeking health care. Her research involves ethnographic fieldwork in large-scale encampments in Southern California, in collaboration with grassroots harm-reduction organizations, to examine how housing policies, drug law enforcement, and health-care initiatives affect long-term trajectories for people who use opioids. Her most recent project investigates the ways that past experiences with criminalization and with health care shape the embodied effects and efficacy of medications for addiction treatment. Her research and advocacy are aimed at reimagining care to promote health and justice.

Rafik Nader Wahbi, MPH, is a community health scientist and educator whose work focuses on the social and political determinants of mental health and drug use, specifically for those who are criminalized, unhoused, displaced, or incarcerated. Rafik studies and writes about how public health and medicine function as tools of social control and capital gain for the state and how they actively co-opt the work of community organizers and grassroots organizations to gain legitimacy. Rafik is part of the Los Angeles Street Care Mutual Aid and specifically serves in Historic Filipinotown. He is an active member of the Los Angeles Kalusugan Collective, or LAKAS, which does local organizing for Filipino and Latino health workers. Rafik also organizes with Craigen Armstrong, who has been incarcerated for over twenty years, and who alongside Adrian Berumen created the Mental Health Assistants program inside the Twin Towers Jail, which organizes folks in the jail for mental health mutual aid.

ARTIST BIOGRAPHIES

Fritz "Zufos" Aragon was born in Manila, Philippines, in 1975. Since 2014 he has operated Urge Palette Art Supplies / Pain Sugar Gallery located in downtown Riverside, California. When he's not trapped at work, you might find him going deaf playing in punk bands. If he's lucky he'll catch up on sleep. Wish him luck.

Edee Allynnah Davis is a Native American trans female, artist, poet, and abolitionist bein' held captive and hostage in the Texas prison(s) system. They are from Southern Cali, a place called San Pedro, in Los Angeles County. Edee is grateful and thankful to be able to work with everyone at ABO, as well as everyone who makes it possible for ABO to operate.

Kill Joy is an artist whose work sits at the intersection where jungle meets desert. Her art practice interprets world mythology and ancient symbolism to highlight issues of environmental and social justice. Kill Joy manages a print shop, La Onda, and art studio, Kitchen Table Puppets, and is based in Houston, Texas, with a practice in printmaking, painting, and puppet making.

Syan Rose is an illustrator whose work plays with representational and surrealist imagery to process systems of violence, honor social movements, and envision a new world. Her debut book, *Our Work Is Everywhere: An Illustrated Oral History of Queer and Trans Resistance*, was published by Arsenal Pulp in 2021. To see more visit syanrose.com or @syanrose on Instagram.

E.T. Russian is a multisensory installation artist, maker of comics and zines, disability justice advocate, and healer. Russian is the author of *The Ring of Fire Anthology*, codirector of the documentary *Third Antenna*, and a featured artist with Sins Invalid. Russian has been published in *Graphic*

Public Health; Disability in American Life: An Encyclopedia of Concepts, Politics, and Controversies; When Language Runs Dry; Skin, Tooth & Bone; and *Gay Genius.* Their work is in the permanent collections of the Library of Congress and the Washington State Convention Center. ETRUSSIAN.COM

Clio Reese Sady is an illustrator living in San Francisco, California. Sady worked for many years as a tattoo artist and uses the skills from tattooing in their comics. Sady is honored to be included in this collection of work and fights for a world without policing.

Kristopher Storey (aka *Kit Brixton*) is a coauthor of *Pets DC: Rise of the Pets*, ABO Comix queer-flux prisoner anthology contributor, zinester, artist, philosopher, surfer, aspiring novelist, punk, and a soccer fan. Kristopher looks to creative DIY endeavors for inspiration and finds adventure and humor in the world, especially the natural or mundane.

Billy Thomas is a white bisexual transgender and a longtime survivor of mental, physical, and sexual abuse. Billy was force-fed mind-altering meds while in the care of Texas CPS. They are surviving capital life and now have twenty years flat done. They look forward to getting early parole with the help of their friend and mentor Casper at ABO Comix.

Glenn "Kinoko" Tucker is still figuring out how to identify themselves. However, their recent acquisition of gender fluidity helped them gain insight into their feminine spirit. Art started for Kinoko consciously as a child. It became a safe place to explore their sense of wonder, curiosity, and sacredness.

INDEX